Reflections of Dance along the Brahmaputra

This volume brings a critical lens to dance and culture within North East India. Through case studies, first-hand accounts, and interviews, it explores the unique folk dances of Indigenous communities of North East India that reflect diverse journeys, lifestyles, and connections within their ethnic groups, marking almost every ritual and festival. Dance for the people of North East India, as elsewhere, is also a way of declaring, establishing, celebrating, and asserting humans' relationship with nature.

The book draws attention to the origins and special circumstances of dances from North East India. It discusses a range of important folk-dance forms alongside classical dance forms in North East India, with a focus on Sattriya dance. The chapters examine how these dance forms play an important role in the region's socio-cultural, economic, and political life, intertwining religion and the arts through music, dance, and drama. Further, they also explore how folk dance cultures in North East India have never been relegated to the background, never considered secondary, aesthetically, or otherwise, but have become expressions of political and cultural identity.

An evocative work, this volume will be of interest to students and researchers of pedagogy, choreography, community dance practice, theatre and performance studies, social and cultural studies, aesthetics, interdisciplinary arts, and more. It will be an invaluable resource for artists and practitioners working in dance schools and communities.

Debarshi Prasad Nath is Head of the Department of Cultural Studies at Tezpur University, Assam, India. Debarshi was the Principal Investigator for a partnership programme with UNICEF India, working on the empowerment of adolescents using folklore as a medium of communication, focusing primarily on folk music and dance. Debarshi's wide-ranging academic areas of interest are evident in his critical contributions from Cultural Theory to Contemporary Cultural Practices. His wide-ranging interests are reflected in his publications, covering areas of translation, literature, folklore, films, societies, and cultures in transition.

Ralph Buck is an award-winning teacher and academic leader. He is on the International Editorial Boards of *Research in Dance Education* (RIDE) and the *Journal of Dance Education* (JODE). He has collaborated with UNESCO in raising the profile of arts education around the world. He initiated, advocated for, and planned UNESCO's International Arts Education Week. He is on the Council for the World Alliance for Arts Education. Ralph's research and publications focus on dance teaching and learning and community dance.

Barbara Snook is a Professional Teaching Fellow and Senior Research Fellow at the University of Auckland where she engages in researching the use of arts integration in primary school classrooms. She is also currently serving as an adjunct Professor at Tezpur University in Assam. Barbara was the Caroline Plummer Fellow in Community Dance at the University of Otago in 2008. She is a successful author of dance textbooks widely used in Australia and New Zealand and was the recipient of an Osmotherly Award in 2007 for services toward the development of dance education in Queensland Australia. Barbara is currently researching the area of dance for older adults.

Celebrating Dance in Asia and the Pacific
Series Editor: **Stephanie Burridge**

Celebrating Dance in Asia and the Pacific is a series that presents the views of eminent scholars, journalists and commentators alongside the voices of a new generation of choreographers working from tradition to create new forms of expression in contemporary dance. It documents and celebrates these artistic journeys that work within the framework of rich and complex cultural heritages. Future titles in this series include Taiwan, New Zealand, and the Pacific. The series is published by Routledge in India and supported by the World Dance Alliance Asia Pacific.

Also in this series:

Beyond the Apsara
Celebrating Dance in Cambodia
Edited by Stephanie Burridge and Fred Frumberg

Traversing Tradition
Celebrating Dance in India
Edited by Urmimala Sarkar Munsi and Stephanie Burridge

Sharing Identities
Celebrating Dance in Malaysia
Edited by Mohd Anis Nor and Stephanie Burridge

Reflections of Dance along the Brahmaputra
Celebrating Dance in North East India
Edited by Debarshi Prasad Nath, Ralph Buck and Barbara Snook

Reflections of Dance along the Brahmaputra

Celebrating Dance in North East India

Edited by Debarshi Prasad Nath, Ralph Buck, and Barbara Snook

LONDON AND NEW YORK

Designed cover image: Barb Snook

First published 2023
by Routledge
4 Park Square, Milton Park, Abingdon, Oxon OX14 4RN

and by Routledge
605 Third Avenue, New York, NY 10158

Routledge is an imprint of the Taylor & Francis Group, an informa business

© 2023 selection and editorial matter, Debarshi Prasad Nath, Ralph Buck and Barbara Snook; individual chapters, the contributors

The right of Debarshi Prasad Nath, Ralph Buck and Barbara Snook to be identified as the authors of the editorial material, and of the authors for their individual chapters, has been asserted in accordance with sections 77 and 78 of the Copyright, Designs and Patents Act 1988.

All rights reserved. No part of this book may be reprinted or reproduced or utilised in any form or by any electronic, mechanical, or other means, now known or hereafter invented, including photocopying and recording, or in any information storage or retrieval system, without permission in writing from the publishers.

Trademark notice: Product or corporate names may be trademarks or registered trademarks, and are used only for identification and explanation without intent to infringe.

British Library Cataloguing-in-Publication Data
A catalogue record for this book is available from the British Library

ISBN: 978-1-032-45238-8 (hbk)
ISBN: 978-1-032-50498-8 (pbk)
ISBN: 978-1-003-39877-6 (ebk)

DOI: 10.4324/9781003398776

Typeset in Sabon
by Deanta Global Publishing Services, Chennai, India

Contents

List of figures   vii
List of contributors   viii
Preface   xii
Author's note   xv
Acknowledgements   xx
Glossary   xxi

Introduction   1
DEBARSHI PRASAD NATH AND BARBARA SNOOK

1 Glimpses of the dance world of North-East India   8
PARASMONI DUTTA

2 Sattriya dance: A narrative of its journey through the ages   22
PRADIP JYOTI MAHANTA

3 Moving objects and thinking body: A dancer's narrative   33
ANWESA MAHANTA

4 Discovering Sannidhi/a confluence: A dance exchange between Assam and Aotearoa, New Zealand   45
ALISON (ALI) EAST

5 Kherai's dance world: Promoting solidarity and tradition   61
MADHURIMA GOSWAMI

6 The dance and the dancers: Tradition and innovation within the indigenous performances of the ritual dance of the *Hudum Deo*   79
PREETINICHA BARMAN

Contents

7 Identity revivalism through folk dances amongst the tribal
communities of Assam 93
MOUSUMI MAHANTA

8 Bihu performance of the Morans of Assam 107
PARASH JYOTI MORAN AND HASHIK N.K.

9 Social media and the politics of dance 121
JAYANTA VISHNU DAS

10 Gender and dance: "Gazing" at the *Doudini* and the female
Sattriya and *Bihuwoti* dancers 136
MOUSHUMI KANDALI

11 Reflections on dance education workshops in Assam: Towards
critical and creative thinking 154
BARBARA SNOOK

12 Echoing the rhythm: Voices of school dance teachers 169
JURI GOGOI KONWAR

13 Dancers' voices 182
GAURAV RAJKHOWA

14 Dance through the performers' lens 195
MANDAKINI BARUAH

15 Studio dance teachers' journeys 220
MAYURI BORDOLOI

16 The performers of folk dances 246
MANDAKINI BARUAH

Index 253

Figures

1.1	Map of the region	9
3.1	Anwesa Mahanta dressed in a male Sattriya dance costume	39
3.2	Anwesa Mahanta dressed in a female Sattriya dance costume	39
4.1	Visiting the Mishing community at Majuli Island, 2015	46
4.2	New Zealand students dressed in local costumes with the Bodos and Tea communities	50
4.3	Male dancers playing female roles. Uttar Kamalabari Sattra, Majuli Island	54
5.1	The Doudini and Bodo community worshipping before the commencement of the ritual	63
8.1	A group of Moran Bihu dancers. Permission given from the Kakapathar Raati Bihu Celebration Committee	109
8.2	Raati Bihu. Permission given from the Kakapathar Raati Bihu Celebration Committee	113
8.3	Chak Chani. Permission given from the Kakapathar Raati Bihu Celebration Committee	113
10.1	Malika Kandali's performance of Mandodari Puche Ravnoak. Photo courtesy of UB Studios Guwahati	151
11.1	Students engaging in dance during the workshop, Pic. Barbara Snook personal collection	163
14.1	Jatin Goswami	195
14.2	Ghanakanta Bor Bayan	198
14.3	Indira P.P. Bora	200
14.4	Ramkrishna Talukdar	202
14.5	Shubhalakshmi Khan	204
14.6	Dr. Lima Das	207
14.7	Dr. Meneka Bora	210
14.8	Dr. Jashodhara Bora	213
14.9	Nganbi Chanu Leima	215
14.10	Sinam Basu Singh	217

Contributors

Preetinicha Barman is an educator, poet, writer, and a classical Manipuri dancer. She teaches English literature at Women's College, Shillong, Meghalaya, India and is associated with the North Eastern Dance Academy in Shillong. She has contributed a number of critical essays and book reviews to research journals as well as book chapters for edited volumes. Her poems are published in various journals and periodicals. *Aiyor Photok* is her collection of Koch Rajbangshi poems. She has recently published a book titled, *Orhan Pamuk: A Critical Reading*. Her present area of research is Koch Rajbangshi folklore and folklife.

Mandakini Baruah is Assistant Professor in the Department of Cultural Studies, Tezpur University. She completed her Ph.D. on Gender and Folklore with special emphasis on the Construction of Womanhood in Assamese Proverbs. Her areas of interest are Gender Studies, Performance Studies, Paremiology, Folklore, and Ethnographic Studies. She has recently edited a book entitled *Women and Urbanity: Cultural Memory of North-East India* published by Tezpur University. Apart from academic discussions, she has also published articles in local newspapers and magazines.

Mayuri Bordoloi is a freelance researcher. She wrote her Ph.D. thesis on "Continuity and Change in the Performance of Bhaona: A Study with Special Reference to Matribhasar Bhaona", where she analysed one of the most important performing art traditions of Assam. Her area of research is Bhaona, the indigenous theatre form of Assam associated with the Sattriya tradition. She has published articles on the performing art traditions of Assam and has looked at how these are reimagined and reconstructed along gender-sensitive lines in changing times.

Ralph Buck is an award-winning teacher and academic leader. He is on the International Editorial Boards of the *Research in Dance Education* (RIDE) and the *Journal of Dance Education* (JODE). He has collaborated with UNESCO in raising the profile in arts education around the world. He initiated, advocated for, and planned UNESCO's International Arts Education Week. He is on the Council for the World Alliance for Arts

Education. Ralph's research and publications focus on dance teaching and learning and community dance.

Jayanta Vishnu Das currently teaches at Tezpur University, India, as Assistant Professor in the Department of Cultural Studies. His area of research is at the cross-sections of media studies, culture, and communication. His most recent publications include "Gender in the Films of Rituparno Ghosh" in *International Encyclopedia of Gender, Media and Communication* (Wiley Blackwell, 2020).

Parasmoni Dutta currently teaches in the Department of Cultural Studies, Tezpur University. The areas of his teaching and research interests are cultural theories, critical heritage studies, and popular and digital culture. His major publications include articles in journals such as *Asian Theatre Journal, Journal of Creative Communications,* and in edited volumes including *The Routledge Companion to Intangible Cultural Heritage*.

Ali East (MPHED) is a New Zealand dance artist and educator recently retired from The University of Otago, New Zealand, and currently Adjunct Professor at Tezpur University, Assam. In 1980, she created the eco-political company, *Origins Dance Theatre* and in 1989 founded New Zealand's first choreographic qualification (now the Bachelor of Performing and Screen Arts, Dance, Unitec, Auckland). Her book *Teaching Dance As If the World Matters* was published in 2011. An interest in dance and cultural communities led her to bring several ethnographic research expeditions to Kerala and Assam. Her current research investigates eco-somatic dance practices and methodologies.

Madhurima Goswami of the faculty in the Department of Cultural Studies is currently working at the Centre for Women Studies, Tezpur University. She is an ardent researcher in the field of Culture and Performance, Indian Poetics, Folkore, and Women's History. She is a trained classical dancer and also a practitioner of varied regional dance forms. She directs an institute of Performing Arts in Tezpur. Her academic research includes interdisciplinary research methodologies drawing on her background in dance and choreography. Her interests lie in the study of dance traditions, dance criticism, creativity theories, and practices.

Hashik N.K. works as Assistant Professor in the Department of Cultural Studies, Tezpur University, Assam. He is a researcher in performance studies and cultural studies, and his research interests are oral narratives, community studies, and performance studies. His doctoral research was completed at the University of Hyderabad, India.

Moushumi Kandali taught for several years in the "School of Culture & Creative Expressions" in Ambedkar University of Social Sciences, New Delhi, before joining her current faculty position in the Department of Cultural Studies at Tezpur University. She has been deeply engaged in interdisciplinary research and documentation in the field of Visual Culture & Art, Literature, and other allied areas for the last two decades. She is well known as a fiction writer with several prestigious awards. Moushumi has published four collections of short stories, three research books on art and culture, and two books of translations.

Juri Gogoi Konwar is a faculty member of the Department of Cultural Studies, Tezpur University, Assam, India. She completed her post-graduation education in Anthropology (Advanced Social and Cultural Anthropology) and obtained a Ph.D. degree on the "Reproductive Health of Women in Upper Assam". Her post-doctoral research was on "Textile Tradition of the *Bodos* of Assam". She has researched "Food Culture of Ethnic Groups of Assam" and "Culture in the Boundaries of India and Myanmar". She has also conducted research on culture and performing arts belonging to different indigenous tribes and communities of North East India.

Anwesa Mahanta is an award-winning dancer and scholar specialising in Sattriya Dance. Her research explores the sociological perspectives of culture inherent in the movement practices and performance narratives of the Northeastern region of India. After completing her doctoral research in Performing Arts and Oral Traditions, she served as an Artist in Residence at the Indian Institute of Technology Guwahati. She was the recipient of a Charles Wallace India Trust Fellowship 2015–2016 where she pursued research at Queen's University, Belfast. Anwesa has written several scholarly articles and was a research fellow at the National Academy of Performing Arts in India.

Pradip Jyoti Mahanta was formerly a Professor in the Department of Cultural Studies, Tezpur University. He is a well-known scholar with areas of interest in the Cultural History of Assam and North East India, Medieval Assamese Literature, and the Traditions of Art in Assam. Dr Mahanta has contributed significantly to a wide understanding of the epoch-making cultural resurgence that came from the Bhakti Movement in Assam led by Sankaradeva (1449–1568 CE). He has written extensively on old Assamese literature and art traditions of Assam. He has authored four books in addition to many contributions to acclaimed journals and anthologies.

Mousumi Mahanta is working as Assistant Professor at the Chandraprabha Saikiani Centre for Women's Studies, Tezpur University, Tezpur, Assam. Her areas of specialisation include Gender and Mental Health, Women's Studies, Sociology of Health, Mental Illness, Anthropology, and Cultural Studies. She has a special interest in ethnographic studies. She has conducted research among the ethnic communities of North East India as part of her academic assignments.

Parash Jyoti Moran is a district leader for the Piramal Foundation. He was an Indian delegate at the World Health Organization's "Asia Youth

International Model United Nations" (AYIMUN) held in Bangkok, Thailand, 2018. Parash participated in India's first International Youth Conference – Telengana Jagruthi International Youth Conference in 2019, held in Hyderabad. He acted as the Chief Guest in the "Raipur United Nations Summit 2019" and delivered a speech on "The role of youth to make India a sustainably developed nation". He is currently the recipient of a Gandhi Fellowship from the Piramal Foundation.

Debarshi Prasad Nath is Head of Department in Cultural Studies at Tezpur University. Debarshi was Principal Investigator for a partnership programme with UNICEF India, working on the empowerment of adolescents using folklore as a medium of communication, focusing primarily on folk music and dance. Debarshi's wide-ranging academic areas of interest are evident in his critical contributions from Cultural Theory to Contemporary Cultural Practices. This range of interest is reflected in his wide range of publications, covering areas of translation, literature, folklore, films, societies, and cultures in transition.

Gaurav Rajkhowa is a cultural studies researcher based in Guwahati, Assam. His doctoral research was on Bhupen Hazarika and the cultural politics of Assamese nationalism. His research interests are in cultural policy, popular culture, ethnic identity, populism, and democracy. Currently as a research fellow in the Department of Cultural Studies, Tezpur University, he is involved in the archiving of folk and popular music practices in Assam. This research involved speaking with folk dance performers to understand how they navigate a performance context framed by state cultural policy, ethnic identity, and rapid commodification of cultural heritage.

Barbara Snook is a professional teaching fellow and senior research fellow at the University of Auckland. She is engaged in researching the use of arts integration in primary school classrooms. Barbara was the Caroline Plummer Fellow in Community Dance at the University of Otago in 2008. She is a successful author of dance textbooks widely used in Australia and New Zealand and was the recipient of an Osmotherly Award in 2007 for services toward the development of dance education in Queensland, Australia. Barbara is currently researching in the area of dance for older adults.

Preface

Celebrating Dance in Asia and the Pacific

Dance in the Asia-Pacific region is a diverse cultural matrix where new contemporary dance occurs alongside continuing traditions such as tribal, folk and court dances, and ritual practices. A continuum that expresses all aspects of life, tradition, and change, dance is also a "meeting point" for modernity and post-modernity, history, and "post-history", the present and the future where complex aesthetic and philosophical challenges are negotiated. Artists are addressing these challenges with integrity and subtlety by developing unique performance styles that are constantly evolving. Working through an empathetic approach that is grounded in regional traditions, the choreographers from the countries of the Asia-Pacific region are at the forefront of developing a new international genre of contemporary dance with unique movement vocabularies and narratives. No dance lover, practitioner, or scholar can ignore the dynamism and explosion of creative energy from this region.

The books in this series discuss the meeting points, intersections, and integration of dance cultures and how choreographers, performers, associated artists, and companies of the region choose to imaginatively invent, blend, fuse, select, and morph these multiple influences. Pedagogy, training, production resources, logistic support, and in some instances imposed restrictions such as censorship all impinge on the artistic process – above all, the passion to create, the need to perform, and the desire to be heard underpin all art. In dance, the body is a powerful means of dialogue that, through embodiment, encapsulates signs and symbols of place and belief. Rather than emulating Western dance forms, there is a palpable confidence in personal creative expressions that are valued, applauded, and enjoyed – the Asia-Pacific choreographers are making evocative and enigmatic dance theatre that touches a human chord and implicitly shows the power of dance to move and inspire us. The complexity of these developments may not seem a big step to outsiders, but to those versed in the traditional forms, these small steps represent giant leaps.

How does an identity emerge from such eclecticism in the Asia Pacific? Dance that is thematically inspired by unique narratives and regional "storytelling" traditions, history, and social issues occur alongside predominately abstract choreography constructed from a diversity of movement vocabularies from the East and the West. Choreographers are incorporating imagery that is metaphoric, symbolic, and iconic to make poetic statements about their world. In this amalgam, memories are embodied, constructed and deconstructed, encoded and decoded into new themes and movement vocabularies in powerful and poignant moments. For instance, across the region, one of the greatest epic stories of all time, the *Ramayana*, a tale that is reinterpreted from India to Bali, Thailand, Cambodia, and beyond, is explored in a myriad of ways. It is revisited and interrogated by practitioners through film, drama, dance, and the visual arts – there is much to contemplate and debate in the interpretation of the characters and the intricacies of the storyline that reveals universal aspects of human frailty such as the struggle between good and evil, weakness and power, lust and greed, the masculine and the feminine, and the search for the soul.

It is timely to be inspired by the breadth and diversity of dance in the Asia-Pacific region. The *Celebrating Dance in Asia and the Pacific* series focuses on themes of evolving contemporary choreography, tradition and change, intercultural research, and practice occurring through artist exchanges, pedagogy, revitalising, and preserving cultural heritage – rich areas for research with implications to readers throughout the global village. An important focus is to highlight the artists' perspective on their work and its cultural and philosophical contexts through the inclusion of a number of Artist's essays in each volume. These insights give invaluable information about the inspiration, intention, and cultural connections for the dancers and choreographers. It is also an opportunity to present their thoughts on the dichotomy between the preservation of dance in their communities and the desire to choreograph contemporary dance informed by traditional and classical forms,

There inevitably remain many tensions, dilemmas, and uncertainties for both artists and audiences where familiar ground is constantly shifting as audiences engage with the new Asian contemporary dance. Rapid changes and the shock of the new may be uncomfortable to some but exhilarating and liberating to others. The strands of all the dance forms coexist and can be imagined as coloured lines merging in a prism. Like in a prism, divergent and vibrant colours come together as a unified bright, white light – a unity achieved through diversity and a celebration of dance in all its forms.

Ultimately, despite divergent views and the polarities of the traditional and the contemporary, there is a sense of respect for all that dance offers – for fellow artists and the passion they all share. Audiences in the Asia-Pacific region and across the world are witnessing continuing traditions that bridge and celebrate rich cultural heritages alongside new explorations and eureka moments for both established and developing choreographers. The words of Carl Wotz, the founder of the World Dance Alliance, epitomise the philosophy and content of the new series by Routledge, *Celebrating Dance in Asia and the Pacific*:

> *Celebrating the variety, the depth and the beauty of human difference through the art of dance.*
> (Singapore, WDA conference 2001)

Stephanie Burridge
Series Editor

Author's note

Until recently, I had never been to India.

As a well-seasoned traveller, I have been asked many times, "have you been to India?", and I have always answered, "I'm not yet ready to go to India". In my heart and mind, I knew India was not just a "quick visit". India would need my full attention and a readiness to receive all that it would offer. I was not fearful, but I was anxious that I did not have a degree of humility, spiritual openness, and time to grasp even a tiny thread of what India was and is in global history and cultural impact. I mean the global reach of India's colour, food, beauty, religions, technology, dance, and music is immense. So yes, I avoided India, as I just never felt ready to connect respectfully with its depth and breadth of culture and with its people.

My good friend Dr Barbara Snook (Barb) and co-editor of this book had visited India and she fully understood my concerns. However, she launched into India with enthusiasm and the openness it deserved. After each of her journeys, she shared her stories and especially told me about the exciting people she met. Barb was often travelling with her and my friend Ali East, and they had visited many dance schools and met many leading dance teachers. Slowly Barb educated me and started to build my confidence and focus such that I would not get overwhelmed.

It was during these many coffee conversations in Auckland, New Zealand, that Barb told me about Dr Anwesa Mahanta and a community of dancers and academics in the Northeast of India. Barb's enthusiasm, my readiness, and the University of Auckland's positive relationships with tertiary institutions in India coalesced in 2019. In turn and via email, Barb introduced Professor Debarshi Prasad Nath and his colleague Associate Professor Parasmoni Dutta, Department of Cultural Studies, School of Humanities and Social Sciences, Tezpur University in the Northeastern state of Assam. After a raft of emails and conversations, the Dance Studies Department, the University of Auckland, and the Cultural Studies Department, Tezpur University, agreed to develop a formal relationship through a Memorandum of Understanding (MoU) that would foster academic exchange and research partnerships.

I was going to India!

In 2019, I headed to Kolkata and it was here that I rendezvoused with Barb. Our destination was Tezpur, but, with flight connections and time differences, and my curiosity, Kolkata marked the beginning of my Indian adventure. We stayed in Kolkata for two days, and we took the role of tourists happily. We secured a driver for the day and he showed us a hint of Kolkata. It was a gentle introduction as we skimmed the sites, but I felt very comfortable and happy. As I expected, the colour, history, humanity, commerce, religion, and blend of old and new were chaotic and magical.

We then flew to Guwahati, the largest city in Assam, where we were welcomed by Dr Anwesa Mahanta and her father Professor Pradip Mahanta, academics in dance and cultural studies, respectively. The next day we headed north to Kaziranga National Park. To be honest I was not ready for this four-hour road journey. It was a dynamic and bone-jarring experience. My sense of road rules and expectations did not match with the local meanings of "keep to the left", "keep in your lane", and "only overtake when the road is clear". However, all the drivers on the roads were on the "same page", and whilst my heart was in my mouth for the entire journey, we were clearly safe with the traffic flowing smoothly and all in sync.

We arrived at our accommodation at Kaziranga National Park. This National Park straddles the Brahmaputra River and it is famous for its wildlife that features tigers, elephants, rhinoceros, water buffalo, turtles, birds, and amazing tall grasses. Yes, I am a tourist and all of this was exciting and of great interest to me. It was also here that we were to meet Professor Debarshi Prasad Nath and Associate Professor Parasmoni Dutta.

We woke early the next morning and embarked on an elephant adventure. The early morning mist and very cool air were exhilarating. The drive into the national park took us through several small villages where the day was just beginning. I loved the opening of shutters, the setting up of small roadside stalls, and the lighting of gas burners upon which breakfasts were cooked. I loved seeing all the schoolchildren immaculately dressed waiting for the school bus or walking to school. I loved the rice paddies and the gentle hills covered with tea. I loved the quality of the light and air as it warmed. It was a beautiful morning. We completed our elephant ride, and we saw much wildlife, but no tigers. They are rare and elusive and indeed the National Park has a focus on protecting them and maintaining their habitat.

I tell you this because this is Assam, and this was my introduction to a rare part of the world rich in natural beauty with unique habitats and cultures. This is Assam, a finger of land reaching northeast, delicately situated between Bangladesh, Myanmar, Tibet, Bhutan, and China. This is Assam, the home of one of the world's largest and most powerful rivers, the Brahmaputra, which flows from the Tibetan mountains through Assam and Bangladesh into the Bay of Bengal. This was Assam, where I was situated, for a very brief week with a job to establish a relationship between two tertiary institutions and foster our friendship and future partnership.

Up to this point in our journey, we had not visited anything "artistic" or cultural in terms of museums, performances, or dance centres. Yet, I felt immersed in culture. The fabric of the women's clothing, the patterns of woven reeds, the flowers in the gardens, the singing in the background, the casual elephant passing on the side of the road with boys astride on their mobile phones, was all culture. It was not until we visited an Orchid centre and saw a lunchtime folk dance performance for tourists that we saw any dance. These kinds of "tourist" dance performances are featured around the world. The dance was fine. They were a group of six young women and men doing their thing with a degree of disinterest. I too was not that interested. I was more interested in watching the family next to our table navigating their lunch and establishing a semblance of order and propriety in a public space. So far away from New Zealand and yet all the same familial concerns and needs.

I need to be clear that while I have never visited India, I have seen much Indian dance. The Indian diaspora is strong and present around the world. I have witnessed very high-quality Indian Kathakali dance, Odissi dance, and Bharatanatyam dance, and so watching relatively bored teenagers in local costumes doing a small dance was great but not because of the dancing.

That evening we met Debarshi and Parasmoni. We had a lovely dinner and spoke about our respective universities, tertiary education systems, dance/culture faculties, families, politics, and life. We shared our paperwork and made sure everything was ready for the formal signing ceremony the next day. Again, we clarified expectations and realities of establishing such international agreements, when distance, economies, and language provide considerable reality checks upon any aspirations.

The next morning, we left Kaziranga National Park and drove south to Tezpur and the University of Tezpur. In making this journey, we returned to the roads and in my mind chaotic driving, but on this occasion, I looked beyond the traffic and focused on the hills, the people, the trees, and then the Brahmaputra River. I cannot tell you how excited I was to see this magnificent and vast river. When I was a 10-year-old boy in Australia, I learned the names of the world's major rivers, and here I was next to one of them. I was so happy, and the river did not disappoint. The bridge we drove over was narrow and long. The river braided as it wound around marshes and islands and then opened into strong swirling currents speeding southwards. In my mind, I listed the other great rivers of the world I had visited: Yangtze, Danube, Darling, Nile, Thames, Amazon, Seine, and now the Brahmaputra.

We arrived at Tezpur University and settled into our university accommodation. The campus was outside the city and set amongst gardens, in a semi-parkland style. Each faculty appeared to have its own building and I gathered that most, if not all the students lived on campus. I walked around the campus and noticed the usual hallmarks of tertiary institutions with most of the students dressed in everyday streetwear. A small part of me was sad that the distinct power of the river was not more evident, but then I remembered that I was here in the dry season, and reflected on many news reports that described the flooding Brahmaputra and the monsoons that too often brought devastation to this part of India and Bangladesh downstream.

The signing ceremony the next day went perfectly to plan. The Pro Vice-Chancellor, Tezpur University, and myself offered speeches and gifts and signed the MOU between our Universities. This was the first agreement that Dance Studies, the University of Auckland, had made with an Indian university and, similarly a first for the Department of Cultural Studies, Tezpur University. As such, it represented an important landmark in our respective histories.

At the core of our new partnership was an agreement to foster academic research and student and staff exchanges. Presently, at the time of writing this chapter, our COVID-19 world has brought to a halt all exchanges, however we have, as evidenced by this book, been able to foster research exchange. A specific point of shared interest has been around community dance and community arts.

In 2020, Tezpur University celebrated the 150th birthday of Mahatma Gandhi. In marking this occasion, the Department of Cultural Studies, School of Humanities and Social Sciences, Tezpur University, held a webinar and invited Dr Barb Snook and myself to speak about community dance and education. Dr Snook and I spoke about our experiences of community dance and how we saw community dance intersecting with Gandhi's vision of community and education. In particular, we drew attention to community dance characteristics of solidarity, significance (Clarke, 1973), and security, and how these are implemented within a dance context. Solidarity speaks to the powerful feeling of unity and togetherness one experiences when participating in a community. Significance recognises that each individual brings something unique and that such diversity is important. Security understands that full participation requires a sense of personal safety to speak, to dance, and to have agency without fear of retribution. It is these values and subsequent practices that we at the University of Auckland bring to education, and we were proud to speak about these on this important occasion.

We recognise that as the relationship between Tezpur and Auckland matures, our interests and connections will grow, but for now, it is our joint interest in fostering community within and through culture that is valued. Dr Snook and I bring our interest and expertise in community dance and dance education with the aim to recognise and foster diversity and participation. The many stories of teaching, learning, and creating dance in the present book speak to the richness of dance and culture in the Northeast of India. We are proud to work with Professor Debarshi Nath and Associate Professor Parasmoni Dutta in creating a book that provides an international platform for sharing the histories and stories of diverse cultures within Assam.

Limiting the sharing of traditions, religious practices, and community issues to a book, a written format brings a degree of frustration. One cannot smell, hear, taste, feel, and embody the details and exquisite moments of culture and the multiple festivals and practices through a book. You really need to be in the villages, in the regions, and on the banks of the red river between the blue hills of Assam. However, as we cannot be in Assam presently, and many of us may not ever have the opportunity to return, hopefully, this book brings to you a small but powerful insight into Assam. As I stated at the outset, the culture and traditions of India run deep and wide like the Brahmaputra, and so to capture them fully is impossible. This book is our attempt to introduce you to artists, educators, dancers, historians, and academic's stories of North East India, and in so doing provide a glimpse of the culture and tradition that defines this corner of India.

Ralph Buck

Reference

Clarke, D., (1973) The concept of community: A Re-examination, *Sociological Review*, 21(3), 32–37.

Acknowledgements

The editors would like to gratefully acknowledge the assistance received from the following people in preparing this manuscript:

1. Dr Ketoukhrieu, Kohima, Nagaland
2. Moses Hongang Chang, Tuensang, Nagaland
3. Shongna Konyak, Mon, Nagaland
4. Gegin Dimingal, Dimapur, Nagaland
5. Zuchano, Dimapur, Nagaland
6. Choilen Phom, Dimapur, Nagaland
7. Levi Keor, Kohima, Nagaland
8. Ngutoli Y Swu, Dimapur, Nagaland
9. Sorito, Pungro, Nagaland
10. Dr Cherrie L Chhangte, Mizoram
11. Kumud Kemprai, Haflong, Assam
12. Prof. Nani Bath, Rono Hills, Itanagar, Arunachal Pradesh
13. Prof. Ashes Gupta, Agartala, Tripura
14. Dr Dakter Esse, Arunachal Pradesh
15. Dr Vandana Thousen, Haflong, Assam
16. Prof. Sunil Kumar Dutta, Guwahati, Assam
17. Laikhuram P. Singh, Manipur
18. Siwani Mech, Research Scholar, Department of Cultural Studies, Tezpur University
19. Munmi Rajkumari, Research Scholar, Department of Cultural Studies, Tezpur University

Glossary

Abhinaya Abhinaya is a Sanskrit word made up of the prefix *abhi* – towards and root *ni* – to carry. Thus, the word means to convey or lead towards. Abhinaya is a performative way of conveying an idea, a theme, a mood, an emotion through dramatic representation.

Abo-Tani An immensely important mythical figure, Abo-Tani is believed to be the primogenitor of the Tani group of tribes living in the states of Arunachal Pradesh and Assam.

Adhyapak A Guru, or teacher, who imparts wisdom to students, particularly in the Sattriya tradition.

Ankiya Bhaona Originally devised by Srimanta Sankardeva, it is a form of traditional one-act play popular in Assam. It is based on mythology and rendered in a stylised theatrical form. Ankiya Bhaona shows the influence of Sanskrit drama and other forms of dramatic entertainment widely prevalent in Medieval India such as *Raasleela, Ramleela, Jatra, Kathakali, Ojapali, Puppet dance,* and *Deodhani*

Bagarumba It is a colourful folk dance of the Bodo community of Assam. Performed by women, this dance form is considered to be the main traditional dance form of the Bodos.

Bailung Bailungs are the priestly class of the Ahom community of Assam. They observe, perform, and preserve the religious rites and rituals of the community.

Bathou Bathouism is an indigenous religion of the Bodo community of Assam. The holy word "Ba" means "five" and "thou" means "deep". This religion is based on the philosophy of five principles.

Bhakat Bhakats are Vaishnavite monks or devotees who live in *Sattras* under the supervision and tutelage of a *Sattradhikar* (Guru).

Bhangimas Bhangimas are unique postures used in several Indian art genres, especially performing arts.

Bhaona Bhaona is a traditional performing art form of Assam. Srimanta Sankardeva, the Vaishnavite saint and reformer, popularised *Bhaona* as a kind of entertainment with a religious message. *Bhaona* is also known as "*Ankiya Nat*" ("*Ankiya*" means one and "*Nat*" means drama or play) and are one-act plays. *Bhaona* stories typically represent the triumph of good over evil, with God's intervention serving as the deciding factor. These plays featured *Gayan* (singers) and *Baayan* (instrumentalists) as well as the *Bhaoriya(s)* (actors).

Bihu *Bihu* depicts many stages in the peasantry's agricultural cycle in Assam. Similar celebrations, such as the Bodos' *Bwisagu*, the Tiwas' *Pisu*, and the *Mishings'* Ali-Aye-Ligang, all revolve around the agricultural cycle. Undoubtedly, Bihu is the most popular festival of the Assamese community. *Bohag Bihu* or *Rongali Bihu*, *Kati Bihu* or *Kongali Bihu*, and *Magh Bihu* or *Bhogali Bihu* are three types of *Bihu* that are celebrated during different stages of the paddy (the primary crop) production in Assam. The *Bohag Bihu* event includes many Bihu songs and dances.

Bihuwati A female Bihu performer is referred to as Bihuwati.

Bor Deori Deoris are one of the major ethnic groups of Assam. The community has divided religious responsibilities among various sub-groups – Bor Deori, Soru Deori, Bor Bharali, and Horu Bharali. A Bor Deori holds the higher position as priest, and he is therefore called the "bor deori" or head priest.

Dasavatar nritya *Dasavatar nritya* is a traditional Sattriya dance form in which the performers portray Lord Vishnu's ten incarnations through their performance.

Deodhani *Deodhani* is a traditional folk dance of Assam. *Deodhani is* made up of two words: "*Deo*", which means God, and "*Dhani*", which means woman. It literally means a woman who has been possessed (Shaman) by God. A *Deodhani* dancer is usually accompanied by an Oja, an Assamese traditional chorus leader.

Dhol and Pepa *Dhol* and *Pepa* are prominent Assamese musical instruments, and the primary instrument of Bihu, the state's largest celebration. *Dhol* is a two-sided drum played with the palms and fingers of both hands, and a short stick called a *"mari"*. *Pepa*, on the other hand, is a wind instrument made of buffalo horn that is often played with fingers manipulating the holes in the tip of the pipe attached to the *Pepa*.

Doudini *Doudini* plays a vital role in Kherai puja. *Doudini* could be a woman or a girl, and no male dancer is permitted to perform with her. The Kherai dance is performed by the *Doudini*, entranced by mantras chanted by the *Deuri* (Priest). The Bodos believe that after being hypnotised, the *Doudini* gains a divine power from the deity that allows her to anticipate and predict the future of an individual or the entire village community.

Eksarana sect of Hinduism *Eksarana sect* means the idea of refuge or shelter in one god. It is a neo-Vaishnavite religious sect pioneered by Srimanta Sankardeva in 16th-century Assam.

Gamosa A traditional cloth generally weaved by the Assamese female folk in their loom. It is a white rectangular piece of cloth having a cross border embellished with floral designs at the ends. The *Gamosa* has various functions in the life of Assamese people. But, most importantly, it is culturally significant for the Assamese; in fact, it is taken to be a marker of Assamese cultural identity. Traditionally, it is used as a socially valuable gift item and also used in religious rituals and social activities.

Guru Shishya Parampara   In Indian religion and culture, the teacher–disciple tradition is known as Guru Shishya Parampara. It is the oral tradition of transmitting knowledge from guru to disciple through a lineage of gurus.

Hudum   *Hudum* is a folk dance performed by the Koch Rajbongshi community of Assam. The Koch Rajbongshis refer to "*Hudum deo*" as their traditional rain god, and they worship and perform *Hudum Puja* to avoid droughts. Only women participate in the rituals.

Hunsari   It is an indispensable traditional folk performance and ritual of the Assamese and an integral part of the Rongali Bihu festivities in Assam. Hunsari is traditionally performed in the courtyards of the villagers led by the elders of the village.

Jyoti Sangeet, Rabha Sangeet, Bhupendra Sangeet   Jyoti Prasad Agarwala, Bishnuprasad Rabha, and Bhupen Hazarika are legends of Assamese culture. The songs written and composed by these artists are collectively referred to as Jyoti Sangeet, Rabha Sangeet, and Bhupendra Sangeet, respectively.

Kherai   For the Bodo people, who live largely in Assam, *Kherai* puja is one of the most important religious events. The major purpose of the *Kherai* puja, which symbolises hope and desire, is to enhance happiness in both individual and public lives.

Khol   The *Khol* is a two-sided drum that is played with both palms and fingers of both hands. Since its employment in diverse folk performances like as *Bhaona* (plays), *gayan-bayan*, *kirtan*, and *borgeets* and as an important musical instrument in Sattriya performances, the *khol* is regarded as a vital component of Assamese culture.

Kirtan Ghosa   It is a compilation of devotional poetic works composed by Srimanta Sankardeva and was meant for community singing in the Eksarana ideology of neo-Vaishnavism.

Mati-Akhora   "*Mati-Akhora*" is the structured grammar that forms the basis of Sattriya dance. These *Mati-Akhoras* are the primary workout patterns, as well as the basic grammatical forms of Sattriya dance. *Mati-Akhora* is an Assamese phrase that refers to ground-based exercise.

Mekhela   A traditional piece of cloth worn generally by the Assamese females. This garment is worn from the waist to the ankle. It is generally worn with the Chador which covers the upper part of the body. The Mekhela is generally folded into pleats.

Moamoriya   In the history of Assam, the famous Moamoriya rebellion led to the end of the 600 years of Ahom dynastic rule. The Moamoriyas were mainly from Moran and Matak communities and they were the disciples of the Moamoriya Sattra.

Namghar   Namghar refers to prayer halls. The word *Nam* means prayer and *ghar* means house. So, Namghar is a "House of prayer", a place for congregational worship in the tradition of neo-Vaishnavism that was popularised by Srimanta Sankardeva.

Nirakar   Nirakar means the one which has no specific form or shape and is incorporeal. The word "Nirakar" is generally used to refer to God, the supreme power, who cannot be confined to any fixed shape.

Nritya   Nritya is the Sanskrit word for dance, but it has a more inclusive sense than dance. It is an expressive genre in which the dancer uses facial expression and body language to represent emotion and ideas while communicating with the audience through rhythmic movements.

Ojapali   *Ojapali* is a traditional song/dance/drama/musical performing art. It is considered one of the oldest forms of entertainment. *Ojapali* is a blend of two words "*Oja*", which means leader, and "*Pali*", which means assistants, who sing and dance. The performances are replete with dramatic conversation and action, often having a space for witty repartees. *Ojapali* focuses on stories from the epics and Puranas, transforming them into a performing style. There are two schools of *Ojapali* based on songs mainly derived from the Ramayana (Sukanani) and songs derived from the Mahabharata (Vyasar).

Purusartha   Purusartha is a significant concept in Hinduism, and it literally means "object of human endeavour". It is a combination of two Sanskrit terms *Purush* meaning "human being" and *Artha* meaning "goal of existence". The four ultimate goals of human life are Dharma (moral principles), Artha (prosperity), Kama (pleasure), and Moksha (liberation).

Sangeet   *Sangeet* means music. However, the Indian sense of sangeet includes both music (singing and instrumental) and dance.

Sattra   *Sattras* are neo-Vaishnavite monastic establishments that function as socio-religious and cultural centres in Assam. They are repositories of traditional religious values and creative expressions associated with them, and they are a vital element of Assamese society and culture.

Sattradhikar   The head of a Sattra, known as the "Sattradhikar", is in charge of maintaining and administering it.

Sattriya   *Sattriya*, or *Sattriya Nritya*, is one of the major Indian classical dance traditions that was developed in Assam and is based on ancient Indian drama and music manuscripts, particularly the Natya Shastra. *Sattriya*, created in the 15th century in Assam by Srimanta Sankardeva, has remained a living tradition. The name of the dance stems from the Vaishnava monasteries where it was performed and practised until Sattriya was officially recognised as a classical dance form in 2000.

Srimadbhagavata Purana   It is an ancient Sanskrit scripture of Hindu religious philosophy and belief. It contains the biography of Lord Krishna till the Kurukshetra war of Mahabharata.

Sri Madhabdeva   Sri Madhabdeva was the disciple of Srimanta Sankardeva. Madhabdeva carried forward the legacy of his Guru and propagated the religious ideology of Eksarana. He was also a saint poet and writer of Namghosa and Bhakti Ratnavali.

Sri Sankardeva Sri Sankardeva was a great Vaishnavite saint, scholar, preacher of Eksarana Dharma, socio-religious reformer, playwriter, and composer of Medieval Assam. Sankardeva led the Bhakti movement in Medieval Assam.

Vaishnava In the Bhakti tradition of Hinduism, a devotee of Krishna or Vishnu is known as a *Vaishnava*. For Vaishnavism, Krishna and his celestial avatars are revered.

Introduction

Debarshi Prasad Nath and Barbara Snook

Introduction

This publication has been written from an ethnographic perspective. While each author has brought their chapter to life based on specific areas of interest knowledge and experience, Gobo and Marciniak (2011) noted that "what distinguishes ethnography from other methodologies is a more active role assigned to the cognitive modes of observing, watching, seeing, looking and scrutinising" (p. 103). While some authors have taken a non-participant observation perspective where the subjects have been observed from a distance, many authors have interacted in the field with the subjects of their study. Interviews have been the dominant method of collecting research data. The methodologies vary in each of the chapters, and we as editors have honoured the authors' different approaches. The academic nature and writing styles vary within this publication, allowing authentic and interesting voices to be heard.

Each chapter is different, bringing to the volume a wide range of topics and perspectives, all united in dance. The content covers discussions on specific classical and ritual dance forms, dance history, philosophical reflections on dance, aspects of religious worship through dance, dance and social media, gender and dance, and dance education. The research is qualitative, and in most cases, the researchers within this volume have conducted their research within their own culture. The value of such research is summarised by King, Horrocks, and Brooks (2019), "theory and philosophical understandings impact on what we believe can be known: these beliefs and understandings then influence how we gather and make sense of information" (p. 10). The "outsider" chapters have been written with the authors clearly locating themselves in regard to their research as, "fieldwork can pose particular dilemmas and contradictions because of the power relations inherent in the process of gathering data and implicit in the process of representation" (Wolf and Deere, 1996, p. 1).

The first chapter provides the reader with an overview of the North East India region and its people. Each of the eight states is discussed, noting the distinctions for each region amongst the people and their cultures. There is definitely no doubt that North East India is not a homogeneous entity, and

DOI: 10.4324/9781003398776-1

this volume does not make any attempt to dispute that. However, we have chosen to introduce readers to some of the diverse dance traditions of North East India, with a special focus on Assam as the book title indicates. Assam itself is not a homogeneous entity. There are many dances of Assam that are not covered in this volume. It is impossible to locate a homogeneous space anywhere in North East India and that is not a matter we have chosen to address. We do include, however, discussions on dance forms from other states of North East India. Several chapters address dances that are found in North East Indian states. Among the artists interviewed in the last five chapters, there are two each from Mizoram, Manipur, and Tripura and one from Arunachal Pradesh.

Chapter 2 provides an insight into one of the two classical dances found in North East India. An expert on Sattriya dance, Professor Pradip Jyoti Mahanta, provides a historical background of this art form, taking the reader inside the religious Sattras where the dance form originated. Anwesa Mahanta, herself a professional Sattriya dancer and academic, addresses the objects in a Sattriya dancer's physical space in her chapter as she reflects upon body and mind through an acceptance of objects and artefacts as being inseparable from movement. In this book, a number of references are made to the Manipuri classical dance form in several of the chapters and a Manipur artist and exponent of Manipuri classical dance has been interviewed in the second section. It may be noted here that Sattriya and Manipuri are two recognised classical dances of India.

Sometimes, in India, and often globally, there is a sense of sacredness and purity associated with classical dance as opposed to folk dances that may not be held in the same regard. Within North East India, however, the difference between the margi and desi forms was never as distinctly and hierarchically marked. Generally, the concept of sacredness may be associated with the desi traditions in North East India by virtue of the fact that most of these dances are connected to rituals and festivals. The Indian division between the margi and desi traditions did manifest itself in North East India with two current classical dance forms, Manipuri and Sattriya, but these dances did not obliterate the folk forms. The desi or the folk dance in North East India was never relegated to the background, never considered secondary, aesthetically or otherwise. For the myriad of village communities throughout Assam and her neighbouring states, folk dances became expressions of political and cultural identity. It is likely that for this reason, the folk dances of Assam are not aesthetically compared with classical dances. Both the desi and margi traditions have their respective places in social life, and they are generally not seen in antithetical terms.

The dance traditions of North East India cannot be discussed in isolation from the dance traditions of India. Broadly speaking, there are two trajectories of the development of dance traditions in the North East: One that is specific to the North East region and the other that bears a close relationship to what was happening in India as a whole, particularly after independence.

While these trajectories may not be exclusive to North East India, they are useful to think about when discussing the relationship between dance and society in the context of the North East region.

Dance has a long history in Indian civilisation that is strangely parallel to the development of India and her relationship with her past. Just as India has struggled with a desire to own or disown her ancient past, she has also struggled to own or disown her dances. It was a complicated process. On the one hand, there was a push to reassert traditional values. There was a growing sense of awareness of a need to restore people's dwindling self-esteem by acknowledging the importance of the country's rich cultural heritage. In contrast, the British as well as the English-educated native elite looked upon traditional Indian dances with scorn and disdain. Some believed that dances reflected the "impurity" that had crept into Indian culture. They considered that these dances were a degenerate form of culture and that the ideal dance form existed in ancient India's sacred spaces such as temples. The postcolonial Indian state thus felt that the need of the hour was to expunge Indian culture of this "impurity". In the eyes of the native elite and the British, ancient Indian civilisation was glorious but it was presently in a state of decay. Dances had to be purged of their "impurity". Ananya Chatterjea (1996) elaborates,

> When the cultural revival movement began in the 1930s, the leaders realised that it was important to weed out this "impurity," as they saw it, from the dancing body, and to link their dance to the classical art described in the *Natyashastra*, the *Abhinaya Darpana*, and other ancient scriptures of performance. In this, they were influenced by Western orientalist scholars who had spoken eloquently about the ancient glories of India's past culture and lamented its present state of decay – an argument which was laden with imperialistic overtones.
>
> (p. 118)

Connecting the dances with these ancient texts gave them legitimacy and allowed the continuation of these practices.

This attempt to draw distinctions between the ancient art-inspired dance forms and other forms of dance very often manifested itself as a tension between high culture and mass or popular culture. A combined project of nationalism, state patronage, and sponsorship ensured "the appropriation of certain regional artistic forms selectively legitimised as 'national' and therefore 'classical'" (Shah, 2002, p. 126). As expected, it was the "classical", "high-cultural" forms that were honoured with the epithet "national".

> The nationalisation of selected intraregional artistic forms as "classical" represented not only the cultural identity of the region, but also the cultural diversity of the newly formed nation-state. This ambitious enterprise of contemporisation, refinement, sophistication, and ablution, in

other words "classification" of certain traditional regional forms meant selective furtherance of one dance at the cost of another, often its own precursor.

(Shah, 2002, p. 126)

In such a scenario, dance scholarship had to make important conceptual distinctions between "high" culture and "folk" culture (or mass culture)

Dance scholarship played an important role in consolidating the cultural heritage claimed by the new Indian state and vital distinctions were made, one of the most significant of which was the line drawn between the classical or margi and the folk or desi traditions.

(Chatterjea, 1996, pp. 118–119)

This division allowed India to connect the margi tradition to the classical art of India while the desi tradition was relegated to the periphery. In subsequent times, there was a desire to "raise" regional or desi dance forms to high-cultural "classical" forms. This was manifested in anxiety for regional communities who wished to belong to the national traditions in order to gain wider political recognition. The recognition of Assam's Sattriya dance as a classical form did not come overnight. It required a prolonged phase of lobbying and consensus generation. When the recognition did come, it was seen as a recognition of the political aspirations of the people of Assam.

For the Indigenous communities of North East India, dance is used to reflect different shades of emotions. There are dances to mark almost every ritual and festival and they are connected to different aspects of the social life of the respective communities. The dances tell stories that include various shades of emotion while the dancers enact everyday actions. Dance for people of North East India, as elsewhere, is also a way of declaring, establishing, celebrating, and asserting man's relationship with nature. Throughout time, dance has expressed man's response to the changing seasons. Dance, in other words, can be a symbolic expression of man's relationship with nature, with symbolism being expressed spontaneously and subjectively. From this point of view, the aesthetic quality of an individual dance is not of any great consequence. Arguably, the spontaneity of dances, particularly of ritual dances, is of far greater consequence than the aesthetics of the dance. Mousumi Mahanta addresses identity revivalism through folk dance in Chapter 7 where she poses the question to the Mishing, Karbi, Tiwa, and Deori ethic groups, "What meanings do members of tribal communities ascribe to their folk dances"?

Several of the chapters within this volume have addressed the many festivals and their dances. In Chapter 5, Madhurima Goswami discusses the Kherai Festival celebrated by the Bodos of the Brahmaputra valley and North Bengal. She describes the dances in some detail with specific reference to the role of the Doudini, a shaman dancer who becomes a temporary embodiment of the spirit of God during the Festival. In Chapter 6, Preetinicha Barman describes the fertility ritual known as Hudum Deo that is practised among the Koch Rajbangshis, a community living in the eastern and northeastern provinces of India. Parash Jyoti Moran and Hashik N. K. discuss the popular Bihu performances of the Moran community in Chapter 8. Bihu is celebrated all over Assam by different Indigenous communities in their own specific ways. There are interesting parallels and contrasts that emerge when one compares the different traditions of Bihu.

It would be wrong to assume, however, that the appreciation of dance is a subjective, internal matter of individual choice. If dances are to be used for educational purposes, and we see a definite and decisive movement towards this, there is a need to lay down objective criteria for their aesthetic appreciation. Best (1975) comments,

> If the "teaching" of art consists exclusively of such activities as giving out the paints and simply allowing the children to express themselves, without guidance at any stage, it is small wonder that the arts are subordinate to subjects of serious study in the curriculum. (This is not, of course, to say that there is no place for allowing freedom of expression in the teaching of the arts).
>
> (p. 12)

Dances must allow for artistic freedom, but it is also important to promote a rational understanding of dance. This may involve the setting up of standards, saying that this movement rather than the other is more pleasing to the eye and explaining why and how this is achieved. Students may be taught to recognise the cultural aspects of a dance and discern meaning. Standards are of course observable, objective phenomena. Thus, while the experience of dance can be a subjective emotion, the educational use of dances calls for observable and objective criteria. Barbara Snook in Chapter 11 reflects from an outsider's perspective on dance workshops conducted in primary, high schools, and tertiary institutions in Assam. In examining five case studies, she reflects on how students may engage in critical and creative processes through dance and how different dance processes may meet the requirements of the new Indian curriculum where students must think both critically and creatively. The development of observable and objective criteria will be a necessary requirement if dance is to be included in the curriculum with a focus on more than performance standards. Having said this, a dance in an Indian cultural context is never really a dance alone as it is primarily a symbol of culture. At a time when the threat of globalisation-induced cultural homogeneity looms large over a myriad of communities in North East India, every dance is a conscious political expression of a culture. People look at every form of dance as a representation of the political strength of a community. This applies not only to folk or ethnic dances but to the "high" cultural classical dance forms as well.

From a historical point of view, we can sense that dances in North East India were originally meant to be participatory. What we are claiming here could be true about dances of all indigenous populations around the world, but we wish to draw attention to the special circumstances of the dances of North East Indian origin. These dances were meant for the communities themselves. Spectator interest emerged much later. Arguably, the dances did not originally allow for a subject/object categorisation. At a later date, however, the process of objectification of these dance forms arose. Dances began to be presented, flaunted even, in the presence of enthusiastic audiences who saw them as an exotic expression of a quaint culture. For the performers too, caught up in a messy world of identity politics, these dances became important in terms of what they did and what political purpose they served. The interests and purposes were wide ranging, from crude commercial concerns to the establishment of political identity. Political identity is addressed in Jayanta Vishnu Das's chapter "Social media and the politics of dance". He poses three questions: Do social media prejudices creep into the representation of dance? Can indigenous dance be framed independently of these representations? How do we deal with authenticity in an era of social media? It was the instrumental use of these dances that gained in popularity. Dance festivals, very often organised by the state, focused on political agendas rather than on an aesthetic evaluation of art. A lot of extraneous concerns have obliterated our view of these dances, these wonderful specimens of the artistry of the people of North East India. Interestingly, Ali East's chapter (Chapter 4) discusses an ethnographic journey from New Zealand to Assam where she and her students travel around the villages and places of interest in Assam, participating in and observing dance in festivals and villages. While such visits can be conducted with respect and appreciation, perhaps it is time we set these dances free, allowing the practitioners to speak out confidently and freely without allowing the message to be cluttered by academic verbiage. The harm has already been done, but we believe that this could be a good opportunity for dance enthusiasts of the region to express their thoughts and engage with their traditions as Moushumi Kandali has done as she addresses the politics of the female body in Chapter 10. She examines the male gaze upon the female Doudini, Sattriya, and Bihuwoti dancers and examines how they are currently situated within the traditional conventions of a patriarchal system. Dance fulfils a need to engage deeply with history and context. Our book is an attempt to provide an analysis of the dance forms of the region and to situate them within their context and, in doing so, historicise them.

The final five chapters of the book are a series of interviews where the author has translated and documented the artists' voices. It is here that valuable new information emerges. Juri Konwar has focused upon the voices of school dance teachers, while Gaurav Rajkhowa interviewed ethnic dancers and Mayuri Bordoloi interviewed studio dance teachers. Mandakini Baruah has written Chapters 14 and 16 recording dance through a performer's lens, and in the final chapter of the book she has recorded the voices of those who perform folk dances.

As stated earlier, in terms of social value there is no distinction between folk dance and classical dance in North East India. They are valued equally. This is not always the case throughout India. Different chapters discuss the many festivals and specific dances that are an integral part of village life. The history and context of dance in this region are complex and the authors discuss intellectual tradition, performance, and celebration of many folk and ritual dances. A recurring theme is a reference to the preservation of traditional dances as changes are observed in a fast-moving society, where technology and entertainment are key. This theme draws together the focus of the book – the past, present, and future of dance in North East India.

References

Best, D., (1975) The aesthetics of dance, *Dance Research Journal*, 7(2), 12–15.

Chatterjea, A., (1996) Dance research in India: A brief report, *Dance Research Journal*, 28(1), 118–123.

Gobo, G., Marciniak, L., (2011) What is ethnography? In *Qualitative Research*, Silverman, D. (Ed.), Sage Publishing. London, 31–63.

King, N., Horrocks, C., Brooks, J., (2019) *Interviews in Qualitative Research*, Sage Publications Inc., Thousand Oaks.

Shah, P., (2002) Where they danced: Patrons, institutions, spaces: State patronage in India: Appropriation of the "regional" and "national", *Dance Chronicle*, 25(1), 125–141.

Wolf, D., Deere, C. (Eds.), (1996) *Feminist Dilemmas in Fieldwork*, Routledge, New York.

1 Glimpses of the dance world of North-East India

Parasmoni Dutta

The region and its people

The title "North-East India" is a colonial legacy, referring to the eight states in India's eastern region in present times: Arunachal Pradesh, Assam, Manipur, Meghalaya, Mizoram, Nagaland, Tripura, and Sikkim. The combined landmass of these states, barring Sikkim, which does not share a border with the other seven states, is located north-east of Kolkata, which was the capital of British India at the time; hence the phrase "North-East India". Today, after several decades of India's independence from colonial rule, this specific nomenclature of the region continues to be relevant, with renewed connotations for both the insiders and outsiders of the region.

Stretching from the foothills of the Himalayas in the north to the Bay of Bengal in the south, this region is noted for several distinctions that make this land, its peoples, and their cultures subjects of interest to a number of academic disciplines. This region has an area of more than 2.5 lakh (2.5 hundred thousand) square kilometres and accommodates a population of more than 50 million people. The contiguous region of eight states, with the exception of Sikkim, is connected to the so-called Indian mainland in the west through a narrow 22-kilometre-wide corridor (often called the Siliguri *chicken-neck*). On its northern, eastern, and southern sides, the region shares international boundaries with Bhutan, China, Myanmar, and Bangladesh. These spatial features, on the one hand, have resulted in an impression of being a peripheral region in relation to the mainland of India, yet on the other hand it makes the region a connecting interface between India and South-East Asia. The cultural practices of the region, including its dance practices, also testify to this liminal characteristic of the region in relation to the cultural practices of the Indian mainland and those of South-East Asia. Secondly, the indigenous communities of the region demonstrate both their individual distinctiveness in terms of their language and cultural traditions, yet also manifest a sense of cultural integration among themselves to conceive the entire region as a singular whole. The intercultural dynamics amongst these communities and their participation in the nation-building process with the so-called mainland India are still an unfinished and ongoing process.

DOI: 10.4324/9781003398776-2

Picture 1.1 Map of the region.

Therefore, the story of North-East India in general, and an account of its dance forms in particular, is indeed too lengthy and complex to be captured in a single chapter, even in its most concise version. Amidst this substantial risk of unwarranted omissions and uncritical generalisations, what is attempted here is an assemblage of representative descriptions and the highlighting of general processes which have been at work in recent history that contribute to shaping most of the dance cultures of the region. While this chapter is intended to be an overview of the dance world of North-East India, the further chapters in this book will outline some of the dances mentioned here in more detail.

A survey of the major traditional dance forms of the eight states

As a complete ethnographic documentation of the peoples and their cultures, particularly the dance forms of North-East India, is not readily available, I am attempting in the following text, a compilation of information, taken mostly from the previous works of various authors, on the major dance forms of the eight states.

The mountainous state of **Arunachal Pradesh,** the largest state in the region, is the homeland of several indigenous communities. Some of the well-known traditional dance forms of the state include the *Aji Lamu* dance of the Monpas that are masked dance-dramas with narrative contents of local Buddhist affiliation. The *Ponung* dance of the Adis is performed by groups of "young girls of the same age group, led by a young man. They form a circle and dance and sing to the jingling of the leader's sword. Their song relates to the creation of crops, domestic animals, man, and society" (Datta, Sarma, & Das, 1994, p. 213). Another dance of the Adis, the Padam Nyani, depicts the daily routine of a housewife through dance. Their *Pasi Kongki* is a dance narration of the bringing of iron from the plains to make dao (a large knife), which is an essential tool for the Adi men for craftsmanship and agricultural works. The *Popir* dance of the Galos performed at the Mopin festival "depicts the myth as to how Abo-tani, the progenitor of mankind, first received various articles for living from the gods" (Datta, Sarma, & Das, 1994, p. 214). The *Hwrw Khañw* dance of the Apatanis was traditionally an all-male dance designed for propitiating the spirits, even though today women seem to perform it more often than men. It is performed during the Morung festival. Among the Idu Mishmis, the *Igu* dance is performed by a priest at a ritual ceremony to chase away the danger of disease or to purify a house visited by death. The Digaru Mishmis have their priest-dance dedicated to the sun god for the protection of man and animals, and another dance is performed by young boys and girls to celebrate the coming of a traditional new year. The *Chalo* dance is performed by the Noctes, singing narrations of their social customs, tradition, and history. It involves dancers clad in colourful costumes, carrying swords and spears, and dancing in a circle. A well-known ritual of the Apatanis is their traditional dance *Roppi*, which is performed after killing an enemy, or any member of the cat family, such as a tiger. It is performed exclusively by men who carry spears in their hands and move around a replica of the enemy. The *Buiya* dance of the Nyishis is performed by girls and boys on the occasion of marriage and the dance is meant to welcome a bride into her new house (Datta, Sarma, & Das, 1994, pp. 213–214).

In **Assam,** the most well-known dance forms in current times are the *Bihu* dance and the *Sattriya* dance. The former is associated with the *Bihu* festival, which is a series of rituals related to agricultural production in earlier times. While the term *Bihu* is a generic one used in an inclusive sense, different indigenous communities of Assam have their own varieties with variations in nomenclature and patterns of performance. Usually, the dance involves performances by boys and girls that symbolically incite the reproductive impulse of Mother Earth so that people get a good harvest at the end of a production cycle.

The *Sattriya* dance evolved as a feature of the Vaishnavite tradition, practised and institutionalised in the monasteries, known as *sattra*s, of Assam. This tradition has existed since the neo-Vaishnavite movement in the 16th century A.D. under the leadership of the versatile guru, Sankaradeva (1449–1568). The solemn respect to Lord Vishnu, in His multiple incarnations, is the central thematic force and purpose of the *Sattriya* dance. It is to be noted that, unlike the other traditional dances of Assam which are mostly put in the category of folk dance, *Sattriya* is one of the recognised classical dances of India. The repertoire of the *Sattriya* includes multiple categories of dances with characteristic gaits, movements, and hand-gestures along with raga and tala-based vocal and instrumental music. The Ojapali dance form which has existed in central and western parts of Assam from a time before the neo-Vaishnavite movement is considered to be the precursor of the Sattriya dance. The *Ojapali* is a semi-dramatic narrative performance involving a master (the *Oja*) and his assistants (the *pali*s, usually two in number, one playing the essential cymbals). A few other notable dance forms of western Assam are the *Kali-chandi* dance, the *Bas-puja* dance, the *Kati-puja* dance, the *Hudum-puja* dance, and the *Kushan-gan*. The *Kali-chandi* dance is performed by a man wearing a mask of the goddess Kali and waving a sword in hand. The *Bas-puja* dance is a vigorous "masculine" dance in which the dancers carry decorated bamboo poles. In contrast to these male dances, the *Kati-puja* and *Hudum-puja* dances are all female affairs in which dramatic depictions of nature and life figure prominently. The *Kushan-gan* is a dance form performed by young boys made up as girls (Datta, Sarma, & Das, 1994, p. 207).

The indigenous communities living in the hills and plains of Assam have their own traditional cultures, including distinct repertoires of traditional dances. The Bodos are famous for their shamanistic *Deodhani* dances (female shaman) performed in their *Kherai* ritual. The dances performed by the *Deodhani* are said to be 18 in number. In these dances, the female shaman dancer performs and may carry a sword and a shield. She also performs "vigorous movements of the head, swinging and tossing the disheveled hair" (Datta, Sarma, & Das, 1994, p. 208). In contrast to the vigour of the *Deodhani*, the *Bagarumba* dance is a very popular graceful dance performed by young girls imitating butterflies. Among the Rabha community, the important dances are *Chathar* and *Pharkanti*. While the *Chathar* is a performance of young men and women on the occasion of the Baikho festival, the *Pharkanti* is a ritualistic ceremonial dance performed on the occasion of death. The Rabhas also have dances related to agriculture and fishing performed by the girls. The Mishing community of Assam are traditionally riverside dwellers and are spread from central to upper Assam. *Ali-aye-ligang* and *Porag* are their two major festive occasions, in addition to Bihu, celebrated with music and dance. In the dances of the *Ali-aye-ligang*, various agricultural processes such as "hunting, fishing, arrow-shooting, rowing, weaving, transplanting and harvesting are suggested" (Datta, Sarma, & Das, 1994, p. 209). The Sonowal Kacharis of upper Assam perform their important dance "singing *haidang* songs in which men dressed in flowing robes dance with gentle movements holding peacock feathers in their hands" (Datta, Sarma, & Das, 1994, p. 209). For the Tiwa community of Assam, the *Sagra misawa* and *Wan sawa* are the most important festivals. The former is a festival of spring and hence it is celebrated with songs and dances of spring, youthfulness, and love. The latter is a post-harvest festival marked with performances by men and women around the sites of ceremonial rice-pounding. The Tiwa version of the *Bihu* celebration is called the *Pisu* in which boys and girls perform the *Boka-nac* in mud. The *Bihu* becomes *Bisu* for the Deoris, their most important performances centring around their chief deities. They dance around the Gira-Girasi in temples, in addition to their performances on agricultural occasions. The Karbis have their most important festive moment in a traditional death ceremony, called the *Chomangkan*. In this highly elaborate ritual, varieties of songs, dances, and narrations are performed by boys and girls. The various dances performed on the occasion involve dancing with decorated bamboo poles, dances by men holding shields and sticks and girls covering their heads in black scarves. Among the Dimasas, the young boys and girls dance in their *Bushu* festival. Rajini gerba and horni gerba are the concluding parts of the community rituals in which the priest (Hojai) cordons off the community area for a certain period (a day or overnight), quarantining the members of the community after invoking the guardian deities of the deities of the area who descend to accept the offerings of the grand traditional worship which is a spectrum of different rituals performed in a series throughout the day. This part of the ritual is performed by the Hojai and no dance is involved in this particular part of the ritual. The Phidimba dance with Seng (traditional sacrificial sword) is performed by the high priests of a Daikho who belong to an indigenous religious institution of the Dimasas. Three priestly classes of the highest order of the Dimasas are Jonthaima, Daingya, and Barowa and their members perform in a *Mishengba* event which takes place every five or six years.

The state of **Manipur** is widely known for its *Manipuri dance* which has been long recognised as one of India's classical dance forms. Four distinct elements can be identified to constitute the present Manipuri dance.

> First, there are the pre-Hindu ritualistic dances of the priestesses, which describe the creation of earth, heaven and man. Second, there is the ancient martial art form of Thang-Ta, which, like the first, is a pre-Hindu ritualistic dance. Third, there is the Rasleela, the cosmic dance of Lord Krishna. Fourth, there are the male-dominated forms, performed to the sound of percussion and cymbals. It accompanies ceremonies like childbirth, marriage and bereavement.
>
> (Manipur, n.d.)

The *Lai haraoba* is the national cultural festival in Manipur which is about "merriment of the gods" and is dedicated to the *umang lai*s or forest deities (Datta, Sarma, & Das, 1994, p. 211). The traditional priests and priestesses are called *Maibas* and *Maibis*, respectively, who lead the dances on ceremonial occasions. In addition to seeking blessings from the deities, the "whole process of creation, procreation, agricultural operation, spinning, weaving, fishing, and playing of games are symbolically reproduced" in the dances of the *Lai haraoba* festival (Datta, Sarma, & Das, 1994, p. 211). Besides the dances in the *Lai haraoba*, the *Thabal-chongba* is a folk dance in Manipur performed by young boys and girls. The *Khubak-ishei* dance is performed with singing, handclapping, and foot movement on the occasion of *Khubak-esei* (*Rath-yatra* or the chariot-pulling festival). Various indigenous communities of Manipur are enriched with their own repertoires of dances.

The Khasis, Jaintias, and Garos are the three major communities in the state of **Meghalaya**. For the Khasis, the most important celebration takes place on the occasion of the *Nongkrem* festival. This is in honour of the ancestral goddess of the Khasis. The festival is celebrated in a place called Smit in the Khasi Hills where women are seen to perform dances in minute graceful movements forming an inner ring, and the performing men form the outer ring around the women. The men dance "holding swords and waving fly-whisks; they take striding steps and engage in a mock combat" (Datta, Sarma, & Das, 1994, p. 213). Among the Jaintias, the *Behdienkhlam* is the most important festival, where "the focus is on praying for the property and good health of the people and on invoking divine blessings for a bountiful harvest" (Festivals and Ceremonies of the "Jaintias", 2019). This elaborate festival is stretched over multiple days and involves cutting, carrying, and the installation of the tall trunks of a specific tree in the Jowai town by spectacularly large crowds. The final day is celebrated with the crescendo in which "both young and old dance to the tunes of the pipes and drums" (Government of Meghalaya, 2020). The *Wangala* is the harvest festival of the Garos celebrated through dances in village houses. In these dances, "the men beat the long drum and some of them dance waving swords and shields, the women dance in a group in gentle steps" (Datta, Sarma, & Das, 1994, p. 213).

The most popular and iconic dance form of **Mizoram** is the *Cheraw* dance, which is also known as the "bamboo dance" among outsiders as the dance involves stepping of young Mizo girls "in and out between and across a pair of horizontal bamboos, held against the ground by people sitting face to face at either site" (Singh, 1995, p. 21). The dance has a variety of patterns and stepping, including stepping made "in imitation of the movements of birds, swaying of trees and so on" (Singh, 1995, p. 21). This dance used to be a part of death rituals in earlier times. However, in present times, it is performed on many other occasions as an art form. Besides this, the *Khuallam* is a Mizo dance performed by men in honour of a guest and the *Chheihlam* dance is performed amidst singing, the beating of drums or tubes or clapping of hands with joy. The *Chailam* and *Rallulam* are two other folk dances of Mizoram, the latter being a war-dance celebrating victory over enemies. Other varieties of war-dance include the *Sarlamkai* and the *Solakia* of the Mara and Pawi communities. There exists a flower dance among the Mizos known as Pârlam, which is performed by girls "dressed in colourful attire with coiffure decorated with colourful flowers" (Singh, 1995a, pp. 24–25)

The state of **Nagaland** describes itself as the "land of festivals" in tourism literature. It is the homeland of several indigenous groups who are placed under the generic term *Naga*. However, several Naga groups are also found outside Nagaland, including pockets of Assam and Manipur. The self-identification of these groups is known to be immensely dynamic and is determined by the inter-group political relations amongst themselves. Their dances are usually associated with one or the other traditional festivals. Some of the important dance forms of the major Naga groups include the *Melo Phita* dance of the Angamis performed by men and women together in the *Sekrenyi* festival; the dance of the Chakesangs in the same festival but performed by men and women separately; the *Sagol Pheikhai* and *Suhtah Lam* dances of the Kukis; *Ngada* festival dances of the Rengmas; the romantic butterfly dance of the Zeliangs; the *Aoleang Lokpu* dance, eulogising victory over enemies, and the *Leisha Lokpu* dance performed by women of the Konyaks. Adding to the many dances of the Naga groups are the *Rukhyo-sharu* war-dance of the Lothas, the *Ghile Kighile* harvest-dance of the Semas, the *Changsang* dance performed during the *Poang LÜm* festival of the Changs, the *MonyiÜ asho* dance of the Phoms, the *Kulu-tsen* head-hunting dance of the Yumchungers, and the *JÜmÜ Nyichi* (*JÜmÜ* – traditional and *Nyichi* – dance) male war-victory dance of the Sangtams (Bhattacharya, 1990, pp. 186–211).

Tripura is the homeland of 19 different tribal communities apart from a few non-tribal communities. The dances of these various groups can be categorised into festival dances, ritualistic dances, and agriculture-based dances (Department of Information, Cultural Affairs & Tourism, Government of Tripura, 2010, p. 156). Some of the well-known dance forms of the state include: *Hozagiri* dance of the Reangs, *Lebang Boomani* of the Tripuris, *Bijhu* of the Chakmas, *Garia* of the Jamatias, and *Cheru* or bamboo dance of the Darlongs. *Gajan* is a festival of the settler Bengali community culminating in Charak Puja, consisting of body piercing and dancing. *Dhamail* is a dance of the Bengali Sylheti community. *Rabindra Nritya* is also a dance of the Bengali community that is part of the heritage associated with Rabindranath Tagore.

For the Himalayan state of **Sikkim**, perhaps the most well-known dance to the outside world is the *Cham* dance – a religious dance tradition of Mahayana Buddhism in Sikkim. This is a spectacular performance wherein the dancing monks put on elaborate costumes, masks, and effigies, visualising protective deities and evils (Gurung, 2020). The major ethnic communities in the state are the Lepchas, the Bhutias, and the Nepalese. The *Chu Faat* is an age-old folk dance of the Lepchas that is performed in honour of Mount Kanchenjunga and four other snowy peaks. Other Lepcha folk dances include the *Mun Hait Lok* dance that depicts the priest controlling the evil spirits, the *Mon-Dryak-Lok* dance that is about the practice of hunting, and the *Tendong Lho Rum Faat* dance that incorporates the narration on flood. The Bhutias perform their folk dance *Chi Rimu* in praise of their beautiful homeland. Their other dances include the *Gnungnala Gnunghey* about the importance of bamboos; the *Tashi Zaldha* dance that involves the offering of white scarves, and the Yak dance that depicts the importance of the animal yak and the life of the herdsmen. The folk dances of the Nepalese in Sikkim include the *Dhan Nach*, or paddy dance, performed by men and women to overcome hardship on the paddy field; *Chyabrung* dance that involves dancing with the beats of the *chyabrung* drum; and the *Maruni* dance performed by young girls during *Deepawali*, the festival of lights (Singh, 1995b).

References to dance in oral, written, and archaeological resources

The act of dancing can perhaps be treated as a universal trait found in every community. Of course, there are individuals who do not dance but it is very unlikely for a community to exist where nobody dances. The patterns, purposes, tastes, values, and ways of making meaning from dance vary between people and places, but dancing, as a cultural form, does exist in every community. The importance given to dance by a community or nation can perhaps be gauged by looking at the manner in which dance is described in various expressive domains such as oral traditions, literary, or historical texts and through archaeological specimens.

In the North-East, folkloric or oral traditional resources are plentiful in the cultural repertoires of all communities. For almost everything in the material and non-material world, one usually finds a myth, legend, tale, ballad, or another narrative form. Myths about the origin of dance are present among several communities. In Arunachal Pradesh, the Tangsas and the Singphos learned to dance from the monkeys and the inhabitants of the sun and the moon, respectively; while the Apatanis, Hill Miris, and Tagins have mythical explanations about the origin of their war dances. The myth of the Sherdukpens tells how the Ajilamu pantomime was created to facilitate the rescue of a woman who was enticed away. The Monpas however believe that the Ajilamu pantomime was created to facilitate the construction of a bridge over a river linking two villages. A legend tells how the monastic dance of the Monpas was first performed to facilitate the construction of a monastery (Sarkar, 1974, p. xiv). In Manipur, the origin of the *Lai haraoba* dance is believed to be from the Koubru hill that was the abode of many gods; and this dance is mythologically described to have emerged during the creation of Meiteis (Singh, 2002, p. 1). In Assam, an oral literary form, called *malita*, is a ballad describing the origin and evolution of specific items. The narrative songs describe the mythical origin of musical instruments like the traditional drum (*dhol*) and the jew's harp (*gogona*). Idioms and phrases used in colloquial Assamese sometimes refer to dancing. For example, sayings such as, "one complains about the floor when one does not know how to dance" or "granny loves to dance and it is now her granddaughter's wedding" revealing that dance is embedded into the day-to-day life of people in Assam. A popular Assamese folktale about "The old couple and the jackals" describes a scene in which an old woman is about to be killed by a group of jackals while returning from her daughter's home. The clever old woman proposed to the jackals that she had learnt a new dance in her daughter's home and now she wanted to perform that dance before her death. The jackals allowed her to dance and while dancing she shouted for a pair of dogs who came and rescued her from the jackals.

References to the North-East Indian region can be found in ancient and epic literatures and various folk narratives. The terms Kamarupa and Pragjyotishpura were used to refer to the state of Assam. In the epic *Mahabharata*, mention can be found about how Arjuna was "fascinated by the dancers of Kamarupa" (Vatsyayan, 1977, p. 169). The *Natyasastra*, a well-known ancient Indian treatise on performing arts written in the period between 1st century B.C. to 3rd century A.D., refers to a form of performance called *Odra-Magadhi* to be "in vogue in the entire north-eastern region covering Anga, Banga, Kalinga, Magadh, Nepal and Pragjyotispur" (Goswami, 2017). Another such treatise, *Abhinaya Darpana* (*the mirror of gesture*) *lasya* (*the graceful feminine dance*) was taught by goddess Parvati to the Assamese princess Usha who in turn taught the art to the milkmaids of western India after she was married to Aniruddha, the grandson of Lord Krishna. Usha's friend, Chitralekha, "used her charm as a dancer to bring Aniruddha from Dwaraka for secret conjugal union with Usha" (Borgohain, 2011, p. 112). A now well-known manuscript, *Srihastamuktavali*, a mediaeval Sanskrit treatise on hand-gestures was found, as a translated work into Assamese in a monastery on the Majuli island. This work is believed to be produced during the neo-Vaishnavite movements of the sixteenth century A.D. incorporating the then "regional dance and music scenario" (Borgohain, 2011, p. 134). Two other important written literary sources have been the *Kalika Purana* of 10th–11th century A.D. and the *Yoginitantra* of the 16th century A.D. that are valuable references to dance and cultural practices of the past in Assam. The chronicles, known as the *Buranji*s, written under different titles by the Ahom scribes at different points of history, also carry information and anecdotes pertaining to the performance of dance in Assam.

A very telling corpus of resources on the prominence of dance as an art in this region in the past is the scattered ruins, temple structures, and archaeological specimens, belonging to different historical periods. Sculptures of dancing figures in different forms and styles depict the prevalence and importance of the art of dancing in this place in bygone days. Some of such archaeological specimens include the figures of Ganga and Jamuna in the doorframe of a probable temple at Dah-parbatia of Tezpur belonging to the 6th century A.D. There are a few other sculptural figures found in Darrang and Guwahati where the depictions of pose, gesture, costumes, and jewelleries reflect dancing characters. In the ruins of Tezpur town, there are a few panels showing a pair of dancers carved within a rectangular frame that captures the par se dance scene (Vatsyayan, 1981). Sculptural renderings of figures of *Devadasi* (temple dancers) are found on the walls of the ancient temples of Hajo, Dubi, Dergaon, and Kamakhya (Sharma Kataki, 1932, p. 44). Noted historian, Pratap Chandra Choudhury, mentioned various archaeological and epigraphic references to the prevalence of the "institution of *devadasis* or temple dancers in the service of the main object of worship, particularly in Siva temples" of Assam in earlier times. "In Assam", as described by Choudhury, "devadasis go by the name of natis, and these unmarried girls were usually supplied [to the temples] by a dancer (nat)" (Choudhury, 1953, p. 538). Mention of the dancing girls of the Kamakhya temple is also found in the accounts of the 18th-century French traveller, Jean-Baptist Chevalier, who describe them as "charming priestesses, with the most beautiful faces and shapes" who "come to initiate the novice to the mysteries of love" (Chevalier, 2008, p. 40). Though Choudhury expressed surprise that the "virgins dedicated for a noble cause" degenerated "into prostitutes and were allowed to defile the temples of god" (Choudhury, 1953, p. 539), Neog opines that the institution of religious dancing flourished in its normal way, but with the fall of local independent rule this fell into abuse after the 17th century (Neog, 2008, p. 341).

Commodification of heritage and dance

In the 19th century with the advent of waves of modernity, the traditional world of the North-East and its cultural contents began to go through radical changes. At the pragmatic level, this emergent modernity in India, including its North-East, was largely constitutive of a few key socio-economic transformations. Change began with the forces of industrialisation, a westernised institutional education, and the gradual emergence of the print media, all contributing to the creation of a new urban culture in India, increasing a vibrant public sphere and a class of elite and educated natives. Subsequently, this new group of elites and educated natives were instrumental in infusing a massive national consciousness among the common people. This cultural nationalism proved to be the most effective tool in India's struggle for freedom that ended successfully in the making of a free and sovereign India in 1947. The resultant processes affected the cultural artefacts of India deeply in terms of their meanings and significance: Artefacts belonging to the world of ordinary traditional life, especially of the rural people, came to be articulated with a kind of heritage value for increasingly urbanised citizens of the country. As rapid industrialisation began to replace the rural landscape with concrete urban edifices, equally proportionate changes in social values and practices occurred. Not only was a divide created between the rural and the urban, but it also resulted in a somewhat perceptual discontinuity between "the past" and "the present". For many, this uncomfortable dichotomy led to a romantic nostalgic longing for the past that had been lost. This was responsible for a new semantic that valued traditional cultural resources, both the material artefacts and non-material traditions of music, dance, and drama – which became indispensable tools for the reconstruction of a lost and desired past. Equally responsible in this regard was the growing pan-Indian nationalist sentiment that necessitated a counter-hegemonic cultural historiography for India with an unquestionably glorious past for all Indians. This was accomplished through the making of a set of nationalist cultural iconographies wherein traditional dance forms, along with other material and non-material traits, are significant. There was a transformation of an array of various ritualistic Indian performance forms into a new category, "cultural heritage". Under this new secular label, various forms of art, including dance, were given great significance. They are now the testimony of a lost glorious past and the markers of Indianness for the outside world. In addition to their aesthetic importance, their sustenance and their conservation for the future became important concerns.

In Assam, nationalist litterateurs, such as Lakshminath Bezbaroa, are credited for bringing the legacies of the Vaishnava guru, Sankaradeva, out of the village prayer halls and into the outside world. This included reconstructions of literary and artistic specimens, various forms of fine arts and performing arts, such as ritual performances of the Bihu and the Vaishnavite dance, drama, and music, as proud symbols of Assamese identity. What is particularly relevant here in the context of dance was the construction of the concept of Indian classical dance in post-independent India. This category included a select number of dances that were then recognised by the new government of independent India as the major forms of art to represent the presumably higher forms of Indian performance tradition, both within and outside the country. The first dance form of North-East India to receive this respectable government patronage was the Manipuri dance and much later similar recognition was extended to the Sattriya dance of Assam. The "construction of the classical, in traditional Indian dance, was forged by the dominant class in India to serve its national ideology" (Chakravorty, 1998, p. 108). These recognised classical dance forms, and many others that were not recognized but demonstrated similar qualities, were characterised by their adherence to long institutionalised traditions and standardised codification through written rules and conventions.

The other important category that began to become equally visible and significant in later decades of independent India was the category of folk dance. In contrast to the classical category, the folk dance traditions were apparently free from the rigid institutionalised structures and were dependent on oral traditions rather than written conventions. In the later quarter of the 20th century, both these categories of dances saw increasing dissemination through various means of public culture and expanding channels of electronic media. What was firmly established in this process was that these various dance forms were no longer attached to the sacred rituals. They became standalone arts, secular and accessible to groups and individuals irrespective of gender, caste, and class. For all constituencies, however, such transformations were never smooth and harmonious. What became evident in later times was that such excessive institutionalisation of the dances, either as classical dances or as intangible cultural heritage, led to a number of undesired consequences. It led to a standardisation of dances which promoted select and fortunate varieties of dance at the cost of many other forms (Dutta, 2017). In Assam, many performers and art connoisseurs believe that the recognition of the Sattriya as a classical dance made the Ojapali a less popular and *less profitable* dance form. Secondly, this also shifted the commanding authority of the dance from the traditional gurus and monasteries to newly opened urban dance schools and bureaucratic offices in the government. The Sattriya, in its monastic form, used to be an exclusively all-male dance. In its proscenium version of present times, this dance is largely represented by the faces of star female performers. While such participation of women in Sattriya is welcomed by all, many also believe that this change is mostly a commodification of the art to satisfy the popular media (male?) gaze, rather than a spirited uplifting through gender equality.

The political narrative of integrated and pan-Indian nationalism faced serious challenges with the rise of ethno-national politics since the late 20th century. The rhetoric of nationalism that had proved to be effectively counter-hegemonic against the western masters of colonialism was also the same narrative of nationalism that emerged as dominant hegemony towards the smaller constitutive ethnicities of the nation. Among the various regions of India, the North-East is particularly known for the assertion of ethnic identities by the various indigenous groups. They vary in intensity against an imposed national hegemony. The most strikingly visible fallout has been the scripting of respective identities by various communities as they promoted their various cultural forms, including their dances. What is currently being experienced in North-East India today, in various forms of cultural articulations, is the ongoing negotiation between the sense of belonging to the nation on the one hand, and to the emergent ethnicities on the other.

As a consequence of coded political negotiations, and because of the ever-increasing values of the traditional performing arts in the emergent culture industry of post-globalisation times, a new festival culture is seen to be in place which involves the showcasing of various cultural artefacts that are packaged and exhibited for popular consumption. With patronage received from both government and private agencies, festivals are effectively intertwined with the network of the tourism industry. These mass cultural events are seen to supersede the erstwhile traditional calendars of dance and music. Added to this, the pervasive outreach of electronic media is also playing a crucial role in shaping the forms of various dances and re-defining the aesthetic norms around these forms. As one illustration of this, the Bihu dance now is less of a fertility ritual in the paddy field; its site has shifted to the floor of the television studio that relentlessly broadcasts reality shows on Bihu dance for most of the year.

What has been discussed so far regards the transformation of local traditional dance forms, once ritualistic activities, into independent arts, thus becoming political capital and economic commodities. However, it should be noted that it has not always been a completely closed and bounded affair, as a cultural link or exchange has been established between the North-East and the outside world. In addition to the traditional Indian dance forms, consumption of performing arts of foreign origin has been there, in varying intensities, since the middle of 20th century through cinema and television, travel, and tourism. With the advent of internet-enabled cyber-culture, such exchanges may undermine territorial boundaries. What can be termed as cultural re-territorialisation or cultural hybridity is apparent, including the culture of dance. This is evident in the increasing experimentation and popularity of categories like fusion dances or dance mash-ups which are seen to populate the current popular dance world of the region

References

Bhattacharya, K. K. (1990). Dances of Nagaland: Script of a Documentary Film. In B. Datta & P. J. Mahanta (Eds.), *Traditional Performing Arts of North-East India* (pp. 186–211). Guwahati: Assam Academy for Cultural Relations.

Borgohain, N. P. (2011). *Female Dance Tradition of Assam*. Guwahati: Purbanchal Prakash.

Chakravorty, P. (1998). Hegemony, Dance and Nation: The Construction of the Classical Dance in India. *South Asia: Journal of South Asian Studies*, XXI(2), 107–120. http://doi.org/10.1080/00856409808723345.

Chevalier, J.-B. (2008). *The Adventures of Jean-Baptist Chevalier in Eastern India (1752–1765): Historical Memor and Journal of Travels in Assam Bengal and Tibet* (C. Dutta-Baruah & J. Deloche, Trans.). Guwahati and New Delhi: LBS Publications.

Choudhury, P. C. (1953). *The History of the Civilization of the People of Assam to the Twelfth Century A.D.* SOAS. Retrieved October 10, 2020, from https://eprints.soas.ac.uk/29600/1/10752572.pdf.

Datta, B., Sarma, N. C., & Das, P. C. (1994). *A Handbook of Folklore Material of North-East India*. Guwahati: Anundoram Borooah Institute of Language, Art & Culture.

Department of Information, Cultural Affairs & Tourism, Government of Tripura. (2010). *Dances & Festivals of Tripura*. Agartala: Department of Information, Cultural Affairs & Tourism, Government of Tripura.

Dutta, P. (2017). Intangible Cultural Heritage in India: Reflections on Selected Forms of Dance. In M. Stefano & P. Davis (Eds.), *The Routledge Companion to Intangible Cultural Heritage* (pp. 230–239). Oxon and New York: Routledge.

Goswami, P. (2017, February 19). *Practice of Raga-Sangita in Pre-Sankaradeva Assam & Sankaradeva Initiation to the Tradition*. Sankaradeva. Retrieved November 5, 2020, from https://www.sankaradeva.com/blogs/195.

Government of Meghalaya. (2019). *Festivals and Ceremonies of the "Jaintias"*. Department of Arts and Culture, Government of Meghalaya. Retrieved November 6, 2020, from http://megartsculture.gov.in/festivals-jaintia.htm.

Government of Meghalaya. (2020). *Behdienkhlam Festival*. Government of Meghalaya. Retrieved November 7, 2020, from https://meghalaya.gov.in/behdienkhlam.

Gurung, P. (2020). Significance of Cham Dance: The Masked Ritual in Sikkim. In S. K. Chaudhuri, S. Maiti, & C. K. Lepcha (Eds.), *The Cultural Heritage of Sikkim* (pp. 223–234). Oxon and New York: Routledge.

Manipur. (n.d.). Ministry of Culture, Government of India. Eastern Zonal Cultural Centre. Retrieved November 5, 2020, from https://ezccindia.org/manipur.html.

Neog, M. (2008). The Dancing Maids of Parihareswara Siva. In M. Neog & P. Neog (Eds.), *Aesthetic Continuum: Essays on Assamese Music, Drama, Dance and Paintings* (pp. 341–345). New Delhi: Omsons Publications.

Sarkar, N. (1974). *Dances of Arunachal Pradesh* (Reprint of 1993 ed.). Itanagar: Directorate of Research, Government of Arunachal Pradesh.

Sharma Kataki, S. (1932). Asamar Pracin Nritya Bhangi. *Awahon, 4th Year, 1,* 44–48.

Singh, K. (Ed.). (1995a). *People of India: Mizoram, Volume XXXIII.* Calcutta: Seagull Books on behalf of Anthropological Survey of India.

Singh, S. K. (1995b). Folk Songs and Dances of Sikkim. *Bulletin of Tibetology,* 104–108. http://himalaya.socanth.cam.ac.uk/collections/journals/bot/pdf/bot_1995_01_full.pdf.

Singh, N. L. (2002). Origin and Evolution of Traditional Forms of Dances in Manipur. PhD thesis, Manipur University, Department of History. Retrieved November 5, 2020, from http://hdl.handle.net/10603/103909.

Vatsyayan, K. (1977). *Classical Indian Dance in Literature and the Arts.* New Delhi: Sangeet Natak Akademi.

Vatsyayan, K. (1981). Some Dance Sculptures of Assam. *Quarterly Journal, 10*(3), 19–35.

2 Sattriya dance
A narrative of its journey through the ages

Pradip Jyoti Mahanta

Atmasanskritirvavashilpani ... .
atmanam sanskurute.

– Aitareya Brahman

(Arts are means of refinement of the self)

Art aims to reveal essential or important elements, or important ideas, in a clearer or more concrete way than real objects are capable. It succeeds in this by employing a set of interconnected parts, systematically changing the relationships between these parts.

– Hippolyte Taine (1865)

Introduction

Indian art of any nature or form, verbal or non-verbal, aural or visual, was envisioned from early civilisations as a means as well as an end when related to self-realisation, refinement, or a dialogue with Divinity. Be it music or dance, drama or theatre, painting or sculpture or any other art form, the arts carry the notion of striving for a higher plane of fulfilment (*purusartha*). Most of the canonical treatises such as Bharata's *Natyasastra* (2nd century BC–2nd century CE) and Sarngadeva's *Sangita Ratnakara* (13th century) celebrate *sangita*, art and artistic pursuit, constituting music, dance, and drama. In this context, it is known as *dharma kamarthamokshadam* (giver of piety, pleasure, prosperity, and liberation) (Sastri, 1953). Religio-secular and social dynamics have been inlaid into any traditional Indian art from their inception and continue to the present day. Seers in the early years of India's civilisation imparted knowledge of religion, philosophy, and other disciplines in their monasteries, innovatively introducing artistic skills and hymnal compositions. These were not merely for exposition of canonical principles, but also to reveal them in a clear and pleasing manner before their young disciples.

The Vedic hymnology along with their interpretive compositions paved the way in evolving the genre of *Samagana*, that is, the mode of singing hymns in sacrificial sessions in honour of deities. This also led to music finding an institutionalised site in religious ceremonies. Prajnananda (1973b) as cited in Prajnanananda (1973a) states, "We are indebted for the Vedic songs and prose (chants) to the poets and Rishis (seers) of ancient India who composed their hymns for the solemn sacrifices" (p. 48). Bharata in his *Natyasastra* refers to the myth of Lord Brahma of the Indian Trinity, who collected the materials for music from the four Vedas and made the structure of the *Gandharvagana*. "This was a new type of music that evolved from 600–500 B.C. from the materials and principles of the *Samagana*" (Prajnananda, 1973b, p. 72). Similar is the myth regarding the emergence of dance in the hands of Lords Brahma and Shiva. The Lord taught Bharata the art of *nritya* and *natya* (dance and drama) and assigned him the role of "scriptor", to write down the knowledge that he received for the benefit of the human world. Setting aside the myths and their supernatural implications, the nucleus of drama is often said to have been contained in the *Samvada* (dialogues) with sections in the *Rig Veda* – dialogues between characters like Yama–Yami and Pururava–Urvashi that were chanted and taught through enactments in sacrificial sessions. Such enactments through institutional pursuits led to the development of *natya* and *nritya* in later years. Scholars such as Manmohan Ghosh (1958) cited in Keith (1964, p. 15) corroborate this view in tracing the history of Indian theatre and dance. Intrinsically connected with such ritual teaching and learning exercises in celebrating the Supreme and worshipping Him is the notion of beauty through visual representation. This is achieved by aestheticising the given text and its performance. Inlaid with this was also the concomitant idea of the sacred and the semi-secular in such presentations. Performances of this nature aimed to please the worshipful God, for visual pleasure of the viewers (devotees), and vindication of the artistic sensibilities of the performers.

True to the Rig-Vedic saying, *rupam rupam pratirupam babhuva – Rig Veda* (forms giving way to a multiplicity of forms) (Dehejia, 2010), multiple forms of art, music, dance, and drama in this context led to the growth of diversity in various parts of the subcontinent in successive stages of history with support and patronage coming from both religious and royal institutions. With increasing social acceptance, some of these art forms such as painting, sculpture, architecture, and music went beyond the confines of the sacred shrines and political establishments, entrenching themselves in the lives of the people. Together with a multiplicity of forms went the flights of imagination in visionary minds, bringing dynamicity and sensitivity in different layers. There was a gradual development in melodic and rhythmic modes, movements and gestures, ascription of emotionalism (*rasa*), innovation and expansion of edifying devices, along with the epistemology of the knowledge related to them. The theory of *rasa* propounded by Bharata in the *Natyasastra* unfolded streams of thoughts and interpretations both within practice and aesthetic formulations as revealed in the works of aestheticians such as Nandikeshvara (*Abhinaya Darpana*), Abhinavagupta (*Abhinava Bharati*), Anandavardhana (*Dhvanyaloka*), and Sarngadeva (*Sangita Ratnakara*). These were documented in different periods of the Christian era. Poetry, music, dance, theatre, and other arts, including architecture, originated and continue in many respects even today as a pursuit of spiritual enlightenment, traversing wide grounds of non-didactic and visual gratification. Along with creative expressions of different art forms, and notwithstanding their divine tenor and intent, these aesthetic treatises (*kalamulashastra*) have over the centuries contributed enormously towards the enrichment of the huge art space successively being enlarged, braving travails of changing time and environment.

The Bhakti Movement was spearheaded by saints and reformers throughout various regions of medieval India. With an unflinching devotion to Divinity, they brought about a new fervour and polyphony in Indian arts, especially in poetry and music. The movement exuded a humanist outlook and a democratic manner of popular participation in religious pursuit. It gave liberty to the individual self, cutting across all barriers in pursuing one's personal God through simpler means bereft of priestly mediation. The saints and composers of the age in extolling devotion to the unity of the Godhead revalidated the inter-webbing of religion with art to the extent of theologisation in emotionalism and art experience (*rasa*). They achieved this mostly through the human manifestation of Lord Krishna, and by integrating it with an emotional exuberance of devotion (*bhakti*). Adopting the language used by the people instead of a canonised and classical Sanskrit in the majority of their compositions, the poets could reach out to the commoners and they built up a trajectory of poetry and hymns in various language traditions.

I felt it necessary to foreground the above discussion in contextualising the subject of Sattriya Dance by placing it in the larger domain of Indian art. Sattriya's emergence and enduring journey through the ages will be discussed, looking at its adaptation to changing times and situations. The phenomenon of Sattriya cannot be viewed in isolation from the terrain of creative impulses preceding it in ancient and medieval India.

The Sattriya tradition

The Sattriya tradition basks in the shine of the green pastoral beauty of nature, with hills surrounding the streams of the Brahmaputra, the red river (*Lauhitya*) providing an overpowering presence. Its history of continuity dates back more than five centuries. The term Sattriya is a composite cultural expression manifested in multiple forms: music, dance, drama, literature, painting, sculpture, and crafts, standing as a unique testimony of a living body of artworks in the cultural history of Assam and of India for that matter. The polychromatic canvas of Sattriya takes into its web an array of varied art forms, and also a distinct lifestyle in the monastic tradition of the *Sattra* that emerged in the wake of the Bhakti Movement in Assam during the 15th–17th centuries.

Srimanta Sankaradeva (1449–1568 CE), saint and preacher, poet, playwright, philosopher, reformer, artist, and composer, was the fountainhead of the Bhakti Movement in Assam. The movement was inspired by the ideal of *bhakti* as a form of spiritual pursuit and was heralded as an all-pervasive cultural resurgence unprecedented in the history of Assam with an efflorescence of all arts, visual and performing. The saint-philosopher with his vision of social harmony and fraternity amidst ongoing conflicts and tensions among diverse ethnic groups, superstitious beliefs, and sacerdotal practices in the garb of religion introduced the faith of devotion (*bhakti*) to the Divinity in the human persona of Lord Krishna. This was enshrined in the *Bhagavata Purana*, a 9th–11th century canonical text. To make the canons and pursuits of the faith an experience of joy, Sankaradeva imaginatively brought in various forms of art and integrated them with the pursuit of *bhakti* in wider platforms of public participation. Towards this end, he composed hymns, epic narratives, and plays and rendered several sections from the *Bhagavata Purana* in Assamese verse, setting them in a performative mode for congregations. The large body of artistic expression, poetry, drama, devotional hymns, and philosophical treatises in melodic verse coming from Sankaradeva himself constituted a huge corpus in this direction, added to which were the works created in the hands of his apostles.

At another level of social organisation during the movement was the institution of *Sattra* with *Namghar* as its epicentre, envisaged by Sankaradeva and his apostolate "as a source of verve and vigour for sustenance of the traditions of religious learning, and the pursuit of art and the new social order born of this resurgent milieu" (Mahanta, 2007, p. 3). The *Namghar* in addition to being the public prayer hall also played multi-polar roles as a seat of learning and theatre. It accommodated other arts as a place for the confluence of all communities on occasions of festivities. The *Namghar* with the sanctum sanctorum placed at one end led to the gradual institutionalisation of music, dance, and drama, after the death of Sankaradeva through dedicated pursuit by the monastic order putting them on a solid foundation to endure for generations as ritual services.

The place of dance in an onward journey of faith

Within this body of variegated expressions comes the *Ankiya Nat* or *Ankiya Bhaona*, introduced by Sankaradeva as a means of drawing the roadmap of his inclusive faith of *bhakti* and its onward journey. Marked by exquisite artistry embedded in its structured form and stylised with subtle combination of music, dance, and drama and other architectonics of theatre, *Ankiya Bhaona* became a powerful medium of popular entertainment with the message of *bhakti* ingrained in it.

As a set of biographical narratives inform us, Sankaradeva mounted his first dramatic experiment *Chihnayatra* (Neog, 1987) in his birthplace, Bardowa, at the beginning of his new journey as a spiritual leader and a playwright-composer. He erected a prayer hall (*Harigriha*) in which he held lyrico-dramatic spectacles with his vision of communicating the kernels of *bhakti* to the multitude in a concrete and pleasurable manner. The dramatist-director of this maiden venture laid the form and structure of the newfound medium, replete with music, dance, and drama and also used painting for creating a visual image of Heaven. In his later plays, however, he gave up the medium of painting or any form of physical scenography focusing more on stylised representations of scenic sequences through music and dance. In raising a spectacle that created wonder in the minds of spectators, Sankaradeva harnessed the services of the surrounding public for furnishing all physical accoutrements; devising musical instruments, masks, costumes; and arranging paper-pulp and colour materials for painting and other accessories. Setting melodic and rhythmic modes, ideation of dance and dramatic stylistics were strokes of his own imagination and creative ingenuity. The spectacular success of the *Chihnayatra* performance with its aesthetic and spiritual appeal established Sankaradeva as a genius with great artistic vision and spiritual enlightenment leaving a deep imprint in the social mind.

Following this novel experiment, Sankaradeva wrote six other plays marked with a more sinewy structure in which dance formed an integral part in the progression of events; entrance – exit, movements, and moments of emotional intensity in respect of the dramatis personae. Even the series of preliminaries in the form of orchestral performances were embellished with dance movements punctuated by intricate footwork and occasional hand gestures. Individual characters and their actions demonstrated variations of flair through dramatic texture to mark the signification of nature and personality inclusive of masculine vigour and feminine grace. Sankaradeva's principal apostle and a prolific composer, Madhavadeva (1498–1596 CE) enlarged the theatre-centric repertoire with a few new compositions for his six plays and introduced another number called *Cali Nac* (Neog, 1987). This was marked with feminine gracefulness and a cadence outside the frame of dramatic performance, which he choreographed for the ceremonial inauguration of the public theatre (*rangavangriha*) in the Barpeta *Sattra* in Western Assam. Thus, through the creative enterprises of Sankaradeva and Madhavadeva themselves, a large trajectory of dance sequences came to the fore that augured a blooming exposition of the art of dance intertwined with the discourse of *bhakti*.

Subsequently, there was a gradual expansion of the religion of *bhakti*, and more and more *Sattras* were established by the apostles of the faith in different parts of Assam. The preceptors and their laity in respective institutions broadened the base of art expression in different directions and founded them as ritual pursuits in support of religious services. In another development, two distinct orders, domestic and celibate, appeared in the *Sattra* system under the umbrella of four different schisms. Although foundational tenets of the faith remained the same, differences began to surface among them in respect of the order of services, festivities, and specialisation of certain arts while music and drama continued to be an enduring exercise in all the *Sattras*. In this voyage of arts, the Kamalabari group of *Sattras* situated in Majuli, a river island of the Brahmaputra, dance found itself deeply rooted alongside other expressive forms.

In a rekindled atmosphere of concomitant pursuit of *bhakti* and art, the monastics of the celibate Kamalabari order, in their wisdom and with a passionate zest, celebrated the greatness of the saints and their monumental work. They culled out dance sequences from the texture of the plays and recontextualised them as special offerings in the ritual services of the calendric occasions of the *Sattra*. The exponents of the *Sattra* drew on collective memory in the process of transmission, rearranging each of the dances by decorating them with frills of rhythmic feats, movements, and gestures. They presented them in new performance contexts without impairing the devotional appeal and structural setting of the original. Dance with its supportive music and in its refurbishment as an independent pursuit found a pre-eminent place in all festivities and came to be a sustained creative engagement in the *Sattra* among the devotee monks. The vocabularies were enhanced with the appropriation of newer rhythmic and melodic mnemonics, movements, hand gestures, and footwork. An oral pedagogy, called *mati-akhara* (ground exercise), was developed to train child monks. Costumes were designed in these celibate *Sattras* that tended to make dance a distinct marker of the Kamalabari group. In most of the other *Sattras*, domestic and celibate, dance continued to remain a part of the *Ankiya Bhaona* performances instead of being an independent discipline of sustained avocation.

The fame and glory of the Kamalabari *Sattra* as a seat of dance spread across its confines reaching parlours of the ruling Ahom court. An invitation was extended to the *Sattra* to present dance on a regal occasion to be held in honour of a visiting Manipuri king in the 18th century (Bhuyan, 1964). Dance was a ritually charged devotional exercise, an offering of prayer at the *Namghar* and the thought of taking it outside the sacred space of the sanctum caused a sense of uneasiness. To avoid causing embarrassment in declining the royal order, the *Sattra* innovatively worked on improvising a new dance, effecting changes in rhythmic patterns and such other allied aspects. It was presented before the royal nobility marking a new chapter in its history. Named as *Rajaghariya Cali Nac*, the dance scintillating with beauty, grace, and movement patterns came to remain as a distinct number in the repertoire of dance in the *Sattra*, without forming a core part of the ritual services.

Sources of inspirational expression

The traditions of art, music, dance, and theatre, emerging from the creative milieu of the Bhakti Movement and shining with ornate grandeur, often raise a reflective question as to what constituted the source and canonical treatises from which the saint composers drew material and inspiration in devising these expressions. Many of the prevailing classical traditions of dance and music in India refer to the treatises like Bharata's *Natyasastra*, Nandikesvara's *Abhinaya Darpana*, and Sarngadeva's *Sangita Ratnakara* in this regard. Even the Sanskrit drama flourishing in the earlier years of the Christian era was founded on the principles laid by the *Natyasastra*.

Sankaradeva often drew on the *Bhagavata Purana* and other puranic texts in introducing the faith of *bhakti* in the Brahmaputra valley. Like a modern academic, he copiously acknowledged the sources in his various compositions. We do not come across such references either in pedagogic or performative levels of Sattra-centric dance, theatre, or music traditions. On closer scrutiny, however, there appear occasional similarities between many of the technical traits evident in the *Sattra* tradition such as hand gestures, footwork, and torso movements in dance. This also applies to the character of *Sutradhara* and the sequential order in drama – use of melodic and rhythmic modes including percussive instruments in music. These similarities are not necessarily direct carry-overs of the canonical principles of the texts. The entire gamut of vocabularies and nomenclatures denoting the technical traits is set in the vernacular, appearing to have been derived from local situations and domestic usage. In the same manner, there are many other traits clearly evident in the *Sattra* traditions and peculiar to them which are not to be found in any other major traditions of Indian dance and music, and also not supported by any of the treatises. It may be possible that Sankaradeva in the early years of his long pilgrimage had come across some of these texts and experienced Sanskrit drama and carried with him the memories of the *sattras* as well as the performance style of Sanskrit drama and adapted them wherever relevant. In an interactive process between the *Margi* (classical) and the *Desi* (regional), the scriptural and the local ingredients became subsumed into the chiselled structure of the *Sattra* arts. This applied especially to dance in the present context, amidst a mixed and multi-ethnic social canvas, with invisible liminal boundaries between the scriptural authority and the local (Mahanta, 2015). What emerges with splendour and majesty is the versatility of Sankaradeva in devising the incredible art space alongside the pursuit of *bhakti* with a wide reach and base.

An appreciation of the Sattra throughout history

Dance continued as an avowed pursuit in the Kamalabari group of *Sattras* forming an essential component of their monastic activities, even braving adverse circumstances caused by social and political upheavals in different periods of the turbulent history of Assam. The changing situations did not diminish the image and impact on the social mind of the *Sattras* at large as hallowed institutions of religion and culture. Annexation of Assam to British India after the fall of the Ahom rule in 1826 as a sequel to the continued Burmese invasions that caused devastation in the social polity in the valley brought sea-changes in administrative, judiciary, economic, and educational fields of the state. The colonial administration took cognisance of the far-reaching impact of the Vaishnava religion and culture on the social life of the people and the role of the *Sattras* in perpetuating peace and harmony among the populace. A status quo was maintained without causing any interruption in the religio-social affairs and functioning of the *Sattras*. The Baptist Missionaries extended their activities from their base at Serampore in Bengal by establishing churches at Sibsagar and Guwahati in the early years of the 20th century. They did not make any dent in the Assamese psyche because of the deep-seated influence of the Vaishnava religion and culture. There was a deep emotive imprint of cultural expression, including the liberal ethos of the *bhakti* faith on the larger Assamese consciousness. This stood as an impediment to the efforts of the Mission in entrenching itself in the Brahmaputra valley. The *Sattras* too, belonging both to the domestic and the celibate orders, left to themselves, stayed away from the colonial state machinery with a sense of benign acceptance of the reality, which in other ways facilitated the sustenance of their pursuits of all activities including art practices. Appreciative remarks by B.C. Allen, a high British official, were recorded in the *District Gazetteers of Assam, Sibsagar* (1905) on the peaceful *Sattra* way of life after his visit to the Garmur *Sattra* in Majuli,

> There are no traces of blood or grease, there is nothing disgusting or grotesque, and the whole place is dominated by that note of decency and propriety which is so marked a characteristic of Vaishnavism in Majuli ... . There is something singularly gracious and pleasing in the whole atmosphere. Everything is fresh and neat and well to do. The well groomed monks are evidently at peace with themselves and the world at large.
>
> (Allen, 1905, pp. 95–96)

This speaks well of the attitude of the British rulers towards the *Sattra* way of life in general. Amidst this environment, dance and other arts continued to flow with abiding religious dedication and fervour even during the colonial regime.

A national awakening of Assam's culture and heritage

The struggle for India's freedom also brought a new national awakening of Indian culture and heritage for reaffirmation of the country's identity as a nation endowed with much civilisation. Amidst this nationalistic resurgence, each region of the subcontinent invoked its past heritage. This manifested in diverse cultural expressions to contribute to the whole of multi-linguistic, multi-religious, multi-ethnic, and multi-cultural matrices of India. In this buoyant environment of reawakening, social thinkers and litterateurs in Assam rediscovered that the Vaishnava Renaissance in Assam with Sankaradeva and his manifold contributions remaining the centre stage was the perfect embodiment of the Assamese mind and its national consciousness (Mahanta, 2015). Such a romantic view of the past as well as the personality of Sankaradeva continued to play a role in the minds of the neo-elites even in the years after independence. Literary and cultural historians made fulsome references to the almost millennium-old scribal tradition of Assamese language and literature, along with its rich inheritance of other fine arts, where Sankaradeva and his age figured pre-eminently. The glorified look at the past brought to the fore an entire range of cultural expressions of the Vaishnava Renaissance as sites of heritage and a newer understanding surfaced in the intellectual arena of Assam. Whereas comparatively speaking, "several music and dance traditions elsewhere in the country had undergone a process of revival and reinstallation" (Vatsyayan, 1992, p. 23), with heritages lost in circulation under adverse social and political conditions, dance, music, and other arts in the *Sattras* continued to be pursued in ritual spaces with a halo of sacred art. The need of that hour was to locate them at the wider social level of acceptance as resources of the heritage of Assam, emulate and learn them outside the sanctum. In the initial years after India's independence, groups of *Sattra* monks were invited to give presentations on public occasions of auspicious nature. These connoisseurs' efforts were taken by public enthusiasts and organisations, in engaging *Sattra* exponents of music, dance, and drama to impart training of these arts to the young generation outside the premises of the institution. It marked a new chapter in the journey of the *Sattra* arts in finding them an enlarged avenue of acceptance, participation, and exhibition.

Along with this new move came a considerable change in the newer performance space of *Sattra* dance and drama in particular. Dance and theatre in the precincts of the *Sattra* remained for ages solely a domain of the male. Female characters were impersonated by male monks and devotees. In the new environment, female dancers and actors entered into the performance space necessitating a refurbishment of the traditional costume and other decorative items for gender-related purposes. Simultaneous changes also occurred in the form of compact and precise presentations on a proscenium stage before an audience, against the illustrative nature of performance at the ritual space of the large *Namghar* in front of the sanctum with spectator-devotees sitting around. Performances of music, dance, and drama in the *Sattra* or the *Namghars* in the villages constituted a duty or obligation on the part of the devotees in the form of an offering to the deity. However, the issues of institutional support coming from the government and other agencies became a sine qua non in respect of these art expressions tending to be invitational exercises. A process of the politics of representation emerged in the secular arena. As a result, the ritual rigour and devotional impulse are often replaced by a showcasing of talent and entertainment of an audience.

The Government of Assam at the state level and institutions like Sangeet Natak Akademi (the National Academy of Music, Dance, and Drama) at the national level undertook various measures towards the extension and promotion of the *Sattra* traditions – music, dance, and *Ankiya Bhaona*. It is worthwhile to remember in the context of the *Sattra* tradition of dance entering a national situation that its maiden exposure was during the first

National Seminar on Indian Dance held in New Delhi in 1958 under the aegis of Sangeet Natak Akademi (Kothari, 2013). The late Maheswar Neog, then a young academic from Assam in his erudite presentation, drew a panoramic pen-picture of the hallowed tradition with select demonstrative performances by a group of monks led by a revered maestro, the late Maniram Dutta Muktiyar of the Kamalabari *Sattra*, Majuli. The exposition, a newfound experience for the scholars, critics, and dance exponents belonging to other traditions of Indian dance, opened up a new vista of understanding at the wider national level. This marked a new chapter in Sattriya's journey from the enclosures of the *Sattra* environment to a larger domain. Celebrated and exponential minds underscored the need to promote this great and living tradition, distinctive in its own right, which propelled the Akademi to adopt various measures in a phased manner to promote it, including giving honours to maestros of the traditions (Neog, 2009, pp. 291–292). At an increasing pace, various other institutions too came up with supportive measures in this direction. In the event of institutional support, signification and increasing exposure, came the need for a comprehensive nomenclature to designate the gamut of *Sattra* dances which otherwise constituted a variety of numbers and segments independent of each other having different names. The term "Sattriya" was chosen through consensus among *Sattra* practitioners and scholarly minds as a qualifying name to denote the tradition born of Sankaradeva's vision. The name was also cultivated and exalted as a hallowed cultural expression of tribute to the saint-composer. Thus, "Sattriya" is a modern appellation coined holistically to identify the entire range of expressions belonging to the *Sattra* system of life and pursuit that received wide circulation at all levels including academia.

Another significant dimension added to the gradual extension of the Sattriya traditions of arts and dance in the present context is that of its academic exploration since the sixth decade of the last century. Founded in 1955 in Shillong, then the capital of undivided Assam, the Assam Sangeet Natak Academy through the initiative of a group of connoisseurs and scholars started a series of activities. They held musical conferences and implemented projects where they documented and interpreted various facets of Sattriya music and dance leading to a set of publications. The universities in Assam opened their doors to young and enterprising scholars for undertaking academic research on diverse portals of the Sattriya tradition of arts resulting in value additions to these forms through academic–practitioner interface. The State College of Music, Assam, affiliated to the University of Gauhati, Dr Bhupen Hazarika, Centre for Performing Arts, Dibrugarh University, and Sattriya Sangeet Mahavidyalaya Jorhat, affiliated to Dibrugarh University, have adopted an institutional curriculum of Sattriya music and dance for undergraduate and postgraduate studies.

The above discussion is a set of pen-pictures of various historical and cultural factors that have been instrumental in shaping the emergence and journey of Sattriya Dance along with its phenomenal presence in the life of the *Sattra* institution, and Sattriya is a pursuit of piety residing in the world outside as a site of Assamese heritage. It is also necessary to put on record that the present discussion is not a complete historical account. Social, political, and literary evidence go hand in hand with Sattriya dance and other arts under the same umbrella.

References

Allen, B. C., (1905), *District Gazetteers of Assam* (Sibsagar), Gauhati, Government of Assam.
Bhuyan, S., (Ed.), (1964 Reprint), *Tungkhungiya Buranji*, Gauhati, Directorate of Historical and Antiquarian Studies, Government of Assam.
Dehejia, H., (2010), *Akriti to Sanskriti: The Journey of Indian Forms*, New Delhi, Niyogi Books.
Ghosh, M., (1958), *Contributions to the History of the Hindu Drama*, Calcutta, Firma KL Mukhopadhyay.
Keith, A., (1964), *The Sanskrit Drama*, London, Oxford University Press.
Kothari, S., (Ed.), (2013), *Sangeet Natak*, Vol. XLVII(1–4), New Delhi, Sangeet Natak Akademi.
Mahanta, A., (2015), Sattriya Dance and the Sastric Memory. In Venkataraman, L. (Ed.), *Sangit Natak Akedemi Journal*, Vol. XLIX (1–2) (pp. 39–52). New Delhi, Sangeet Natak Akademi. ISSN 0972-494X
Mahanta, P., (2007), *The Sankaradeva Movement: Its Cultural Horizons*, Guwahati, Purbanchal Prakash.
———, (2015), *Bezbaroa's Writings on Sankaradeva, Vaisnavite Religion and Philosophy*. In Śarmā, M., & Nath, D. P. (Eds.). (2014). *Lakshminath Bezbaroa: The Architect of Modern Assamese Literature: Issues of Nationalism and Beyond*. Perfect Imagers for Centre for Assamese Studies, Tezpur University.
Neog, M., (Ed.), (1987), *Guru Carita Katha*, Guwahati, Gauhati University.
——— (2009), *Jivanar Digh Aru Bani* (2nd edition), Guwahati, Chandra Prakash.
Prajnananda, S., (1973a) Third International Congress for the History of Religions.
Prajnananda, S., (1973b) *The Historical Development of Indian Music: A Critical Study*, India, Firma K.L. Mukopadhay.
Sastri, P. S., (Ed.), (1953), *SangitaRatnakana*, Vol. IV, Madras, Adyar Library.
Taine, H., (1926), *The Philosophy of Art* (1865), Paris, Hachette.
Vatsyayan, K., (1992 Reprint), *Indian Classical Dance*, New Delhi, Publications Division, Government of India.

3 Moving objects and thinking body
A dancer's narrative

Anwesa Mahanta

Introduction

> Looked at again and again, half consciously, by a mind thinking of something else, any object mixes itself so profoundly with the stuff of thought that it loses its actual form and recomposes itself a little differently in an ideal shape which haunts the brain when we least expect it.
>
> (Woolf, 2003, p. 98)

From objects in physical space to the space within, a dancer raises a narrative through the manipulation of choreographic content. The dance weaves a texture that emotes reflective thoughts, providing a panoramic vision, both within and outside of the body. As a professional Sattriya dancer, I speak to my own personal experience in order to philosophise and reflect on the union of body and mind through an acceptance of objects and artefacts as being inseparable from movement.

Objects, commodities, and cultural artefacts surround our habitat, with which there is daily human contact through our senses, perceptions, and actions. We select objects of our choice, expressing something of ourselves, drawn from a sense of desire, familiarity, and connection. A simple example of a personal living space provides a glimpse of this affective dimension of a spatial frame through chosen objects. I personally collected wooden sculptural motifs from Chidambaram in Tamil Nadu, celebrating a memory of my visit to the place and as a mark of respect to the sculptural marvels of the temple architecture that deeply moved me. Dance subjectively involves "a deep connection within the framework of an object-subject relationship where the expressivity and representational nature of an object is experienced by the perceptivity of the subject" (Siegel, 2006, p. 355). Dance finds its expression in different spaces as a ritualistic performance form depending on its presentational contexts. The choreographic narrative of a dance form, however, is connected through cultural motifs, artefacts, and objects.

The arrested movements found in the manuscript folio of the Sattriya dance tradition and the motivational dimensions of performing bodies in practice can be seen in painted forms. Sattriya dance inspires both mediums in its expressive content. Poet, Saint Madhavadeva, the principal apostle of Srimanta Sankaradeva, was so moved by an artisan's workmanship as revealed in a set of wooden carvings on the door of Namghar (a hall for prayer and social activity), that he spontaneously uttered that he too would carve these motifs of creepers in his poetry. The association between the body of the dancer and the object in relation to the space can be seen in various artistic contexts. The objects can stir emotions, creating a mobility through perceived notions that mediate a bodily expression. Virginia Woolf's leading statement guides us to the important cues of this process of perception, conception, mobility, transformation, belonging, becoming, and representation (Woolf, 2003). Tuan (1980) relates to "the interplay of an object/cultural artefact and body/mind relationship in the multi-layered representations of the material and the mental" (p. 462). As a dancer, I am able to relate to the construct of an artefact. As I begin to present my dance as a Sattriya disciple under the tutelage of a teacher addressed honorifically as Adhyapak, the oscillation of the object as a material and mental construct in a paradigm of performativity and belonging begins. As a token of respect, a disciple offers a gamocha (a traditional cotton garment with floral motifs and a red border) with a betel nut and areca leaves in a sorai (a bell-metal tray with sacred usage), in expectation of a wonderful journey ahead.

"The longing of being" (Bell, 1999, p. 2) is part of a new system of knowledge that is responded to by an acceptance of an offering by the teacher. When performing, a mutual sharing of gamocha provides the object with an assumed symbolic identity and a sense of belonging and acceptance. In this present chapter, I research nuances of embodiment through my insight as a Sattriya practitioner. A narrative of a dance form and its perspective by a practitioner cannot be viewed in isolation without philosophical speculation and within the context of physical affairs of the land and its people (Vatsyayan, 1983, p. 3). As I weave in tangible dimensions of the material culture of the Sattriya tradition, I also explore and analyse the mobility of the object in stirring the creative imagination of the dancer, which helps to define the spatial body and the narrative of the dance and the dancer.

Spatial frame and visualisation of objects

> Wherever your eye falls – for it will fall on what you love – will lead you to the questions of your life, the questions that are incumbent upon you to answer, because that is how the mind works in concert with the eye. The things of this world draw us where we need to go.
>
> (Reilley, 2000, p. 25)

The first line defines a spatial frame for an object that the mind creates, imbuing it with a performativity. Inspired by Upanishadic thought, especially seen in various dance forms of India, it is important to relate the multiple frames of the dancing body within the physical space reaching out to the infinite space in an organic interaction of mind, matter, sense, and spirit (Vatsyayan,

1997). An echo of these philosophical speculations forms the foundation of Indian classical dance. Manifestation of the flexible form is thus a finite part of the infinite and its objective is to invoke the experience of the omniscient and the infinite. Nevertheless, by analysing Reilley's quote, we can perceive that an emotional attachment towards an object may lead towards a motion of time and space within a psychical state. This happens through the visualisation of an object creating perception and a stirred imagination. Through dance, a dancer may apply the abstraction of body movements to emote an infinite spatial existence seeping from a physical form. For instance, the Ramayana outlines how the Hara Dhanu (the bow) is lifted by the prospective groom of Sita as a statement of valour, honour, and chivalry and with the blessing of Shiva. This cosmic design reiterates how multiple emotions are interwoven within a physical containment of a bow. Medhi (1997) cites Sankaradeva's play *Sri Rama Vijaya* where it is thus stated:

Ohi mahesaka dhanu: gagana hante parala tadanantara akashi bani sunalah ohi dhanuta je guna dite paraya taheka mathe kusuma mala diye sita swami baraba, iha satya jani jatna karaha.

(p. 255)

(This bow of Shiva fell from the sky with an oracle, "one who can bend the bow with the string will be adorned with the nuptial garland by Sita". Knowing this truth (O Kings and princes) you try yourself).

In the ancient Indian performance treatises such as the Natyasastra and Sangita Ratnakara, there are specific suggestions about the spatial dimension and décor regarding paintings, ornamented pillars of skilful craftsmanship, floral adornment of the space, and bell-metal lamps. Inspired by such references, a dancing space is usually designed with an architectural frame and curation. The dancing body in its minutest of movement performs in relation to the physical space. Whether sitting, standing, half sitting, reclining, or bending, the dancing body is situated in a space and traverses through a range of expressions and emotional relativity from the finite to the infinite, said to the unsaid, form to the formless. Right from the beginning, it is noted in the first lesson when a dancer is learning a traditional dance such as Sattriya, the teacher situates the dancing body on the earth and bends it towards the sky, connecting the main source of energy – the naval to a cosmic energy. Traditionally, when engaging in dance training in the Sattra institutions of Assam, the Namghar orientates the dancing body in space and time quite spontaneously. However, in urban dancing spaces, the physical space is framed in such a way that material objects such as instruments, iconographies of deities, or picturesque frames of idols are placed to evoke the same spirit and matter. In the history of Indian dance traditions, despite each one having a different narrative, the genesis of the tradition finds its roots in a ritualistic form within the temple spaces. Hence, within a modern context, in a studio or on a stage, the dancer tries to invoke the engagement of the form and the content through an introduction to iconic representations of artefacts that connect to the metaphysical form of dance.

In the context of living dance traditions such as the Sattriya, where the dance is still performed as a ritual ceremony in prayer halls (Namghar), the spatial frame reflects different dimensions. There is no idol worship, and the sanctum sanctorum contains the Srimadbhagavata Purana (a principal text of Vaishnavism) or the Kirtanaghosa (a volume of poetic compositions) with an ideational belief of Nirakar (formless). Hence, the dance repertoire is philosophised with the idea of absorption of infinity through fluid movements, circular representations, a soft-footed nature, and a balance of grace and energetic vigour. The references and readings of the cultural narratives and artefacts, such as manuscript paintings, engravings on the walls of temple sites, and the Namghars, provide me as a dancer a feel of constant oscillation between the outer and the inner space. The formless takes on a form to assist in an understanding of a microcosmic unit of the macrocosmic whole.

When interviewed, Hari Prasad Saikia Barbayan, a Sattra inmate, said that the Namghar, for him, is a "space of connect". While it is a space where you connect to several minds, the spatial exhibits of the Namghar also make it a heritage reservoir site. With the artefacts and motifs connecting him to the philosophy of the Sankaradeva Movement, the space with the gathering becomes both a living site of heritage and socio-cultural space. The artefacts are not just objects kept in the museum. Here, the physical space leads towards the visualisation of the objects in a mental space. The material objects represent the aura of the space and invoke a sense of longing to be in that space. When this occurs, "it defines the mobility of the object in its spatial frames of transit and transition" (Svasek, 2014, p. 2). People buy the idols of gods from the temples, or the Bhagavat Purana, venerated as a holy book from book stalls. The Gamocha with a sacred motif inscribed on it is bought from a Namghar.

The existence of the body: subject–object

The body exists in the space, but the space also inhabits the body. Merleau Ponty (1962) discussed a body in movement while inhabiting space,

> Movement is not limited to submitting passively to space and time, it actively assumes them, it takes them up in their basic significance which is obscured in the commonplaceness of the established situations.
>
> (p. 102)

While bodily actions are ingrained in the body's system, the body also absorbs the cultural values of society through the subjective experiences of human interactions and the materials of their surroundings. The body interestingly wears a social costume in sync with the social construct of the body image.

In the Sattriya dance tradition of Assam, the concept of the body would be defined as a union of masculine and feminine qualities, as penned by Sri Sri Madhavadeva in Nam Ghosha – *prakriti purusha duiro niyanta Madhava* [Thou art the soul of and loving friend of both men and women]. Both the male and female genders are guided by Lord Krishna. As a dancer trained in the Sattriya dance tradition, I have experienced the changing of costume in order to adapt to a new subjective experience of a body conceptualised with the perceptions of social, cultural, and philosophical expectations. The theory of performativity refers to the establishment of identity through a form of role-playing in which we present ourselves according to "our perceptions of the cultural expectations of what we should be" (Spivey, 2004, p. 115). Perceived as a patra (empty vessel) in treatises such as the Natyasastra, with the rigour of practice and training, the individual adapts a dancing body to the core thoughts, principles, and ideals of a particular dance form. The training involves a sensory experience of embodying a new cultural narrative through movements with an active participation of body and mind. The rehearsed actions of the body become so much a part of the sense experience that meanings become created through the body. It is much like a "touch" and "feel" experience where the body exposits a powerful medium of knowledge and where the sense of contact happens through the thinking body. As Springay (2005) stated, "It is a mode of inquiry that dislocates binary opposites questioning the role the body plays in the construction" (p. 35). Further, as an expressive note of this bodily existence, aharya or the external décor of the body comes to the fore. Indian dance traditions have distinctive costumes that signal as markers of a particular tradition. In Sattriya, where the dance form is divided into male and female dances, costume marks a difference with the respective representations. While the performing body remains the same, the gestural interpretations and the framework of ornamentation and décor change with costume. I remember my training process, where I was constantly asked to interpret the movements with both vigour and grace depending on the content of the narrative and build up a psychological framing of the body. The differences in the costumes further enhance the psychological framing of the dancing body, so much so that now I feel my representation of a male dance number is incomplete without the costume and the jewellery. A dancer's body embraces the use of these artefacts and individually shapes the décor of the presentation through the choice of colour and size of the material to enhance the beauty of the performance. Hence, each performing body has a different visual narrative pertaining to the context and the body. The costume or the jewellery prepared within different spatial–temporal frames adds the narrative content of the weaver and designer. To view this apart from the context of dance, the woven design would just be a cultural commodity or an artefact. Once the dancer weaves in these units as an organic part of his/her narrative, the commoditised socio-cultural object becomes embodied into the absorption of the aharya (the inspiration or breath) of the dancing body. The jewellery and the attire become synonymous with the dance form, inter-relating the tangible and the intangible. While the aharya is an organic component of the art form, it also represents the cultural artefacts of the region itself. In Sattriya, the costume of the dancer is woven by weavers from Sualkuchi, who embody cultural narratives as they weave patterns in the dress material. The gold ornaments are prepared by khanikars of Upper Assam, mostly from Nagaon and Jorhat, who in a similar way would prepare sets. The flowers made of pith come from the Goalpara region and all reflect the cultural narratives of the region.

From the audience's point of view, a dancing body is for viewing, which transforms the "subject into an object" in the spectator's gaze. However, unlike a scopophilic spectacle, here the body of the dancer demands participation from the audience in terms of the audience's reception of the dancer's thoughts and interpretations of the narrative. A successful interaction would create the rasa sannidhi or confluence of emotions aroused with the performance. In a large performance space, the nature of performativity transforms each existent being as a thinking body in a process of sensory experience. An intersubjective space (Benjamin, 1986) is constructed – where the bodies step out in their respective costumes into the aharya of the thinking bodies sharing a dialogue of emotional involvement and engagement through a sense of "self" constructed in relation to actions and reactions, presence and absence, perception, and reception. The reception of the audience sharing their individual narratives of the performance enhances the significance of this intersubjective space, irrespective of physical time and space.

There are several personal incidents from my dance diaries where persons from the audience have shared their thoughts following the witnessing of the narrative and a few also have experienced cathartic experiences during the performance. One such personal experience was during a Sattriya session at Queen's University Belfast, as part of my academic module "Love, Hate and Beyond: Emotions Culture and Practice". The module's objective was to discuss wider theoretical perspectives on emotions. While relating the emotive situations in daily life, I tried to translate various emotive layers through movements taken from the vocabulary of Sattriya dance. Towards the end of the discussion, a dance piece was presented where the nayika, or heroine, expresses her deep love towards the protagonist drawing on various analogies of nature. Written in Brajabuli, a poetic language that evolved during the Bhakti Movement of Eastern India, the poem was interpreted with facial expressions and body movements. The students responded to the piece very well and came up with thoughtful questions. Weeks later one of the students happened to meet me in a grocery store, and the student as an observant performer narrated his thoughts on the piece shown and how the emotions shown in the piece left a deep imprint in his mind. While the dance and the subject mobilised the emotional significance of the content, the movements both depicted and perceived by the onlooker channelled an "interconnectedness through emotive mobility where the audience is aware of the active engagement of the performer in mobilising their thoughts and emotions"

Moving objects and thinking body 39

Picture 3.1 Anwesa Mahanta dressed in a male Sattriya dance costume.

Picture 3.2 Anwesa Mahanta dressed in a female Sattriya dance costume. Images, Deepak Mudgal.

(Albright, 2013, p. 75). There are many personal narratives where dance movements move minds and emotions on various levels.

> a person whom I met and who shook me up, herself being moved and I was moved to see her moved and she, feeling me moved being moved in turn ... Helene Cixous.
>
> (Albright, 2013, p. 75).

Space and the extended body

> We find it familiar to consider objects as useful or aesthetics as necessities or vain indulgences. We are on less familiar ground when we consider objects as companions to our emotional lives or as provocations to thought.
>
> (Turkle, 2007, p. 5)

During my fieldwork with the mask performers of Bharigaan, a dramatic performance by the Rabha community of Assam, the performer Bachan Rabha said during an interview, "there's always a call from these masks and I realise that it's time for me to perform". The comment was overwhelming for me to see the connection of the performer with the masks and the cultural artefacts of his community. The mask is not merely a cultural object but an embodied artefact that responds to the call from within. "These masks become expressive modes of 'transformation' and 'transcendence' and represent the being suggested by the mask" (Sheppard, 2001, p. 27). I questioned how the masks with static expressions helped him in his performance. The performer smiled and said, "The masks guide me in my moves." The performer determines the structure of the dance around his character and curves his movements to embody and enliven the character. The mask is now an extension of the whole body, where the connection to the audience is through this embodied vision.

In some performances, even the dancing space on the stage is decorated with lamps, sculptures, and idols of gods and goddesses. While it is not mandatory to include these iconic images, the practitioners may use them as extended elements of the performing body. The national broadcasting television channel, Doordarshan, arranges cultural motifs such as manuscripts, painted masks, and textiles when designing sets for a telecast of Sattriya dance. Depending on the conceptual framework of the choreography, artefacts in the form of props are used in the performance space. They form an organic part of the narrative that functions as a tool in developing the environmental atmosphere of the whole stage. The use of props in choreography adds another dimension to the entire thinking process and the actions of the performer. The shapes of the extended bodies create an artistic image and connotations of the conceived idea. The body's spatiality here encompasses a "subjective spatiality of situation showing the larger existential framework of the 'my body is in the world'" (Preester, 2007, p. 353). Dance scholar Arshiya Sethi stated during a personal interview with the writer several years ago in 2016 that the dancing body with its moves is "constitutive for space, a bodily and external form, one system". She proposed that, as a Dhyana Padam or symbol of the sanctum, the sculpted images of deities such as Nataraja, Krishna, Jagannath, or a replica of Agnigarh (fire arch used in Sattriya tradition), lead one into the essence of dance. Moreover, this usage started as a moment of redesigning the space, with the props and rangoli (painted artwork on the floor) to give a sacred look to a proscenium stage to "throw back the temple linkages of the dance started by the pioneers of Bharatanatyam like Rukmini Devi Arundale" (Sethi, 2016).

From the iconic images and painted imageries, props are also used as narrative content informing the performance, where the functional tools shape the body of the performance. A Sattriya performance ritualistically begins with an aarkapor (white screen) where two persons hold a piece of cloth and the performer stands behind it which draws the distinction between the real world and the constructed space of the performance. Interviewee Sethi (2016) further states,

> The piece of cloth in other Indian classical dance contexts is also seen sometimes as a veil of a woman, or as a baby, and in dance forms such as the Kuchipudi, a way to depict Ardhanarishwara, a dance representing the deities Shiva and his consort Parvati, expressing a male and female union. Ghunghroos, or the dancing bells are used as an audio prop. In a similar vein I place the kumbha or diya, (brass plate and pot). The kumbha and the diya were part of established rituals that the devadasi (female servant of a deity) would perform. The kumbh aarti (group singing) was such a central part of the devadasi's ritual practices that there was a conscious attempt to use it to draw a line of distinction from Bharatanatyam.

In Sattriya, the dancer wearing the aachal (veil) may not necessarily use it physically but would refer to its existence through body movements in the course of dance.

Object spatialisation and dance narrativisation: Moving outside and within

From the structural framework of material existence, dance, through its expanded vocabulary, creates a spatial framework of its own. Through internalisation of material existence, the dancer reinstates the objects and artefacts used as part of the narrative to build up a creative truth – a reality of the performance space. Between the movement of the objects and the performing body, the motion created is more of an inward experience conveyed externally contributing towards a sensory experience. Bharatanatyam danseuse Rama Vaidyanathan expanded on this topic during an interview,

> For me keeping an idol of the Nataraja within my sight in the dance space is inspirational at various levels. Apart from the fact that He is

supposed to be the Lord of Dance, His standing on the right foot with the left leg raised infuses in me a kind of inexplicable energy. For me He is all about balance, all about maintaining the equilibrium of creation and dissolution. When my eyes fall upon the Nataraja idol while I dance, I am reminded of creating that same balance in my dance. Not just a physical sense of balance, but also the balance of my mind, body and soul which is essential for every dancer to master. Gazing upon his svelte and taut frame, his calm countenance amidst the frenetic activity of creation with one hand and destruction with the other, I am reminded of finding my own equanimity of static and dynamic. Because dance is not all movement, it is also stillness and what better example to teach us than Lord Nataraja Himself who manifests the ultimate balance. When I look at Him, I realise how important it is for dancers to master the art of control. We need to be in control of our body, mind and senses and not even for a moment can we falter on that. Lord Nataraja is the supreme example of control, the Adi Yogi and of course the cosmic dancer – every morning before I begin my practise I prostrate before him and utter a silent prayer, asking him to grant me the sense of balance and control that He has.

The ritualistic observance of a Sattriya performance with its pre-ritual events includes offering respect to the scriptures, with lamps signifying the lighting of the way towards enlightenment. The objects used during the course of a performance are viewed in a particular way, unlike the normal objects mostly kept in the Namghar. The curation of the objects inside the Namghar aims to create an environment of supra-reality of heavenly space. The main sanctum of the space with its motif reflects the iconic representations towards the steps to higher realisation. The simhasana (sculpted wooden artwork) placed in the sanctum sanctorum is curved with representational motifs of a lion governing an elephant. This representation indicates thoughts controlling existence. The Bhagavata (treatise) at the top of the iconic image speaks of formlessness. Performance and the embodiment of the philosophical interpretations of the Bhagavata are important in displaying how the body from a material existence becomes connected to a supreme formless consciousness. The decorative frills and patterns are the realities of that existence.

With the realisation of the thinking body there is a synaesthesia, a blurring of boundaries – a "synthesis of imagined and material experiences occur where the body delves deep into the movement of meaning making" (Carlson & Pajakowska, 2001, cited in Springay, 2005). Personally, I feel that when I stand as a Sattriya dancer for that purpose, I engage myself into these networks of thoughts where my body continuously shares a dialogue with the history, cultural artefacts, and iconic images, formulating a narrative, an inspired story of my own amidst the setting. The dance itself becomes a "model path for thinking where dancing and dance-seeing are a kind of knowledge of the sensory effects of movement in general" (Traube, 2012, n.p.). With an engagement of the historicity and expression of the movements, touching, together with the expressive forms of artefacts, the body undergoes the "process of thought". The interpretations of the thinking body are reflected into the performance, which becomes significant in carrying forward the legacy in the present. Traube (2012) notes Laban's statement that

> A dancer is a human being who consciously strives to weave clear intelligence, deep feeling and strong desire into a harmoniously balanced yet interactively moving whole, thereby weaving in a dynamic unity of mind and body.
>
> (n.p.)

I would like to refer to my own training experience of learning abhinaya (mimetic expressions). The words suggested – "Look my friends, Krishna, the child, is playing with the coconut shell". To narrate the line with movements, my body actually had to undergo a thought process and a sensory experience of holding a coconut shell. I incorporated space in my body for the object along with the narrative content of the movements. The imprints of the outer world were translated with the choreographic intent of the dancer through perception and visualisation, allowing the body to think and respond to a material presence. The thinking body in its understanding of various spatial frames narrates the sensory experience of the perceived and conceived with her visual objective drawing a "dynamic unity of mind and body" (Traube, 2012, n.p.). George (2007) states,

> It is not only our bodies that enter the world of performance; it is, even more significantly, our minds, which step across a threshold from one set of assumptions about one kind of reality into another.
>
> (p. 27)

Personally, in interpreting a 500-year-old dance tradition introduced in a different historical and cultural context and in a performative situation, I connect to my lineage. I take the history of the past to philosophise and internalise the movements where the lived body is truly "dancing the becoming" according to Nancy (2005), as cited in Traube (2012). In this process of reflection, "body-thought" objects or the material units outside are spaced inside, and the living experience of motion mobilises the dance of the dancer.

> Labour is blossoming or dancing where
> The body is not bruised to pleasure soul,
> Nor beauty born out of its own despair,
> Nor blear-eyed wisdom out of midnight oil.
> O chestnut tree, great rooted blossomer,
> Are you the leaf, the blossom or the bole?
> O body swayed to music, O brightening glance,
> How can we know the dancer from the dance?
> W. B. Yeats

References

Albright, A., (2013), *Engaging Bodies: The Politics and Poetics of Corporeality*, Middletown, Wesleyan University Press.
Bell, V., (1999), Theory, Culture and Society. *Sage*, 16(2), 1–10. Retrieved from http://sagepub.com at Queen's University on April 20, 2016.
Benjamin, J., (1986), A Desire of One's Own: Psychoanalytic Feminism and Intersubjective Space. In T. Lauretis (Ed.), *Feminist Studies/Critical Studies*, Macmillan Press, 78–101.
Carlson, F., and Pajakowska, C., (2001), *Feminist Visual Culture*, Edinburgh, Edinburgh University Press.
George, E., (2007), Performance Epistemology. In J. Keefe & S. Murray (Eds.), *Physical Theatres: A Critical Reader*, Abingdon, Routledge, 26–31.
Medhi, K. (Ed.), (1997), *Ankavali*, Lawyers Book Stall, Assam, India.
Merleau-Ponty, M., (1962), *Phenomenology of Perception*. (translation Smith, C.), London, Routledge.
Nancy, J., (2005), *Alliterations: Conversations sur la Danse*, Paris, Galilee.
Preester, D., (2007), To Perform the Layered Body: A Short Exploration of Body in Performance. *Janus Head Amherst: Trivium Publications*, 9(2), 349–383. Retrieved from http://www.janushead.org/9-2/DePreester.pdf.
Reilley, M., (2000), *The Barn at the End of the World: The Apprenticeship of a Quaker, Buddhist Shepherd*, Minnesota, Milkweed Editions.
Sheppard, W., (2001), *Revealing Masks*, Berkeley, University of California Press.
Siegel, S., (2006), Subject and the Object in the Contents of the Visual Experience. *Philosophical Review*, 115(3), 355–388. Retrieved from http://www.people.fas.harvard.edu/~ssiegel/papers/msocproofs.pdf.
Spivey, V., (2004), Sites of Subjectivity: Robert Morris, Minimalism and Dance. *Dance Research Journal*, 36(1), 113–130. Retrieved from http://www.jstor.org/stable/30045072.
Springgay, S., (2005), Thinking through Bodies: Bodied Encounters and the Process of Meaning Making in an Email Generated Art Project. *Studies in Art Education*, 47(1), 34–50. Retrieved from http://www.jstor.org/stable/25475771.
Svasek, M. (Ed.), (2014), *Moving Subjects, Moving Objects: Transnationalism, Cultural Production and Emotions*, New York, Berghahn Books.
Traube, S., (2012), Dancing Is Thinking: Philosophy and Dance. Retrieved from https://www.goethe.de/en/kul/tut/gen/tan/20509666.html.
Tuan, Y., (1980), The Significance of the Artefact. *Geographical Review*, 70(4), 462–472. Retrieved from http://www.jstor.org/stable/214079.
Turkle, S., (2007), *Evocative Objects, Things We Think With*, Massachusetts, Massachusetts Institute of Technology.
Vatsyayan, K., (1983), *The Square and the Circle of the Indian Arts*, New Delhi, Abhinav Publications.
Vatsyayan, K., (1997), *The Square and the Circle of the Indian Arts*, New Delhi, Abhinav Publications.
Woolf, V., (2003), Solid Objects. In S. Dick (Ed.), *Virginia Woolf – A Haunted House, the Complete Shorter Fiction*, London, Vintage.

4 Discovering Sannidhi/a confluence
A dance exchange between Assam and Aotearoa, New Zealand

Alison (Ali) East

The aim of the field trip

The aim of the field trip was to introduce students to an introductory ethnographic reconnaissance (Wolcott, 2008). A Summer School course titled *Dance Ethnography: International Field Trip* offered students the opportunity to study community dance throughout Assam, with particular emphasis on the relationship of dance to community life. In the process, however, students came to learn as much about themselves and each other as they did about community dance. They found themselves "foreigners" without the familiarity and cultural touchstones of home (East & Rajendren, 2009).

> We are airborne – re-routed, reassigned, re-assured, re-connected. This is a well-organised group – not fazed by our last-minute change of plans, and not knowing what will ensue. Laura, Lucia, Tukohirangi, Rebekah and I will find ourselves together for the next three weeks. This is the beginning of our adventure, the commencement of our story. At Kolkata airport I discover that my group are a bunch of card sharks. They generate much interest with their hilarity and happy exclamations for two solid hours. We have been flying for 24 hours and I know that I am feeling pretty ragged, but I am happy to have arrived here in India. It is familiar and I am comfortable with these people – hearing Hindi, Bengali, Assamese and watching the women, graceful and serene in their beautiful saris and north eastern attire. Unlike us, they are resigned to waiting for hours, to last minute changes of plans and coping with discomfort while tending to babies, young children and their own aged mothers.

> We finally arrive at Guwahati, collect our luggage and make our way to the exit. I am scanning the crowds at the door for the familiar face of our KALPA hostess, Dr Anwesa Mahanta. Half an hour later she is still nowhere to be seen. I am about to ask the guard if I can borrow his cell phone when she is there, with two drivers and my friend and dance colleague, Dr Barbara Snook from The University of Auckland, whose flight was not diverted and delayed. Apparently, the only bridge to the

DOI: 10.4324/9781003398776-5

46 Alison (Ali) East

Picture 4.1 Visiting the Mishing community at Majuli Island, 2015. Image: Santanu Mahanta.

airport was blocked due to construction – a situation that would later prevent us from attending an official function. Our delay has meant no recovery day and we are due to teach a workshop for several hundred children at 9.00 am the following morning. However, that very evening, and somewhat bedraggled from our long flight, we are invited to the house of well-known traditional musician and instrument maker, Dr Prasanna Gogoi, only to be confronted by TV cameras and expected to participate in a traditional celebratory "bihu" performance. We oblige happily, albeit slightly sleepily, picking up the steps as only dancers can.

The concept of Sannidhi/a confluence

Our KALPA hosts led by Professor Pradip Mahanta and his daughter Dr Anwesa Mahanta provided their considerable expertise throughout our three-week journey. They have spent many years travelling and researching traditional performing arts throughout the entire region of Assam. We learned that there are some 22 distinct ethnic communities, each with their own language, religion, weaving, building style, dance, and music. These are largely farming communities whose livelihoods to this day depend on the land.

As a way to frame the collaboration between the University of Otago and KALPA (an organisation dedicated to the promotion of Literature, Art, Culture, Social Harmony and Cultural exchange' within Assam), our hosts named it "Sannidhi – a Confluence", an encounter, or intersection of cultures and ideas. This idea in turn influenced the way that my students viewed their field trip experiences, focusing more on those strong moments of confluence than the detail of one dance form or another. Each exchange, whether in a village or school classroom, was seen as Sannidhi.

The notion of "confluence" stayed with me as we progressed on our journey. I recognised multiple dimensions of confluence as also being those between researcher and researched, the known and the unknown, between past and present, tradition and innovation, religion and art, thought and action, ideas and experience, and between teacher and student or initiate and guru. It was about who we became as we encountered new relationships. In this sense, the confluence was also within ourselves. Travelling to new places is a transformative experience if we are open and reflexive (Lean, 2009).

Trans-locational teaching and learning

When students travel away from home to study the dance of others as "trans-located" (East & Rajendren, 2009) or "situated" learners (Brubaker, 2011), they not only gain an understanding of the role of dance in other communities, but a greater appreciation of their own cultural values and danced expression. In the process, they also learn key attributes of empathy, compassion, and co-operation with and for others and the world (East & Rajendren, 2009). They come to understand people's relationship to the land and the integral connection between work, worship, and dance. We realise how the idea of confluence is also a political position as we witness the challenging juncture of eastern and western ways of being.

Our hosts helped to provide a cultural context for our study of community dance by taking us to temples, museums, and ancient ruins where traces of the dances' origins could be seen sculpted into the stone walls. It was as if the stone masons of hundreds of years ago understood the importance of preserving dance for future generations. Our hostess demonstrated some of the moves we saw and we danced on the ruins, imagining that we were ancient goddesses and gods of the past. I wrote in my journal at the time:

> After driving through miles of rice fields and small villages we arrive at the ancient remains of the ruins of the Madan Kamdev Heritage site. Engraved on these stone ruins are important records of the dances of the past. Here the excitement of our hostess Dr Anwesa Mahanta was infectious. As an expert in Assamese Sattriya dance, she was able to point out the important links between the gestures in the carvings and the Assamese classical dance forms of today. We marvel at the age of this historic place and yet are appalled at the lack of concern for the dumping

of garbage everywhere surrounding this sacred site. Sadly, this concern will become a theme throughout our journey.

Later, we visited the Srimanta Sankaradeva Temple and Cultural Museum with our host, Professor Pradip Mahanta. We were not used to the concept of pilgrimages to sacred places, to the reverence with which they are regarded, or the crowds of worshippers and religious trinket sellers lining the steep roadside. We were also not certain that we would ever see our footwear again, having stacked them in a shed full of a million other shoes.

We travelled across the Brahmaputra River to the Sualkuchi Weavers' village where we were introduced to the highly regarded Assamese craft of traditional silk weaving. The women of the village learned their extraordinary weaving skills from their elders through many years of patient apprenticeship. In my journal, I note,

> This is a very different kind of tertiary education (craft-village campus) and I hope the weavers are well-recognised for their skilled work – and well-paid for their long working hours.

There was little time for rest or reflection though, somehow, we managed to rally ourselves for the next day's programme and headed off with our drivers and hostess to the Nagaon Harvest Food festival, where there was a ritualistic burning of a giant straw sculpture. We were almost burned alive, as we were shoved forward to the front by our enthusiastic hosts. Some less auspicious events, however, will be remembered from this day as we experienced being strangers abroad (Kaeppler, in Buckland ed.), 1999) I recorded,

> When the female students return from the public toilet, they are stopped by a young woman, who insists on adjusting each of their 'wrongly folded' traditional attire. Once again, we are swamped by TV media as we struggle to eat with one hand at the official table.

> Our driver Monju and Videographer Santanu invite us to each of their home villages to meet every single member of their extended families and receive tea and sweets. One family had arranged for a performance of dance and music to take place, including a spontaneous dramatic rendition by our driver's amateur actress mother. We are overwhelmed by the generosity of everyone and climb back into our bus. The day, it turns out, has hardly begun.

Cultural exchange

As my students joined in Assamese dances and ceremonies, they shared their own dance styles with each community and engaged in individual conversations and informal interviews. Some valuable lessons of tolerance and appreciation of difference were learnt – along with a broadening of understanding regarding their own individual cultural backgrounds as citizens of Aotearoa, New Zealand. Our Maori student found a way to share aspects of his cultural dance outside of its traditional context. While he struggled a little with this at first he was, however, able to see the relevance of sharing his culture with Assamese people. Tu was later to comment:

> Because I come from my own ethnic [Maori] background I was able to find similarities and differences between the culture in Assam and my own Maori culture. I was able to provide them with a little insight into the Maori worldview ... . As I now reflect on the trip to Assam, India, I realise that it has heightened my desire to learn more about my own culture and make sure that my culture will not only survive, but will one day thrive again.

Another student, highly trained in European classical ballet, learned to perform her dance in remote village settings in bare feet on an earthen surface without the usual classical music accompaniment. At the private studio of Dr Goswami, this student, Rebekah, taught a ballet class to the Indian classical dance students, commenting at the similar disciplinary rigour required for each genre, and the ease with which the students learned the ballet form. She recalled,

> The student's technique of the ballet steps was very good. I don't think they found ballet difficult. However, my pointe shoes sparked an interest. Dancing on one's toes in stiff shoes was something completely new to them.

Dancing with village communities

After another long drive through farmland and small villages of mostly bamboo and mud houses, we arrived at the village of the Bodo people and found members of the Bodo and Tea Garden communities assembled in a large field in anticipation of our visit. A large group of young women wearing bright orange and red costumes and another group dressed in red and white were lined up ready to share their dance with us. An ensemble of musicians was gathered to one side with a variety of woodwind, string, and percussion instruments, none of which were familiar to us. Their high-pitched trills and metallic beats were easily audible across the whole field. I recorded:

> The dance begins and we are astonished to see the slender, beautifully attired dancers each wielding two large machetes that they swing overhead. I wonder whether this is a remnant of a time when women fought in tribal battles. A graceful butterfly scarf dance (Bagarumba, a dance about love) follows before we are also draped in local attire and taught a less formal circle dance accompanied by much laughter by all. Naturally,

50 *Alison (Ali) East*

we are once more graciously treated to tea and sweets in our host's family home.

We learned later that these two distinct communities were not accustomed to dancing together. Had we facilitated a cultural sannidhi by our presence? Laura commented:

> Dancing with the Bodos and tea community made me feel more accepted into the community. I noticed that simply observing created a barrier between the performers and us. Once we crossed it and joined in their dance, we felt a part of their community. Although we may appear and speak differently, we can move and connect without words, ultimately creating a social bonding relationship.

Back on the bus, we were on the road again, this time to meet the Deori Community. Here the concept of sannidhi was particularly evident in the playful relaxed engagement with members of this welcoming village.

> Having watched a demonstration of dance and music, the bending and swaying circle dances of the young women, our students are, again, whisked away to a small bamboo hut where, accompanied by much giggling and chatter, they are dressed in local costume and invited into the

Picture 4.2 New Zealand students dressed in local costumes with the Bodos and Tea communities. Image: Barbara Snook.

dance. The group hardly notices that they are speaking different languages in this joyful sharing of dancerly passion. They are young people of a similar age, though with vastly different life paths. Dancing in long tight skirts, mekhela chardas (two-piece sari), and with cloth wrapped around their breasts, completely altered the movement possibilities and changed the somatic experience for the athletic 'kiwi' students.

At Sipajhar, the village of the Ojapali artists in the Darrang district, our sense of sannidhi found new meaning as we were welcomed into the courtyard, offered tea and sweets, and treated to a series of extraordinary displays of musicianship and dance theatre by men of all ages and three young women. The girls performed the Deodhani, tossing their long shining black hair in a display of sensual grace. The Oja, lead singer narrated an ancient saga (into which the story of our presence was spontaneously woven) with the accompanying Pali singers and drummers, playing a fast-paced hypnotic rhythm in support. We learned that this semi-dramatic form of Ojapali has been performed since the 12th century, and that it has provided a vehicle for social commentary, blended with the religious scriptures and epic tales (Nor et al., p. 6). I was introduced to the elderly wife of the recently deceased dance master, who invited me to chew pan. I lent her my glasses and she was amazed at what she could see.

In a hilarious exchange with the older male dancers we were taught the difficult wedding dance, Dhepa Dhuliya, of fast-moving interwoven pathways around and through between each other as our interpreter did her best to explain the sequence in English.

The ongoing preservation and sustainability of these traditional village artforms is a source of much concern for Cultural Studies researchers in Assam, (Goswami, 2015; Mahanta, 2018), and we wonder whether our presence and fieldwork, as outside foreigners, might bring some visibility and recognition to these highly skilled artists.

> Barb and I have woken early, our aging bodies unable to lie on the hard boards and thin mattresses provided at our hotel. The others are still sleeping as we slip into our clothes from the day before and climb down steep stairs to the hotel café. This is a dingy concrete room, open at one end onto the street where the cooker is located. We order black tea and lemon which duly arrives. The first cup is sickly sweet, but once our driver appears and is able to translate, the second cup is better – no sugar this time. Breakfast consists of puri and chickpea curry and is delicious. The driver and his assistant have slept in their van and probably had a more comfortable sleep. (We had arrived in this small dusty town around 4.30pm the previous day, checked in and ate "lunch" which was served as dinner). As Barb and I sit in the red-painted café with matching plastic chairs and tables an entire busload of travellers pours in for breakfast. I

marvel at the chef's ability to produce a full breakfast for all these people with one gas burner.

Majuli Island

We woke early, took breakfast on banana leaves at a roadside café, and drove the distance to catch the Majuli ferry. Accustomed to the choking bureaucracy and health and safety rules in Aotearoa, New Zealand, we watched in horror as our large heavy traveller van was loaded onto the barge along with other vehicles and several hundred-foot passengers.

> I look around for life jackets and notice about ten of them –rather ancient and probably now unseaworthy – hanging along the wall of the cabin. Who would get those, we wonder, if we were to take in water? I am almost certain that the only swimmers are amongst our group. However, after an hour of slow drifting down the Brahmaputra river we come alongside another barge and everyone disembarks up the sandy slope. As we drive across several kilometres of sand we learn how the island is rapidly being washed away by the summer rains.
>
> Our hotel is built on concrete stilts, several metres above the ground, under which small goats are grazing, and everywhere there are stop banks, on which simple bamboo dwellings have been built. Yet this sacred place is home to thousands of farmers, fine crafts people and monastic sattras. How do they all (cows, goats, pigs, chickens and people) cope with the annual floods we wonder, when much of the island may soon be underwater?

At the Mishing community on Majuli Island, we were invited up into one of the large single-roomed bamboo houses to taste and witness the making of rice wine. The loosely woven bamboo floor was strong enough to hold our weight, though we had never been in a house where one could see through the widely spaced slats to the ground and watch pigs and chickens passing by beneath the house. A woman was weaving on a wooden loom under the next house while a man and a woman were threading up a loom on the pathway. The dancers were each wearing their own beautiful handwoven costumes in different colours and motifs. As I watched the movement of the dancers, I imagined that I could see the graceful swaying of the rice in the fields, the bending action of planting, the sewing of seeds, and the action of cutting and then thrashing the stalks. Theirs is a dance totally of this place and derived from their daily toil. There appeared to be little separation between the artistic performance and the daily farming work these people did. The fabric worn by the women and men had been woven here, the cotton yarn grown, spun, and dyed and the silk sourced from nearby. The act of weaving and the patterns created are said to have spiritual significance as a metaphor for the interwovenness of life and the universe. The Mishing community had taken time out of their extremely busy day to welcome us and perform their dances. Before leaving, we implored the women to sell us some of their woven cloth. Each item had taken at least two months to weave. It is a major source of women's income and we were pleased to have such beautiful products.

The Sattra communities

We learnt from our hostess, Dr Mahanta, that one of the main religions of Assam revolves around the monastic Sattras where young boys are trained in the rigorous arts of drumming, theatre, and dance arts. It is a rare thing for a westerner to witness this daily ceremonial practice in the performance space and we felt deeply privileged.

> At the Badala Padma Ata Sattra at Narayanpur, having removed our shoes, we are ushered into the namghar (large open-sided hall) where we sit cross-legged on the concrete floor. This is our first Sattra experience and we don't know what to expect. But, as the chanting, drumming and cymbals enter our ears and chest we are overtaken by the vibration and rhythm. Though we don't yet understand the significance of this performance, we know that we are privileged participant/observers. A rich display of drumming and acrobatic dancing by young initiates follows. This is indeed embedded community dance and we are excited to understand more.

At the Natun Kamalabari Satra in Majuli Island, we were invited into the dance master's house for tea and then treated to a demonstration of training practices by young monks. We learned that these young boys are offered to the Sattra as young children to be raised and educated by the monks, and, in the process, avoid the poverty and hardship of their family's circumstances. Since the arts are admired as a form of conveying religious meaning, these young boys receive rigorous training in the performing arts of theatre, music, and dance. Then, having completed formal education, they often become teachers of these arts. Once again, we find ourselves questioning our own tokenistic valuing of community arts in Aotearoa, New Zealand, and the reverence with which the Assamese people still view these practices.

In the celibate order of Uttar Kamalabari, a special performance was being prepared. We were invited to watch three young males transforming themselves with makeup and wigs as they assumed the female roles required for the re-enactment of one of the mythological sagas from the Bhakti manuscripts of the Vaishnava faith. Their attention to detail was astounding and soon even their mannerisms and voices changed to that of beautiful women. In a time of gradual acceptance of transgender status in the west, we were amazed at how seamlessly these novices flowed between assuming masculine and feminine identities.

54 Alison (Ali) East

Picture 4.3 Male dancers playing female roles. Uttar Kamalabari Sattra, Majuli Island. Image: Barbara Snook.

I attempted to record the experience in words, writing as I watched, trying to capture the rhythm and content of the dance, practising "performing" writing, though I soon reverted to my video camera.

> The monks, wearing white robes sway as they play two-ended drums, rock from side to side, turning occasionally. The beat becomes faster, then slows, as the monks progress down the room, sanctifying it, preparing the space for the dance. I wonder if the dance-master (who is also drumming) has invented this stepping and swaying routine himself, or whether it is something unchanged through millennia.
>
> Step jump turn, plié with bent lifted leg, turn full circle. Quivering hands come away from drums momentarily, creating a visual rhythm – two feet to one foot with step across the front – or a toss across front with one leg. Now a big jump turn, walk in a circle while cymbals and drumming continue and now they kneel to play, picking up the tempo. All of this – the music and the dance – is all Sattriya, a dance form associated with the Sattras. Now the dancers begin. They are wearing gold dhoti with blue blouses, orange head crowns and an array of beads. All are male. Their moves are similar to the preceding musicians – with many turns, jumps and deep pliés, arms bent, elbows out and fingers turned up in a

distinctly Burmese style. Their hands are painted with a red circle on the palms and red fingertips.

Testing sannidhi

As a teacher of western post-modern dance forms, I was curious about how the Assamese students might engage with the physical improvisational form of Contact Improvisation. At Dibrugarh University, I seized the opportunity to conduct a combined workshop with the Performing Arts and New Zealand students and was immediately impressed with their openness and willingness to engage with this non-rhythmic dance form. Both groups, men and women, played together in the simple act of sharing weight, paying attention to the movement of a partner, sensing without directing (in this spontaneous dance, no words are needed). I wrote at the time,

> This is a true sannidhi, confluence of bodies, of equal participation of genders, size, weight and ability. We laugh at the joy and playfulness of the experience of healthy physical intimacy and at the sheer pleasure of intuiting this dance together.

After a spontaneous concert of music and dance by the Dibrugarh students, we waved farewell to our new friends from the bus, wishing we had had more time to come to know each other better. Our journey was almost over.

> There were many other encounters, too many to recount here, yet all contributing to the rich experience of the three week journey that could only be couched as an introductory reconnaissance (Wolcott, 2008). Undoubtedly though it has contributed to a new appreciation for the cultural diversity of Assam and, in the process, given us a new perspective on our own cultural community within Aotearoa, New Zealand.

Being or doing ethnography? Establishing communities of shared interest

When one group is studying another, when they are sharing the same performing space (be it a classroom or village compound) participating in the same dance, and learning from each other, a new community of shared interest is established – though the only shared language may be the dance itself. Pam Burnard (2006) uses the term "reflective community of practice" (p. 8). In the process of dancing together with each local group, the students became both "insider and outsider, friend and stranger" (Frosch, 1999, p. 264) and, in the process, gained rich insight into the lives of their dancing friends. The ensuing "reflective conversations" between them, despite having no common language except through our interpreter, served to enrich the sense of individual and group identity as each came to know themselves through their conversations with others (Madison, 2012, p. 11).

As dancers and beginning ethnographers, the students utilised their combined skills as critical interpreters of their own, as well as others' actions. Their artist's ability to position themselves as both performer and audience, or in ethnographic terms, participants and observers; to engage, as Grushka (2005) suggests, in "a multiplicity of interpretive positions" and to "become critical interpreters of their own actions" (p. 354) enabled rich somatic reflection. She contends that "artists ask questions ... which are often as much about *who they are* as what they know" (p. 354). In their collective questioning, students discovered as much about each other as those they had gone to research. Madison (2012) describes a shift from "Participant-observer" to "co-presence" or what Spry (2006) refers to as the "performative I". By opening ourselves to others in the form of performances or participation, we moved from the "ethnographic present" (viewing an artefact suspended in time) to the "ethnographic presence" (Madison, 2012, p. 199). We were acknowledging and honouring the living presence of the many people we met along with their art.

Citing Dwight Conquergood, Madison (2012) contends that ethnography is always about negotiation and dialogue and resists conclusions, "It is [she suggests] about making a difference in others' lives ... and about recognis[ing] both differences and commonalities." (p. 10–11). Through their communication with others, my students brought themselves, as well as those they had come to study, "more fully into being" (p. 11). In her course reflection, Lucia wrote:

> Generally I feel as though I have grown personally on a much deeper level than I had expected. Countless moments of insight into Assamese lifestyle and the smaller [ethnic] communities has enabled me to understand what life is like for families in less privileged areas and has made me think about giving back to the community in New Zealand.

The sharing of observations, sensations, and ideas greatly enriched students' individual experience in the field and this was evident in their written reports. As Emerson et al. (1995) affirm, "no two persons participate in and experience a setting exactly the same way ... there is always more going on than the ethnographer [alone] can notice" (p. 86). Researching together enabled the students to ask questions of each other later to seek clarification regarding what they had heard, seen, or felt. It provided an informal form of reliability testing and cross-checking of information, so necessary in undertaking ethnography (Davies, 2008, p. 97). Our dancerly interactions provided opportunities for the interweaving of their own and each other's perceptions into the research discussion. Our combined and varied memories form a somatic mosaic of felt memory.

Somatic sensibility and embodied participation

As dance ethnographers, our challenge was in how to translate the sensuous experiences of dancing (response to different rhythms, different surfaces, and different movement language) into words, to tease them apart yet without losing the essence and wholeness of the moment. Theresa Buckland (2006) describes a "weaving of somatic and verbal detail, [of] linking bodily sensation with the other senses and with verbalisation" (p. 106). Along with our rich participatory experiences, we had to acknowledge our lack of cultural knowledge. We were dependent on our local informants and limited written material to fill in the gaps in our understanding. Madison (2012) has spoken of performing writing. It was helpful for us as dancers to see the entire ethnographic research experience as performance (Denzin, 2003). As dancers trained in various forms of somatic practices and human anatomy and physiology, our perceptions were both inward and outward. We "felt" the placement of feet on the earth and noticed how different this felt from dancing on a sprung wooden floor. When we danced on the hard concrete surfaces of many venues, we learned how to land lightly so as not to jar our joints. We noticed the springing agility of the old Ojapali performers and how they seemed younger when dancing. We registered the coolness of our local dance partner's hand compared to ours that were hot and sweaty. As we attempted to adopt the curved graceful posture of Bihu, we noticed how much longer and bulkier our western bodies were. Our ears found themselves tuning differently to the multiple rhythms and timing of ethnic instruments. Ours was a multi-sensory ethnographic experience and we struggled to find the words to express its nuances or to identify a methodological construct to accommodate it all. Every activity and event, from the hard beds, spicy food, the pot-holed roads, and challenging toilets became part of this body-centred dance research, recorded as somatic memory. Even our dreaming here seemed relevant.

It has become evident that our lasting impressions have contained more of the *taste*, *smell*, and *feel* of things and less about the details of the dances we came to study. Lucia's reminiscences from 2015 were all about the senses:

> The smell of burning at the Bihu festival; The sickly-sweet taste of local handmade sweets; The warm caring hands of nurturing women wrapping my sari; The feel of cold concrete on my knees as we kneeled at ceremonies; Dancing barefoot in the grass with the Bodo community.

As dancer ethnographers, we sensuously experienced a somatic embodiment of each culture as we simultaneously uncovered more layers of ourselves (Cohen Bull, 1997; Fraleigh, 2004; Fraleigh & Hanstein, 1999; Ness, 2004). Maarit Llonen (2003) suggests, "A dancing person is like a mirror, simultaneously revealing something of herself and about the other" (p. 565). This embodied knowledge of self/other created a new kind of cultural meaning and mutual understanding (Novak Bull, 1990; Shapiro, 2008).

Conclusion

As John Van Maanen (2011) attests, "The magic of telling impressionist tales is that they are always unfinished, [yet] with each retelling we discover more of what we know" (p. 120). Only a small portion of our many rich encounters could be included here. In returning to the recorded material – photos, videos, and notes from nearly five years ago, I realise how much I learnt from our brief tour, and yet how little I really know about these rich and diverse cultures of Assam. We were graciously invited up into raised bamboo huts for rice wine, to chew pan with the old men and women, to have tea and sweet cakes everywhere, to participate in sacred ceremonies in the Sattras, to offer workshops and to learn the dances of each ethnic group that we encountered. We took an elephant ride through a herd of endangered rhinos, learned to wear Assamese clothes, and eat with our hands. We were reminded, by authors such as Joan Frosch (1999), that dance ethnography is much more than just the study of the dance – it is the holistic study of an entire culture.

By travelling to another culture, students are able to look back and acknowledge their own with more clarity, appreciation, and understanding. These opportunities have helped to forge positive relations with institutes and universities in places that would not normally feature on our world map and yet who have much to teach us that is highly valuable and relevant to us here in Aotearoa, New Zealand.

Acknowledgements

I would like to acknowledge Professor Pradip Mahanta and Dr Anwesa Mahanta for hosting us in 2015 and for their continuing support; Dr Barbara Snook and my former student participants Laura Hight, Lucia Mckewan, Tukohirangi Pini and Rebeckah Wilson for their contributions.

References

Brubaker, J. (2011) Undergraduate political communication in action: Volunteer experiences in a situated learning course. *Innovations in Education and Teaching International*, 48(1), 3–12. 10.1080/14703297.2010.543775.

Buckland, T. (Ed.). (2006) *Dancing from Past to Present: Nation, Culture, Identities*. Madison, WI: University of Wisconsin Press.

Burnard, P., & Hennessy, S. (Eds.). (2006) *Reflective Practice in Arts Education*. Dordrecht, the Netherlands: Springer.

Cohen Bull, C. J. (1997) Sense, meaning and perception in three dance cultures. Chapter 14. In J. C. Desmond (Ed.), *Meaning in Motion: New Cultural Studies of Dance*. Durham, NC: Duke University Press, pp. 269–287.

Davies, C. H. (2008) *Reflexive Ethnography: A Guide to Researching Selves and Others* (2nd ed.). London: Routledge.
Denzin, N. K. (2003) *Performance Ethnography: Critical Pedagogy and the Politics of Culture*. Urbana and Champaign, IL: University of Illinois, Sage Publications.
East, A., & Rajendren, B. (2009) Trans-locational dance study: The educational efficacy and outcomes of a trans-cultural field trip from the University of Otago, New Zealand to South India. *Published Proceedings, WDA World Dance Alliance Conference*, New Delhi.
Emmerson, R. M., Fretz, R. I., & Shaw, L. L. (1995 [2011]) *Writing Ethnographic Field Notes* (2nd ed.). London: University of Chicago Press Ltd.
Fraleigh, S. (2004) *Dancing Identity: Metaphysics in Motion*. Pittsburgh, PA: University of Pittsburgh Press.
Fraleigh, S., & Hanstein, P. (Eds.). (1999) *Researching Dance*. Pittsburgh, PA: University of Pittsburgh Press.
Frosch, J. (1999) Dance ethnography: Tracing the weave of dance in the fabric of culture. In S. Fraleigh & P. Hanstein (Eds.), *Researching Dance*. Pittsburgh, PA: University of Pittsburgh Press, pp. 249–280.
Goswami, S. (2015) *From Ritual to Performance: A Study of the Sattriya Performance Traditions of Assam as Intangible Heritage with a Special Reference to the Kamalabari Group of Sattras*. A Thesis submitted in Part-fulfilment of the requirements for award of the degree of Doctor of Philosophy, Tezpur University Napaam, Assam.
Grushka, K. (2005, August) Artists as reflective self-learners and cultural communicators: An exploration of the qualitative aesthetic dimension of knowing self through reflective practice in art-making. *Reflective Practice*, 6(3), 353–366.
Kaeppler, A. L. (1999) The mystique of fieldwork. In T. J. Buckland (Ed.), *Dance in the Field*. Chippenham, Wiltshire: Antony Rowe Ltd, p. 28.
Lean, G. (2009) Transformative travel: Inspiring sustainability. Chapter 12. In R. Bushell & P. J. Sheldon (Eds.), *Wellness and Tourism: Mind, Body, Spirit, Place* (pp. 191–205). New York: Cognizant.
Llonen, M. (2003) Bodily flashes of dancing women: Dance as a method of inquiry. Qualitative Inquiry, 9(4), 554–568. 10.1177/1077800403254223.
Madison, S. (2012) *Critical Performance Ethnography: Method, Ethics, and Performance* (2nd ed.). Thousand Oaks, CA: Sage Publications, Inc.
Mahanta, A. (2018) Understanding the paradigms of Sattriya dance and dancer in a changing space. In P. Chakravorty & N. Gupta (Eds.), *Dance Matters Too: Markets, Memories, Identities* (pp. 231–257) , New York: Routledge.
Ness, S. A. A. (2004) Being a body in a cultural way: Understanding the cultural in the embodiment of dance. In H. Thomas & J. Ahmed (Eds.), *Cultural Bodies: Ethnography and Theory*. Oxford: Blackwell, pp. 121–144.
Nor, M. A. Md; Kebudayaan, Pusat; Penerangan Kementerian, Kebudayaan Komunikasi dan. (2012) *Dancing Mosaic: Issues on Dance Hybridity*. Kuala Lumpur, Malaysia: Cultural Centre, University of Malaya: National Department for Culture and Arts, Ministry of Information, Communication and Culture, Kuala Lumpur: City Reprographic Services 2012.
Novak Bull, C. J. (1990) *Sharing the Dance: Contact Improvisation and American Culture*. Madison, WI: University of Wisconsin Press.

Shapiro, S. B. (2008) *Dance in a World of Change: Reflections on Globalization and Cultural Difference* (Sherry Shapiro editor). Champagne, IL: Human Kinetics.

Spry, T. (2006) A performative – 'I' copresence. Embodying the ethnographic turn in performance and performance turn in ethnography. *Text and Performance Quarterly*, 26(4), 339–346.

Van Mannen, J. (2011) *Tales of the Field: On Writing Ethnography* (2nd ed.). Chicago, IL: University of Chicago Press.

Wolcott, H. F. (2008) *Ethnography: A Way of Seeing* (2nd ed.). Plymouth: Altamira Press.

5 Kherai's dance world
Promoting solidarity and tradition

Madhurima Goswami

Introduction

The Bodos are the eighth largest tribe of India and are a dominant ethnic group of the Brahmaputra valley and North Bengal. Known as Kiratas in the prehistoric age, they belong to the Tibeto-Burman language family of Mongoloid origin. They travelled from Mongolia (Tibet) to the plains of Assam and were originally "animists" (a belief that objects, places, and creatures all possess a distinct spiritual essence), but through the ages, a section of Bodos converted to other religions. The Bodos respect the roles of the arts and understand their benefits to individuals, communities, and their contribution to social cohesion and social justice. Members of the community who have been working outside their state come back home during Kherai to participate in the celebration. They settle all kinds of matters in front of Bathou Brai (the traditional god of the Bodos), regardless of whether it is a sin or a good deed. They take blessings from all the senior people of the village. They participate in the ritual dances and show their solidarity.

Gathering stories

The observations and analyses used in this chapter are based on data that was collected in the Bodo village of Dhekidol, 20 kilometres away from Tezpur in the Sonitpur district and from the Dhekeri Botola village. My principal interviewee was Sri Tajuram Narzary, a community elder who shared his family genealogy showing that some 150 years ago, an Ahom (elder) came from Sivasagar, settled in this village, and married a Bodo girl. Since that time, Kherai has been celebrated. As little literature exists regarding the Kherai festival of the Bodos, this research seeks to preserve cultural history through the voices of the people themselves.

The Kherai festival

The word "Kherai" when broken into two parts: literally means "Khe" (sky) and "rai" (to invoke). During the ritual, the Bodo gods and goddesses are invited down to earth to accept offerings from the villagers. A regular space

DOI: 10.4324/9781003398776-6

within the village acquires a special status within a particular time frame. The entire arena (Kherai Sali) becomes an alternative cosmos breaking the continuity of profane space and is transferred into a cosmic plane. During the Kherai, the entire pantheon of the Bodo gods and goddesses are invited to the earth to be with their community and to listen to their woes.

The performance cycle of Kherai constitutes and recapitulates the major events in the life cycle of the Bodos. These events mainly depict the rhythm of their daily lives, their histories, their fantasies, and the way in which they imagine their world. Through this, the community makes an attempt to bridge the difference between heaven and earth. The Bodos create linkages to fill the voids that have been created by loss or a shifting of memories. The community members spend years practising their performance traditions and they have also devised strategies over the years to review their own performances and to adapt to new environments in order to infuse an energy and a spirit that is spontaneous and fresh in their performances.

Kherai is a folk dance that belongs to a non-classical tradition. It contains some codification, but retains enough flexibility to allow dancers to carry out their own interpretations. Bodo gods and their characters are presented in sequence, building up to a battle and then a victory dance. While putting it this way may describe the sequence in which the dance episodes unfold, it does not do justice to the polyphonic nature of the performance. What the dance seeks to do is not so much as narrate a story that already exists in different forms in the oral tradition, but to present a series of images that are strung together by Bodo instrumental music.

The making of the Kherai arena (altar) space for performance

A clearing or a suitable place in a village is selected for the Kherai ritual performance. In earlier times, it was held in a dense forest. It is believed that the altar symbolises a holy road from heaven to earth or from earth to heaven. The philosophy indicates a holy link between the god in the heavens and humans on earth. The space as such has no specific attribute, other than a clearing on which to hold a ritual.

During my stay in the village, I was told about a big tree trunk on which were inscribed some letters regarding the Bodo ancestors. The tree was chopped off by the villagers some years ago for timber, and where the tree stood, a prayer hall (Namghar) was built. The tree's remaining part is cemented into a column within the Namghar structure as an authentic presence. This also stands as a traditional testimony.

The sacred space is irreducibly marked out and distinguished from the profane space; therefore the sacred cannot be interpreted in any terms other than the religious. The Kherai acts as an architectural signifier of sacred space.

Picture 5.1 The Doudini and Bodo community worshipping before the commencement of the ritual.

The villagers understand that the sacred space is as much about process and encounter, rather than simply a place or a structure.

Within the Kherai ritual space where a host of activities take place such as the chorus, the music, the dance, and seemingly unrelated comic interludes, the mixing of human and non-human worlds permits a simultaneous presentation of alternative viewpoints. The performance of Kherai satisfies an ardent search for expression. The Bodo community members in the ritual space are fully aware of the surroundings, instinctually maintaining a critical distance from each other, indicating a distance from their possible predators. Through their bodies, they intimately intermingle with their surroundings. Within the homogeneous space they imagine rivers, pathways, forests, and mountains, which define movement possibilities.

Doudini: Mediator between community and God

The Doudini is a shaman dancer, a temporary embodiment of the spirit of God. A Bodo woman in her mid-to-late sixties performs the role of Doudini in the Kherai ceremony. The community addresses her simply as *Nasoni* (dancer) or as Doudini, depending on the status ascribed to her by her particular society. She acts as a medium between the community and God and many roles are enacted during the course of the ritual. She is believed to be possessed with divine power and dance is an important way of conveying this power.

While in the field, I interacted with the shaman dancer, Dalimi Boro, a village woman who has been entrusted with the performing of the ritual for the past two decades. She stated,

> I perform for my village and for the district also. Other villages pay me at a rate of two thousand rupees per festival. In a season I may get two or three ritual events to perform. I perform it religiously, but very often with contempt these days.

During my stay in the village for fieldwork, Dalimi stated that she was not going to continue performing the ritual. Consuming raw blood these days makes her sick. Moreover, a part of the money has to go to the village committee or otherwise she is not allowed to carry on as Doudini. A few years ago, her husband deserted her. Her two sons left her on pretext of working in the city and she was left alone. Dalimi's experience is not that of all Doudinis, however, she brings to attention the fact that in her case, being entrusted with the role has played a role in the disintegration of her family unit. The village had experienced trouble in finding a Doudini to conduct the ritual, and it is therefore even more important that this chapter records the authentic voices of the community at this time.

The Doudini's dance performances

Dance is an ancient art conveying an infinite range of meanings through postures and movements. The basic features of the Doudini's dances are rhythmic movements in space with demonstrations of special footwork skills. A Doudini's independent expressive merit is challenged when she attempts to gesticulate the content of the lyrical text during the dance. The priestess or the Doudini performs a symbolic interpretation for the audience to understand. She shows the ordinary person in commonplace situations at the beginning of the ritual dance, and in this instance the movement does not necessarily synchronise with music; instead, it can be admired for the suppleness of the human body, the rhythmic foot movements, and the suggestion of human emotions through gestures.

In one section, the Doudini carries a pair of live pigeons, criss-crosses her hands, and continues dancing while interacting within the space. She lifts the pigeons as though they are to go up into the sky and finally, they are let loose. This symbolism is about the welfare of the community. She performs a gesture of salutation and then proceeds to the next act. Each of her acts contains thought-provoking content. The movement in Kherai is highly stylised, based on the principles of counterpoise, which frequently calls for the opposite of what one would normally do following a particular gesture in order to make it intelligible and convincing to the audience. There are however opportunities for the Doudini to inject the dance with her own interpretations.

The Doudini and others wear masks that portray the dominant moods of the characters they represent. The Doudini's costume, oiled hair, and colouring add to her expression. The masks contain features that are delicately modelled showing expressions that are serene or benign. The body and the hand movements are natural and not exaggerated or stylised. The following describes the hand gestures and gait used by the Doudini.

Hand gesture

The hand gestures used for holding pigeons, offering, placing a burning wick inside the mouth, and salutation are understood at a basic level. They do not express the moods of the characters. The movements are conducted naturally and are quite literal. Mood is conducted in terms of the styles of movement displayed through the torso, the legs, and the arms.

Gait (chali)

On the day of the ritual, the Doudini enters the sacred arena in a normal state and quickly moves into a daze or stupor. She supervises the ritual arena inside the Namghar and then starts a gradual dance with a salutation to the gods and by offering a pair of pigeons in the name of peace and welfare in the village. Each of the dances she performs is associated with a character type and each episode portrays a different set of characters so that there is an interweaving of different styles of movement. The characters are classified by the moods they embody. They are largely heroic, godly, or divine.

The walking (chali) which is used throughout the dance is a half-crouched position, interspersed with high leaps, jumps, and somersaults. The feet are placed flat on the ground and the steps move in a curved direction going three steps forward and three steps back. As Doudini circumnavigates the entire arena, the Bor-deuri and the Bailung follow her and there is a long community queue following these religious officials. The circumnavigation is known as Labdinga in Kherai.

Initiation ritual

During my fieldwork, I observed that the Doudini has a calm face when she enters the ritual arena. She remains silent for the entire period and exchanges communication through the language of gesture. She stays in a serene mood throughout the ritual event but can become disturbed when things go wrong for her. For instance, if the ritual music is not in accordance with the mood of a particular moment, she abruptly stops and commands the accompanists to correct the rhythmic beats. She waits till they are able to play the right music. The audience believes that she is experiencing spiritual exaltation due to a spiritual possession. Her spiritual authority is well established within the community, and she negotiates her religious authority despite her everyday life as a housewife.

The following sections form the initiation ritual.

1. Tel bati: A cup of blood is placed on the Doudini's head. She moves clockwise and anti-clockwise, drinks the blood, and the first dance comes to an end.
2. Paro uruwa: A pair of pigeons are held with both hands. The Doudini dances with the pair, making them fly high and low. She makes circular movements and then finally takes the live pigeons in her hands and throws them up to the sky.
3. Taruwal ghurua: The Doudini takes a pair of swords in her hands and with wrist movements clockwise and anti-clockwise keeps turning the thungris (swords) and finally digs them deep in the ground.
4. Suli ghurua: The Doudini bows her head over the thungri (sword) and starts throwing her head in a frenzied manner until she gradually moves into a trance.
5. Salita khowa: The dancer lights a wick and places the burning wick inside her mouth, while keeping rhythm with her feet. Finally, she takes a deep breath and exhales.
6. Mekhela pindha: A dress is placed on the thungri (sword). The Doudini takes the dress and moves it around her body with encircling movements. She uses her hands to hold the skirt, a gesture of women wearing mekhelas.
7. Koloh loi: The performer carries a pitcher filled with sacred water on her shoulder. She moves right and left to the tune of the kham (traditional Bodo drum) and siphung (traditional Bodo flute) and performs the act of sprinkling the holy water.
8. Thungri nac: The Doudini takes out a pair of thungri from a pit and balances them in both hands. She moves the swords in the air with one thungri in front and one at the back as though enacting the art of self-defense. One sword is placed at the thighs and the other behind her back.
9. Paro uruwa: The Doudini dances with a pair of live pigeons as before and finally makes them fly. The dance ends with folded hands and the Doudini leaves the performance arena.

The Doudini's preliminary performance initiates and energises the ritual. The audience takes it as a warming up for the entire period of the ritual, and this is an indication to the audience as to how successfully the Doudini will perform her part. Later, in a larger space, an elaboration of the entire ritual performance takes place. The audience's anxiety and the enthusiasm are related to how well the Doudini performs. The audience is capable however of orienting themselves in any situation by accepting the performed tricks on faith, treating them as signs of evidence of something greater than the dance itself.

Kherai comes alive in the movement activities of the shaman dancer as she demonstrates her wit, skill, and expertise in the space to win over the deities. She has a social responsibility of mediating between God and the community. When interviewed, Bodo scholar Kameshwar provided the following descriptions of the dances.

1. Bathou gidingnai
   The Doudini moves around the altar of the Bathou several times, dancing slowly to the tunes of siphung (flute) accompanied by the kham (drums) and jotha (cymbals).
2. Chotrali
   The Doudini dances holding a sword in her right hand and a shield (dahal) in her left hand as she moves around the altar of the Bathou. She is believed to be demonstrating the war dance in the name of the goddess of war, Ranachandi or Ranphagli.
3. Khapri chipnai
   It is believed that the Doudini demonstrates tactics as to how a person can save himself from an enemy attack in the battlefield. This dance is related to the Bura-ailong, the bodyguard of Bathou Maharaja.
4. Khoijama phonai
   In this dance, the Doudini demonstrates tactics as to how to destroy the enemies on the battlefield.
5. Gandoula bonnai
   This dance is related to the Manasu or the Manasa god. The Doudini shows how to subjugate the enemy.
6. Chanalaw bana
   Through this dance the Doudini shows the preparations for a battle. This dance is related to the powerful God, Abla Khungur.
7. Khamao barkhonai
   To worship Rajkhandra, the God grandson of Bathou Brai, the Doudini climbs upon the drums and dances on them.
8. Dao thoi longnai
   After a chicken is sacrificed in the name of God, the Doudini drinks the blood of the sacrifice in a cup (khuroi) and dances accompanied by a flute, and later bows before the God.
9. Mashakhaori moshanai
   This dance is related to the God Khoila, the messenger of Bathou Brai.
10. Maoji mambrand galena (the spotted cat dance)
    This is performed by a family for the recovery of an ill family member.

The dances described above are the main dances that are performed by the Doudini in Kherai once she becomes fully engrossed in her activities. Narzary (1996) describes a different set of dances that have certain set preliminaries in the initial stages and are danced by the Doudini. The following descriptions are from my observations while in the field at Dhekidol. I have attempted to include different interpretations that exist and that speak to the complexity of the Doudini's role.

Most of the non-verbal communication that is carried out is spontaneous. As such, the movements do not enhance the texts they accompany. They are basically abstract ideas and vibrations of the inner self. The Doudini consciously moves her body and limbs in space in a meaningful manner. Some movements she has learnt from her peers, while other movements have been carved out from her understanding of space and time. During the act of climbing a hill, she takes three steps forward and three steps backward. Her hands also go up in the space indicating an experience of a pathway up a hill. She tilts her head as she takes the curved pathway and tries to hold the air in a unilateral dimension. Since she performs the acts before the public, she is enacting the sequences for the community to see and enjoy, so she makes sure that there is an artistic flavour in the entire display of the act.

Movements are mimetic in ritual theatre. The Doudini becomes a tribal girl when she comes from the hills to the plains. We can say that these movements belong to the larger activity system that the onlookers understand. The mimetic movements of the tiger, ants, birds, and other animals are part of the ritual dealing with biodiversity and the fertility of the land. Besides dance, there is also drama content involved in the ritual. A story is told through realistic means in which the community members enact a story using their bodies to showcase various incidents. Through years of practice, they come to understand where particular acts have to be performed. The subsidiary members also know how they have to behave during some of the moments where their participation is needed.

The dancers work on developing their agility and flexibility throughout the year so that purity and preciseness of the movements replicating everyday life are well established. The Doudini and her co-performers perform acrobatic movements.

Doudini's choreography

Though the nature and the attributes of the gods and goddesses are not generally known or discussed, Doudinis seem to make some intelligible choreography and the community appears to understand its meaning and importance. Doudinis are experienced artists, and their knowledge is embodied in their conduct of the creative process. It informs the way that she relates to her co-dancers, how she generates movement material, manipulates and edits that material, and binds a variety of choreographic elements within an emerging work.

It is not a case of having a set-theoretical knowledge of what should be done in a choreographic situation and then putting these ideas into practice, nor is it a question of envisaging the work in theory and then finding a physical form to illustrate that idea. Rather, the intelligence of the choreographer's action is embedded in the doing of which she may or may not be reflectively aware. This knowledge is created through dance. Ryle (1963) accords weight and value to the doing itself, instead of requiring a theorisation of practice to render it epistemologically respectable. The embodied actions of the Doudini give her dance credence as a thoughtful activity. To assume that theory must be the driving force behind thoughtful choreography would be to succumb to what Ryle (1963) calls "intellectualist fallacy and to ignore the intelligence intrinsic to practice itself" (p. 12).

Different Doudini personalities may display a number of conflicting moods that may be displayed in different episodes of dance. While the narrative must be adhered to, the divine attendants or the associates of Doudini will assist her in creating the performance.

Bathou, the presiding deity, is visually portrayed through the Siju plant (*Euphorbia neriifolia*), but his heroic deeds are displayed by the divine attendants of Doudini (Lampha–Lamphi).

The structure

Following is a description of the structure of Bathou dumonai mosanai (raising the altar for Bathou's consecration).

Before the creation of this universe, there were five elements: earth, air, water, fire, and ether, and according to the classical tradition, this dance is the reverse of the folk tradition. A formless god is imagined. Five pairs of bamboo strips and 18 bamboo poles are used to prepare the Bathou altar, and the entire preparation of the altar is demonstrated through the dance.

Bathou kharnai mosanai (Laying of the Bathou altar and sprinkling of holy water)

> After the raising of the altar, a seat is laid for the Bathou by the sprinkling of holy water, thereby purifying the inner self before the commencement of the dance ritual.

Paizam banai mosanai (Laying of the seat)

> After purification of the body, and when the seat is laid, one is expected to bend his knees and initiate God's services.

Bathou gidingnai (Re-incarnation and spiritual change of the body)

> A depiction of childhood, youth and old age are shown through dance to show that life is dynamic, not static.

Kherai golao (Limitless service)

> The creation is given significance.

Kherai gusungnai – (Service)

> The dance shows how people perform different services to survive.

Gandula bonnai mosanai (The dance of a fly is restricted)

> The guali insect cannot fold its wings, so it keeps hopping from one place to another. Man with disinterested contemplation also moves from one place to another. The dance is performed to control people's senses.

Khezoma phonai (Driving away of the amroli/jamoli insects)

> The jamoli insects make their homes with their saliva. They show some skills and live their lives with contentment. Like them, human beings too need to live in unity. The dance reflects this sentiment.

Dahal thungri sibnai mosanai (Moving of dahal and thungri)

> For the security and defence of our own bodies we need weapons to protect us. Dahal is the remover of all obstacles. The dancers' wrists move the shields and the swords to show that they are driving away their enemies. They shake their hands vigorously as if enemies are confronting them. The wrists move in clockwise and anti-clockwise directions. No sins of the world should touch the body of a community member.

Govo khungriao gana mosanai (Dancing over a sharp-edged weapon)

> In earlier times people used to test valour and truth through dangerous plays or tricks. Enemies would not dare to inflict any injury on someone who is truthful and religious. The power needed to stand on the sharp-edged sword needs terrific courage. It is expected that members of the community could also protect themselves by showing how brave they are.

Arkhala janai (Consuming fire)

> The dance shows people that once you are engaged in the dance and "ignited", you can perform difficult tasks with ease.

Daukhe longnai (Consuming of cock's blood)

> Uncontrollable and powerful enemies resort to drinking their own blood to show their indomitable strength. The priestess drinks the blood of a sacrificed cock in one go, but at times when she is not able to consume the blood, she lies unconscious in the ritual arena.

Gorai dabrai nai (Horse)

> Our body is made of various parts. The dancers move around in a circular motion, signifying a strong horse while participants think of their own bodies.

Xat hengra sifai na (Lessons in life)

> In this world, we are all born as third category people who are lured by property, wealth, children, and possessions. But, people cannot rely on hopes and ultimately one has to leave everything behind.

Nao bonai (Boat rowing dance)

> Life is an imaginary boat in which our bodily form goes from one place to another. Some day we will reach its end. We will complete our lives on earth that day.

Raigung sibnai (Religion)

> It is difficult to see religious turmoil in the state. It is true that religion is very narrow and anti-religious people try to transgress the religious boundaries making it difficult for them. However, religious bondage can never be negated.

Khamao barkhona mosanai (Dance over the mardala kham)

> One who does not have a spiritual mind cannot do religious works. The Doudini is able to dance on the kham only because she has a pious mind and she knows that the kham is an instrument of the gods. She makes sacrificial offerings of worship to the Kham.

Ranchandri mosanai (Victory in religion)

> Religious teachings can be difficult to understand. Finally, when realisation is achieved, there is celebration. It is said that the Bathou followers won a religious debate that upholds this belief. People as a mark of bravery, dance Ranachandi with enthusiasm and celebrate their victory in holding to their religious beliefs.

Jaraphagala dia (The punished father-in-law)

> The Doudinis show the mental condition of the punished father-in-law. Once he is driven away from home, he wanders from one place to another. The Doudini performs frenzied movements during her travels.

The varied images of the Kherai festival include remarkable encounters and various feats of the Doudini. The actions or dance of the priestess in the ritual space include the following.

1. A serene and calm Doudini enters the arena after a ritual bath where she washes her feet, touches the ground, and is seated by her attendants. The chants of Hari-Bol (chant the name of God) fill the air.
2. The lamphi (dance associate) helps the Doudini to get dressed; her hair is oiled and combed. Vermillion is put on her hair parting, and red colour is also smeared on her cheeks.

3. Ritual ornaments are placed on the altar.
4. Invocatory music (Saraswati seu) is played on the kham accompanied by the jotha. This marks the beginning of Kherai and the sanctification of the entire environment.
5. The Doudini marks the opening by standing on a low stool and performing movements that purify the ritual dress she is wearing. The dress embodies the shamanistic spirit.
6. She sanctifies herself by putting a burning wick in her mouth, which also testifies to her supernatural power and strength.

The performers

The villagers take recourse to their folk traditions for the sake of understanding the dance. The movement dimension in the Kherai festival communicates with specific supernatural beings and the ritual is carried out to obtain specific ends. The same vocabulary of movements performed in a different manner will have a different meaning when performed by a different set of performers. The resultant movements create a beautifully shaped folk dance that gets its form from the creative processes of the people.

The movement is performed following a circular path. The performers (community members) walk and move in a formation encircling a right-angled structure. They show the crossing of a river, moving inside a boat, climbing a hill, coming down to the plains, the passing of the entire year, pleasurable moments with community members, the movements of wild animals, survival tactics, killing of wild animals, and the skill needed to track wild animals in a forest. During my observations, I was informed that the movement technique employed by the community members was mainly of their own creation.

It is essential that community members follow the priests, as it is a belief among the Bodos that it is very easy to come to earth but very difficult to make your way out of it and the priests may know the way. This is portrayed by moving in a clockwise and an anti-clockwise direction. The frame is open and flexible, and the people can join in at any moment of the ritual. Labdinga is a dance of joy and fulfilment. After every sacrifice that is offered to the gods, a Labdinga is performed on the earth by the community to mark joy. It is also used as a linking device to provide smooth transitions between the Doudini's performance sequences. As each sequence ends, she makes her offerings to God.

The varied images that Kherai presents are of remarkable encounters and various feats of the Doudini. The various actions or dance-like movements of the priestess in the ritual space include a narrative where Bathou (Lord Shiva) becomes a tiger, then a bear, and the Doudini disguised as a hunter performs the heroic deed. The audience knows beforehand that at the end of the narrative, the disguised hunter will reveal himself as Shiva, but the dance must portray Bathou's godly character which is known to all.

The various encounters in the Kherai ritual space include the following.

1. Doudini's fights with evil spirits.
2. The Doudini must consume blood in one go. The Doudini will lie dead/senseless if she is not able to drink blood.
3. The Doudini performs a dance signifying a playful session with a wild bear and finally overpowers him.
4. In spite of the deadly ants (amroli), the Doudini manages to climb down a hill.
5. The Doudini tears off the neck of a sparrow with her teeth.
6. She kills birds with a single arrow.
7. The most interesting grand finale of the ritual is when Doudini tries to de-spirit herself. A band of ten young boys hold her back as she tries to exert her strength attempting to leave her spiritual body and become a human once again. This much-awaited sequence bears testimony to the sacredness of Kherai. The Doudini is lifted up and all her accessories are taken out of the arena. It is believed that if this is not done in a timely manner, Doudini will not regain her senses and she will not come back to earth again.

Music

Bodo music has a unique tone, sound, and feeling that is aurally transmitted at all religious and social functions of importance. In the present time, as an expression of a community's feelings, folk music has become more important than artefacts. Where it was once viewed as an accompaniment to a dance, it is now valued in its own right. Every context can give rise to meaning in a folk song. For instance, the specific musical instruments used by the Bodos as accompaniment create music contextualising the event. The sound of the flute (siphung) for the Bodo community represents the incantation or the prayers of the community. The sound of the drums (kham) is the rhythm of the Bodo people. The sound produced by the cymbals (jotha) makes one attentive about one's state. This sound is basically used for concentration. Serja (Bodo traditional violin) brings in the melody to the song. The songs are shared among the folk groups as events in people's homes or at community gatherings where most people take an active role, by interacting as listeners, players, dancers, or singers.

Currently, the Bodo community is involved in a cultural revitalisation trend that has emerged over the last hundred years. This has led to self-conscious efforts to preserve their heritage of folk music. It has also become important for the elderly to pass it on to the next generation. Emotions, symbols, and rituals from the past are learned aurally and associated in some sense with modern life. Measures are being adopted to conserve Kherai music as a marker of ethnic identity. The Kherai music in general is very different from the other varieties of music in Bodo folklore.

Kherai music is folk religious in nature. The entire repertoire of Kherai music can be divided into various types. Each music type accompanies the Doudini's specific action. If the music is not played according to her actions, the dancers stop their dancing. Some tense moments may prevail during various junctures of a ritual dance. The following categories were observed during the fieldwork in this research.

Types of Kherai music

1. Serene calm music is played on the flute to welcome the gods and goddesses at the beginning of Kherai. The same music is also played during the offering of sacrifices. The kham (Bodo traditional drum) provides a rhythm and control to the whole piece.
2. Labdinga music is played after every sacrifice and at every propitiation. It resembles Bagarumba (springtime music) and is generally played during the spring festival representing victory and happiness.
3. The trance music prevails throughout the ritual performance. Whenever the Doudini goes into a trance, the kham (drum), siphung (flute), and jotha (cymbal) are played together in a thumping manner until the Doudini regains her senses.
4. Performances that move to the right are often for bodily transformation at the ritual altar and must adhere to a strict tempo.
5. Certain expressions like jumping, chasing, crossing a river, or walking are characterised by different music underlying the emotions of the movement.
6. Clockwise and anti-clockwise movements have different music.
7. The beginning and ending frameworks are always the same. The music then follows the action of the community members where sometimes the music is created spontaneously.
8. There are not too many variations in the music, for example, a single piece of music can become background music for the entire ritual. Different stories are enacted to the same music.

The use of music in the Kherai ritual usually has links with a performance, but on some occasions, there is no direct link between the Doudini's performance and the music. Part of the altered state experience can be improvised. Different orchestras and conductors may use musical variations or improvisation of the same written score, but there is stability in repeated performances of a piece in an aural tradition. It has also been found that certain patterns of rhythm, tone, and melody can induce physiological responses (such as thumping music during any kind of transformation). The kham beats played in different tempos lead to different emotions being expressed. The performers over the years have become accustomed to the overall structure of the music, and the specificity of the tones in particular sequences is well known by the participants. All the music can be controlled within a range of four to seven beats. The change from one type of music in a particular sequence to something different in another sequence progresses in a linear sequence. Every episodic structure has music that is well considered taking care of the underlying emotions of the episodic content.

Dance as restored behaviour

Numerous folk dances have become well known inside and outside of the state. This has been at the cost of stylistic variations that were once a part of these dances. Some of the more difficult dances are no longer performed, as the Doudinis are not accomplished in performing them, or they have been erased from their memory.

According to Schechner (2002), the process by which a dance has been reconstituted is called "restored behaviour". Restored behaviour is a "living behaviour" that has been reconstructed from the outside and viewed, "independent of the causal systems that brought them into existence" (p. 34). Restored behaviour is likened to putting on a mask or a costume in order to stand outside of one's own history and observe it objectively. I observed in the Thelamara (Dhekeri Botola village) area that the community had already started creating an event for the Kherai dance depicting their histories and lives. They were also experimenting with cultural images outside of their traditions. For example, scenes of different types of work were added, along with hunting and working in the fields in order to provide a picture of authentic daily life.

The priest in the Borbil region has started training groups of young girls and boys to teach them the traditional dances of the Bodos. These groups give performances inside and outside of the state. This has also brought some economy to the village. It is perhaps with a touch of irony that one notes the activity of reconstructing historical traditions. The dance now returns to the people who started out by being objects of the discourse. The discourse produced by writers has now become a part of what is constituted as restored behaviour. The writings can serve as mirrors through which the dancers see their dance as an objectified form on which they can now reflect in an effort to both preserve and interpret traditions.

Categorisation of Kherai dances

According to the Bodo scholars I met during my fieldwork, namely, Kameshwar Brahma and Bhaben Narzary, there are 18 official dances performed during the Kherai ritual, but there are many more that may be performed throughout the ritual. For the purpose of research, I have categorised the dances as follows:

1. Adorning dances
2. Linking dances
3. Sacrificial dances

4. Trance dances
5. Propitiating dances
6. Invoking dances
7. Mimetic dances
8. Emerging dances
9. Theatrical dances

These categorisations can further be arranged into three types:

1. Primary dances
2. Secondary dances
3. Mimetic dances

Primary dances invoke the main deities and consorts as possessed. These dances fully depict the nature and attributes of the deities.

Secondary dances appease the minor deities and may be used as linking devices in between the sequences. These are also used as participatory dances as they make an allowance for the public (onlookers) to participate. They primarily accompany the priest and the Doudini.

Mimetic dances are performed by two characters known as Lampha (male) and Lamphi (female) who act as the Doudini's associates and relievers in the ritual. Both the characters imitate the Doudini's actions in a light vein. The community is entertained by their jocular feats. The associates' body language provides a form of comic relief for the spectators as a contrast to the vigorous acts of the Doudini. The Doudini's dances are a visual manifestation of social relations and engage an elaborate aesthetic system.

Conclusion

A movement system must be adhered to in order to make communication possible where there are definite codes, rules, and regulations. In the Kherai ritual, the way the performers gather in the ritual arena is also a part of the ritual norm. A group of performers take the lead in almost all the patterns of performances. Their work is to facilitate the performance of the official priests. These performers do not tell the actual story but act as passive receivers who enjoy the performance of the main performers. They have learned what they know by watching, observing, and participating.

The community is not generally aware of the multiple abstractions that take place in the performance. Although it is said that the gestures communicate, it can be difficult to understand what is being communicated at certain points. However, Doudinis express many gestures that are understood by people. One such gesture is when she de-spirits herself she moves her hands in such a way that clearly shows that she is letting the spirit go out of her. Here the hands tell the story.

Some performances use the space in a restricted sense or make it more concentrated. It creates the image or illusion of a vast space beyond that is larger than life. The small space provides a sense of security. Space holds a tension and resistance as the body of the mass moves through it and shapes it. Space is transformed into fields, heaven, a ritual altar, a resting place, pathways, and a transformation platform. Dance and mime continue to carve the volume and the size of space.

The most important feature of the Kherai performance is when audience members have a sudden urge to join the performance. They initiate their involvement with a quick release of energy before the regular flow of movement or gesture commences. The energy release is the urge and it gives motivation to begin their movement and gesture. This also attracts the spectators' attention. To make it more convincing for the audience, the performers need to play their parts with vigour.

While aesthetically pleasing for everyone, the movements can also indicate that they belong to a specific culture. It entirely depends on the spectators as to how they interpret the movement. They might empathise, recognise the culture, be moved to participate, or simply admire the dance as an artwork.

While the movements may not be understood by everyone, all of the community want to see them preserved as they have been created by their people and references their ethnic or cultural identity. With repeated observations of the choreographic dimensions, the movement system can be understood and located within a larger activity system. A formal teaching and learning system is not practiced. The community members have been observing these dances since childhood and have regularly participated in the dance.

It is difficult to separate the aesthetic from the articulation of meaning in the various dances. To manage this effectively, a good knowledge of the socio-cultural backgrounds combined with an appreciation of presentational skills is required.

The attraction in the ritual is not the ritual itself, but the way the community dramatises it by evaluating the acting capacities of the members and the musical accompanists. Geertz (1973) discusses how these are exclusive meta-commentaries, in this case, on Bodo society. Whatever be the plot, or the context, whether drawn from folklore, myth, oral traditions, or historical accounts, they are strictly "reflexive". The reflexivity of performance dissolves bonds and creatively democratises society.

Since these community performances are not taught through institutionalised learning, people spontaneously join the group. Since the framework is flexible, anyone can join and leave the performance at any time. Dance is a symbolic medium and is specifically a part of unique human communication in social and cultural systems. It is also true that as a system it operates through tradition that creates meanings that can be changed or adapted to a new situation. The community understands these conventions of social and cultural constructs as they are a part of it.

In conclusion, the performative aspect of the Kherai ritual is a rich and important aspect of the Bodo culture. With an ethnographic text in their minds, they participate in a performance that in turn becomes a workable script. Their technical knowledge of the performance, sense of music, theatre, dialogue, dress, sets and props, performance sequences, and spontaneous improvisation all came together in a logical sequence. This is an ethnographic dance/drama, where not only the individual characters but the social processes of life are given importance. Every aspect of life however small or insignificant is shown in the dramatic ritual. The focus is on the action, such as a priestess preparing for a ritual by taking a ceremonial bath or offering food and love to a sacrificial animal before a sacrifice. Where there is abundance and prosperity, the dancers demonstrate gaiety and joy by jumping on and thumping mother earth.

References

Geertz, C., (1973), *The Interpretations of Cultures*, Basic Books, New York.
Narzary, B., (1996), *Kacharir Samaj Aru Samskriti*, Bina Library, Guwahati.
Ryle, G., (1963), *The Concept of Mind*, Hutchinson, London.
Schechner, R., (2002), *Introduction to Performance Studies*, Routledge, London.

Interviewees

Dalimi Boro
Kameshwar Brahma
Bhaben Narzary
Sri Tajuram Narzary

6 The dance and the dancers
Tradition and innovation within the indigenous performances of the ritual dance of the *Hudum Deo*

Preetinicha Barman

Introduction

India is rich in cultural heritage, and this is largely to do with performance traditions broadly classified as being traditional and modern. Vatsyayan (2007) classifies traditional performances as "folk" and "classical". She marks the distinction between them stating, "the first implies community participation and the second refers spontaneously to systematised methods of expression – which imply the community" (p.2). Vatsyayan (2007) further elaborates, "folk performances are correlated to 'tribal/village' while 'classical' performances relate to the urban sophisticated" (p.2). Although this distinction exists, both the classical and folk performances are indigenous to India's native culture. Throughout time, certain folk dances have undergone changes. However, many folk dances have retained their originality in terms of the form, festival, ritual, or celebratory context.

Dance assists in understanding the diversity of humanity. Dance, like humanity, shifts, changes, and responds to diverse contexts and needs. Throughout the ages, dance in India has been classified, theorised, and practised, providing a rich history of diverse dance genres that meet varied ritual, artistic, social, and spiritual functions.

A fertility ritual known as *Hudum Deo* is practised among the Koch Rajbangshis, an ethnic community living in the Eastern and North Eastern provinces of India. Dance is an integral part of this ritual, which is primarily religious and exclusively carried out by women who sing and dance around the totem of the rain deity *Hudum Deo* as they pray for rain. Apart from the ritualistic dimension, the songs and the dances also include secular meanings that speak to the desire and longings of the womenfolk. The dance forms of *Hudum Deo* draw upon movement patterns from their tribal legacy and the agrarian life of the community. The movements reflect both similarity and differences with other Rajbangshi dance forms.

The dance performances of *Hudum Puja* have strong cultural traditions and expectations yet remain flexible. They are the carriers of the old

DOI: 10.4324/9781003398776-7

traditions yet are adaptable to change as reflected in the contemporary dances of *Hudum Deo*. The dancers follow certain movements established in the past by earlier dancers. While these patterns are broadly followed, the dancers of today are also able to create new patterns. An innovative form is always welcome, except that the new form must comply with the basic pattern of the circular movement around the *Hudum Khuti*. Regulation and innovation go hand in hand which is a common feature of most of the Koch Rajbangshi folk performances. The dance sequences in all the regions are almost all the same; they start with *Jagan* and end with the dances of thanksgiving and celebration of rain. This chapter examines the ritual of *Hudum Deo* revealing the coexistence of tradition and innovation as danced by the women who perform this ritualistic dance in North Eastern India. This chapter also includes the voices of several women interviewed, who give insights into their lived experience.

The ritual of *Hudum Deo*, popularly known as *Hudum Puja*, is done during a period of prolonged drought. The agrarian community of the Koch Rajbangshis are always dependent on rain and drought is distressing for them. *Hudum Deo*, the rain god, must be appeased at any cost. Hanley (2010) points out, "Asian dances have been intertwined with religion throughout history ... dance was often seen as a way to placate the gods/spirits and narrate the struggle between good and evil" (p.8). In the context of *Hudum Puja*, dance performances, in essence, aim at placating the god *Hudum Deo*. Symbolically, this male god is regarded as the progenitor of fertility. The appeased *Hudum Deo* showers down as rain to make the arid land fertile. This is enough motivation to embark on the ritual that is carried out through drama, song, and dance. In this unique cult, the women devotees remain naked throughout the ritual. They are led by the chief priestess of the ritual known as *Ekkushiya* (the mother of only one child). At night, they gather in an agricultural field, usually far away from human habitation. The distance and the darkness are supposed to conceal the naked bodies from the gaze of the men who are excluded from the ritual. In some regions, the ritual lasts for seven nights. The second week of the ascending moon (*Shuklapaksha*) is the time for the ritual. The exclusionary aspect of the ritual bars the entry of all the males while also maintaining restrictions on the participation of virgin females. Through the process of inclusion and exclusion, the aura of the ritual is created so as to focus on the sole objective of fertility. The naked female body, in this context, serves as the symbol of the parched soil, left arid and fallow for lack of rain.

There are certain other communities around the world who also follow rain-making rituals, and in such fertility rituals, women often play a pivotal role by miming agricultural activities. Frazer (2009) referred to several such traditions among communities such as, the Pshaws and Chewsures of the Caucasus and villagers of Armenia, Georgia, and Transylvania. Regarding the ritual in Transylvania he comments, "In a district of Transylvania when the ground is parched with drought, some girls strip themselves naked, and led by an old woman, who is also naked, they steal a harrow and carry it across the fields to a brook, where they set it afloat" (p.172). Though these cults bear a similarity to *Hudum Puja*, it should be noted that the song and dance performances of the *Hudum Puja* exceed these other cults in terms of visual as well as semiotic representation. Frazer (2009) states, "A similar rain-charm is resorted to in some parts of India; naked women drag a plough across a field by night, while the men keep carefully out of the way, for their presence would break the spell" (p.172). No clear indication is found in Frazer's *The Golden Bough* as to which community of India he refers to. However, as Lavanya Bhakat (2014) points out in her essay, "Rajbangshi Nareer Hudum Puja", besides *Hudum Puja* there are very few such traditions in India that engage naked women in fertility cults. She mentions however, that in the *Meghrani Brata* of Bengal the women follow rituals while naked and that the *Katyayani Brata* has a similar tradition (p.62).

The *Hudum Deo*: How it is danced

Right at the beginning of the rituals of *Hudum Deo*, a plantain stump is erected by the *Ekkushiya*, as the symbol of *Hudum Deo*. The dance performance surrounds this totem known as *Hudum Khuti*, meaning the pole of *Hudum*. Besides this, there are a pair of sholapith idols known as *Hudum* and *Hudumi* (*Hudum's* wife). The dance is performed in a circular formation which reflects the original nature of the dance. The movements reflect the miming of agricultural activities such as tilling the land, harvesting, and carrying bundles of crops. The hand, legs, and waist movements usually follow certain daily activities such as, thrashing, pounding, and winnowing. The symbolic significance of this apparently simple dance form is layered with meaning. The *Hudum Khuti*, around which the dance is performed symbolically embodies the active male power while the equally active forces of the dancers attempt to pacify this power. The pole symbolises the phallus representing male fertility. The image of the pole of *Hudum* comes very close to the pole dance called *Dombaley*, which is related to a fertility cult of the Wattals of Kashmir. In the *Dombaley* the dancers also move around a pole, but in this case the dancers are exclusively male. Vatsyayan (2010) considers the "pole" of this dance as "a symbol of fertility and continuity, and dance movements to be the representative of the cyclicity of life" (p.32). In the case of the dances of *Hudum Puja*, the concept of the cyclicity of life is regarded as the prime motion of life around the fertility god. The very concept of fertility holds and controls life, therefore, the fertility god is placed at the centre of the cycle.

At the commencement of the ritual the participant-priestesses place the *Hudum Khuti* over a clay platform made of the soil of a prostitute's threshold. The platform is cleaned by the water collected in a winnow by five prepubescent girls from the rooftops of five houses. Certain objects such as, the nest of a black drongo, husks, cobwebs, dust particles stuck in an elephant tusk, elements carried by a whirlwind, the pubic hair of a polyandrous woman, and other objects are buried inside a pit dug under the platform. Promila Ray, a veteran *Gidali* (female lead singer) noted that these objects are regarded as culturally specific fertility symbols, which are supposed to excite the deity. The dance of the naked priestesses signifies the same objective. It's an erotic orgy of dance performed to animate the *Hudum Deo* to respond to the call of nature and shower rain. The chief priestess, the *Ekkushiya*, as the mother of only one child represents the unfertile soil that was once fertile and bears the prospect of fertility. If rain showers down, germination and reproduction would follow as rain is read as being the semen of *Hudum Deo*. Rain, in this context, is afforded the dimension of being a fertility stimulant. Semiotically, the naked bodies of the priestesses represent the boundlessness of nature. They are the natural forms of nature, unclad by the trappings of culture. As Das (1994) points out, the women return to their primitive selves. They do not hesitate to become as bare as nature herself while they invoke the rain god. Das (1994) considers the hugging of *Hudum Khuti*, which is an essential part of the dance performance, to be the semiotic representation of the appeal of the soil for union and fertility. The other movements of the dance, the hand and body gestures also tend to signify the associations with sexuality, fertility, and reproduction. Almost all the songs and dances are led by the *Gidali* or the lead singer. Sometimes the *Ekkushiya* herself happens to be the *Gidali* of the group. The others follow her steps in singing and dancing. The songs tend to be choruses while all the dances are group performances. This is a typical feature of most of the Koch Rajbangshi folk performances.

The structure and songs of *Hudum Deo*

The first night of the ritual is known as *Jagan* (the awakening). This ritual is divided into three parts: *Namani* (descending), *Jagani* (awakening), and *Bashani* (establishing). For each ritual there are specific dance performances, all slow in rhythm. The *Namani* songs are usually the songs of invocation meant to address the deity asking him to descend on earth. Certain *Namani* songs and dances would ridicule *Hudum* for not showering rain while others would even threaten him and his consort. Such a song is:

Swargo thaki namil Hudum	Translated: From heaven descends
amanche diya paon,	*Hudum* and puts his feet on stage,
Hudum name Hudumi name	*Hudum* descends, *Hudumi*
Arao name Madankam Deo	descends, and descends
Bhakto palite namil Huduma	*Madankam Deo* (the god of
Thakurer chetta	eroticism and love). To take care
Jadi karis ang mang sang,	of the devotees, Hudum's phallus
Mochhorang tor Hudumirmang	has descended. O *Hudum*, if you
(Barma: 29)	do any nuisance we'll squeeze
	your *Hudumi's* vagina.

Usually the *Ekkushiya* sings this as a *mantra* (chant). Thus, an erotic atmosphere is suggested right at the beginning. The mantra itself is beyond the separating of categories such as the sacred and the profane. This example is a typical feature of the rituals, songs and dances of *Hudum Deo*.

After this formal invocation, the women who accompany the *Ekkushiya* dance in slow motion and bathe her on a winnow (an implement made of bamboo, used for winnowing of grains). While being bathed, the *Ekkushiya* spreads her legs symbolising her readiness for the sexual act of union with *Hudum Deo*. The winnow itself is a yonic (pudendal) symbol. It is filled with water that *Hudum Khuti* has already bathed in and it is dropped down *Ekkushiya's* body. The priestesses sing a song while pouring the water on the totem:

Hudumer ghar saat bhai	Translated as: *Hudums* are seven
Karo dekhong pani nai,	brothers, but none has water
Boil peti megh re tui khatambar	(semen) inside him, O cloud, you
Mor gaodhowa jaldeng	are so fat and rigid. I give you the
jalpaankar. (Neogi: 33)	dirty water I bathed in. Drink it.

This part of the ritual known as *Jagani* is the awakening of the deity where the deity is ridiculed right at the beginning for not giving rain. In some villages of North Bengal there is another ritual that is followed after the bathing and installation ceremony. In this ceremony, the *Ekkushiya* sits down over a plantain leaf, spreading her legs. The other priestesses cover her genitals with clay and make a clay mound. Then one of the participants dresses up as a man and sows seedlings on the mound (see Dilip Barma). The others then start a specific song and dance item around her. Such a song is:

Indraraja gosaire ekjhaske jal de	Translated as: O lord *Indraraj*,
Raktopujur jhela dhuiya sondang	give some water. I am smeared
mandire (Barma:30)	in blood and gore. Only after
	washing this I can enter the
	temple.

Here *Hudum Deo* is referred to as *Indra*, the Hindu God of Thunder as well as the king of gods. The blood and gore refer to the menstrual cycle of women. This is an attempt to invoke rain as the priestess needs to take a bath to clean herself before entering the temple. The dance that accompanies this song is volatile with erotic gestures as the song itself is replete with overt sexual symbols.

Following this, the deity *Hudum* and his consort are invoked with offerings of flowers, tulsi, fruits, milk, rice, and other goods. The priestesses sing songs of welcome while they move the bamboo sieve adorned with earthen lamps and incense in front of the idols and the *khuti*. According to *Gidali*, Promila Ray, Baran songs and dance follow in the Sukatikhata village in the Dhubri district of Assam and some other areas. The Baran, a typical welcoming dance of the Koch Rajbangshis, is not usually followed. In cases where the Baran dance is not performed the chief priestess moves her hands in a circular motion while holding a sieve (a typical gesture of welcome or Baran). In the absence of a male professional drummer, others may beat their tin drums or any other instrument available to them to produce a sound effect. This part, as well as the offerings of flowers, is accompanied by typical songs. The priestesses, led by the *Ekkushiya*, dance in a slow rhythm and offer the particular object that is mentioned in the song. A typical song of this phase is as follows:

Oki Devaraj	Translated as: O *Devaraj*, come
Jeighate chailon bati	through the bank where you are
Oi ghaate aiso re.	welcome with the lamps on the
Oki Devaraj he	sieve. O *Devaraj*, come through the
Jei ghate phul tulasi	bank which shows the offerings of
Oi ghaateaiso re. (Ketoki Ray)	flowers and tulsi (basil leaves).

The hand gestures of the priestesses show a *mudra* indicating the *ghaat* or river bank. The performers follow the rotating of the sieve in which earthen lamps are placed along with offerings of flowers and tulsi leaves as they utter, "phul-tulasi". In this context, the reference to *Devaraj* or *Indra* is quite crucial. During the *Jhijhian* dance of Bihar, Lord *Indra* is invoked in a similar way during the time of drought. Chawla (2014) mentions that in this ritual the songs are basically prayers and the theme behind the dance is that they sing and dance to please the Lord of Rain with their deep devotion, and on responding to it [rain].

In the case of *Hudum Puja*, unlike the *Jhijhian* dance, women devotees do not just bow down in front of the deity and pray for the boon of rain, but attempt to allure and satirise him, thus enforcing the showering of rain. The dances of *Hudum Puja*, unlike other dances, show the mingling of the sacred and the profane. In this context, it is pertinent to say that the reference to *Indra* must be a later introduction as *Hudum* and *Indra* cannot be the same god. As Bhattacharya (2011) discusses, *Hudum* is sometimes referred to as *Indra*, while sometimes as *Barun*, but both *Indra* and *Barun* are Aryan gods, while *Hudum* is a non-Aryan folk god. This reference would seem superficial, as *Hudum* is rather a combination of both the deities as he carries out the duties of both. Bhattacharya (2011) further refers to Birendranath Datta, according to whom the very nature of the rituals of *Hudum* reflect that he is a folk god of fertility (p.108). It can be assumed that under the influence of Hinduism, the names of the mainstream Hindu gods are used as equivalents to the folk gods, but there are a few songs where *Hudum* is referred to as *Devaraj* or *Indra*.

The dance in a circular formation around the *khuti* begins right after the appeasement of the deity. The circular movement of the dancers provides a symbol of the ceaseless yearning and compulsion of the priestesses. When I interviewed the Rajbangshi folklorist, Dipak Kumar Roy, he said that the circular movement is taken from the pattern made by the revolving sun. This pattern is central to and original to this dance. In this sense, the yearning of the priestesses is as incessant and universal as the revolving of the sun. However, many other folk dance forms of India contain circular formations. This pattern is evident in dances such as *Thabal Chongba* and *Rasleela* of the Meiteis; *Khongi Lam* of the Kuki Chins of Manipur; *Kimbku* dance of the Chang tribe of Nagaland; *Nongkrem* dance of the Khasis of Meghalaya; *Radha Khandi* of the Bandus of Garhwal; *Hurka Nritya* of the villages of Kumaon; *Phumaniyan, Kud* and *Svegi* dances of Jammu; *Dombaley* dance of the Wattals of Kashmir; *Jhijhian* dance of Mithila (also Nepal); *Garba* and *Dandiya* of Gujarat; *Giddha* and *Sammi* dances of Punjab; *Khoria* dance of Haryana; *Mathuri* dance of Andhra Pradesh; and, the *Kolkkali* dance of Kerala. In each of the above dances, the circular pattern is accompanied by specific gestures and movements that reflect their particular tribe. In the dances of *Hudum Deo*, while maintaining the motion, the devotees put the right leg ahead and then take a back step. They move their waist in a roundabout gait and change their hand gestures according to the wordings of the songs.

The deity now is regarded as the beloved, around whom the female lovers move and dance. He becomes the centre of their passion and longing. The nature of the songs combines ritualistic practices with clandestine fantasy; honour to *Hudum* is replete with sensual appeal. Hence, the dancers would make gestures representing sensuality. An example of such a song is as follows:

Hilhilaisekomortamor
Shirshirachhegao
Konthekonagelee
Hudumerdekha pao. (Ray, 2017: 193)

Translated as: My waist is shaking, body is rousing. Where do I go to meet my *Hudum*?

In the song, body parts of the dancers are erotically described, along with sensual passionate movements. At times the *Ekkushiya* comes out of the circle (the others maintaining the line) and hugs the *Hudum Khuti* passionately while singing of her desire for the deity addressing him as "*Alpo Bayosher Hudum Deo*" (my young *Hudum Deo*). Apart from her, any other priestess can also come and hug the pole passionately. In this context, Neogi (2014) comments, "This apparently looks as if a beautiful temptress, surrounded by her fays attempts to seduce the meditating lover so far indifferent to her moves" (p.31). Neogi (2014) further adds that the dances of *Hudum Puja* are always accompanied by a number of songs, that are indecorous and replete with primeval humour. Their basic purpose is to enchant which is the prime means of worship in this ritual.

All of the dances performed on the very first night of the ritual reflect the *Lasya* (slow) tempo of dance. In the song of welcome, the hand movements reflect the leaf-like gesture of the *Patra Mudra*. Though untouched by classical refinement, the dances of *Hudum Puja* unconsciously reflect certain categorical divisions and patterns of classical Indian dances. The *Patra Mudra* is the same as *Pataka Mudra*, common to most of the classical Indian dances such as, *Bharatnatyam*, and *Classical Manipuri Nritya*. In the welcoming dances of *Hudum Puja*, the mudra copies the shape of a leaf. It is definitely not adopted from any classical form. Similarly, the *Lasya* gait owes its origin to the ritual's theme for the first day, that is awakening and appeasement of the deity. Where certain classical styles appear, they are merely coincidental. This is evident from the fact that the dancers of *Hudum* are unaware of any kind of classical tradition, and the *Hudum* dance is an ancient tradition.

During an interview with Bhuban, Chandra Ray, a veteran Rajbangshi folk dance teacher, commented that the performer-priestesses of *Hudum* may not even be aware of the idea of *Taal* (rhythm), *Sam* (beat), or *Phak* (offbeat). It is quite natural for the dancers to imbibe the patterns that they have adopted without consciously being aware of the classicism associated with them.

After the *Jagan*, other rituals and dances follow on the subsequent nights (sometimes even during the day). The priestesses continue going to the fields (the ritual space) every night until the *Puja* is over. On each of the nights, there are performances around the pole of *Hudum*. The songs of this period focus on the prospect of rain. The priestesses invoke *Hudum Deo* demanding rain. They use different gestures like pointing towards the bare sky indicating that there are clouds and mime the falling of rain and taking showers. Such a song is as follows:

Kala Megh, dhwalaMegh, Translated as: Clouds, black and
Meghsodor bhai, white, you are siblings, Give us
Ekjhalakpani deo water so that we can take a shower.
Gao dhubar jai. (Ketoki Ray)

Some other songs, like the song relating to Hudum's wedding, are also performed.

Hudum Hudumir biyat genu Translated as: I have gone to the
Kaner sona daan panu wedding of *Hudum* and *Hudumi*
(Bhattacharya 111) and have received a gift of earrings.

In this song, the *Hudum* is praised for being generous enough to donate something valuable like earrings. The suggestion is that he has a large heart, and the prospect of rain would be another instance of his generosity. The dance that matches the song is full of gestures of rejoicing and merrymaking. The scope of merrymaking is in fact, one of the basic dimensions of the dances of *Hudum Deo*. Though the erotic dances have the aim to excite the deity, the element of humour and rejoicing are designed to induce the priestess-dancers to join in the rituals. Hence, the ritual space may become a platform of jocundity. Schechner (2003) discusses the intimate relationship between "entertainment and ritual" considering rituals to be the platform for people "to engage in behaviour that would otherwise be forbidden" (p.173). He states that, "even the 'forbidden behaviour' is 'permitted' as well as 'encouraged' and 'rehearsed'" (p.173). In the rituals of *Hudum Deo* the erotic dances are not rehearsed and they are accepted uncensored while being performed.

In certain regions of North Bengal, the *Hudum* priestesses visit the houses of the villagers. They beat tin drums or ring bells to alert the men folk about their coming so that they will go far away from their houses or remain hidden inside. When the group of women enter the house, they sing specific songs and dance accordingly. These songs and dances may include *Bari Dhoka* (entering the house) and *Bari Ghura* (visiting the house) or *Para Berani* (visiting the neighbourhood). A typical *Bari Dhuka* song is:

Hudumnacheke, Huduminacheke Aagduwareke! Paasduwareke?" (Barma:31)	Translated as: *Hudum* dances, *Hudumi* dances, but who is at the front door, who is at the back door?

In this dance, the women of the household take part and they are invited by the *Gidali* or *Ekkushiya* to join them. The *Gitthanee* (lady of the house) gets a special invitation to join the dancers. Elements of folk journalism can be found in these types of songs, as in some songs the singer-dancers would indulge in social criticism or satirising, instead of concentrating only on the *Hudum*-based songs. Like the dances of the first day, these dances also include circular patterns and formations. The house yard is wetted with water before the performance, but here the rhythm is not as slow as the *Lasya* tempo of the first day. The dancers leap occasionally lifting one leg, while the other leg is dragged to touch the first. The legs make splashing sounds as the leaping and touching continues. The splashing sound is an indication as to the yearning for more water that rain can provide. In these dances the leg movements are used more than the hand gestures.

The last day of the ritual is either the third or the seventh day. It is known as *Deoghar Parva,* meaning the episode of the deity. If the rain has already started falling, the ritual is limited to three days and nights. Otherwise, it would continue for seven days and nights during which there would definitely be rain (all the interviewees confidently confirmed this). The priestesses would gather in the field on that last night and cook sweet-rice with milk (*payas*). In between the cooking and the distribution of *prasad* (sacred food), the orgy of the dance continues. The naked priestesses express their gratitude to their *Hudum Deo* as rain showers down. The maddening dance of these women reflects what is happening. They light up a torch and place it up high to make the space below completely dark. On this occasion, they repeat all the dance items that they had performed so far, as well as add some new items that are in the manner of rejoicing and thanksgiving. The rhythm increases in tempo from *Lasya* (slow) to *Madhya* (medium) to *Uddam* (fast). Thus, there are *Therk* (fast dance performances with hopping or jumping) to *Chatka* (songs with a fast rhythm and an explicit rhyme scheme). In this context Sharma (2009) observes, "The dance rhythm moves from *Bilambita Laya* to *Madhya Laya* and then reaches at the *Druta Laya* towards the end" (p.68). The *Lashya* tempo of the dance corresponds to the movements of the slow running rivers of the plain areas, while the *Uddam* tempo with jumping steps owes its gait to the hill areas. The dances of the various Naga tribes reflect similar styles of jumping steps with exceptions in the movements of the hands and torso. The ethnic community of Koch Rajbangshis belongs to both the plain areas and the hilly terrains, and they perform two contrary gaits according to their natural surroundings. While dancing in the *Uddam* tempo, the dishevelled hair of the dancers judder over their naked bodies giving them a jocular look as if the parched nature is rejoicing at her rejuvenation, as if the long-bereaved woman is celebrating her gratification of desire. The juddering of flaunted hair can be compared to that of the *Deodhanis* or priestess-dancers of the *Deodhani Nritya* of the Kachari tribe of Assam. Ray (2017) states that, "in *Hudum* dance sometimes the *Shringar Rasa* or the aesthetics of eroticism rises to such a height that the dancers lose all their senses and faint" (p.192).

Once the rain pours down, the ritual space turns into a muddy field. That incites the dancers even more. Two amongst them would act as a pair of bullocks while the third dancer acts as the farmer yoking them to till the land. They then bring a pair of ploughs and ladders to till and even the land. Though it is a mime, dance movements enliven it. The act of sowing seeds also reflects some dancing patterns. They mime farming acts such as thrashing stalks, winnowing, reaping, even while dancing in the circular motion. These actions serve as the dancing steps and gestures. Moreover, during other songs and rituals they also move and bend in ways that reflect similarity with the movements during agricultural activities. Later, at the end, the *Prasad is* distributed to all, including the men folk who would be allowed on this occasion to come to the field. By this time, the priestesses would be fully dressed and have finished the rituals.

Many dances depict agricultural activities as performed in the *Wangala* festival of the Garos. Agrarian communities usually imitate steps from agricultural activities. The rituals performed often follow the agricultural work actions, seasons, needs, and roles. The concept of fertility in *Hudum Puja* works as a correlative objective connecting the ritual, the women, and the prospect of agricultural productivity.

One important aspect common to all types of *Hudum dances* is that they do not strictly follow the traditional pattern of the other Rajbangshi dances. In the case of most of the other dances, a Rajbangshi female dancer would always keep her legs closed, and avoid the steps of jumping or hopping. This is not the case in the dances of *Hudum Puja*. However, at times they do follow the usual patterns of Rajbangshi dances and maintain the 2 ½ step, which is typical of the Rajbangshi dance steps. The step is called 2 ½ because the dancers move two full steps and a half step (ending before the step is complete or full). The dances of *Hudum* may show variations depending on the spatio-temporal location of the ritual.

During my interview with Sarathi Ray, a veteran *Gidali* and *Ekkushiya*, she pointed out the dual nature of the dances of *Hudum Deo*. In all the dances that they perform, the dancers must strictly follow the circular movement of the dance around the *Hudum Khuti*. If the ritual continues for seven nights, the priestesses have to carry on in the same formation for all the nights. At the same time, the dances reflect flexibility as the dancers can adopt any dance gesture matching with the songs. Ray refers to some old-time dancers who might join in occasionally but would maintain their own steps and patterns from their bygone days. The dancers may also follow the rhythm of the beats they make with simple and bare musical instruments that are easily available, or made by themselves. Ray refers to a pair of *jhamtas* (a pair of wooden instruments played with the hands) which are made by her group members. The typical items performed in North Bengal are *Bari Dhoka*, *Para Berani*, and *Pathariya Nach* that are examples of extraneous songs and dances. These dances reflect the scope for local variations and interpolations.

Conclusion

The tradition of these dances is beyond articulation, in terms of the teaching–learning or training process. As Durga Das Mukhopadhyay (2017) writes, "Tradition plays an important role in the creative artistic process, particularly in the field of folk performing arts. Folk art is functional and spontaneous" (p.54). It is the tradition through which the dancers imbibe the art. These dances are not taught at any particular institution or under a recognised dancer. As Ray (2017) points out, "in the Rajbanshi culture the women-centric folk dances are free from 'Gurubadi' or teacher-centric traditions. Dances are taught by and learnt from grandmothers, aunts, sisters and such female relatives" (p.187). This is affirmed by the *Ekkushiya Gidali,* Sarathi Ray, who acknowledges both her maternal and paternal aunts as the informal teachers of her performing skills. As she says, the new participants of the folk rituals learn the dances and songs from the previous *Gidali* and other performers by means of participation rather than through training. They have cultivated the knack of improving their performing skill while following other performers and imitating their movements.

From a sociological point of view, *Hudum* dance emerges as a scope of liberty for the dancers who carry out the ritual in a closed space unhindered by social codes. As Paul (2019) states, "Though confined within the patriarchal structure of the society, the Rajbangshi women reflect personality and freedom in the case of the folk rituals and worship" (p.76). The tendency of managing a household through the appeasement of the deities is a common obligation that the Rajbangshi women accept with their usual forbearance. Therefore, for the common good of an agrarian society, women come out during the drought-driven days, organise themselves, and carry out the essential task that is the ritual worship of *Hudum*. The ritual itself also offers them a space to express their emotions and exhibit their skills. The circular motion of their dance places all of them on a level plane where they can identify themselves with one another. Descutner (2010) observes:

> Dance is not only movement selected and determined as significant for its beauty and interest as physical performance, it brings experiences that occur in the here and now into a culture's mythic and spiritual worldviews, reflecting ancient religious beliefs and practices while embodying them in present day performance.
>
> (p.21)

A similar view is shared by Vatsyayan (2010) who speaks of the connotative meanings associated with the steps, gestures, and movements of a dance. She states,

> (The) seemingly simple, unselfconscious movements of the human body signify complexities, which may be traced back to many dimensions of a physio-psychical level living through a millennium of antiquity. The context and the performance of the contemporary situation are vital and immediate yet historical, or remote antiquity is of equal significance. Thus, spatially they can be observed. Temporally they have to be related to different orders of time – the immediate physical and mythical.
>
> (p.19)

At the physio/socio/spiritual level, *Hudum* dances reflect a number of realities – the agrarian life of the community that are largely dependent on rain, the dependence of the seemingly patriarchal society on womenfolk for its functioning and sustainability, the urge of reproduction, the primeval desire and aspiration for a space for the manifestation of inner urges. The priestess-performers not only connect to the deity through their dance, but draw parallels between the deity and the devotee. The passionate orgy replete with dance reaches a certain stage when the deity and the devotee are in the same psychological and emotive space. The hugging of *Hudum Khuti* and the *Therka* dance under the rains are the visible symbols of this union. The dance of *Hudum Puja*, in this context, is connotative of a past way of life that the Rajbangshi society must have experienced. Dev (2016) considers the ritual of *Hudum Deo* and similar women-oriented rituals of the Rajbangshis to be reflective of their primitive life that "carries the concepts of the chastity of women, their prime status in agriculture, the urge of reproduction, family welfare, as well as their primordial passion" (p.95). The dances are simple as evident from the gestures, steps, and gait of the dancers. However, the naked female dancers in the context of this particular ritual seem to exert tremendous power over the deity which forces him to shower as rain. As I have mentioned in an essay, entitled "Culture in the Banality of Nudity" (Barman, 2007), "the naked female body attains the authority to regulate the divine ordinations. This ritual turns into a celebration of the banal body and a ceremony of possessing power" (p.58). In another essay on fertility cults, Barman (2016) stated that the fertility rituals of the Rajbangshi women,

> reflect the collective belief system of the community that is based on the power of women to control the natural phenomena. Those rituals also highlight their capacity to orient fertility and productivity and their mutual responsibility in the lines of social development.
>
> (p.153)

This speaks to an ancient system of economic equity and matriarchal control over production that existed in the past. The change of social structure and building up of a new socioeconomic hierarchy might have changed many beliefs and practices, leaving residues that offer only glimpses through certain rituals. The dance and the ritual of *Hudum*, in this sense, carry a great significance when passing on age-old values.

In its contemporary context, *Hudum* dances provide an emotive space for the participating women, where they can express themselves and share their female bonds. The antiquarian relevance however, hints at the existence of a larger space for women and a sphere of their socioeconomic dominion. Thus, the rituals and the dances of *Hudum* represent a certain timelessness as they bring an ancient world into contemporary times. Every performance of *Hudum* dance is a renovation of an archaic dance that accommodates itself within both the contemporary and agricultural traditions and beliefs held within that specific community.

References

Barma, D., (2017) *Lokaoitijhya: Hudumdeo O Urbaratantra*, in *Lokasanskriti: Utarbanga O Asom*. Ed. by Biplab Kumar Saha, Kolkata, Chhaya Publication.

Barman, P., (2007) Culture in the Banality of Nudity: Women Body, in *Hudum Deo, Protocol: Journal of Translation, Creative and Critical Writings*. Ed. by J. Prodhani, Tura, Department of English, NEHU, Tura Campus.

———, (2016) *The Fertility Cults and the Sphere of Women: Rituals of Hudum Deo and Kati among the Koch-Rajbanshis*, in Women's Writing from North-East India, Eds. by Namrata Pathak and L. C.Gracy, Guwahati, MRB Publishers.

Bhakat, L., (2014) *Rajbangshi Nareer Hudum Puja*, in *Rajbangshir Basanta Utsav*. Ed. by Alokesh Chandra Ray, Dhubri, Banamali Prakashan.

Bhattacharya, M., (2011) *Hudum Puja: Ek Narikendrik Anusthan*, in *Loka Sangskritir Suvash*. Ed. by Dwijendra Nath Bhakat, Golakganj, Centre for Ethnic Studies and Research.

Chawla, R., (2014) *Folk Dances of India*, New Delhi, Life Span Publishers and Distributer.

Das, D., (1994) *Goalpariya Loka Sanskriti Aru Lokageet*, Guwahati, Shri RajenSarma.

Descutner, J., (2010) *World of Dance: Asian Dance*, Philadelphia, Chelsea House Publishers.

Dev, R., (2016) *Koch-KamatarPrachinItiha*, Kolkata, S.S. Publications.

Frazer, J., (2009) *The Golden Bough: A Study of Magic and Religion*, The Floating Press, http://en.bookfi.net/book/1128118, accessed on 06.10.2020.

Hanley, E., (2010) *Introduction to the World of Dance: Asian Dance*, Ed. by J. Descutner, Philadelphia, Chelsea House Publishers.

Mukhopadhyay, D., (2017) *Folk Arts and Social Communication*, New Delhi, Publication, I&B, Govt. of India.

Neogi, P., (2014) *Rajbangshir BasantaUtsavatNareer Bhumika*, in *Rajbangshir Basanta Utsav*. Ed. by Alokesh Chandra Ray, Dhubri, Banamali Prakashan. (the song cited is translated by Barman, P.).

Paul, P., (2019) *Kochbihar Jelar Lokasanskritite Rajbangshi Naree*, in *KochbiharerSahitya O Sanskriti*. Ed. by Narendranath Ray, Kolkata, Chhaya Publication.

Ray, D., (2017) *Koch Biharer Lokanritya O Nareesamaj*, in *Lokasanskriti: Utarbanga O Asom*. Ed. by Biplab Kumar Saha, Kolkata, Chhaya Publication. (the citation translated by Barman, P.).

Schechner, R., (2003) *Performance Theor*, London and New York, Routledge.

Sharma, N., (2009) *Bharatar Uttar-Purbanchalar Paribeshya Kala*, Guwahati, Banalata. (citation translated by Barman, P.).

Vatsyayan, K., (2010) *Traditions of Indian Folk Dance*, New Delhi, Clarion Books.

———, (2007) *Traditional Indian Theatre: Multiple Streams*, New Delhi, National Book Trust.

Interviews

Anjalee Ray, a participant of *Hudum Puja*, Sukatikhata village, Dhubri District, Assam, interviewed on October 10, 2020.

Bhuban Chandra Ray, Veteran Dance Teacher and Kushani, Baniyamari village, Dhubri district, Assam, interviewed on January 18, 2020.

Dipak Kumar Roy, Professor and Folklorist, Department of Bengali, Rayganj University, West Bengal, interviewed on September 28, 2020.

Ketoki Ray, village veteran and insider of Rajbangshi folk life, Gauripur, Dhubri district, Assam, interviewed on March 10, 2006.

Promila Ray, veteran *Gidali* of *Hudum Puja*, Sukatikhata village, Dhubri District, Assam, interviewed on October 10, 2020.

Sarathi Ray, *Ekkushiya* and *Gidali* of *Hudum Puja*, Khekshiyali village, Dhubri district, Assam, interviewed on September 20, 2020.

7 Identity revivalism through folk dances amongst the tribal communities of Assam

Mousumi Mahanta

Introduction

Many heterogeneous groups of people call Assam their home. Each community holds a unique traditional culture with different languages, ancestry, customs, and history. There is a special relationship between people and nature in the state of Assam. People build their relationships with nature – trees, land, water birds, and animals – through different rituals, customs, and expressive behaviours, with dance being the most commonly used medium of expression. Dance is also used to reflect people's way of life. Farmers work hard to harvest the land, often facing challenges and difficulties through natural disasters such as floods and droughts. Farmers try to overcome these natural calamities by performing ritual dances to the beat of traditional instruments.

The people feel grateful for God's blessings of the sunshine, rain, wind, and the food that they obtain from nature. They consciously or unconsciously move their limbs in a rhythmic manner to express joy and gratefulness to their gods and goddesses. These movements often take the form of folk dances of people living in Assam. Their folk dances evidence the collective tradition of each community rather than being expressions of individual excellence. While there are various rhythms, musical arrangements, dance styles, dress patterns, and inherent traditional or religious beliefs throughout Assam, within individual communities of Assam, people all work together to collectively support their community traditions.

When people are in crises, be that social disorder or socioeconomic need, it is often their culture that provides comfort and security. The tribal communities of Assam, such as Bodos, Mishings, Tiwas, Sonowal Kacharis, Rabhas, Karbis, Hajongs, Deoris, have their own unique cultural traditions that have been used either by themselves or by the government in shaping the development of their community. Different multicoloured costumes support vibrant and special dance forms that not only safeguard the identity of communities, but also fulfil the community's spiritual, political, and religious aspirations.

DOI: 10.4324/9781003398776-8

Methodology

The research question driving this chapter is, "What meanings do members of tribal communities throughout Assam ascribe to their folk dances?" This qualitative research engages in a reflexive methodology through a constructivist lens. Pouliot (2007) purports,

> Constructivism is a post-foundationalist style of reasoning which emphasises the mutually foundationalist style of reasoning which emphasises the mutually constative dialects between the social construction of knowledge and the construction of social reality ... and should be inductive, interpretive and historical.
>
> (p.359)

Interviews were the primary method for gathering data. They were used to gather opinions, beliefs, experiences, and historical knowledge for the purpose of, "exploring the meanings that people ascribe to actions and events in their cultural worlds, expressed in their own language" (Roylston & Choi, 2017, p.235). Participants were selected on the basis of their willingness to participate and their knowledge of the subject matter. The participants were drawn from the areas of Chandubi, Bokakhat, and Majuli in Assam. Interviews were collected from performers of the Rabha ethnic group of Chandubi within their home settings. Due to the Covid-19 pandemic, it was not possible to conduct face-to-face interviews of all participants. Telephone interviews with cultural experts and researchers from the Mishing, Karbi, Tiwa, and Deori ethnic groups were conducted.

Ethnographic profile of the people

The Deoris reside on the plains as opposed to the many tribes who live in the hill regions. They are a major tribal community in Assam (Deori, 2015). The people reside throughout the upper valley districts of the Brahmaputra river and belong to the Sino-Tibetan family of Mongoloid stock (Phukan, 2019). The community has maintained their racial traits, language, religion, folktales, and traditional beliefs through many centuries. The people of the Deori tribes are mainly categorised into four groups, namely *Dibongia*, *Borgoya*, *Tengapania*, and *Pator-goya* (Phukan, 2019). The Deoris are one of the oldest tribes of Assam.

Tiwa

The Tiwas are one of the prominent "Scheduled Tribes" of Assam. Traditionally, Scheduled Tribes lived outside the wider Indian society, yet interacted with other tribes and the wider society (Xaxa, 2010). The Tiwas are one of the leading plain tribes living in the Brahmaputra Valley of Assam.

The Tiwas in Assam form two groups on the basis of their habitat – the Plain Tiwas and the Hill Tiwas. The Hill Tiwas live in the district of Karbi Anglong and in some areas of Khasi and the Jaintia Hills districts of Meghalaya. The Tiwa community belongs to the Tibeto-Burman linguistic family, and they have their own languages (Patar, 2009).

The Tiwas of Assam are very proud of their distinct sociocultural life. One special characteristic of Tiwa social life is the institution of Dekachang. This structure is usually built in the middle or at the edge of a village from where the people can easily view the entire area. This bachelors' dormitory or Dekachang is considered the principal traditional institution for educating youths in the social and cultural conduct of a tribal society. It is very common among North East Indian tribes. The bachelors' dormitory is known as Dekachang or Shamadi of the Tiwas, where Tiwa cultural elements are practised and preserved (Patar, 2009).

For the Tiwas, the most sacred religious institution is the *thans* (temple) where they worship their presiding deities. Even today the *thans* such as Mahadeosal Than, Basundhari Than, Deosal Than, and the Kumoi Than in the Morigaon district of Assam are considered very sacred.

Rabha

The Rabhas belong to the Indo-Mongoloid group and have similarities with members of Bodo groups such as Garos, Kacharis, Meches, and Hajongs. The Rabhas are one of the indigenous tribes of Assam. They live in different parts of the state of Assam along with bordering states of West Bengal, Meghalaya, and a few areas of Bangladesh. Some of the Rabha clan groups have adopted cultural and linguistic elements from other communities with a loss of their own identity and have now moved to the folds of the Hindu Assamese caste system. Some Rabhas however have been making efforts to preserve their unique culture and identity through mobilising the masses (Mandal & Roy, 2013).

The agricultural practices, food habits, and belief systems of the Rabhas reflect on an accumulation of features from both the Aryan and Mongoloid cultures. The Rabha society is matriarchal and the village economy is based on agriculture where both men and women work in the fields. The women wear colourful clothes that they weave by themselves. They also commonly wear beads and silver ornaments. The Rabhas celebrate three main festivals, and observe Farkanti in remembrance of the dead kings of their clan. In the various festivals, both men and women sing and dance to the tune of local instruments such as the *karra* (flute) and *singa* (pipe). They brew a local beer called *junga*, which is consumed not only in religious festivals, for birth, death, and marriage, but also on a daily basis. The Rabhas prepare as many as ten different varieties of beer. The traditional economy of the Rabhas in general, is based on agriculture, forest-based activities, and weaving (Basumatary, 2010).

The Karbis

The Karbis are one of the oldest of the many Tibeto-Burman races inhabiting the province of Assam. In Assam, they live in the Karbi Anglong district. Some of them live in pockets of North Cachar Hills, Kamrup, Nagaon, Sonitpur district and in the Khasi and Jaintia hills of Meghalaya. Linguistically they belong to the Tibeto-Burman group and use the Karbi language.

The Karbis wear colourful clothing. The dress of the man is similar to the Khasis of Meghalaya. The man wears a turban, dhoti, a sleeveless striped jacket with a long fringe covering the buttocks and coming around in front. The woman wears a petticoat (pini), secured round the waist by an ornamental girdle. The upper part of the body is covered with the *ji-so*, a wrapper passing under the arms and drawn tight over the breasts (Anam, 2000).

The Karbis have always been agriculturists who are accustomed to jhum cultivation. Rice, sugar cane, jute, mustard seed, pineapples, orange, and bananas are the major crops. They also practise terrace cultivation.

Ancestor worship and belief in reincarnation is a significant feature of their belief system. They also believe in divination and magic. There are a number of gods in the Karbi pantheon and are worshipped in different ways, at different times, and in different places.

The Rongker is the compulsory annual village festival, held at the beginning of cultivation (June), or in some villages during the winter season. Goats and fowls are sacrificed to their gods in the festival (Anam, 2000).

Mishing

The Mishings comprise 17.8% of the total tribal population of Assam. They generally inhabit the Sivasagar, Dibrugarh, and Lakhimpur districts of Assam. They have their own language, culture, social customs and traditions, religious faith, and practices. The Mishings believe in Abo-tani, their ancestor, who is believed to be a son of Mother Sun and Father Moon of the heavenly abode. Some of them have adopted aspects of Vaishnavism, following the Sankaradeva bhakti movement in Assam while some others have adopted Christianity.

Ethnic identity of tribes of Assam

At times, groups of people may consider themselves marginal within a larger society. Driven by feelings of discrimination, suppression, or negligence by a principal group, the marginal group may look for differentiation in order to establish their own identity. They start demanding acknowledgement and distinction through cultural traits. Such cultural traits are seen through language, social customs, traditions, belief systems, food, lifestyles, dresses, ornaments, and performing arts. Colonial authorities tried their best to keep the tribal communities of Assam away from the freedom movement, but the tribal communities of Assam were involved in the freedom struggle and made a significant contribution towards the national movement. The British established colonial administration on tribal lands. From that point on, the tribes of Assam were forced to assert their unique ethnic identities. Ganguly (2001) states,

> The tribal communities never reconciled themselves to their subjugation by the British. Their micro-level freedom struggles continued and they consistently asserted their respective ethnic identities and insisted on enjoying exclusive control over their resources like land, water, forests, minerals etc.
>
> (p. 5)

Dance forms of the communities

The Karbis have many dance forms. Dances performed during the occasion of *Chomangkan*, the death ceremony, are very popular (Bordoloi, 1982). *Banjar Kekan* (Pyre Dance) is performed during the *Chomangkan*. The *Banjar* is a thick seven-feet-high piece of bamboo, smoothed and ornamented. Green leaves are inserted on the bamboo post and three bamboo sticks are projected from three sides. Small baskets are made of split bamboo pieces with tiny flags and other materials hanging from them. Six four-feet-long bamboo pieces are ornamented and decorated with leaves and are then fixed around Banjar posts. These posts are called *Seroso* (Bordoloi, 1982). The Banjar posts are planted together near the funeral pyre of the clan member one week before the commencement of the death ceremony. The number of *Banjars* and *Seroso* are increased if the death ceremony is for a few people belonging to the same family (Bordoloi, 1982). Young men dance around the Banjars. Through their gestures, the departed souls are welcomed to the home of the host of *Chomangkan* for their customary purification. The dance is also performed in order to return the soul to its heavenly abode during the last evening of the *Chomangkan* (Karbi Cultural Society, 1977).

It is taboo for boys and girls of the same clan to dance together, side by side. Traditionally, a young male must dance with a girl once in his lifetime. There is a belief that if a boy fails to do so in his lifetime, he must face the humiliation of dancing with his mother-in-law in his eternal abode. This belief is the same for his female counterpart; she will be forced to dance with her father-in-law. This dance is performed with a degree of humour revealing that entertainment exists in both the real world and beyond. *Nimso Kerung* is a traditional dance of the Karbis performed during the *Chomangkan* ritual. It is the first dance that any adolescent will perform with the opposite sex. Both boys and girls choose to dance with the partners of their choice whom they feel that they may marry in the future. The young girls wearing black scarves accompany the boys later in the dance where they are interlocked and dance rhythmically to the drumbeats of the traditional drummer or *Duhuidi* (Teronpi & Das, 2016).

The *Hen up ahi kekan* (Bamboo Shoot Dance) is another prominent dance form of the Karbis. The Karbis are provided for abundantly by the hills, where bamboo shoots and other varieties of vegetables and fruits are plentiful. They collect bamboo shoots from nearby hills during the month of September and store them in funnel-shaped structures called *Hen-up ahi*, crafted out of bamboo, for fermentation and distillation. The fermented product is taken out after three or four months and distributed throughout the community as a food item. It is during the taking out of this product that the *Hen-up ahi kekan* is performed. Happiness and joy is displayed by the tribal youths signalling completion of the whole exercise that was the outcome of their collective efforts (Karbi Cultural Society, 1977).

In the past young unmarried youths (male and female) would form a group and embark on *Jir-Kedam*, in a joint community paddy field. During this time, they build a *Terank*, a camp where the youths stay throughout the year. They select the land, clear the land, and till the land and sow the seeds of rice and any other allied crops. They take up activities like weeding, guarding, etc. until the time of harvesting. It is during this stay in the *Terank* that the youths learn the art of cultivation, art, craft, and culture, and young women learn the art of weaving and other domestic chores. During harvest, after the rice is threshed and winnowed, it is placed in cloth sacks and tied at the corners in readiness to be carried on the shoulders of the young men from the threshing ground to the granaries. Following the harvest, they would be in a mood for celebration. The dance in this celebration is called, *Hacha Kekan* (Harvest Dance).

The *Baikhu/Baikho* festival is celebrated among the Rabha Community of Assam. During the *Baikhu/Baikho* festival, boys and girls perform the *Chathar* dance. This dance is very sensual, energetic, and cheerful and is performed during the spring season in the *Baikho* festival. It is celebrated in order to conciliate the deity of wealth (*Baikho*, acclaimed for her ability to bring forth rain and keep the community in good health. Some of the people of the Rabha community inhabit the hills and depend on a shifting cultivation. During the shifting of their cultivation, cultivators sing and dance *Hamjhar/Girkay* for merrymaking to ease their hard labour. They use agricultural implements during the performance of the dance (Rabha, 2011).

Rabhas usually perform during the death ceremony known as *Farkanti* that is steeped in folklore. Once upon a time, male Rabhas left their communities to fight in wars and most of them did not return. There were concerns that their clan would likely disappear. The wives of the lost warriors started searching for their lost husbands and headed to the battlefield, but they lost their way. Suddenly their husband's souls showed them the path in the form of birds, *Manchelengka*, *Tandalengka*, and *Badadika*. The women finally reached the place where their husbands' dead bodies were lying. From that time during death ceremonies, the women perform *Farkanti* as a sign of respect to dead souls, and as a promise to safeguard the clan. In the *Farkanti* dance, female performers perform some colourful movements with swords and shields (Rabha, 2011).

Khuksi is a ritual dance connected to the festival of *Baikho* in the Rabha community. The festival is celebrated during the months of May and June. The *Baikho* deity is worshipped through rites and rituals, music and dance. Games, dancing over a fire and merrymaking are remarkable aspects of the festival where both males and females participate. The ritual objects have a deep connection to everyday life. The *Khuksi* dance starts at a slow pace. Young males and females gather in their traditional attire to perform. They dance around a real or artificial tree placed in the area, and after a certain period of time, they break the tree by jumping over it so that they can destroy it. Later, the boys apply rice powder to their faces and change their costumes into a white attire. They gradually dance faster, becoming more and more vibrant with their moves, and start dancing over burning coals scattered everywhere in the field. There is an element of fear in this dance and a nervousness amongst the male performers. The women performers finish the dance by pouring traditional wine from a traditional kettle over the burning feet of the male dancers to sooth them (Rabha & Rabha, 1981).

Ali-ai-Ligang is the most popular of the festivals of the Mishing tribe. It is associated with planting of paddy seeds. Ali means seeds, Ai means fruits, and Ligang means sowing *Ali-ai- Ligang* is celebrated on the first Wednesday of the Phagun month in mid-February (Chetia, 2021). *Gumrag* is one of the most prominent dances performed during the *Ali-ai-Ligang* festival. Community life is represented through the *Gumrag* dance. The symbols of hunting, fishing, arrow shooting, transplanting, and harvesting are included in the performance. Girls usually show symbols of weaving, dressing, combing hair, and applying facial makeup through dance steps. All the people in the community, irrespective of age, gender, wealth, social status, or marital status perform together in *Gumrag*.

Porag is another important festival among the Mishing community. *Porag* is a post-harvest festival and is referred to as *Nara-singa Bihu*. People from neighbouring villages are invited to take part in the festival. Dancers and drummers from all of the nearby villages perform in good humour exaggerating a sense of competitiveness, but the performance always ends in harmony.

The *Mishing Bihu* dance is an artistic dance form. Both boys and girls dance for fun during the Bihu festival. The *Mishing Bihu* is performed mostly in kitchen areas in a distinctive rhythmic style as the participants sing Mishing oi–nitam (love songs).

Bihu is known as *Bisu* among the Deori community. There are three *Bisus*: *Magh Bisu*, *Rangali Bisu*, and *Kati Bisu*. *Bisu* is celebrated every Wednesday of the month, as Wednesday is considered an auspicious day among Deoris. They also worship Shiva (Gira) and Parbati (Girasi) in a festival full of prayers, devotions, and celebrations known as *Bohag Bisu*. This dance is mainly celebrated in temple courtyards by everyone in the community. The women playing the roles of Goddesses perform the *Deodhani Nritya*

(Deodhani Dance) to the beat of the *Dhultang*, one of the Deori's important musical instruments. This dance is related to many rituals. *Goshani*, the main goddess, is given *Muhudi* (mouth freshener) during the performance. She is offered mouth freshener for purification and refreshment unlike other *Deodhani* dances where there is animal sacrifice. She is then asked about the future of the state, village, and people by the priest. *Goshani* tells the past and future and delivers good and bad omens for the people, state, or the country. The dance concludes with all people dancing joyfully. During the festival period, the *Husori Bihu* is performed in every household (Deori, 2016). The following dances are also performed: *Deodhani*, *Bihu* dance with *Hasoti Geet*; *Bihu* with *Abor Bo' Geet*; and *Bihu* with *Bihu Bisarjan Geet*. Every dance has particular songs of specific ritualistic importance (Deori, 2016).

The colourful spring festival of Tiwa is the *Sagra Misawa*. The youths of the hill regions of Tiwa and neighbouring areas dance in the festival with essence, passion, and love. The *Bihu* is known as *Pisu* by Tiwas. The *Buka nac* (Mud Dance) is a popular dance where young people assemble together near a muddy spot and throw mud at each other. The mud cools and soothes the body. Over a period the slinging of mud has become a source of fun for the youths. In North East India the throwing of colours, rice powder, and mud at each other during some festivals such as Holi is very common (Patar, 2009).

The Borot festival is an important song and dance festival among plain Tiwa communities. The Borot festival is celebrated during a full moon in the *Pushya* month (December–January). This festival is celebrated on the Teteliya hills of Jagiroad, and *Pandal* (temporary shelters) are constructed, wherever the festival is organised. This festival is celebrated with prayers and worship. *Kuwari* (young girls) and *Ayoti* (young women singers) play important roles in the festival. A *sarailau* instrument is used to accompany the dance. It is a clapping device made of bamboo or wood with birds and animal motifs carved into it. The *Mukha nritya* (Mask dance) is another important dance performed in Borot festivals with *Phulbari* (bamboo posts lit with fire, and fire embers). These dances are very lively (Patar, 2009).

Identity revivalism through dance performances

Assam is a fertile land where agriculture is the main source of livelihood for the communities, and where ethnic communities welcome seasonal changes through various rituals, activities, and festivals. Cultures are expressed through dress, ornamentation, and architecture. Tribal communities reflect their everyday lives through folk dance and such rituals are important within every community. Folk dances are very vibrant, rhythmic, and spontaneous to encourage mother earth to absorb their energy to be more productive.

Each community has its own unique dances. Gradually these dances have become important identity markers within the communities. The process of identity revivalism through dance started after colonisation. All communities (Karbi, Mishing, Deori, Tiwa, Rabha) and their folk dances were originally performed as rituals for religious purposes. They now perform in ceremonies, for entertainment as well as for devotion. Taboos and regulations remain attached to the dances; for example, young men dancing with girls from the same clan is prohibited in the *Nimso Kerung* dance of the Karbis. Gradually however, all expressive forms are being transported to the modern-day proscenium stage context in order to preserve identity.

Most communities of North East India including Assam were not assertive of their ethnic identities in the pre-colonial period. The communities tried to improve their social, economic, and political status through a reassertion of their traditions and culture. Through folklore and folk dance, they tried to strengthen their ethnic identity. Since 1953, the Government of India has undertaken the initiative of nation building through the promotion of folk dance in public performances. Folk groups from every state perform in a parade in Delhi to represent the identity of the particular state (Pereira, 2017, p.136).

In Assam, folk dancers were encouraged to perform their local dances in parades. The communities came out with their folk dances and enthusiastically performed in public. Assam's *Sahitya Sabha*, a literary organisation established in 1919 is another platform, where folk groups were given space on the stage. Folk groups from the Tiwa, Mishing, Deori, and Karbi communities prepared their items for standardised performances. *Bodo Sahitya Sabha*, a literary organisation, was established in 1952 to preserve and promote the language, literature, and culture of the Bodo community. Later, *Bodo Sahitya Sabha*, began promoting other folk dances along with folk dances of the Bodo community. The transformation of identity through the institutionalisation of dance started gradually in Assam. Though some of the ritualistic aspects were absent in standardised dances, the dances expressed a metaphoric representation of objects used in rituals and festivals. In Assam, month-long Bihu festivals are observed through stage performances where mass audiences gather. Assam has gained global recognition and a unique status and identity through the vibrant and colourful performances of Bihu dance. The Borot, Gumrag, and Chathar dances have received special attention and gradually these dances have acquired special recognition throughout India for their colourful dresses and vibrant dance patterns. These dance forms are arranged in a very disciplined and standardised way for stage shows so that they are accessible for better understanding of the general public. A prominent cultural institution of Assam, the Srimanta Sankaradeva Kalakshetra of Guwahati was established in 1990 for the preservation of art and culture in the state of Assam. They invite groups of folk dancers to give public performances in their different festivals. Mileswar Patar (2009) states,

> In recent times Borot dance, taking the shape of performing arts, entered the stage due to the tireless efforts of Tiwa Kanthimari Samat, and have

received national and international recognition. In Srimanta Sankaradeva Kalakshetra the Borot festival is celebrated.

(p.46)

In this way the communities of Rabha, Tiwa, Karbi, and Mishing are able to communicate their identity through the above-mentioned dance forms.

Folk dances are given a platform by local governments for the purpose of supporting tourism. Private and government agencies organise and promote folk performances in tourist locations such as hotels. In this way dance not only fulfils the initiatives to display the identity of a community, but also fulfils the government's agenda to promote the identity of India. In an interview with a community leader of the Mishing community it was revealed that some folk groups of the Mishing community perform in tourist resorts in the Kaziranga National Park during the tourist season.

In the Kaziranga National Orchid and the Biodiversity Park, different groups of the Mishing community perform, *Gumrag, Porag, Mishing Bihu* while the Karbi community perform *Hen up ahi kekan, Hacha Kekan* throughout the year to attract tourists (Interestingly, this is one of the performances that Dr. Ralph Buck and Dr. Barbara Snook would have seen in the Kaziranga National Orchid and the Biodiversity Park that Professor Buck writes about in his Preface). The tourist information officer of Chandubi Kamrup stated that they invite local folk dance groups of the Rabha community to perform in front of national and international tourists during December to April. A local Chandubi folk performer, Mashya Rabha, informed me that they perform different forms of Rabha dance such as *Farkanti, Hamjhar*, and *Chathar* in the Chandubi festival. In tourist lodges and other institutions throughout India, different Bihu dances are staged, creating dances for different events such as silver jubilees and golden jubilees where the performers are paid for their performances. The Government of Assam's Ministry of Cultural Affairs sponsors folk festivals in order to fulfil tourism goals. The Majuli festival and Dehing Patkai festivals are organised by the Government of Assam with arts and crafts of the folk communities displayed for the audience. Large numbers of tourists participate in these festivals.

Knowledgeable persons from each of the communities are used as guides to organise forums, mostly for safeguarding community identity through a preservation of language and culture. The following organisations, Mising Agom Kebang (MAK), Takam Mising Porin Kebang (TMPK), and Takam Mising Mime Kebang (TMMK) work towards linguistic and cultural preservation and socioeconomic advancement of the Mishing community.

There are further links between politics and culture. Folk dances are reciprocally mobilised politically both by political parties and by local communities. Community people of all ages, both male and female, perform *Gumrag Mishing Bihu* in front of political leaders. Political leaders use the opportunity as an avenue for communicating their political interests while the community take it as an opportunity to raise their economic and developmental issues in front of the political leaders. It is common to showcase folk dances of the communities in political meetings. *Mishing Bihu* is often a popular choice by MAK, TMPK, or Mishing Sahitya Sabha.

A political relationship with the varied and diverse cultural traits in each community has continued after colonialism with dance playing a major role in fulfilling political agendas. Besides the Mishing community, other tribal communities also helped in the propagation of their individual folk dance forms. Karbi political and social organisations such as Karbi Nimso Chingthur Asong (KNCA), and Karbi students' organisations often start their meetings with Karbi dances. The Karbi Cultural Society, established to develop Karbi traditional culture is the active body organising Karbi youth festivals which are the oldest ethnic festivals where all traditional dance forms are showcased with other colourful ethnic cultural components. The society recently organised workshops of Karbi folk dances to disseminate the knowledge of the dance forms among the youth of their communities, and in so doing, supporting the maintenance of Karbi culture.

Deori Sahitya Sabha, All Assam Deori Students Union, Deori-Chutia Sahitya Sabha, and Deori Jatiya Gana Abhibartan are the organisations which claim political rights for the Deori community. These organisations have tried to impart the message of the community's identity through preservation and promotion of the unique dance form Deori Bihu and Deodhani. The Rabha community has also been trying their best to establish and strengthen their identity through the preservation and propagation of their cultural dances. The Sodou Rabha Kristi Sanmilan is continuously organising folk dance workshops among the youth of the Rabha community in different areas of Assam, and in doing so trying to build knowledge of their culture and preserve their tribal identity.

Community people living in urban areas now celebrate most of the popular festivals of the community such as Ali Ai Ligang, Borot and Bisu festivals in their urban localities. They celebrate the festivals with dance and music. Guests from all other communities are also invited. Performances are simulated in an artificial context while seeking to maintain authenticity.

The Sangeet Natak Akademi is the first national academy established for preserving the cultural heritage of India and it was where the institutionalisation of folk dance and music began. One of the major objectives of the Sangeet Natak Akademi (established in 1953) is to revive and preserve the folk traditions of the various regions of the country. It also aims to encourage and promote the folk culture of the community.

The Sangeet Natak Akademi along with the Government of India's Ministry of Cultural Affairs, has been continuously organising folk festivals all over India. Folk artists from different states are recognised, and have been given fellowships. Research is also conducted on folk performances. Gradually, institutionalisation of performing arts has developed in Assam, starting with the establishment of a Centre for Studies in Performing Arts at the Dibrugarh

University; the Department of Performing Arts, Assam University; and, the Mahapurusha Srimanta Sankaradeva Viswavidyalaya, Nagaon.

Recently, the Department of Cultural Studies, Tezpur University, has embarked on a collaborative project with Samagra Shiksha, Assam, and UNICEF, Assam, to disseminate positive messages in society using the medium of folklore by training school-going adolescents of different ethnic communities of Assam. It is expected that along with helping to tackle social issues, this initiative will help to foster a process of revitalisation of folk cultural expressions, particularly folk music and dance.

The digitisation of folk performances is another major means of maintaining community identity. Video and audio recordings of folk performances are documented either at live community performances or recorded by media houses for publicity. There are regional channels in Doordarshan (DD North East), where folk performances were first broadcast. Recently there was a rapid increase of commercialisation of folk cultural expression, particularly with the rise of satellite television and then social media. People from inside or outside of communities are using social media platforms to make popular their particular dance patterns, food habits, dress, and customs. On the Mishing Aikya Samaj and Mishing Tribe Facebook pages the Mishing tribe promotes Mishing food, dress, and dance. The Tiwa Tribe Official is another prominent Facebook page where the videos of the Borot festival and dance, and the Tiwa Tauling dance are uploaded for viewers. The Greater Karbi Tribe is one of the popular Facebook pages for Karbis' where videos, photos, and descriptions of Karbi folk performances (Hacha Kekan, Lengpum Sok Chon) are uploaded for promotion of the dances. The Deori Tribe and Rabha Tribe have two official pages that promote the art and culture of their communities. Folk dance videos of popular artists of Assam are uploaded onto YouTube with an aim to popularise the dances. The Mishing, Karbi, Rabha, Deori, and Tiwa communities have very rich colourful dresses and ornaments associated with their dances and festivals. Such colour helps in capturing digital audiences' attention.

Conclusion

The proliferation of folk dance in Assam has been instrumental in extending social solidarity amongst and across cultures and with this proliferation has been a rejuvenation of cultural values in social spaces. The rapid increase of the commercialisation of folk performances however has increased the risk of misapplication and misunderstanding of art forms. While there are obvious benefits, there is a need for communities of Assam to become aware of the dangers. There are threads of concern that have arisen along with the commercialisation of folk performances, such as copyright protection and the ethics in regard to ownership of art forms and performers' rights. The increasing drive of powerful political groups may bring negative outcomes to the communities and difficulties in maintaining the traditional heritage of Assam. The ebb and flow of nationalism has worked as an overwhelming force that has shaped patronage in a remarkable manner. Folk dances are rightly viewed as the main, authentic, undiluted expression of local values and world views in every community of Assam. Supporting these communities in protecting and enlivening their dance is therefore one of the most important strategies that local and national governments and tertiary institutions could implement.

References

Anam, N., (2000), *The Enchanting Karbi Hills* (1st ed.), Guwahati, Angik Publication.
Basumatary, P., (2010), *The Rabha Triba of North East India, Bengal and Bagladesh*, New Delhi, Mittal Publication.
Bordoloi, B., (1982), *Chomangkan: The Death Ceremony, Performed by the Karbis*, Guwahati, Tribal Research Institute.
Chetia, K., (2021), Me-Dam-Me-Phi and Ali-Ai-Ligang, Cultural Identity of the Tai-Ahoms and Misings of Assam. *International Journal of Creative Research Thoughts*, 9, 739–744. https://ijcrt.org/papers/IJCRT21A6066.pdf.
Deori, B., (2015), Identity Formation and Political Assertion among the Deoris. *International Research Journal of Management, I.T. and Social Science*, 2(3), 5–10. https://sloap.org/journals/imdex.php/irjmis/.
Deori, F., (2016), *Deori Samaj Sangaskritir Safura*, Tinisukia: The Assam Computer Press.
Ganguli, J., (2001), Ethnic Issues, Secularism and Conflict Resolution in North East India. In B. J. Deb (Ed.), *Ethnic Issues, Secularism and Conflict Resolution in North East India* (2nd ed.), New Delhi, Concept Publisher, 5–8.
Karbi Cultural Society, (1977), http://karbiyouthfestival.com/, Accessed on 12 December 2020.
Mandal, B., Roy, M., (2013), The Rabha and Their Social Movement (1925–1950): A Case Study of North Bengal. *IOSR-JHSS*, 10(3), 5–8.
Patar, M., (2009), *Aitihya and Samakal*, Guwahati, Ak Bak.
Pereira, C., (2017), Religious Dances and Tourism: Perceptions of the "Tribal" as the Repository of Traditional in Goa, India. *Etnografica*, 21(1), 125–152.
Phukan, M., (2019), The Deori Tribe of Assam: A Socio-cultural Study. *International Journal of Applied Research*, 5(8), 234–236.
Pouliot, V., (2007) "Sobjectivism": Toward a constrctvist methodology. *International studies quarterly*, 51 (2), 359–384.
Rabha, B., (2020, 1 December), The Folk Dances of Rabhas. https://bipulrabha.blogspot.com/2011/03/folk-dances-of-rabhas.html, 1 March 2011, Accessed on 1 December 2020.
Rabha, P., & Rabha, S. (Eds.), (1981), *Dev Devi Aru Rabha Samaj*, Kamrup, Rabha Sahitya Gosthi.
Roulston, K., & Choi, M., (2017), Qualitative Interviews. In U. Flick (Ed.), *The Sage Handbook of Qualitative Data Collection* (pp. 233–249). London, Sage Publications Ltd.
Sangeet Natak Academy, https://sangeetnatak.gov.in/sna/introduction.php, Accessed on 9 December 2020.

Teronpi, B., & Das, K., (2016), The Politics of Festival-Tracing the Origin and Growth of Karbi Youth Festival: Search for Identity. *IJRDO-Journal of Social Science and Humanities Research*, 1(3), 1–14. https://www.ijrdo.org/index.php/sshr/article/view/66.

Xaxa, X., (2010), Commonalities and Identification as a Tribe. In T. Tiba (Ed.), *Scheduled Tribes of North-East India and Development*, New Delhi, B.R. Publishing Corporation. 53. 2019-05.

List of interviewees

1. Matshya Rabha, a community performer
2. Minati Doley, cultural activist
3. Jyotimala Doley, community youth and researcher
4. Siem Phancho, community youth and researcher
5. Priyanka Bordoloi, community youth and researcher
6. Apekhsita Sonowal, community youth and researcher
7. Danny Gam, Tourist information officer, Chandubi

8 Bihu performance of the Morans of Assam

Parash Jyoti Moran and Hashik N.K.

Methodology

This research demanded participatory as well as non-participatory observation. Interviews with active participants and other knowledgeable persons of the community were undertaken, gaining a snapshot of the Bihu festival and other aspects of Moran culture. This ethnographic approach suited Parash's insider position as a Moran. Interviews were undertaken as a talking partnership, and being a Moran was advantageous in developing rapport. We were aware however, of maintaining some relationship boundaries as researchers, in order to maintain some objectivity, and not allowing notions of "self, intersect with those of the people studied, affecting the formulation of knowledge and its interpretation" (Sherif, 2001, p.437).

It seems astonishing that there is very little written material available on the Morans and their culture. Most available material is found in souvenir shops, and tourist magazines. A few books exist and these provide key references in this chapter. With the dearth of in-depth research works on the culture of the Morans, it is timely that this chapter furthers our understanding of Moran culture.

Morans: An overview

Morans are considered to be aboriginal people of Assam (Sarma & Mahanta, 2016), but the origin of the word "Moran" cannot, in our minds, be satisfactorily verified, due to a lack of written evidence. There is a myth among the Moran people that an old woman of their community had the supernatural power of giving life back to dead people. She was given the epithet "Moran" meaning; Mora (dead) + and (bring back), literally stating that she could call back a dead person to life.

A British colonial officer, Sidney Endle (Endle, 2010) proposed however, that a few centuries ago, three brothers named Moylang, Moran, and Moyram, inhabited the Hukang Valley in the upper reaches of the Chindowin river (Dohutia, n.d.). While the eldest of them remained, the youngest, Moyram,

DOI: 10.4324/9781003398776-9

migrated to Nepal and the middle brother, Moran, crossed the Patkai range entering Assam and settling near the Tipuk river of the Doomdooma region. Dohutia (n.d.) discusses Endle's belief that the title Moran thus came from the name of their progenitor. Today, the Morans are still to be found in the surrounding area of the Tipuk river.

Morans are Indo-Mongoloid people. A British civil service officer Edward Gait (1981) mentions that the Morans had their own language, which was akin to that of the Kacharis, but that over the course of time, they gave it up in favour of Assamese. According to a linguistic survey of India, the Morans belong to the Sino-Tibetan or Tibeto-Chinese language family (Grierson, 1903). Presently, Morans have retained their own ancient language while speaking Assamese in their daily life. The Superintendent of Ethnography in Assam, Major Gurdon, also identified an affinity of the Moran language with that of the Bodos through linguistic evidence (Grierson, 1907).

The Indian folklorist, Birinchi Kumar Barua (1969), discusses the fact that the original home of the Morans was in western China near the Yang-tse-kiang and the Huang-Ho rivers. The Morans living in Tinsukia have the peculiarities ascribed to and identified as Moran, while those living in other districts have adopted rites and customs of other communities. The present Moran population measures 3.50–4 lakh (350,000–400,000).

Morans are a patriarchal community and descendants are traced through male family members. Among the Morans there are about 138 clans or social groups. The clans were socialised for different kinds of trades and walks of life and in some cases the clans can be identified by their surnames. The Morans follow the Mahapurushia Vaishnavism religion propounded by Sankaradeva. Sri Aniruddha Deva, a former disciple of Sri Sri Sankaradeva, the founder of the sect. The Morans were the first of eastern Assam's tribes to have been converted into Vaishnavism of the Aniruddha Deva sect, popularly known as the Mayamara sect. The conversion into Vaishnavism happened more than 400 years ago, during the time of the religious Guru of the Mayamara, Vaishnava Satradhikar Sri Sri Chaturbhuja Deva, at Puranimati near the present Jorhat district. As the Morans are exogamous people, an intra-clan marriage is regarded as a crime. Monogamy is a prevalent practice among them, although polygamy is not wholly ruled out.

The Bohag or Rongali Bihu is the only Bihu festival of the Morans. In the greater Assamese society, there are three Bihus, which are Bohag or Rongali Bihu, Magh or Bhogali Bihu, Kati or Kongali Bihu. While other Bihus are not celebrated, Morans hold Bohag Bihu at a different time to other Assamese communities. The Bohag Bihu of the Moran people is always started on a Tuesday in the month of Bohag for a week or more, according to the Assamese New Year Calendar. The date is fixed according to the formal decision or holy order of the Moran Gosain (a holy chief of the tribe). Morans celebrate Bihu with dance, song, music, and merrymaking.

Bihu among the Morans

Morans celebrate the Bohag Bihu as a time-honoured custom as well as a socio-religious festival. The celebration of Bihu as a socio-religious festival contains some unique characteristics from ancient times as well as more contemporary characteristics. The Morans were once worshippers of Kesai-Khaaiti, so the celebration of Bihu begins with a dedication to her at the Kesai-Khaaiti Than of Sadiya.

Morans do not celebrate Bohag Bihu from the first day of Bohag because they believe that they lost their beloved King and Captain on that day, while he was bestowing blessings to the Ahom Bihu team (a neighbouring ethnic group in Assam). This is a historical belief and it is believed that this delay respects the lives they lost on the first day of Bihu. Hence, they do not observe Bihu from the first day as do other Assamese communities.

The celebration starts from the first Wednesday of Bohag with the celebration starting only after the Baik (words) given by the Satradhikar Gosain (holy chief of the community), to whom the people have allegiance. The Gosain is the person who decides the date, the duration of the celebration, and all other matters pertaining to the festival. There are also cases of celebrating Bohag Bihu in one village at different times to another. This may happen when different Gosains or the Sattras decide on different dates for celebrations of Bihu. Their followers simply follow the dictate of the chief of their own Sattra.

Picture 8.1 A group of Moran Bihu dancers. Permission given from the Kakapathar Raati Bihu Celebration Committee.

There are reasons why the Morans opt for the first Wednesday of Bohag to celebrate the Bihu, and these include:

1. Morans, before they converted to Vaishnavism, gathered together on the first Wednesday of Bohag at the Kesai-Khaaiti Than of Sadiya, to offer sacrifice for the well-being of the society and to welcome the new year, and then to celebrate Bohag Bihu. Even after conversion to Vaishnavism, the Morans continued to obey their old traditions. They are well-known for their devotion to their Guru.
2. According to another legend, the Moamoria rebellion happened because of the cruelty and suppression meted out by the Ahom rulers to Vaishnava gurus. In 1769 A.D. Ramakanta, son of Naharkhura Saikia (a great warrior of Moamoria rebellion) became the king of the Ahom Kingdom. Raghab Moran, a brave warrior and leader of the Moamoria rebellion became Borboruah and married the widow of the King of Rajeswar Singha. But Raghab Moran was killed by his wife Kurangonayani on the 13th of April, 1770 A.D; that day was a Tuesday. Not only that, along with Ramakanta, his father Naharkhura Saikia and others were also killed in the uprising. After this sad incident, it was decided not to celebrate any joyous festival, even Bihu. So now, the first day of Bohag is a time of reflection and preparation as a sign of respect to those who were killed.
3. The most unfortunate and sad case for the Morans was that their religious gurus, Shri Shri Astabhuja Dev and Shri Shri Chaturbhuja Dev were also killed by the Ahoms on that day. Therefore, Morans celebrate the Bihu after a period of mourning, which was ten days following the death of their beloved gurus. Since then, the practice of celebrating Bihu on a Tuesday has been strictly followed by the Morans. When the 13th of April does not fall on a Tuesday, the Tuesday following the 13th April is fixed for celebrating and takes that day as Bihu Uruka (Bihu-Eve-Day).

For the celebration of Bohag Bihu the Morans need a Tuesday as Uruka, Wednesday as Goru Bihu (dedicated to the cattle), and Thursday as Manuh Bihu (dedicated to people). The last day of the celebration is observed as Bihu-Uruwa (completion of Bihu festival) day.

On a Tuesday, Mongole Uruka, the Morans observe the Shri Chaturbhuja Dev Tithi, a religious holy ceremony in the village Namghar to pay their respects to their revered gurus. On the day of Uruka, people clean their houses, Randhoni Ghar (kitchen), Gohali Ghar (poultry house), and their tools. Young boys go to the forest to collect necessary vegetables such as turmeric, brinjal, bitter gourd, and other items to make Chat-mari, (tiered bamboo whips) along with Torapat for pogha (tree-leaf to make rope for cattle), makhiyati (luck plant), and tangloti (holy rope plant). Aged people indulge in games such as Dhal-Korhi or Daposi (traditional games) for the well-being of society at the Namghar field. The games run from the first to the last day of the festival. They believe that if the game finishes very quickly then it is not a good sign for the community's welfare in the coming year. If the playing of the game becomes very confusing, then they believe that is also a bad sign. They offer betel nut to the deity and play the games again until there is a happy ending.

The very next day of the Uruka is called Goru Bihu. During this day, the cattle are bathed and tied with new rope. Along with the cattle, elephants are also bathed. This ceremony is held in a nearby river or in a big pond. After the bathing of the cattle, the Chat-mari (bamboo whips) are exchanged. A clever person will change his three-line Chat-mari with someone else's eight-line Chat-mari. Later the Chat-maris are hung from the roofs of their dwelling houses. On the day of Goru Bihu, all young and elderly people play Koni-Jujj (an egg-fight) with the eggs of hens and ducks. They believe that the first egg from the hen or duck is comparatively harder than the subsequent eggs, so they save the first egg to fight in the games. Eggs are then fried with amrali-tup (ant-seeds). Customarily on the eve of the Bihu they also prepare a curry of one hundred and one vegetables, called akh-ati-hak. The whole house is purified by Makhiyati as they believe that this activity will chase away all disease and evil from the house. In the evening Khermuthi (bundle of hay) is lit in front of the house. Burning this bundle of hay, the villagers believe, will be helpful in killing unwanted insects of the home. On this day, elderly people observe the Shri Astabhuja Dev Tithi in the Namghar and Sattra. A group of young boys and girls come to their guru and ask his permission to start the celebration. A Bhakat announces the dictates of the Gossain. After acquiring the permission for the celebration of the Bihu from the Namghar, a team of young boys with an older boy, go to every girl's house and request that their parents send their daughters to the Bihu. They promise to bring them back home safely. From this day, they begin the celebration of dancing, singing, beating drums, and playing flutes in the Bihughar.

Thursday is the Manuh Bihu. On this day the young ones present Bihuwan to their elders and give respect. The elders also give "ashirvad" (blessings) to the young ones. All the villagers, especially the Soroniya devotees who are initiated, go to the Gosain Ghor and take ashirvad from their religious guru, Jiodhan. During the Bihu celebration period the women remain busy in their "Randhoni-Ghar" (kitchen) preparing different types of Bihu cakes.

After seven days of celebration, the Morans observe a Bihu-Uruwa ceremony. They again go back to the Sattra or Namghar. This time they make their way singing and dancing from the Bihu-Ghar to the Namghar. After that, they sing and dance in front of the Namghar, where all villagers and guests come to observe Bihu.

Morans celebrate Bohag Bihu in different ways. The variations in the celebration of the Bihu are listed below.

1. Dhormo Husori
2. Bihu Husori
3. Bormoga or Log Bihu
4. Raati Bihu

Dhormo Husori

This Moran celebration is not common to all Assamese people. The Dhormo Husori is different from other forms of Bihu. While on the one hand, it is a typical traditional religious Bihu, only the elderly and Soroniyas devotees can take part in it. The religious people who take part keep themselves away from women other than their mothers, wives, and mothers-in-law. Religious Bihu songs are sung by the singer and the songs composed by the Moran religious preachers, including Phul Konwar and Moni Konwar Geet. In this Bihu, non-religious songs are strictly prohibited. All members of the Bihu team wear specific dresses and the singers are known as Bor Namati, Pali Namati, Dholia, and Talia as per the roles they play. In the other forms of Bihu, anyone can change their role but, in this form, from the beginning to end, no one can change or break their allotted role. Morans believe that, if anyone is to truly pay respect to this Bihu team, then any problem can be solved by the deity through the Dhormo Husori.

Bihu Husori

The Moran Husori party does not include girls, unlike some other Assamese communities. It is performed by the young boys only. In the Bihu Husori, all types of songs that speak of love, nature, comedy, or relationships can be sung by the members and enjoyed by the community.

Bormoga Bihu or Log Bihu

This Bihu includes young boys and girls who are invited by families to perform the Bormoga Bihu in their houses. The host welcomes the party in a traditional manner and prays for blessings by way of performing dancing and singing. They believe that if they please the party, then they will be blessed by God. The party of girls and boys are offered Bihu cakes. In this Bihu, there are two groups, one of boys and the other of girls. They start singing and dancing simultaneously in front of the house. Then the boys' group sing and play music and the girls start dancing to the boys' music. The ritual is known as Log Bihu because the boys and girls dance and sing together.

Raati Bihu

Raati Bihu is the main part of this festival. This section of the festival provides a unique identity to the Moran tribe. This Bihu is performed at night by young boys and girls in the Bihughar. In the Bihughar, there is a bamboo

Bihu performance of the Morans of Assam 113

Picture 8.2 Raati Bihu. Permission given from the Kakapathar Raati Bihu Celebration Committee.

Picture 8.3 Chak Chani. Permission given from the Kakapathar Raati Bihu Celebration Committee.

Chati (a knot) in the centre of the house. The boys sing Bihu on one side of this Chati and girls sing on the other side. The Chati acts as a divider between them. In this Bihu the boys and girls begin by taking positions in the Bihughar and they start singing and dancing, each group remaining in separate spaces. The youths start to sing holding hands in a circle. In no situation do they cross the imagined Chati divide. After midnight, the youth from the neighbouring villages arrive at the host village to enjoy the Raati Bihu. Outside the house, the guest youths are invited to sing by the local youths and the local boys present them with a long bamboo "dang" pole and "Chak-Chani" bamboo stick to play music to accompany their song. The village girls then start to dance to the rhythm of the song.

The people of the Moran community begin the arrangement of Bihu long before the spring season begins. The youths of villages go to nearby forests to collect wood, bamboo, and other items to build a two-room open-shed house, traditionally known as Bihughar. For the Moran people, Bihughar is not a place of dance and music performance only, but it is also a sacred space. If someone wants to address the Bihu team or invite the Bihu team to their home, then they have to go to the Bihughar and the team also has to go there to accept the invitation. As they respect this house as a sacred place, they never do anything unethical in the Bihughar.

A Moran gamosa with its own distinctive features is worn by the boys and girls at the time of Bihu. The boys' gamosa is completely white in colour. The boys wear dhoti and Enga-Chula or a white shirt. The girls wear a black "Kaliya-Riha" and "Methoni". Methoni is worn around the bosom; the length of the Kaliya-Riha is to the knee, which helps when they are dancing. The girls wear "maduli" (a drum-shaped ornament) around their necks, known as "dugdugi" and "kontha". They put seasoned flowers in their hair and wear a garland of flowers or leaves. Boys have no particular ornaments, but they tie coloured Rumal (handkerchiefs) on their wrists. In Moran Bihu, musical instrument such as "dhol" (drum), "pepa" (flute), "Xutuli" (flute made of soil clay), "gagana" (jew's harp) and "veena" (bamboo musical instruments played by women) are used. Chak-choni is made from a bamboo stick and is a well-known musical tool for the Morans. The rhythm follows the lyrics of the dhol (drum) and the sound suggests a form of redemption.

> Ghini Tighini Ti-Ghini Jaang Jaang Jaang
> After that the beat of the Dhol for dance steps follows.
> Ghini Tighini Ti-Ghini Taak Taak Taak

The instruments include:

Pepa: The indigenous Moran Pepa (hornpipe) was made of a special leaf called Jangu-Pat. They originally used buffalo horns, but these are no longer in use.

Xutuli: The Xutuli is a flute instrument of the Morans and is made of bamboo. It has three holes, to make it easier to play and is usually played in a slow rhythmic manner.

Taka/Gagana: The female dancers play the Taka (an instrument made of bamboo) with their song. The difference between the Assamese Taka and the Moran Taka is in its size. The Moran Taka is much longer. They also play Gagana, a sweet musical instrument made of bamboo.

Songs of the Morans

Morans love their song, music, and dance. They observe their folk, social, and religious festivals with songs accompanied by music and dance. As Bihu is the major community festival, during the period of Bihu they sing "Bihu-Geet" at their Bihughar. The songs are very meaningful, reflecting their feelings towards love, nature, and many things related to daily life. The young boys and girls try to attract each other by melodiously and slowly singing love songs. In the Moran Bihu song, a sweet slow rhythm is found. Without stopping, they sing the Bihu songs throughout the day and into the night, as it gives them immense pleasure. The following are classifications of such Bihu songs, which are more often than not, content-oriented:

(a) Songs of prayer and supplication

On Wednesday, the Moran Youth themselves make their Bihughar (space for the event). For the Moran the house is for events and sacred at the same time. While making the house for the event they pray to Sankar and Madhaba (the religious guides) to give more power and save them from any inauspicious incidents. They believe that Sankar and Madhaba will protect the Bihughar. Sankar is Srimanta Sankaradeva, and Madhaba (Madhabadeva) was the chief disciple of Sankaradeva.

As a part of the song they mention that the beams of the house are named after Sri Sankardeva, and the truss or "Maroli" is named after Madhabadeva.

On Thursday they sing and pray to Pranehori (God) to forgive them if they have not built the sacred house properly, because they made it only from the tree leaves (Geregua pat) collected from the local forest.

(b) Pad (beginning song)

A Bihu dance performance of the Moran generally starts with these songs. The songs reveal the important three days of the week, Tuesday, Wednesday, and Thursday. The Bihu eve must fall on a Tuesday, so the first song they sing is "Uruka", the second day is Goru-Bihu, and the third day is Manuh-Bihu. After the Pad, they continue to sing the next type of Bihu song or Bihu Geet or Bihunam.

While starting the event, the boys will start by saying to their friends that it's the beginning of spring season; and the very next Tuesday is Uruka, where are you all? Come let's prepare for our fest, because Bohag Bihu is around the corner.

The girl will call their friends to start the event by saying that thereju (a fruit of local forest) has already ripened and it's a sign of the advent of Bihu, let's start the celebration.

(c) Songs of love and attachment

The majority of Bihu songs are about love. The sentiment of love runs throughout the songs with excellent poetry of youthful exuberance. Love songs are sung by young boys and girls in exquisite melodic patterns accompanied by the vigorous rhythm of the Bihu dance, where two lovers communicate their love through songs.

When they first see each other the boys sing: We meet here at this event and we know each other from the first eye contact. Let's share what is on your mind. I am anxious about how you will respond to my call.

The girls will reply to the boys in the following manner: You are singing a sweet song and your voice is too kind. Love draws me towards you but I feel shy to speak.

If they fall in love with each other after they meet, the girls present tamulpan (betel nuts) to their lovers and the boy will say, "Your gift of betel nut makes me crazier; I am missing you every second of my life". Then the girl replies that from the first day of our meeting, I have secretly loved you, now it is difficult to live without you. The intention of both is to get together in future and make a family for life.

After love, they promise to continue loving and the boy sings another song: Here they showcase their love for each other and promise each other to live together forever. They are saying that they will build their house through their love, and happiness.

> Chokure Chinaki Holung Nu Jene Tene,
> Bihurenu Khulate Pai,
> Monore Chinaki Dibine oi Nidio,
> Chintainu Marise Khai …
>   The girls reply …
> Oti Morom lage Tumare bihunaam,
> Arru Morom Lage Matat,
> Oti Morom Lage Bihute Dekha Pale,
> Matibohe Nuarung Lajat …

After they meet, they fall in love with each other. The girls present betel nuts to their lovers, and the boys accept the betel nuts as a gift and then start to sing:

Ki Khuai Pogola Korili Lagari,
Hate Kata Tamulor Logot,
Khangte Hungte Uthungte oi Bohungte,
Tuloinu Pori Thake Manat ...
The girls reply ...
Jidina Chenaiti, tukenu dekhilung,
Antarote Sobiti Tholung,
Hidinare Pora Janibi Chenaiti,
Moiyu Tumare Holung ...

After love, they promise to continue loving and the boys sing:

Morome Amoni Kore Muk Logori,
Nepabi Toi Muk Beya,
Ture Oi Logote, Kotam Moi Chirodin,
Jody Kore Ishare Daya ...
The girls respond saying,
Akhare Chakiti Jolam Buli Bhabisung,
Amarenu Notun Ghorot,
Monore Akhati Puram Buli Bhabisung,
Ajiban Tumare Logot

The Husori song:

The Husori songs are performed as an invocation to God.
    The meaning of the song is to take blessings from God. Here they mention that God first created the world then he created humans. The same God created this event in our minds so why should we not observe it? Let's celebrate Bihu and celebrate the lord's creation. Again, in this song they say that nature gives us the weather to celebrate, trees are growing older and birds are singing new songs. To attempt to describe God's creations using human words is useless. Let's celebrate Bihu, as Bihu is here only for a single month. If we don't celebrate now, when will we do it?

        Hei ... Prothome Ishare,   Shristi Shorojile,
            Tarpsat Sorojile Jiwo,
      Heijan Ishare,   Bihukhon Oi Sorojile,
           Aminu oi Nepatim Kio ...,
    Heeii ... Chote Goiye Goiye,   Bohage Palehi,,
            Phulile Oi Bhebeli Lata,,
    Koinu Koi Thakile,   Uroke Nopore,
           Amarenu Bihure Katha ...,
    Heei.. Bihute Ahile,   No-Pani Bahile,
           Gosenu halale Pat,

> Bihu Thake Mane, Bihuke Binabi,
> Bihu Gole Binabi Kak ...
> Concluding Couplets

At the end of the performance, the songs turn into blessings. The families that are in trouble pray for blessings by offering betel nuts wrapped in banana leaves, in a kneeling position in front of the husori team. While receiving the betel nut, a youth from the husori team receives it by singing and dancing. They bless the family by praying to God for the family's wellness and purity. It's believed in the community that the performers of the husori are as pure as God's own child, like Krishna himself. Krishna is regarded very highly in the form of Hinduism that is practised here.

Some songs are associated with the Bihu Uruwa performance: Bihu Uruwa is the final ceremony of all the Bihus. On this day, all girls and boys gather in the Bihughar. All the village people come to observe and witness the ceremony. The boys and girls start their Bihu in the same way, but on the final day, they sing different songs. The boys hold hands in a circle and start singing:

> Heeii ... Hasati Oi   Luitor Hihu,
> Ajije Jabogoi Bohagor Bihu ...
> Heeii ... Bihu Jy Oi   Bogoli Oi ...
> Bihu Kene Kori Rakhimnu Oi ...
> Heeii ... Hasati Oi   Raidang Bengenar Pat,
> Eman Din Gaiyu   Rokhabo Nuaru,
> Agani Jolise Gat ..."
> Heei..Hasati Oi   Raidang Bengenar Pat,
> Ajije Jabogoi,   Bohagor Bihuti,
> Agani Jolise Gaat ...

The girls respond with their song.

> Heei ... Kauri Gol   Godhuli Hol,
> Amaru Jabore Homoye Hol,
> Heeii Bogakoi Bogoli   Kolakoi Kekh,
> Bohagor Bihukhon Ajiyei Hekh ...

Through the songs the youth express that the Bihu season is going to end, as this is the call of nature. We celebrate this Bihu from our heart but we can't hold onto it. We dance and sing, and now our body is crying along with our hearts. The girls respond with their song.

Songs that have reference to stories

Historical incidents of the Moran people find a place in these songs. Their aspirations are expressed as they narrate their history. By singing this song, they remember their soldiers who died in the Moamoria revolution for their people. They took arrows in their bodies to save their motherland. They sing that they are not forgotten and they are acknowledging the sacrifice they made for their community.

"... bortupor gulibur kus pati dhorili,
nijore jiban de, dekhkhon rakhili,
  atayao pahori jua ny hori oi,
  gobindai ram ..."
"... Dhum Dhum Kori Gulibur Futile,
Amare Ronuwai Habati Dhorile,
Jy Jody Jaok Buli Jibantu Arile,
  Kalaloi Jatitur Naamtu Rakhile ...'

Traditional Bihu songs, such as these, are transmitted from one generation to the other. The songs are sweet to listen to and very simple to understand. Through the Bihu songs, Morans try to express their feelings of love, joy, and sorrow and share valuable information about their history, lifestyle, wars, legends, agriculture, and natural disaster. These songs are like a mirror of the social life of the community.

Conclusion

Arguably, human beings are the most cultured creatures on the planet. Their life is not only a simple biological progression from birth to death, but also a social movement from one stage to another, marked by special ceremonies and festivals. Bihu is a composite festival concerned with the general welfare of society. The Bohag Bihu is an important festival for the Morans, through which they glorify youth and love, and express a yearning for union. The Morans celebrate their Bohag Bihu not only as a festival of joy and merriment but also as a social-religious festival. Although in the truest sense of the term, "Bihu" is a non-religious festival, to the people belonging to the society of the Morans, there is a religious fervour included within the whole festival. By including religion and history, the people succeed in keeping the memories of their saints alive. Bihu festivals remain one of the most important means for articulating and archiving Moran culture. The beautiful strains of music, the heartfelt dancing, and associated rituals keep Moran culture alive as it is passed from one generation to the next every year.

References

Barua, B., (1969) *A Cultural History of Assam*, Lawyer's Book Stall, Assam.
Dohutia, S., (2016) *Introduction to the Morans of Assam* (3–296).Banalata, Dibrugarh, Assam, Translation from the Assamese original, Sun Gogoi.
Endle, S., (2010) *The Kacharis*, Akansha Publishing House, New Delhi, Reprint.

Gait, E., (1981) *The Census of India*, Volume 1, Government Press, Calcutta.

Grierson, G., (1903) *Linguistic Survey of India Vol III*, Calcutta Office of the Superintendent of Government Printing, Calcutta.

Grierson, G., (1907) *Reviewed Work of the Khasis by P.R.T. Gordon*, Cambridge University Press, Cambridge.

Sarma, G., & Mahamta, S., (2016) The Moran Community of Assam: Historical Development and Cultural Practices. *Intellection: A Bo-Annual Interdisciplinary Research Journal*, 4(2), 99–115.

Sherif, B., (2001) The Ambiguity of Boundaries in the Fieldwork Experience, Establishing Rapport and Negotiating Insider/Outsider Boundaries. *Qualitative Inquiry*, 7(4), 436–447.

9 Social media and the politics of dance

Jayanta Vishnu Das

Staged television performances

Television and performance have a long history of interdependence in the Indian context. Dance as the epitome of entertainment has always provided a commercial aspect of any television programming manifesto. Early Indian films created an initial dance template where the story was carried forward through dance segments. They are an integral part of the narrative structure. Indian films draw their inspiration from traditional theatre forms, where dance and song were integral to the storytelling idiom. It also helped that in the initial years of Indian cinema a majority of the stories were adaptations of Indian mythologies, considered a mainstay in theatre traditions. Dance had always been an integral part of conveying mythology through storytelling and, therefore, the screenplay of the mythologies lent themselves easily to song and dance routines. There were few parallels in western cinema other than the Musical Theatre genre often reproduced on film. Dance traditions were integral to the Indian theatre traditions and the dance routines in classic adaptations were mostly classical and traditional Indian dance forms, such as the *nautanki* or *jatra* and have become major Indian traditions. Since the advent of sound in films, song and dance in popular Hindi cinema, now known as Bollywood, has been a focus, and some would even argue, the key features of its on-screen acumen (Gehlawat & Dudrah, 2017). Song and dance are integral in maintaining a tradition of Indian cinema with its own grammar, with a perceived predominance of song in the narrative. Both song and dance combine to produce a distinct storytelling idiom as evident from the narrative structure of Hindi cinema. Iyer (2017) argues, "the dynamic figurations of the body wrought by cinematic dance forms produce unique constructions of narrative, stardom, and gender" (p. 124). Bollywood has produced dancing stars such as Shammi Kapoor, Helen, and Zeenat Aman who are known for their dancing skill.

The proliferation of dance in the 1980s and 1990s period owes much of its influence to television. Breaking out from the confines of Indian films, television provided a new meaning to dance, and dance liberated itself from the predominance of song to stand as a separate entity. As opposed to being part of the storytelling process, dance in contemporary television stood out

DOI: 10.4324/9781003398776-10

as an independent performance narrative. Different dance maestros found prominence due the liberal approach of the state broadcaster Doordarshan towards Indian performing traditions. There were several programmes dedicated to major Indian traditions of dance. The stage was created for dance and other performing traditions. Dance in particular transcended into popular territory as its viewership increased and it is important to note that the popularity of commercial Indian cinema also stretched the boundaries of dance to express itself in novel manifestations. Fusion dance and the intermixing of western forms with traditional Indian dance forms was tolerated and accepted to be the new normal.

The advent of satellite television in the 1990s was a key "arrival" point of modernity in India (Cullity, 2002). The country was not only opening itself to new ideas but economically too, the direction of the country was shaping itself for a break from the old. Chakravorty (2010) notes, "India is going through tumultuous change. In a world where borders are no longer possible, classical Indian and popular dance films coalesce to foreground postmodern hybridity" (p.169). The old and new, found new territories, norms, and boundaries in which to clash over. This struggle for negotiating a new identity was found in almost all spheres of Indian life. New urban centres opened up, cinema was changing, new jobs in the private sector were created, and foreign brands were available, which had been unthinkable a few years earlier. Naidu (2006) opined, "India is a world leader in several areas – its indigenous built communications satellites have been successfully launched, it has the best computer software in the world, and its telecommunication technology has successfully reached the most remote rural areas" (p.68). Change need not be assessed from the binaries of good or bad but rather as a negotiating point of establishing new identities in a modern fast-paced changing situation.

The far-sighted changes that took place within the context of Indian life did not happen overnight but rather, occurred through a relatively slow process. This was also true in the way in which dance was perceived and performed in the context of Indian television. Reality television in this milieu was a novel experiment of entertainment mixed with creativity. Dance was emancipated from the confines of a cinematic storytelling process, to itself becoming the story. Most of the formats of dance-based reality television programmes echoed each other in style and content. These shows provided the stage that dance had lost in its cinematic avatar. Reality shows fashioned new categories of dances and dancers, and imaginative concepts were spawned in turn. These new categories of dance echoed the sentiments of the new India that was created in post-1990s India. Old boundaries of dance were being redrawn, gharanas (a social organisation linking music to dancers by lineage) were increasingly becoming liminal categories, and music was reshaped meeting the sentiments of new audiences. This is what I would term as the post-dance era of Indian television. Historically, prominent forms of dance media have been the screen-based dances in film and television, mainly from Hollywood dance musicals and Bollywood films to the dance films of Maya Deren, Charles Atlas, David Hinton, Thierry De Mey, and others, from dance for camera.

(Bench, 2010, p.184)

The audience shaped the process of creativity in a dancing tradition in a major way. It challenged old hegemonies, fashioned new idioms in concert with the times, redrew boundaries, and stretched the limits of the understandings of what constitutes dance. Dance became part of an increasingly contested territory where media, audience, economy, and globalisation forces were key to the new dance that was increasingly becoming discernible from the old. Staged dance in television was a performance of spectacle where the audience was central to whatever was done, as it was the audience who brought in revenue for television. "The habitus that connected identities to territorial locations has been reconstituted and deterritorialized" (Chakravorty, 2010, p.170).

One of the major shifts with the coming of Indian satellite television channels was a new economic shift in television advertising. The new economy brought in advertising revenue that demanded programming more attuned to audience choices. Reality dance shows are a complex result of these chains of economic consequences of the Indian globalisation story.

Assamese television introduced new dance reality formats in line with the global trends of programming. In essence, local dance traditions were co-opted into a pattern of commercial dance shows. DY365, a Guwahati-based satellite channel introduced the reality show DY Bihurani which introduced a local traditional folk dance, Bihu, to a reality dance competition paradigm. The folk dance forms of Northeast India were no longer confined to villages but became an essential element of connecting the region to the rapidly globalising world. This model of introducing folk dance was not only confined to television but was also cloned in social media. The format's success can be understood by the fact that increasingly most channels had their own versions of such shows. Chakravorty (2010) argues,

In this new form of practice (originally created by DJs mixing various musical tracks to create new hybrid forms), high and low, classical and folk, Indian and western cultural forms absorb, influence, co-opt, plagiarize and cannibalize one another.

(p.171)

Audiences were hooked not only for the entertainment value, but emotionally too as they supported those they felt should win.

These competitive programmes opened the way for those who had no other avenue through which to showcase their talent. The rags to riches story line echoed through most of these reality shows created far more than just dance shows. The small-town talent who migrated to the city to showcase their skill echoed the new age migration of skilled workers from the rural to the urban communities. The new economy provided jobs in the urban centres for youths coming from smaller centres. Jobs were available in the private sector in novel areas such as Business Process Outsourcing (BPO), Information Technology (IT), and knowledge sectors, creating a new class of educated urban youth who formed the new middle class. The audiences constantly demanded new content for entertainment, new narratives of hope. Schiller (1989) cited in Gamson et al. (1992) points out, "commercial concerns dictate important elements of media content, prompting a privatisation of culture" (p.380). Privatisation is an ongoing process constituting large media organisations, capitalism, and a burgeoning consumer culture that constantly demands more content. The story of dance reality shows fulfilled this appetite for novelty and success stories as a result of the creativity and talent that emerged at this time.

Performing dance in the virtual sphere

> "After all, isn't the body of the dancer precisely a body dilated along an entire space that is both exterior and interior to it?"
>
> (Michel Foucault, 2006, p.232).

Gangnam Style by the Korean pop singer Psy became an anthem for millions of people on YouTube. Psy's "Gangnam Style" went viral, with more than 3.8 billion views and counting, and it also spawned a multitude of memetic content that parodied, referenced, or remixed the original (Soha & McDowell, 2016). It created viewership records on YouTube. People consumed not just Psy's music, but his dance moves gained traction and were imitated the world over. Dance as a virtual category has an intimate connection with the camera. The ability to create and record for posterity gives dance performances longevity, otherwise lost in the process of performance. People can watch recorded videos, replay them several times, share with friends, and in the process, they attach emotion to it, even imitating the dance.

Works of social dance media present themselves as evidence that dance is to be shared, copied, embodied, manipulated, and recirculated. In the virtual world of a networked society, any creative process creates and attracts attention (Bench, 2010). This refers to not only the original dance, but spoofs of dance videos and memes of the original that are circulated widely. Social media has transcended audience boundaries and connected performers to unchartered territories of fans. Soha and McDowell (2016) argue that,

> From the very beginning, YouTube provided a platform for people to post and share culture, like dance videos, styles, and techniques. Today the dance crazes of the world spread virally through the social media networks of the Internet in addition to late night dance halls. In the digital

age, people have gravitated toward participating in both the celebration and transformation of cultural phenomena online, and, as always, people want to dance.

(p.9)

The process of being seen in the virtual world in contrast to the real, is a completely different category of being for the dancer. Evaluation by mouse click, points, and written comments drive the process. An informal struggle for recognition is thus taking place as expressed by a user (Peters & Seier, 2009, p.194). To be seen in the virtual does not necessarily mean only the act of watching for the consumer. It constitutes other categories of emotion linked to the act of seeing in ways that are complete departures from the behaviour of live audiences. "Historically different media have always played a decisive role in historically different self-relations. Processes of mediation are, thus, not only intimately linked to processes of subjectification; they are also their prerequisite" (Peters & Seier, 2009, p.187).

Dance is not just performative but is a counter-hegemonic category in social media. The fluid temporality and spatiality lend dance to newer traits inherent in social media such as the "going viral" trend. There is not just an audience for a performance but the imploding structure of social media allows a performance to reach an infinite number of people. Dance thus, is no longer just a category that happens in real time, but a simulated reality, performed an infinite number of times in the defined spatiality of social media networks. In the process of creating a viral dance video, the technology starts by capturing the dance on a camera. The next process is to edit it in a non-linear manner, then to the act of uploading it.

> The computer is thus always a node in this arrangement – as a medium of reference to existing texts, poses and videos already in circulation – and at the same time, as a medium of distribution of the performance in the future.
>
> (Peters & Seier, 2009, p.193)

The point of departure is in the networks themselves and not necessarily in the performative act. Networks are the new power structures that lend legitimacy to the act. The "dance act" is subscribed to by viewers, watched, saved for later, shared, and thus is constantly creating new territories of viewership and experiences. The very essence of the dance process bypasses the hegemonic control of the television economy that dictates the choice of programme, timing, length, and creative process. According to Gamson et al. (1992) "Gramsci's (1971) enduring contribution was to focus our attention beyond explicit beliefs and ideology to see how the routine structures of everyday thinking contribute to a structure of dominance" (p. 381). The sense of democratisation of the production and distribution process itself created the first-level playing field. The performer has a notional control over their creative process, yet it is a complex structure of digital domination of user-based production, a logic of neo-capitalist control of creative output.

If the performer has control over their creativity on social media, so too the audience controls what to watch and what not to watch. The audience is no longer simply a viewer of the performative act but also a user. They exert control over the content, its virality, creative process, and popularity. The simplistic decision whether or not to watch results in a complex chain of network reactions that ultimately decides on what appears to watch next in an algorithmic process. Our freedom to watch is after all as good as a mathematical formulation that drives us towards the next choice. This in fact is the initial user's choice rather than an audience choice. Whereas the audience was a political entity that negotiated choices, the user constitutes a mathematical probability dictated by the social network. Thus, large media organisations are an important part of how we consume and perform dance in the virtual sphere.

Everybody is a performer

Who is a dancer? The answer does not emanate from the dance itself, but from philosophical discussions upon which much of the meaning-making processes of present times are dependent (Best, 2004; Redfern, 2007). Hence, what is authentic, or rather, what constitutes the idea of authentic representation of dance is not clear.

Does dance come to occupy an authentic sphere in the realm of new media representations? Or, is it a constructed agenda, or even a reflection of reality? The answers to these questions are problematic and depend on the context. In the realm of changing new media representations, dance indeed occupies a central territory or space. It becomes a negotiated space to reclaim lost territory by youth and elderly alike. Facebook, YouTube, TikTok, Twitter, and WhatsApp are the new spaces of negotiation when enforcing the political. Increasingly, what was once considered classical or sacred in terms of dance has been challenged. The hegemony of the old structures is increasingly questioned. Dunner and Moser (2008) cited in Peter and Seier (2009) state, "the increasing technologisation of the media has not caused an impoverishment in subjective interiority; on the contrary, it has generated a greater variety of self-referentialities" (p.189). Digital networks provide an alternative to the old by bypassing old power structures and in turn creating potential for the future. The way in which we understand the political category of the performer is thus redefined in a remarkable manner.

Increasingly, audiences become the performer or the user in the new media sphere. While the performer in the old sense derived legitimacy from training and allegiance to a certain tradition, the new performer is a creative user, and the camera becomes the tool of engagement. The old differentiation between a trained dancer, or a classical dancer to that of an amateur are dissolved constantly. Dr. Arup Senapati was seen performing a break dance to a popular Hindi film song at a medical college in Assam fitted in his PPE kit for his Covid-19 patients. The video went viral immediately and the doctor's efforts were seen as a departure from the normal by providing his patients with something out of the ordinary. A popular Assamese song *Mon Hira Doi* from the 1982 Assamese film *Bowari* was remixed by Neel Akash in 2020, and has created a plethora of dance covers on social media. The song has become popular among contemporary dancers and there are multiple dance covers available on YouTube. While the song itself was always popular, it transformed itself to a dance number in its new avatar creating new dimensions of popularity. In this process, we see rap versions of Bihu emerging as distinct from the original folk dance as evident from the popularity of these dance videos.

Technology collapses boundaries and power structures that existed, and as Peter and Seier (2009) observe,

> The difference between professional and amateur does not seem particularly applicable here, for it is questionable whether the so-called amateurs judge themselves according to professional standards, or according to the commentaries and answers of other users listed on the YouTube website.
>
> (p.193)

This process of transfer of power is more of a political reorganisation of space rather than a creative transfer. Each node in a social media network has equal power in the balance of the new power structures. Thus, while equality is achieved in the balance of nodes, overall equity is something of a utopian concept.

The increasing popularity of social media amongst new and upcoming dancers point to a new balance of power. There is an increasing recognition of the ambitions of the everyday performer. Talented dancers have emerged who use technology to showcase their skills that otherwise may have not been acknowledged. Short videos have been increasingly produced and consumed in an unprecedented manner over the last few years. Viral applications have fuelled this phenomenon. Our attention span has shortened too, with an increase in the consumption of digital media. The duration of videos is increasingly calibrated to a size that the audience can relate to. If the video is a little longer in duration the audience may lose interest and move on. While content is supreme in this network, the time duration, interesting opening sequence, placement in the video thread, and similarity to other videos are determining factors of success.

The craze for short video applications

The introduction of videos and short animated gifs on Facebook and Instagram are indicative of a gradual shift towards content-based everyday performances. An individual may be considered as a "microcelebrity" (Senft, 2008) based on their "curating, rearranging and recirculating" abilities to brand their image. Abidin (2015) introduces the term "Influencers" to define micro-celebrity with a large number of followers who wield much influence. This media term is used by media houses to reach wider audiences. Increasingly, the popularity of video-based content has been driving the social media economy in India. The nation has been exposed to new genres of video content that were non-existent before the advent of these social media networks.

We come across D.I.Y. videos of every shade and hue, and reaction videos have become very popular, specifically in the gamers' world. There are also comparative culture videos, travel diary videos or travelogues, cuisine-based videos, make-up and fashion videos, hobby and enthusiast videos, extreme sports videos, cult-based videos, "did you know" or knowledge videos, children's videos, role play videos, animation videos, and pornographic videos. Some of these genres themselves spawn an exponential number of sub-genres and arguably, some sub-genres themselves become genres. The content in the second most popular type of video is dance. "Dancing videos usually refer to the creators who make moves in accordance with the rhythm of the music" (Yang, 2020, pp.37–38). The exponential growth in video-based content also points to the growth in digital platforms that encourage video content creation and the generation of revenue from such media. YouTube, for example, has a specific earning mechanism for channels based on the number of views. The content-based software industry has boomed from this, where growth is based on user-created data and revenue. While digital networks might recognise content as data creation, for users they are a platform to showcase talent.

Short video applications such as TikTok, Josh, and Starmaker have based their business formula entirely on the potential to create user demand for videos. These 10-seconds to 1-minute videos not only provide fame, but lead to sponsorship or advertising deals based on popularity. For example, by 2019, TikTok had garnered 120 million downloads. This was later banned by the government of India as part of the larger ban on a number of Chinese applications. TikTok created dance sensations who would gyrate to songs and lip sync them for 10-second videos. "The iconography, rituals, spaces and lifestyles of youth culture can be seen in TikTok's trends, most notably its dance and stunt challenges" (Kennedy, 2020, p.1070). These were not your star performers but everyday neighbourhood people. Sanjeev Shrivastava, a teacher by profession became an overnight dancing sensation imitating Bollywood actor Govinda's famous dance steps to the song *Aap ke aa jane se*. His video uploaded in 2018 garnered almost 30 million views on YouTube. This use of technology also percolated the class and caste barriers of the Indian social system. The creativity and talent of the performers made some of them famous and they were referred to as "TikTok stars or celebrities". Dinesh Pawar and his wife Lakhimi from rural Maharashtra have 3.5 million followers. Srivastava (2018) stated,

Videos recorded of them in a simple background depicting the location of a village or the fields, attired in regular clothes with no makeup and dancing to Bollywood songs, caught people's attention.

(P.1)

They are everyday celebrities or micro-celebrities from India's margins. The increasing popularity of such short and focussed content-based video platforms redrew the boundaries of how we perceive and perform dance. Dance has become a commodity of exchange in the increasingly crowded market of content currency. Such content is incessant, direct, and catchy capturing the attention of the viewer. Papu and Puja from Assam were TikTok celebrities from Assam whose videos garnered huge views on the video app. After the ban they migrated to different platforms taking their followers with them. Today, their videos are on YouTube under the channel name Papu MDR and have millions of views, despite these videos being no more than dance reprisals of popular songs. They have earned popularity in their own right based on the reach of the platform they chose. It has brought them recognition and through this, they have also acted in original music albums.

Their popularity, however, is a constant endeavour to stay relevant in a crowded market. The moment interest starts to fade the content loses out to the crowd of other such content already available. "YouTube is probably the most prominent example of a media practice that allows the individual to record the minutest details of his or her life and to distribute them" (Peters & Seier, 2009, p.187). A perfect example would be the proliferation of "home dance" as opposed to the choreographed or classical or professional dance. They are minimalist videos often shot in backyards without the finesse of a professional video. "Backdrops for playbacks are often simply the rooms as they are. The 'filmic' space depends on the possible camera positions, and cameras built into laptops are often used" (Peters & Seier, 2009, p.192).

The discourse of being viral is a momentary affair with popularity. Fame is temporary and fandom is refashioned in terms of the new digital economy. The individual becomes important as a political entity empowered to consequently make change of one's own fate. The network's nature is fluidic and constantly oscillates between different versions of being popular, famous, and in turn viral. What is viral today however, might not be relevant in the next moment.

There is no doubting the fact that dance and other performative acts have found a new political sphere to negotiate that may lead to fame and popularity. This can be gauged from the massive use of such applications in the Indian situation. TikTok celebrities not only thrive in the new digital medium, but also migrate to other platforms, taking along with them their millions of viewers and users. The ban on TikTok in India in 2020 saw a migration from one platform to another in large numbers. New applications emerged. As one closed down, even more stars appeared, and new talents were recognised, creating a continuum of an ever-performing talent pool in the social media scape. As Appadurai (1990) argues,

> One of the ways to comprehend globalisation is through the mediascape. This terrain of movement of people from one media to the other is an economic category that can only be imagined in a networked society.
>
> (p.2)

The political economy of dance in social media

Dance is not just a category of performance. It needs to be understood as a cultural industry category in the ever-changing world of media. Dance has always been a popular creative form, and media has a symbiotic relation to it. The success of dance as social media content relates to its relationship to popularity, in terms of the creation of new dance videos as well as its popularity. The logic of the capitalist media is in its profit-making potential. More of what sells is produced to better exploit the demands of the market. This logic is a hallmark of the production process in social media. The concept of a sharing of the profits is a differential that creates a division within several ecologies of social media players. Some networks do share monetary profit from the revenue generated from the content created by the user, while others do not share revenue but only provide the user with a platform to showcase talent.

One of the most popular content-sharing platforms is YouTube, a platform that has been around for a long time. Soha and McDowell (2016) point out, "With over 1 billion active users uploading 300 hours of video content every minute of every day, and billions of page views each day, YouTube has begun to challenge television as a central source of audio-visual content, especially among the younger age groups" (p.1). Wasko and Erickson (2009) argue "many have heralded the video-sharing website as a democratising media platform that would convert media consumers into producers, and reshape the entire landscape of media" (p.372). YouTube has channels that are individual Google accounts where content creators can upload and publish content. Viewers can subscribe to these channels, and whenever a new video is published from the subscribed feed, they get an update. Viewership and subscribers, determine the popularity of any individual video or of the channel. "However, various techniques adopted by the site to enhance advertising privilege some videos over others" (Wasko & Erickson, 2009, p.382). YouTube provides the marketplace whereby professional producers, amateur producers, laymen, individuals, groups, and societies become publishers of content. Andrejevic (2009) writes about being able to publish familiar music videos and copyrighted movie clips with original user-generated content. Such content may receive the widest possible views because of the popularity of the platform itself, however, the economy of publishing is in itself a concern. Google runs a programme of sharing revenue that is generated from content by any particular channel. These norms are well laid out, but have changed over the years. Their model has been accepted in the creative content industry. Facebook has also launched a revenue-sharing programme in recent years. As Andrejevic (2009) points out, "One of the advantages of an interactive platform for the delivery of commercial content is that it enables the capture of increasingly detailed information about patterns of user behaviour and response" (p.415).

The explosion of video creations and their adoption by social media audiences created new opportunities in the economic realm. The sharing formula is roughly 45% to 55%, wherein platforms such as YouTube and Facebook keep 45% of the revenue and the rest is shared with the content creators based on advertising revenue generated from the users content. Soha and McDowell (2016) cite Mark Andrejevic (2009) and Toby Miller (2009) both of whom "have criticized this 'basic bargain' for social media users as inherently exploitative, suggesting that what appeared to be a free and open cultural space was actually a brilliant way to have user producers" (p. 2). The content creators have to sign up for these partnerships or sharing programmes by accepting the laid-out norms of the network. Wasko and Erikson (2009) comment that, "Users are encouraged to use music or video footage in the creation of videos, without penalty in order to capitalise on YouTube's viral marketing potential" (p. 381). Various companies use contests to inspire users to create content that falls in line with promotional media.

The model is such that the independence of the creators is ensured. The model is free from governmental control, and does not necessarily undergo censorship. Bagdikian (1990) argues however that a private ministry of information has emerged in the last few decades focussing on large media giants. The censorship and control does not necessarily stem from government, but from powerful private structures of profit. While this utopia of economic empowerment and independence drove the participation of new media, critics would argue that social networks have become too large for comfort. As Andrejevic (2009) states, "YouTube represents a site of hope, or a firm foundation for contesting the replication of the forms of governance, control and exploitation that characterise the emerging interactive economy. It is simply to assert that the contested status of YouTube has something to tell us about the nature of the struggle" (p.409).

Dependence on the algorithms of these networks, copyright issues, sharing of revenue and limited search exposure have been criticised as grounds for too much network influence in determining what we see and how we see. The control is overarching, our lives have become dependent on choices that we make based on predetermined choices made by them. Wasko and Erickson (2009) explain,

> One of the most worrisome aspects of YouTube's monetisation strategies is the commodification of labour. This issue arises most acutely when we consider how advertisers and media companies exploit users for profit.
> (p.383)

Staging local at global festivals: Taking Assam to the world

Much of what is mediated as dance for a global audience in the tribal traditions of the Northeast of India is through the numerous festivals in each state of the region. It is not out of place to find foreign tourists mingling with local dance performers and taking photographs. These festivals are generally government-funded tourism endeavours that project a certain image of the state, its people, and culture. Some of the major festivals that need to be mentioned are the Hornbill festival in Nagaland, Dambuk festival, Sangai festival, Majuli festival, Brahmaputra festival, Nongkrem dance festival, and the Chapchar Kut festival. The dance traditions form a major point of attraction in these festivals. George Haokip (2012) reiterates, "North-East India has been a land of immense ethnic confluence for centuries, eventually leading to an inter-regional and intra-regional ethnic divide. It is an undeniable fact that North-East India has nurtured diverse ethnic groups with their varied social structures, religious affiliations, political aspirations and world views" (p.217). It not only projects the culture of the indigenous population, but reinforces the idea of the exotic in a visual sense. The visual metaphor is an important trope while expounding the nature of a relationship between self and others. Photography was one of the earliest traditions of ethnography and was practised originally by colonial ethnographers. As Thomas Metcalf (1995) observed in relation to such representations, "much of the effort of ethnological classification was directed by a search for 'scientific' precision, the recording of exact images with photography logically complementing the compiling of statistical information" (p. 117). While we may have temporally shifted to newer sensibilities of capturing precision, in the shift from capturing to staging, our methods might have not changed much.

These festivals are well documented in social media with their own independent pages and content. The common theme running across all these territories of divergent tribes and their representation is their culture. It is placed at the forefront of any mediated image of the region. The rich community dance traditions of the region are essential to such a representation. These images foreground unity, brotherhood, a richness of tradition, and ethnic identity amongst other such qualities. This works as points of departure for the tourists who visit these festivals.

Difference is used as a tool for attracting audience and tourists, and dance creates a visual metaphor. What was once captured through the lens of the colonial ethnographer, is today staged for the world to see. Not only in person, but also through social networks and other media outlets. Documentaries, news clips, travelogues, and video vlogs are the new representative idioms towards such a representation of the region. These new media forms create essentialised boundaries between self and other. The other might constitute people from the same tribe who are not performing or not trained in particular traditional performances. Thus, the bamboo dance (Cheraw) or the war dance of the Naga tribes, that we receive as an audience, creates not only the outsider–performer relation, but also what we might consider performer–non-performer binaries.

Conclusion: Authenticity in the realm of representation

What is authentic in representative reality? Baudrillard (1988) argues that dramatic vicissitudes in the technology of reproduction have led to the implosion of representation and reality. In the postulations of Hall (1997), representations are not merely reflective of the real world. Dance is a creative category of everyday performance. To determine authenticity of this political category we need to critique our understanding of media and its representative aspect. Sartre cited in Woodhouse (2000) defines authenticity as "choosing freely without rationalising or pretending that someone or something made you choose the way you did, and fully accepting the consequences of your choices" (p.150). Peters and Seier (2009) argue that "processes of subjectification in new media necessarily repeat and vary older and other forms of mediated processes of subjectification. The points of comparison are thus not unmediated subjects, but relations of the self that are mediated in a different way" (p.189). The moment mediated categories are created and propagated, reality is recreated and refashioned in new terms. Pallud and Straub (2007) cited in Wang and Skovira (2017) argue "the word 'technology' seems to jar with the word 'authenticity', in that technology connotes things that are fake or simulated whereas authenticity connotes things that are natural and real" (p.1).

There cannot be multiple realities but only copies of the same reality. If we consider reality from the perspective of the viewer, we are forced to understand reality as a lived experience. The meaning-making process is an attempt by the viewer to locate the dance in their own milieu. "Increasingly, the former (technology) becomes dominant, as 'simulacra' are substituted for a reality that has no foundation in experience" (Gamson et al., 1992, p.374).

The viewer generally assigns meaning from their own experiences and contexts. "One needs to take a closer look at the relationship between practices of the self and media apparatus. Dance videos can be understood as 'auto-mediated' practice that not only represents a model of the self, but generates and multiplies self-referentialities" (Peter & Seier, 2009, p.201). The context of technology representation of the authentic, is thus clouded under the suspicion of falsities. Simon (1969) argues that technology was "man-made as opposed to natural" (p.4). We have to reorient and refashion the tools and methods of our understanding of the authentic in this changed context of a networked reality, and dance is no exception to this new paradigm of understanding.

References

Abidin, C., (2015). Communicative Intimacies: Influencers and Perceived Interconnectedness. *Ada*, 1–16. https://adanewmedia.org/2015/11/issue8-abidin/

Andrejevic, M., (2009). Exploiting YouTube: Contradictions of User-Generated Labour. In P. Snickars & P. Vonderau (Eds.), *The YouTube Reader* (pp. 424–440). National Library of Sweden.
Appadurai, A., (1990). Disjuncture and Difference in the Global Cultural Economy, *Public Culture*, 2(2), 1–24.
Bagdikian, B., (1990). *The Media Monopoly*. (3rd ed.). Beacon.
Baudrillard, J., (1988). *Selected Writings* (Ed.). Mark Poster. Stanford University Press.
Bench, H., (2010). Screendance 2.0: Social Dance-Media. *Participations: Journal of Audience and Reception Studies*, 7(2), 183–214.
Best, D., (2004). Aesthetic and Artistic: Two Separate Concepts: The Dancers of "Aesthetic Education" Perspectives. *Research in Dance Education*, 5(2), 159–175.
Chakravorty, P., (2010). Remixed Practice: Bollywood Dance and the Global Indian. In P. Chakravorty & N. Gupta (Eds.), *Dance Matters: Performing India*. Routledge. 185.
Cullity, J., (2002). The Global Des: Cultural Nationalism on Mtv India. *Journal of Communication Inquiry*, 26(4), 408–425.
Dünne, J., Moser, C. (Eds.), (2008). *Automedialität. Subjektkonstitution in Schrift, Bild und Neuen Medien*. Fink Verlang.
Foucault, M., (2006). Utopian Body. In C. Jones (Ed.), *Sensorium: Embodied Experience, Technology, and Contemporary Art*. MIT Press. 232.
Gamson, W., Croteau, D., Hoynes, W., Sasson, T., (1992). Media Images and the Social Construction of Reality. *Annual Review of Sociology*, 18(1), 373–393.
Gehlawat, A., Dudrah, R., (2017). The Evolution of Song And Dance in Hindi Cinema. *South Asian Popular Culture*, 15(2–3), 103–108.
Gramsci, A., (1971). Selections from the Prison Notebooks (pp. 373–393). In Q. Hoare & G. Smith (Eds.), Int. Publ. New York.
Hall, S., (1997). Representation, Meaning & Language. In S. Hall (Ed.), *Representation: Cultural Representations and Signifying Practices* (pp. 15–64). The Open University & Sage Publications Ltd.
Haokip, G., (2012). On Ethnicity and Development Imperative: A Case Study of North-East India. *Asian Ethnicity*, 13(3), 217–228.
Iyer, U., (2017). Dance Musicalisation: Proposing a Choreomusicological Approach to Hindi Film Song-And-Dance Sequences. *South Asian Popular Culture*, 15, 2–3, 123–138.
Kennedy, M., (2020). 'If the Rise of the TikTok Dance and E-Girl Aesthetic Has Taught Us Anything, It's that Teenage Girls Rule the Internet Right Now': TikTok Celebrity, Girls and the Coronavirus Crisis. *European Journal of Cultural Studies*, 23(6), 1069–1076.
Metcalf, T., (1995). *Ideologies of the Raj*. Cambridge University Press.
Miller, T., (2009). Cybertarians of the World Unite: You Have Nothing to Lose but Your Tubes! In P. Snickars & P. Vonderau (Eds.), *The YouTube Reader* (pp. 424–440). National Library of Sweden.
Naidu, Y., (2006). Globalisation and Its Impact on Indian Society. *The Indian Journal of Political Science*, 67(1), 65–76.
Pallud, J., Straub, D., (2007). *Real vs. Virtual: A Theoretical Framework for Assessing the Role of Authenticity in Visitor Interactions with Museum Technologies*. In Proceedings of the 13th Americas Conference on Information Systems, Keystone, CO.

Peters, K., Seier, A., (2009). Home Dance: Mediacy and Aesthetics of the Self on YouTube. In P. Snickars & P. Vonderau (Eds.), *The YouTube Reader* (pp. 424–440). National Library of Sweden.

Redfern, B., (2007). Philosophical Aesthetics and the Study of Dance as an Academic Discipline, *Research in Dance Education*, 8(2), 187–201.

Schiller, H., (1989). *Culture, Inc.* Oxford University Press.

Senft, T., (2008). *Camgirls: Celebrity and Community in the Age of Social Networks*. Peter Lang.

Shrivastava, S., (2018). *Dabbu & My Wife Dancing on Govinda's Song Aap Ke Aa Jane Se*. Youtube. Retrieved from https://www.youtube.com/watch?v=Fs54NYdpJkY on May 31.

Simon, H., (1969). *The Sciences of the Artificial*. MIT Press.

Soha, M., McDowell, Z., (2016). Monetising a Meme: YouTube, Content ID, and the Harlem Shake. *Social Media + Society*, 2(1), 1–12.

Srivastava, S., (2020). Stars of TikTok, Safe Haven for Artistes, Voices on India's Margins, Speak Out on Sudden Ban. *ThérapieWire.in*. Retrieved from https://thewire.in/culture/chinese-apps-ban-tiktok-stars on July 1.

Wang, W., Skovira, R., (2017). *Authenticity and Social Media* [paper presented]. Twenty-third Americas Conference on Information Systems, Boston.

Wasko, J., Erickson, M., (2009). The Political Economy of YouTube. In P. Snickars & P. Vonderau (Eds.), *The YouTube Reader* (pp. 424–440). National Library of Sweden.

Woodhouse, M., (2000). *A Preface to Philosophy* (6th ed.). Woodhouse.

Yang, Y., (2020). *Understanding Young Adults' TikTok Usage: Real People, Creative Videos That Makes Your Day*. University of California.

10 Gender and dance
"Gazing" at the *Doudini* and the female *Sattriya* and *Bihuwoti* dancers

Moushumi Kandali

Introduction

> *Dance is an ideal laboratory for the study of gender, because its medium, the body, is where sex and gender are said to originate; it is where the discourse of the "natural" and the "cultural" thrash it out. Dance is the significant clue to the management of the female body in any given time and place. Furthermore, the politics of dance as an institution, sometimes dominated by women, more often dominated by men, demands its own inquiry.*
>
> (Daly, 1989, p.294).

There are many questions that one can critically address while deliberating upon the dynamics of gender in relation to dance. I will examine the gender dynamics of the female shaman-dancer of the Bodo community of Assam, known as the *Doudini*. Alongside the *Doudini*, I will also examine the gendered subjectivity of the *Bihuwoti*, the female performance of the *Bihu* dance of Assam, and the female *Sattriya* dancer, who dances the only classical dance form of dance in the Brahmaputra valley of Assam.

In order to create a context, I have critically mapped the historical transition and transformations of female dancers within their respective dance traditions and examined how they are situated in terms of the power dynamics within the traditional conventions of a patriarchal system. This attends to the recurring necessity of reclaiming the often "absent" or marginalised position of the female dancer in some dance traditions.

The transitions that the three dances in question have undergone were both empowering and ideologically challenging during the ushering in of a new global culture within a post- globalised era. Transformations and transitions have been triggered by the hegemonic culture industry of the west and the changing patterns of the global market economy along with an unprecedented advancement of technology and extension of mass media. The traditional societies in India which were mostly patriarchal in nature have now become more accommodating to the idea of gender equality and gender bending, paving ways for newer gender-neutral spaces for artistic expressions. However, it has also brought forth cultural shock and conflict with a pull between tradition and modernity.

New challenges arose in negotiating power equations in the new order, where entangled forces of a complex consumerist capitalist culture opened the way for newer modes of oppression. If a dancer had to once negotiate with a patriarchal system within a small community, now the challenges are to devise new ways of negotiation within a broader and more complex post-global system where patriarchy remains strong. One such challenge for the female Assamese dancer concerns the negotiation of traditional gender roles within the dance traditions on the one hand, and on the other hand, to devise strategies of transgression in order to incorporate newer roles within "modern/contemporary" dance. The challenge was to find a middle ground without falling into the trap of cultural essentialism. Within this culture, there is a constant bombardment of mass media production leaning towards a "popular" audience, and an overwhelming presence of a contemporary cyber culture.

One of the most pertinent questions in this research was to check if the female performers representing each tradition were subjected to gaze and voyeurism, and how this has been diffused, diluted, and negotiated at times to reclaim an empowered position as a female subject/performer. The body is the sole medium for a dancer, from which the representation and meaning production of a particular culture, tradition, or community is reflected. Within this context, the cultural connotations of the female body in a dance are difficult to critically analyse without looking at the spectator's role as the bearer of a gaze and as an experiential being who participates as the other half of the performance, producing certain meanings and in turn constructing a collective convention.

Methodology

This qualitative research was designed as a comparative study within a land where more than a hundred cultural groups and dances are vibrant living traditions. An examination of the conditions through which behaviours have developed and the relationships between each of the three dances involved in the study posed questions to be answered (White, 1978). The research was conducted over several years of direct field engagement where my role was as an observer and participant with an aim to research primary and secondary data and review the available literature.

Much of the content in this chapter derives from my own experience in the field, and it is from an insider's position within the context of *Bihu* and *Sattriya* dances. The comparativist mode of analysis is applied between each of the dance forms and also between the historical and contemporary version of each of the dances where I have compared and contrasted the gender roles played by the female dancers of three significant dance forms. I have attempted to achieve a saturation of data through a comparison of interviews and through my years of experience in the field (Constantinou, Georgiou, & Perdikogianni, 2017).

It is important to take into account the complexity of analysing gender across cultures. I acknowledge the imperialistic danger of imposing one's own agenda upon another culture, or having certain presuppositions or perceptions about another culture leading to mis-representations and mis-interpretation. As Mahler and Pessar (2001) state,

> Gender is not the sole axis which power and privilege revolve; differentiations based on race, ethnicity, class, nationality and other identities also play roles, often in conjunction with gender.
>
> (p. 443)

For this reason, my study identifies the complexities of the cultures surrounding the three dance forms, so that the application of a feminist gender lens may be applied.

Interviews formed the dominant mode of data collection. I interviewed five major practitioners of the dance forms, and scholars who have made their mark as experts in particular dance forms. The scholars/dancers/interviewees/informants (including myself and my own statements based on first-hand observations and findings) preferred to be identifiable in this study and hence their real names are used in the present study. J. Konwar, M. Kandali, M. Goswami, J. Gandiya, and I. Daimari are considered cultural ethnographers who can shed light on the historical trajectories and individual empirical experiences. I have applied a narrative ethnography through a feminist lens. Little research about these three dances has been conducted from the perspectives of gender and feminist discourse. I have referred to seminar proceedings, unpublished research in progress, and relevant literature.

Within the aforementioned conceptual framing, this research applies notions of gaze and voyeurism (Roy, 2005) as a central prism to allow critical perception and theoretical understanding. While it is possible to compare studies of gender dynamics in India across other areas (Nandigama, 2020), I have, to date not uncovered any major research studies where gender dynamics have been analysed and problematised to create a sociopolitical understanding of the cultural contexts related to dance traditions. Currently, researched articles are historical mappings with ethnographical or technical understanding of the formalistic and stylistic aspects of the dance forms, following the standard canons of Indian aesthetics and their primary texts and treatises.

Doudini

The *Sattriya* and *Kherai* dances (where the *Doudini* is the central performer) have evolved under a rigorous institutionalised grammatology. In the Bathou religion, that celebrates the *Kherai* festival, the main dance role is played by a *Doudini* who performs different dances and falls into a trance where she receives the required divinity to act as a mediator between the people and the gods.

During my field observations, I concluded that some communities addressed the main dancer as *Nasoni* and some as *Doudini*, depending on the status ascribed to her in her particular society. Her role in the *Kherai* ritual is a realistic portrayal of the spirit, and the "self" emerges from a longstanding practice of the tradition. The collective self emerges through community expectation and the individual self through her personal dance expression. This ritual creates a self-representational model foregrounding the notion of community. Through a powerful envisioning, the *Doudini* emerges from within the collective.

The *Bihu, Kherai,* and *Sattriya*

The Brahmaputra Valley is rich with multiple dances where female dancers have historically played significant roles. The *Bihu* is a free-flowing dance style, and in recent times is staged within a set performative convention where female dancers are extremely important and an integral part of the performances. Likewise, the *Kherai* dance of the Bodo community is an energetic spectacle where female dancers have always played a pivotal role. The *Bihu* dance is significant in the Brahmaputra valley as it shares a stylistic commonality among most of the cultural communities of Assam. It is representative of a unified assimilative expression across ethnicities. Most of the ethnic groups celebrate *Bihu*, and the *Bihu* dance of each community manifests itself through similar body movements, hand gestures, positions of the feet, and movements. As Konwar explained,

> Bihu has been a dance tradition where both male and female participate. Sometimes they perform separately as Lora (male) Bihu or Suwali (female), and sometimes they perform together. Female dancers have always added colour grace and rhythmic vibrancy to the Bihu dance form thereby playing a very important role.

Whereas the *Bihu* and *Kherai* dances rely on female dancers, the *Sattriya* was once a male dance tradition, until a radical departure in the 1960s when female dancers were allowed to perform and be included in the tradition for the first time.

The *Sattriya* dance emerged as an expression of faith in the Sattras and as an integral component of worship. It emerged during the mediaeval period of Assam (the 15th century) as a part of the neo-Vaishnavite Bhakti movement led by the Bhakti saint, scholar, artist, writer, and social reformer Srimanta Sankaradeva and his prime disciple Sri Sri Madhavadeva. These two saints established the Sattras (Vaishnavite monasteries) all over Assam and brought with them a rich repertoire of multiple art forms to propagate the ideals of Vaishnavism amongst the common people, thereby creating an unprecedented upsurge of cultural renaissance in the valley. Since that time, Sattras have become systems of the neo-Vaishnavite religio-cultural order. They are a hub for multiple art forms such as manuscript painting, wood carving, dance, and theatre. *Sattriya* music and the *Sattriya* dance formed an important part of the worship system.

Sattriya dance has been thriving as a living dance tradition for almost six hundred years. As a classical dance (with a set of dances), *Sattriya* has a definite grammatology and structure with different manifestations in terms of body movements, hand, and foot gestures. Abhinaya (emotive facial expressions) is based upon the Indian classical aesthetic texts such as Natyasastra, Abhinaya Darpana, and Srihastamuktavali along with infused elements from local indigenous local cultural expressions.

Unlike *Sattriya* and *Kherai*, the *Bihu* dance tradition has seen several paradigm shifts over the centuries due to many socio-politico-cultural factors. It is important to map these historical shifts in the context of *Bihu* so that we can understand and critically examine the changing role of the female dancers in this particular tradition. The *Bihu*, a seasonal and an agricultural festival of Assam, is celebrated by almost all the ethnic groups and it is a unique example of a festival of acculturation, signifying a synthesis of multiple cultures, where religious/ritualistic components of various ethno-racial groups are assimilated. It has been celebrated in the pre- and post-harvesting period for hundreds of years as recorded in the Buranjis (the historical accounts) of the royal Ahom Kings who ruled Assam for six hundred years until 1826. There are different types of *Bihu* dances, such as the Jeng or female *Bihu*, where only the girls perform; the male *Bihu*; the Log Bihu where both male and female take part; and, the Huchori, where a group, including elderly people visit every house in the village in the evening to sing and dance *Bihu* in the courtyard of the household, with religious and spiritual intonations to give blessings and offer prayer for the prosperity and well-being of the society. Rati Bihu or the *Bihu* performed in the night by groups of young boys and girls was once an effervescent tradition that dwindled at the advent of British colonisation.

The gender dimension

Despite having an expanded scholarship around dance in Assam, there is a dearth of literature focusing on the gender dimension or feminist philosophies around the gender dynamics in the aforementioned dances. Kandali (2011) places the *Sattriya* dance in context.

> The Sattra institution is basically a male tradition and system. Only males were allowed to stay and practice the Vaishnavite lifestyle. Sattriya was performed strictly within the Sattra premises as a means of devotion

to the supreme Lord and as a medium of expression for the philosophy called Bhakti. Bhakti was the central philosophy propagated by the Bhakti movement of India, of which the sattra culture of Assam was also a part, where only the male monks played the dominant role within the Sattra. Therefore, an outside performance of Sattriya in a broader public arena was an unthinkable affair prohibited by the Sattra cultural conventions. Due to a reformist movement in the 20th century, new age ideologies, such as liberal ideas about gender equality arose. Some progressive minded male dancer/trainer Gurus started teaching female disciples to learn the Sattriya dance style.

(n.p.)

Further to the above, in our interview, Kandali reflected on this history. "It was indeed a very challenging period in the sixties when women started to learn *Sattriya*. Almost the entire society was against the female dancers who tried to learn the dance form."

As Kandali stated in her interview, it was in the year 1960 when a few girls namely, Punyada Saikia, Kunja Dutta, Niru Dutta, and Gulapi Dutta of the Garhmur Xoru Sattra area of Majuli came forward to learn *Sattriya*. They encountered many obstacles. The legendary guru, Rakheswar Saikia Borbayon of Shri Kamala Bari Sattra had started teaching these girls in Majuli, but he faced great resistance and objection. The Sattradhikar, or the Abbot of the Sattra and some monks of the monastery along with certain sections of society severely criticised him for teaching the female students which compelled him to leave the Sattra. In 1963 he left the Sattra and settled outside, but kept spreading the *Sattriya* culture to the outside world.

It was a new awakening in the cultural arena of Assam. Though the numbers were very few, women came forward to revolutionise the classical dance world of Assam under the leadership of Raseswari Saikia Babayan. During this period, according to guru Jatin Goswami, dancer Putuli Hazarika of the Bhekulimari village of Majuli, came forward to learn the dance and completed the entire course to become the first trained female *Sattriya* dancer. Kamala Sharma (now Kamala Goswami) also made her mark as a prominent female dancer of *Sattriya* during that period.

During the 1960s, under the leadership of the late Jibeshwar Goswami, more female dancers, namely Makhoni Goswami, Binu Goswami, Dipali Goswami, and Purnima Goswami started to learn *Sattriya* and even performed outside Assam at various places throughout India. Gradually many more females came forward to learn the dance form, despite not all of society welcoming this change. Some sections of society became antagonistic. Some educated and reputed families of Assam refused to allow their sons to marry a female *Sattriya* dancer.

Gradually however, the scenario changed in the following decades when great *Sattriya* scholars such as Dr. Maheswar Neog (1998) and others encouraged the female dancers and took upon themselves the responsibility of establishing them as trained dancers. As observed by Kandali, Guru Jatin Goswami, Suren Goswami, and other noted artists encouraged the female dancers. Gradually the Sattra monks also started to teach females and society began to accept and recognise the female *Sattriya* dancers. From the 1970s onwards, a group of dancers namely Deepali Das, Saradi Saikia, Pushpa Bhuyan, Dolly Patowari, Tanjua Devi, Indira P.P. Borah, and Garima Hazarika emerged in the scene to usher in a vibrant momentum to the larger cultural domain. Now almost all the sattra gurus and the male gurus outside the sattras welcome the idea of allowing the female dancers to be a part of the tradition thereby bringing in a major unprecedented shift (Borgohain, 2011).

Following the 1970s, many more female dancers came forward to enrich the tradition, not only in the field of performance, but also in terms of scholastic engagements making significant contributions. According to the interviewees in the present study, there are currently many female dancers actively engaged in *Sattriya* performance as well as intellectual deliberations at multiple levels from imparting knowledge through their institutions, to keeping the dance legacy moving forward. This has come up as a vibrant strand of cultural activism through organisational endeavours, where new methodologies for aesthetic meaning productions are attempted, examined, and applied. In a post-modern global condition of theorisations and hybridised cultural conditions, they are also negotiating intersectional realities through meditative, imaginative, and creative interventions without distorting the original classical format of the tradition.

While the female *Sattriya* dancers became a part of the tradition after almost five hundred years of exclusion, the *Bihu*, female dancers have always played a significant role with equal partnership in both performative rendering and compositional or choreographic endeavours.

The first phase of *Bihu* that dates back to the pre-mediaeval period was mainly of the Raati (Night) *Bihu* where prayer to the fertility goddess and ritualistic dance depicting youthful love, passion, and desire predominated. The songs and the body gestures expressed the joyfulness of being in love, the physical craving for the paramour, and the intimate bond between human being and nature. The second phase was manifested in the reflections of the new sociocultural developments and changes that became evident in the expansion of the Vaishnavite Bhakti movement propagated by the Bhakti saint scholar, writer, artist, and social reformer Srimanta Sankaradeva. *Bihu* underwent a definite departure in its third phase during the rule of the Ahom King Rudra Singha who was a connoisseur of music, art, and culture both in North Indian and in other south-east Asian traditions. Up to this time, *Bihu* was an agriculture-based cultural affair with restricted spectatorship. When the King started a new practice of performing *Bihu* in the Royal courtyard in an open space with a broader spectatorship, he paved the way for a new tradition of Huchori. Here a group of performers would go in a procession to the court, and on their way back, the bureaucratic elite would invite them to sing, dance, and shower blessings. Later transitions followed after the Burmese invasion, the advent of British colonisation and the treaties of Yandabo between the British and the Burmese in 1926.

The British attempted to ban *Bihu* as an obscene and vulgar expression, with ardent support from a section of the new elite aristocratic class of Assamese intelligentsia and neo-literati during the 19th and early 20th centuries until it was reclaimed, and given a rightful position by middle-class Assamese. In 1941, for the first time in Assam, *Bihu* came to be celebrated publicly in the affluent Assamese town of Sivasagar. After one decade, Radha Govinda Baruah, known as the Iron Man of Assam, organised a grand gala of *Bihu* celebration.

This new practice became immensely popular, spreading throughout the state and brought forth a new form for the staging of *Bihu* with associated changes and transformations in props, settings, lighting, and choreography.

Bihu dance became spectator-centric with an essential aim to entertain the audience. The spontaneity that was visible earlier in open fields and courtyards was eventually lost by modern-day performers. "Stage Bihu" became a neon-glittering spectacle with a million-rupee budget. The spectacle further accelerated with the fashionable accommodation of *Bihu* in the music of the Assamese Film Industry. "In the decades between 70's to the 90's, most Assamese movies featured age old *Bihu* songs that flew through the generations orally, accompanied by a distinctively traditional score" (Kandali, 2016).

The Bihu-oriented Video Compact Disk industry is flourishing in all areas, with millions of dollars in annual turnover, thereby further enhancing the status of *Bihu* as a grand public spectacle. This trend started in the 1990s and has continued to develop in popularity. Buoyed up by the economic boost of the tea and oil industry and advancement of communication technology, an affluent and socio-politically powerful section of the urban population started to act as power players in the collective spaces where they began investing money in the festivals or sponsored events related to *Bihu* and thereby bringing influential change to the society. A mushrooming of *Bihu* committees sponsored by the affluent business class through large corporations, further enhanced the making of the spectacle of *Bihu*. New practices were devised or strategically created that were not part of the original *Bihu* tradition such as the *Bihuwoti* competitions among the female dancers where one female dancer would be crowned as the Bihu Rani or the Bihu Queen with a trophy and prize money comprising several lakhs of rupees. With transformations over time, *Bihuwoti* became the central player in cultural re-enactment, and with that came different expectations when viewing the female dancers. *Bihu* is now a comparatively secular performance/enactment with popular cultural attributes and qualities within the permissible elastic liquidity of the "profane".

The *Doudini*, the central dancer/performer of the *Kherai* dance tradition, has played a noteworthy role over many centuries. The *Kherai* dances operate within a sociocultural set grammatology and dense structure, similar to *Sattriya*. Both *Sattriya* and *Kherai* are ritualistic dance performances or mythico-spiritual enactments performed within strict religious conventions. For many centuries, *Kherai* with its profound religio-mythical grounding has adhered to a sacred system of ritualistic performance within a set structure where the *Doudini* carries the responsibility of becoming the medium between the mundane world and the higher realm of divinity.

Daimary and Goswami reflected upon the ritualistic enactment of the *Kherai* noting that it has undergone many subtle changes. Daimary and Goswami both observed that the *Kherai* Puja was originally organised for three days, however the number of days is decreasing according to the changing lifestyle of the people where urbanity has rapidly been encroaching on rural and pastoral life. In several areas, it has been observed that animal sacrifices have been replaced by offering of flowers known as *Bibar Bathou*. If this new tendency of replacing old ritualistic practice continues then undoubtedly the role of the *Doudini* is going to change and the existence of *Doudini* in its original form is endangered. Already anthropological, sociological, cultural, and other associated disciplinary studies have shown that radical changes have brought transformations to the folk life of the people, and many indigenous ethnic tribes are losing their traditional style of living, livelihood, and lived experiences amidst the aggressive proliferation of a modern life-style (Baruah, 2003). Due to the impact of the cultural globalisation of the last century, certain unprecedented changes have been witnessed in the traditional and ethnic societies of India and the indigenous lived experiences of the people.

Keeping in mind the ethno-historical backdrop and the contextual transitions and transformations that the three dance forms under discussion have undergone, we deliberate upon the question as to how "Gaze" and "Voyeuristic" spectatorship comes into play in the current climate. Since the 1990s, *Bihu* has seen two distinct trends. Firstly, live Spring performances are completely new during the annual *Bihu* festivals called Bohagi Utsavs, (Festival of Spring) along with a new festive-extension known as Bohagi Bidai (Farewell to Spring). These performances have arisen in response to the sheer commercial pressure of the current competitive market of the music industry and the newly emerging celebrity culture.

The other trend is that of releasing and launching Bihu Video Compact Disks with a narrative plot and music. Most of the *Bihu* videos use musicians, singers, and composers who compose *Bihu* songs and dances where the female dancers perform as the lead. In the larger context of spectatorship, it is similar to what is seen in its more influential mainstream counterparts such as the Hollywood or Bollywood film industries. The spectatorship is built upon the largely male-oriented, patriarchal, middle-class ethos and values that play upon the elements of voyeurism, fantasy, and sublimations of urges and desires (Sahoo & Kandali, 2015).

The desired object is often the female protagonist who is usually the *Bihu* dancer. Herein the reading of the representation of female subjectivity in the

Bihu Video Compact Disks and the play of the male gaze and female objectification through the prism of feminist critique becomes most applicable and relevant. This can also be viewed in a broader critique regarding the dynamics of power politics in the consumerist bonanza of a culture industry of *Bihu* (CDs and VCDs) through Adornoesque dialectics (Kandali, 2016).

To substantiate the argument that this dance form is now catering to the commercial demands of the culture industry and subsequent objectification of the female body through the *Bihuwoti*, I point out the unfortunate dwindling of the once-vibrant male *Bihu* traditions of Lora-Huchori and Mota-Bihu, have been marginalised by the promotion of the female Bihuwoti.

As Konwar observed in our interview, the once-vibrant Lora Bihu which we had observed as a significant part of *Bihu* celebration during our parents' time and in our childhood till the period of late 1960s and 1970s of the 20th century slowly began to become side-lined.

Reference to Lora Bihu has hence disappeared, as female dancers have gained more attention as lead dancers with male dancers as supporting players. This applies to *Bihu* stage performances and also in the popular narrative-plots of the Bihu VCDs, where the dominant male spectatorship is real within the culture industry. At present, there are hundreds of *Bihu* festivals all over the Brahmaputra Valley with the adorning of the *Bihuwoti* as the Bihu Kuwori (Bihu Princess) and Bihu Rani (Bihu Queen) with no male dancer or Bihuwa crowned as Bihu Konwar (Bihu Prince) or Bihu Roja (the Bihu King).

All the interviewees made comments about the demise of the involvement of males in the Lora Bihu. They noted that *Bihu* is a changing form in the contemporary global culture industry. From various collective accounts including my own childhood memories, one can say that the male *Bihu* tradition was once one of the most vigorous, effervescent, and multi-layered dance performances where dancing, singing, and playing instruments in a frenzied trance would keep the spectators spellbound for hours in a heightened euphoria. Although there are no specific references available regarding the stylistic rendering and formalistic analysis of Lora *Bihu*, the knowledge to which I refer has been handed down through a shared cultural repository of understanding. I am a bearer/inheritor/cultural participant in this knowledge.

It is evident that the contemporary live *Bihu* performances on the stage are different from the original dances. The camera-controlled projection of a dancer's body in the VCD/music videos very often cater to the demands of the dominant spectatorship. There is no doubt that *Bihu* is now a dance of celebrated love with underlying erotica, and that the female body/figure/subjectivity of the *Bihuwoti* has seamlessly transformed into an anatomy of seductive presence providing ample scope for the play of the male gaze and voyeuristic imagination under the projection of the camera lens (Butler, 1990).

Bihu is a dance form within the realm of the "profane" and this perhaps allows a certain liquidity and seamless transformation without too many restrictions because of the already inherent code of conduct permissible for expressing love and erotica. The religio-ethical codes of conduct designed for the dance forms, which belong to the realm of the sacred, include *Bihu*, *Sattriya*, and *Kherai*. These dances are bound to this realm of the sacred and within the spiritual domain, the dancers dance to the gods and not for the male onlookers. Even if there are some subtle suggestions of Shringara (the Sanskrit term and the canonical concept for the emotion of erotics/erotic play), they are intended to be the extended dimension of the central emotion of Bhakti (devotion) or emotive manifestation of eternal and transcendental/metaphysical love of God. One might wonder as to what role gaze and voyeurism can play in such a regimented structure of a sacred tradition dedicated to the Divine and for the larger collective social well-being of the community.

Goswami, spoke of her observation that, "despite the temporal and temporary transcendence from the mundane to the ethereal, the *Doudini* as an empowered "deity" becomes the mediator between God and Human". A *Doudini* has to perform around 18 dance forms, and before her performance, she is beautified in front of the crowd. She is adorned with ornaments and has to change her dress in front of the public. She is accompanied by male members in the early morning before dawn in the village pond for a bath. Daimary and Goswami spoke clearly,

> The Doudini does not enjoy liberty throughout the entire process of the ritual as she is bound to perform every act set by the system, so much so that she has to forgo her dignity in front of the public that also violates the Criminal Act, 2013 Offence 354C: Voyeurism. The body of the Doudini is not a matter of privacy, rather she belongs to the public. In the case of Doudini, who is also called a Nasoni (dancer), changing clothes in front of the public is not a taboo. A woman's body is rather exploited in the name of Doudini, though she attains a high post during the period of the ritual. Her body is likely to experience pain during the ritual, as she has to dance and perform her acts on the edge of a sword. Though the ritual is performed both by female shaman and a male priest, there is no equal division of labor as the Doudini has to perform more acts compared to the male priest.

Whether it is the female subjectivity of the *Doudini* or the *Bihuwoti*, the realm of the sacred or the profane, or the terrain of the religious or the secular, one thing that becomes a common manifestation is the controlling of the body of the female dancer by the hegemonic agencies. This also includes the subjugation of the body to the currents and undercurrents of voyeuristic gazing within the context of spectatorship.

When we extend our critical inquiry to the dance form of *Sattriya*, a complex dynamic of spectatorship unfolds. *Sattriya* is currently performed in two different spaces, one is the private space of the Sattra premises where it is an everyday enactment. It is a devotional act for the Divine Lord Vishnu, performed as an intimate ritualistic offering to the Supreme God, as a rendezvous between the devotee and devoted, where the spectator's role is absolutely minimal or nil. The other space is public, where the *Sattriya* is enacted as a performing art with an overwhelming presence of spectators. The recording or live telecast of such public performances have added another dimension to the issue of spectatorship, making it complex and multi-layered. In both the spaces however, be it private or public, the strict grammatology has been maintained keeping to the conventions and set structure despite some visible changes in terms of duration, props, costumes, and make-up, lighting and other scenographic elements. A pertinent question that arises is, what alterations can be seen because of the participation of the female dancers, that was previously only dominated/danced by men?

Besides ushering in a much-needed radical change in terms of sociopolitical justice for gender equality and gender-representation, has there been any discernible change in terms of the aesthetic and performative dimensions? *Sattriya* has a unique feature of distinctly categorising two sets of dances as Purusha (Male/Masculine) and Prakriti (Female/Feminine) through various expositions of basic stance (*ora*) as *purush/mota ora* and *prakriti/maiki ora*, with some whirling movements (*pak*) and jumps (*jap*). Some dances are specifically attributed as male or female, such as the male Krishna Nach and the female Cali and Mela Nach. Most interestingly and most importantly, female impersonation by male monks has been an integral part of *Sattriya* tradition, both in the theatrical as well as the dance performances, where the female dances and characters are attributed with *lasyabhaba* or feminine gracefulness, unlike the male dances which are mostly vigorous in nature. As such, the aesthetician Bharata Muni (1937) laid down conventions about different types of impersonation in his classic treatise called *Natyshastra* that is regarded as the basic foundational text for all the Indian classical dance forms. In this text, Avirupanurupini has been described as impersonation, where a man assumes the character of a female. Based on the Natyashastra conventions many Indian classical dance forms including *Sattriya* have been following Nayashastra, and it has been practised with such artistic finesse and aesthetic precision that there is mention of a very fascinating anecdote in Guru-Carita, the biography of the Assamese Bhakti Saint Srimanta Sankaradeva. In this narrative, it is said that the female characters played by the young monks in Ganakkuchi under the direction of Sri Sri Madhavadeva were so perfect that people started believing they were young female dancers and the Koch king Raghudeva had to send some *kotwal* (police officials) to investigate the matter as it was considered anti-traditional and scandalous. The *kotwal* finally discovered that they were none other than the male *bhakats* (devotee or monks) with false wooden breasts and hair. Whether it is the natural biological body of a female dancer or the conditioned body of a male dancer made effeminate by training, the voyeuristic gaze must have played its part in shaping the nature and quality of the performance.

Although the *Sattriya* dance is basically a classical dance with a dominant trait of spirituality and religious devotion, impersonation of the female characters in the dramas or the dance, performances are also about feminine attributes and graceful body movements that can entice any spectator when performed outside the remote interior of the Sattra premise. Once the female dancers are in a broader public space, the spectatorship changes and with it, the audience's different reception of the dance. The matter here is not so much about the body (whether male impersonating female or a female as biologically given), but that of the space where the enactment is exposed to a larger spectatorship comprising different kinds of spectators who have different orientations and inclinations, unlike in the Sattra premises where the spectatorship is trained and oriented towards Bhakti. As such, new meanings of the dance are made by "new" audiences.

The influence of the "view" or "gaze" is a powerful agent causing a constant evolution of *Sattriya*. The spectators in broader collective public spaces which could be an urban-scape, cyberspace, or a social media audience, belong to a very vast, complex, and secular strata where the dance appreciation might be purely aesthetic or just for entertainment. The body of the female dancer may, in such circumstances be seen through different lenses and perspectives, forming different points of view or gazing and voyeuristic pleasure. How does the female *Sattriya* dancer respond to such a situation and seek ways to deflate, dilute, or distract the gaze?

An observation by Deborah Hay (1989) three decades ago still finds some resonance and relevance in giving us a direction for critical reflection in this context.

> The greatest challenge is to figure out, and then to verbalize the ineffable experience of the dance spectator to find the clear, accurate and necessarily poetic language to express how it is that a dancer's focus, or the way she activates her skin, or the palpable feeling of the spatial environment, signifies a particular way of seeing and being seen. In the effort to theorise the alternatives to the male gaze, we need to think a lot more about performative presence. Presence is the silent yet screeching excitement of physical vibrancy, of "being there". It is one of the thrills of watching dance, to see someone radiate pure energy, whether it is in stillness or in flight. Questions abound: What constitutes presence? How do we know it when we see it? Is it pan-cultural, or is it highly coded? How is it related to the structure of spectacle? Why is it so seductive? Does that seductiveness demand possession? Can that seductiveness be derailed? There seems to be an affinity between presence and the male gaze.
>
> (p.23).

Deborah Hay opens up interesting yet very complex questions about "presence"; the "seductiveness" of the "present" body along with a significant question about the affinity between presence and male gaze. In focusing upon the central issue of spectatorship and the male gaze, she articulates and critically dissects the concept of the male gaze by focusing on the comparative circumstantial complexity of the dancing female body and that of the body of a female in a celluloid frame. Ongoing examination of the impact of the "gaze" on the *Sattriya* dancer is necessary as the dance moves into ever-shifting public spaces (real and digital) and away from the ritual and educative space of the Sattra.

The concept of male gaze comes from feminist film theory (Daly, 2002). In films, the female performer is literally an object on celluloid. She has no presence in the movie theatre, she cannot look back at the spectator and is thus rendered passive. In dance, the situation is not as clear-cut. The dancer does have a literal, if not always effective presence. S/he can participate in a give-and-take situation/condition with the audience. Ann Daly (2002) stated,

> A highly accomplished technician looks anything but passive. Nevertheless, the dancer becomes more than just a technician within the stage frame. S/he becomes part of a dense thicket of completely familiar quotes and conventions that conspire to position her/him as the willing object of our desire. We need to face squarely the risk factor in trying to jam those conventions, as much of the beauty and pleasure of dance as we know it is tied up with the erotics of display and spectatorship. There are times and places, however, when the conventions are in such flux that it seems possible for the gaze to be unfixed and for the performer to elude possession. I don't happen to think we are living in that time and space. Our existence is too over coded.
>
> (p.297)

Daly (2002) goes on to say that,

> The theory of the male gaze has obvious implications for dance, and dance has much to offer for the development of that theory. In films where the concept of the male gaze originated, the performer is flat on a piece of celluloid. In dance the performer is live. How does that affect the dynamics of the male gaze? Is the male gaze more vulnerable to be dismantled when the performer is live? How can a dancer – who fundamentally displays his/her body for the viewer, avoid being objectified? Does some dance create a literal and metaphorical space in which spectator and performer can share the dance together, on equal terms, rather than the one serving her/himself up for the other? Are there dancers who have been able to achieve this?
>
> (p 298).

Conclusion

Pondering this intriguing yet complex possibility of achieving a metaphorical space for the dancer and the spectator to thrive on an equal partnership of unified aesthetic experience, I have attempted to answer the questions posed in the context of *Sattriya*. I have based some of my understanding on an interview with *Sattriya* dancer, and scholar, Dr. Mallika Kandali. Based on Kandali's (2015) performative experience and scholastic exploration, I agree with her proposal that *Sattriya*, despite all associated baggage of voyeuristic possession and play of gaze, has a central Bhava. The overwhelming presence of Bhakti as the principal driving force acts as a kind of spiritual rein over the spectators by creating an ambiance of metaphysical transcendence and a space of deep devotional substratum. As Madhavadeva, the principal disciple of Srimanta Sankaradeva wrote in one of his lyrical composition of Borgeet, "Bhokoti xoman boli naahi aar kahaya Madhav gati nander kumar" (Bhakti, or the emotion of devotion is the ultimate emotion for the Vaishnavite philosophy and the way of life). Sattra culture and *Sattriya* dance performances indoctrinate and inculcate this emotion as an absolute finality thereby deflating and diluting the opportunity of titillation for the spectator. Kandali (2015) also pointed out that she has often attempted to experiment within the traditional parameters of *Sattriya* grammatology and philosophy by bringing in significant social issues such as ecology or gender as an attempt to re-appropriate and re-contextualize the elements of the sociopolitical in the religious as an intervention. In one instance, in one of her own compositions "Mandodari pusoyo Ravanak" (Mandodari questions Ravana) she enacts an encounter between the epic characters, Ravana, who abducts Sita, the wife of Ram, and Mandodari, Ravana's wife. The issue of gender inequality and gender discrimination is very intensely and poignantly narrated. In the performance choreographed and composed by Dr. Kandali, Mandodari questions her husband Ravana as to why he had to abduct Sita, and why women in the world had to face unfairness and be physically hurt in the process? In this composition, she impersonates both Ravana and Mandodari and the focus of the spectator keeps constantly shifting from the gendered body of Ravana to Mandodari.

The passivity of the female body is deeply challenged in the live performance as a vigorous statement seeking gender justice. The dance rattled the spectators by making them critically conscious of their own gaze and voyeurism. A parallel can be drawn with the interventions by the "Guerrilla Girls", in the modern western visual art scene. These girls, over the last five decades, paint or put up the face of a guerrilla on highly sexualized and eroticised bodies of female figures in famous paintings by the male artists over centuries bringing an awareness to their own gaze and voyeuristic pleasure.

The answer to the research question that I have tried to explore herein is not so easy to arrive at. The constant dilemma of negotiating the traditional indigenous ethos and value systems and the transitional repercussions brought forth by colonisation and cultural globalisation makes the artistic praxis more complex and challenging. There remains a challenge when performing in a new space of transformed spectatorship with the subsequent challenge of diffusing any kind of unwanted or unwarranted gaze. In all

Gender and dance 151

Picture 10.1 Malika Kandali's performance of Mandodari Puche Ravnoak. Photo courtesy of UB Studios Guwahati.

three case studies of *Sattriya*, *Bihu*, and *Kherai*, the female dancers have to face these challenges in this contemporary cultural order. However, to devise strategies and negotiation, the practitioners would benefit from a critical consciousness and understanding of the complex realities of both the contemporary global culture as well as one's own indigenous cultural milieu. Through a comparative mode of analysis, we observe that the female dancers of *Sattriya* have made certain attempts at probing these challenges as seen in experimental performances discussed.

With steps drawn from a set grammatology, the focus of *Sattriya* is of the religio-cultural order. The *Bihuwoti* dancers have a more difficult challenge of diffusing the gaze with a deeper gender consciousness. In the case of *Kherai*, the existence of *Doudini* itself has now become a challenge. The female dancers of this dance would also benefit from reclaiming their empowered position to continue where patriarchal gaze and voyeurism could play an oppressive or dominating role. However, there are no easy ways, nor easy answers in considering a course of action. It is hoped that the female dancers will find other ways in the course of time through meditations and mediations.

Due to the unprecedented pandemic situation of Covid-19 in 2020 and 2021 it was not possible to conduct more field studies or interviews with more practitioners. It is suggested that more time be invested in finding a way forward for dancers. While I have made a critical attempt to map and understand questions through gender and feminist discourse, more conceptual and theoretical engagement with many other theories such as the Affect Theory, Reader's Response Theory or Reception theories would assist in further understanding the emerging roles and meanings of these dances in Assam. Keeping these possibilities in mind as a future research project, I would like to sum up this chapter with a quote cited by Landing (2012), from the legendary artist and dancer Isadora Duncan (1903) which is relevant even today.

> The Dancer of the future will dance not in the form of nymph, nor fairy, not coquette but in the form of women in its greatest and purest expression. She will realize the mission of the women's body and the holiness of all its parts. She will dance the changing life of nature, showing how each part is transformed into the other. From all parts of her body shall shine radiant intelligence, bringing to the world the message of the thoughts and aspirations of thousands of women. She shall dance for the freedom of women.
>
> (n.p.)

References

Baruah, S., (2003) Citizens and Denizins: Ethnicity, homelands and the crisis of displacement in North East India. *Journal of Refugee Studies*, 16(1), 44–66.

Borgohain, N., (2011) *Female Dance Traditions of Assam*, Purbanchalprakash Publication House, Guwahati.

Butler, J., (1990) *Lana's "imitation": Melodramatic Repetition and the Gender Performative*, University of Texas Press, 9. DOI: 10.10.5555/gen.1990.9.1.

Constantinou, C., Georgiou, M., Perdikogianni, M. (2017) A comparative method for themes saturation (CoMeTS) in qualitative interviews. *Qualitative Research*, 17(5), 571–588.

Daly, A., (2002) *To Dance Is Female: Critical Gestures*, Wesleyan University Press, Middletown, Connecticut.

Daly, A., (1989) *Critical Gestures: Writing on Dance and Culture*, Wesleyan University Press, Middletown, Connecticut.

Hay, D., (1989) *Playing Awake: Letters to My Daughter*, T.D.R.1988, Cambridge University Press, 33(4), 70–76.

Kandali, J., (2011) *Curating Indian Visual Culture: Theory and Practice, Seminar Presentation, ACUA, Association of Academics, Artists and Citizens for University Autonomy*, Fine Arts Saroj Naidu School of Arts and Communication, University of Hyderabad, Hyderabad.

Kandali, M., (2015) *Mandodoro Puch Ravanoko Dance Performance at Rabindra Bhavan, Organized by the Indian Council for Cultural Relations and Cultural Affairs*, Government of Assam, Guwahati.

Kandaki, M., (2016) Imagining the community: The making of the spectacle of Bihu, Nezine, accessed through www.nezine.com.

Landing, K., (2012) Isadora Duncan: A revolutionary dancer, webpage of the National Museum of Women in the Arts. http//nmwa.org/blog/Isadora-duncan-a-revolutionary-dancer/.

Mahler, S., Pessar, P., (2001) Gendered geographies of power: Analysing gender across transnational spaces. *Identities*, 7(4), 441–459. DOI: 10.1080/1070289X.2001.9962675.

Muni, B., (1937) Rupanusarini Natyashastra. *Asiatic Society*, 2, 28–32.

Nandigama, S., (2020) Performance of success and failure in grassroots conservation and development interventions: Gender dynamics in participatory forest management in India. *Land Use Policy*, 97, 103445.

Neog, M., (1998) *Sankardeva and His Times: Early History of the Vaishnava Faith and Movement in Assam*, Lawyers Book Stall, Guwahati.

Roy, A., (2005) The male gaze in Indian television commercials: A rhetorical analysis. In Carilli, T. and Campbell, J. (Eds.), *Women and the Media: Diverse Perspectives*, University Press of America Inc., Oxford. 3–18.

Sahoo, S., Kandali, M., (2015) Amusing oneself to death and/or imagining the nation: VCD films in assamese. In Goswami, R. and Dutta, M. (Eds.), *Eight Glorious Decades of Assamese Cinema*, Assam Book Syndicate and Publishers, 39–55. Guwahati.

White, D., (1978) Comparisons as cognitive process and the conceptual framework of the comparativist. *Comparative Education*, 14(2), 93–108.

Interviews

Daimary, I., Goswami, M., (2020).
Gandiya, J., (2020) Telephone interview.
Goswami, M., (2020).
Kandali, M., (2020).
Konwar, J., (2020).

With thanks to Dr. Madhurima Goswami and Dr. Mallika Kandali for access to their unpublished doctoral theses on Khrai and *Sattriya* dance, respectively.

11 Reflections on dance education workshops in Assam

Towards critical and creative thinking

Barbara Snook

Introduction

This chapter reflects on dance workshops conducted in North-East India, and how those workshops promoted creative and critical thinking. In respect to the recent education curriculum changes in India that endorse a move towards the promotion of critical thinking and creativity, a section on integrating dance activities across the curriculum is introduced and examined within the research study. While educationalists may support the idea of dance integration in classrooms, little is known about 'how' to implement creative dance activities that promote learning in different discipline areas. For this reason, I have outlined 'what' I did during the workshops in the five case studies within this research. The case studies range across primary secondary and tertiary education, with one case profiling a workshop conducted with primary school teachers.

Methodology

This qualitative research acknowledges my vantage point of western privilege. Denzin and Lincoln (2008) state that,

> Sadly, qualitative research, in many if not all of its forms (observation, participation, interviewing, ethnography) serve as a metaphor for colonial knowledge, for power and truth.
>
> (p. 1)

This study acknowledges a "Pakeha" (non-indigenous settler population in New Zealand) perspective, and through reflection attempts to recognize 'self' in a respectful and useful manner. In that the Indian government has introduced a school curriculum that calls for creativity and creative thinking, it is believed that this research may be useful to teachers and learners. Rather than provide research derived from a western context, this study was conducted in Assam, India, and I approached Linda Tuhiwai Smith's (2012) questions with integrity: "Whose interest does it serve? Who will benefit from it?" (p. 10). I make no assumptions in responding to these provocations, instead hoping that the intention to add to a body of knowledge around creative thinking and learning is of value. The study was approached with a good heart and a clear spirit (Tuhiwai Smith, 2012).

Reflective practice is at the heart of this research. While educators must continuously reflect upon their own practice in terms of teaching delivery, this research values reflection as a meaningful way of examining the learning that took place within several different classrooms across Assam. Qualitative research however, is born out of a wish to understand the other, and this research examines five different case studies.

> For reflection to genuinely be a lens into the world of practice, it is important that the nature of reflection be identified in such a way as to offer ways of questioning taken-for-granted assumptions.
> (Loughran, 2002, p.33)

The learning that took place within this study is identified through constructivist theory. For the students and teachers who took part, the experience of the workshop was new to them and they generated their own rules and responses to accommodate new understandings. This method of learning involves cooperation, experimentation, open-ended problems, and real-life scenarios in which the learners discover learning on their own through active involvement with concepts and principles (Bruner et al., 1956). As constructivism is a theory about learning rather than a description of teaching (Fosnot, 2005), it is an appropriate lens through which to examine the outcomes of this study.

In order to discuss the outcomes that took place through new learning, an auto-ethnographic approach was adopted, and in so doing I acknowledge my relationship to the collective experience. As auto-ethnography is about both the research process and the product of the approach (Rambo & Ellis, 2020), it is particularly suited to this study where dance as an approach to developing critical and creative thinking is examined.

Fostering creative thinking

Creativity is complex, and while it is possible to recognise a creative object, describing the brain activity associated with creativity is elusive (Fisher, 2004). Sternberg (2001) suggests that, "Creativity refers to the potential to produce novel ideas that are task appropriate and high in quality" (p.360) while Boden (1998) proposes that "creativity is a puzzle, a paradox, some say a mystery" (p.15). While definitions of creativity are both broad and complex, research on the relationship between arts and creativity stresses that, "artistic and aesthetic concerns cannot be "optional" for any one of us" (Richards, 2007, p.500). Creativity is more than a buzzword. "It involves high-level cognitive processes which include innovative problem solving, an outcome of which comes from divergent thinking, and the possibility of multiple solutions" (Keun & Hunt, 2006, p. 35). This research proposes that when students engage in dance, there is a direct relationship between the movement developed and critical and creative thinking and learning (Fasko, 2001; Keun & Hunt, 2006). When students engage their bodily kinaesthetic intelligence to solve problems, critical and creative thinking skills are developed (Buck & Snook, 2020(b); Richards, 2007).

Developing critical and creative thinking skills through dance requires a valuing of the process associated with the creation of movement. Rather than developing exceptional skills in performance, the focus is on working collaboratively to problem solve, "with no requirements for participants to compete with each other or to be "technically good", although some participants may very well be very good dancers" (Buck & Snook, 2020(b), p.291).

While dance in education is viewed within an educational structure, the creative dance referred to in this research shares commonalities with community dance. Amans (2017) summarises community dance of the 21st century as having, "a focus on participants, collaborative relationships, inclusive practice, opportunities for positive experiences, and celebration of diversity" (p.9). The positive experiences that creative dance activities offer are for all students. Nobody is left out, as each person engages at their own level of dance expertise. One could state, if you can walk, you can dance, but in this instance, this dance is also for those who may not be able to walk. Inclusivity is at the heart of dance when working creatively and collaboratively.

Dance/arts integration

For almost a decade, I have been researching the possibilities and advantages of arts integration. During my doctoral study (Snook, 2012), it was evident that although teachers valued dance in the New Zealand arts curriculum, very few teachers were implementing dance in their classrooms, relying instead on whole school performance productions. Unfortunately, this means that the curriculum intentions as outlined in the New Zealand curriculum are not being met. A performance meets the New Zealand curriculum objective of "Developing Practical Knowledge". A whole school performance is not necessarily inclusive as not all performance opportunities can be equal. The New Zealand Arts Curriculum objectives of "Understanding dance in context", "Developing ideas", and "Communicating and Interpreting" are very likely not being met at all in many cases. My research revealed that primary school teachers were focused on the many other discipline areas that they were expected to teach, but all agreed that if they could use dance across the curriculum, then they would. This seemed to me a little like valuing dance but not teaching it. There was a gap to be bridged, and my ongoing research has looked at how best this could be achieved. How could teachers learn "how" to teach using an arts integration pedagogy?

Dance or arts integration means using an arts or dance-based process to teach a concept in a different discipline area, maths through dance as an example. The focus is on the learning in the discipline area. Through a dance integration pedagogy, students work collaboratively to problem solve and are free to develop creative ideas without any fear of being "wrong". Arts integration is a difficult concept to grasp. Some may imagine that through a dance performance, students can demonstrate what they have learned. This is not the case. The John F. Kennedy Centre (2010) provides a definition:

> Arts integration is an approach to teaching in which students construct and demonstrate understanding through an art form. Students engage in a creative process which connects an art form and another subject area and meets evolving objectives in both.
> (p.1)

This definition supports the work that we are doing at the University of Auckland, with one difference. Rather than expecting teachers to meet evolving objectives in two subject areas, arts and science as an example, we focus on the one area such as science, with the arts being used as the method only. While this may seem as though the arts are being devalued, we instead promote the teaching and learning of the arts disciplines in their own right. We also believe that where teachers are using arts integration, they will become more confident in teaching the arts (Snook, 2021).

As advocates for creative classrooms "where students learn through cooperation, problem solving, creative thinking, and most importantly an enjoyment of the learning process" (Buck & Snook, 2020 (a), p.98), we have conducted research that investigates our claims. Research was conducted at a six-teacher rural New Zealand school where the teachers and students engaged in arts integration over a two-year period. As generalist teachers often have little understanding or experience of using the arts as a process and tend to view arts in silos of performance and presentation (Buck & Snook, 2016), I worked in the school at intervals providing professional development and support during the two-year period. An arts integration expert was also employed to demonstrate lessons and support the teachers in creating their own.

Our study employed both qualitative and quantitative research methods to investigate whether arts integration increased students' social empowerment and intellectual engagement and we also analysed the effects of arts integration on academic performance. We worked alongside our Canadian colleague, Brittany Harker Martin, who provided scientific evidence. The key findings of this study are listed below:

1. Teacher resistance to arts integration can be overcome with embodied knowledge through experiential professional learning;
2. Arts integration is engaging for teachers and students;
3. Teachers who feel ownership over their arts integration pedagogy will practise it;
4. Arts integration is socially empowering; and
5. Arts integration has a positive impact on student academic performance, specifically maths and writing (Martin, Snook, & Buck, 2018).

Our research adds to the growing body of knowledge (Appell, 2006; Burnaford, April, & Weiss, 2013; Gullatt, 2008; Rinne, Gregory, & Yarmolinskaya, 2011) that has proved conclusively that the arts are vital when creating creative and critical thinkers in school classrooms. While this research promotes success in a western context, when implementing arts integration in Indian classrooms, care would need to be taken to ensure that it serves to enhance the strength of the cultural education system already in place.

The new Indian curriculum

The Indian government has recently announced a new curriculum that promotes creativity and critical thinking. This is in line with Singapore's Ministry of Education's Thinking Skills, Learning Nation (TSLN) where new creative directions are aimed at preparing students for the challenges of the 21st century. While the "rich heritage of ancient and eternal Indian knowledge and thought has been a guiding light for this policy" (Government of India, 2020, p.4), the curriculum should also be, "Holistic, Integrated, Enjoyable and Engaging" (p.1). The introduction to the National Education Policy (2020) states,

> It is becoming increasingly critical that children not only learn, but more importantly, learn how to learn. Education thus, must move forward toward less content, and more towards learning how to think critically and solve problems, how to be creative and multidisciplinary, and how to innovate, adapt and absorb new material in novel and changing fields.
> (p.3)

"The teacher must be at the centre of fundamental reforms" (Government of India, 2020, p.4). Research suggests that it is important that teachers be involved in determining how professional development happens in India (Darling-Hammond, 1999; Klein & Riordan, 2009; McKeown, Brindle, & Harris, 2019; Whitworth & Chiu, 2015). This may be difficult for Indian teachers who have themselves been educated in a system that valued rote-based learning, and they have then gone on to teach in a similar manner. In the old system, there are right answers, whereas in a system valuing critical thinking and creativity, there may not always be right or wrong answers, but many different ideas. While there are provisions made in the National Education Policy for professional development, unless it is ongoing, regular and well understood by the facilitators, change may be slow within classrooms. Klein and Riordan (2009) discuss how teachers implemented professional development in a school that is based on Hahn's "Outward Bound" philosophy (outdoor education challenges):

> The school embraced a philosophy of impelling students into experiences that pushed them to discover their capabilities [and the school] promotes rigorous and engaging curriculum, active, inquiry-based pedagogy, and a school culture that teaches compassion and good citizenship.
>
> (p.62)

While it would seem that the school's philosophy was well understood by the teachers who had chosen to teach at this school, it was found that the "teachers' beliefs about their content area seemed to have direct implications for how much they implemented" (p.75).

There are many obstacles, such as assessment as an obvious concern, and that may inhibit a full implementation of the creative aspects of the new Indian curriculum when it comes to measuring creative and critical thinking. While the limitations within a chapter prevent an examination of the extent of the difficulties in curriculum change, China has implemented a similar approach to India in their school curriculum. While wishing to introduce critical thinking skills and creativity, China also values its history and Confucius' ideals, and like India, China has a history of leaning towards the attainment of skills that meet short-term examination needs (Dello-Lacovo, 2009). It is suggested that India may benefit from understanding the difficulties experienced in China when implementing curriculum change as the country moves forward towards the development of critical and creative thinking skills. Like China, India has been making moves towards more student-centred learning over many years. During the 1990s there were government interventions that aimed to reform the education system in India (Sriprakash, 2006). One of the greatest difficulties would seem to be India's huge population. Sriprakash (2006) discussed case studies that were a small "drop in the bucket" when considering schools and students throughout the country. This chapter now moves on to examine five case studies, and in so doing adds "more drops in the bucket" to borrow Sriprakash's metaphor above.

Five case studies

Case Study One

The first workshop took place at a public primary school in Guwahati, the morning after my arrival in the country for the very first time. I recall walking through a car park with many school buses, more than I had ever seen before in any one place. I was with my colleague, Ali East from the University of Otago, four of her students, and our host Anwesa Mahanta from KALPA (an organisation dedicated to the promotion of literature, art, culture, social harmony, and cultural exchange within Assam). As outlined in Chapter 4, Ali and I were in India with Ali's students on an "ethnographic reconnaissance".

We were honoured with a formal welcoming ceremony (felicitations) that took us by surprise, as we are not accustomed to such attention in our own country. The room was relatively large and had a raised stage at one end where the felicitations took place. The students sat quietly on the floor observing the ceremony. Both Ali and I had agreed to conduct workshops and I began the morning's activities. Teachers and administrative staff observed from the stage. The 50 students appeared to be around ten years old.

I began with short warm-up activities that required the students to work in pairs, and small groups. It seemed important to start with simple activities that were easily explained so that I could ascertain the level at which I could position some challenges. Following some warm-up games to break down barriers, we began by clapping the syllables of our names around in a circle. Students were then asked to create a separate movement for each syllable of their name and then teach them to a partner. I demonstrated what I meant by showing separate movements for the syllables in my own name. All went well. The students understood the instructions and quickly applied themselves to the task. Once they had learned the movements for their partner's name, each pair put both sets of movement together and performed them together. They were further challenged by then being placed with another pair where they learned all four sets of movement and performed the movement together as a continuous dance sequence. They were also given a new instruction to create their own structures for the dance. These included: who would dance where, would they move through lines, create a circle, or something else drawn from their own imaginations. The students enjoyed themselves throughout. There was much laughter and full engagement from every student. Each group was given an opportunity to perform for the rest of the group at the end.

At one stage while the students were busy creating their work, Anwesa came to me looking genuinely amazed. She stated, "I can't believe that you have them creating their own choreography, and so quickly, and they are having so much fun". She appeared to recognise in that moment, that when there is no right or wrong way of responding to the task, or need to be technically competent, then the students became fully engaged in the moment as they worked with others. Other teachers were very taken with the way in which the children engaged, working together, solving problems, and above all the students demonstrated a high level of creative thinking. There was no sense of students being too shy to perform. Some teachers joined in and others came to watch when they heard the sound of children having fun.

The workshop continued with a limerick activity to demonstrate how dance can be used to teach other concepts in other discipline areas. For each activity, it was a matter of taking the time to explain and then check for understanding before starting and then moving through each task relatively quickly. Students were given a tight time frame in which they were to create their choreography. Because of this, they got onto the task straight away and listened to each other without wasting time. It is always possible to extend the time if need be, but I was aware that having a tight time frame and always moving forward was a good strategy I had developed over years of experience. Where students had invested time and energy it was important to give them an opportunity to show what they had made by performing for the class. This appeared to be a highlight for the students.

Case Study Two

The second case study took place in the same school, but this time it was for the teachers and not the students. I had explained that it would be a professional development workshop for teachers, but when we arrived, chairs had been set out in the space. A few teachers came in and sat down. I explained that we wouldn't be using the chairs and began moving them to the back of the room. Those teachers left the room. Time went by, some teachers popped their heads around the door and then disappeared. Some stayed in the hallway outside and others disappeared altogether. This was not a good start. We went into the hallways and encouraged the teachers to come into the room. By the time they felt reassured and had entered the space, we had lost quite a bit of time and I had only 40 minutes left in which to conduct the lesson.

I started off with an "ice-breaker", the game of clumps. The teachers walked in the space and when a number was called, they had to run and quickly make a group, bobbing down together when they had the required number. I explained that this activity was a fun introduction to maths for young students. There was much laughter and barriers started breaking down. The next activity required small groups to create three frozen shapes. I asked that they didn't use a circle as that was too simple, however many groups did include a circle as one of their three shapes. The teachers appeared to be nervous about getting it right, but once they saw what other groups were doing, they relaxed a little and could see what was required. Although I believed that I had explained the group shape exercise quite clearly, the teachers appeared to overthink what was required. Perhaps it was difficult for them to be expected to do something so simple? We went on to the limerick activity that I had facilitated with the students in the earlier workshop. At this point, the teachers began displaying some elements of creativity. They certainly appeared to be having fun, especially when they watched each other's performances. Unfortunately, at that point, the time was up.

Case Study Three

Two years had elapsed since I had been in India. This workshop took place at a University in Guwahati where my "now" close friend Anwesa Mahanta was an "Artist in Residence". She taught students the Indian classical Sattryia dance. The students did not achieve credits for their achievement in this course, but every student was required to choose at least one subject from a group of offerings in order to complete their studies. Dance was one of these offerings. Anwesa invited me to conduct a workshop with her students in her dance studio. Dance was not a major course of study for these students, but they were there because they had chosen to be.

Approximately 25 students attended the class. We warmed up with games and I then worked through some creative tasks leading up to a "Spider Dance". The object of the exercise was to have them understand how to create a ternary structure for dance, by creating an A section, a B section, then a repeated A section. We began by sitting in a circle and I taught them the nursery rhyme, "Incy Wincy Spider" with all the actions. This spider climbs up, falls down, and then goes back up again, just as in a ternary dance form. Each person was then asked to suggest something that a spider might do (e.g. scuttle, weave, drop, bite, etc.). Once we had each come up with a word, students were divided into pairs and asked to create 30 seconds' worth of movement that demonstrated what a spider might do. Once completed, they were then asked to create a separate B section with different spider movements, only this time they needed to completely change the way that they used dynamic elements and space. If most of the dance had been performed in one place in the A section, then the pair needed to use the whole space in the B section. If movements had been slow and flowing in the A section, then they needed to be sharp and fast in the B section. Once again, the pairs created 30 seconds worth of movement. Once complete, the students rehearsed running the A, B, and then A sections together to create their dance. Each pair was given the opportunity to perform their dance, different music was played for each pair and chosen to elicit laughter and enthusiastic dance.

The exercise was a huge success. There was much laughter and students had clearly enjoyed themselves. When creating movements that a spider might do, the students moved right away from getting steps right, or looking good, and they were really creative in what they came up with. Each pair worked together to think creatively and come up with solutions. This group of students responded to the task with both energy and enthusiasm, despite the fact that the dance they had been learning with Anwesa was classical Indian dance technique.

Case Study Four

This case study was conducted at a public rural primary school close to Tezpur. I was taken to the principal's office and was invited to take tea.

I naively declined the invitation thinking that I didn't have enough time as we had been late in arriving and I needed to get into the classroom and start the class. The tea and cakes arrived anyway, and I sat and took the time to partake in this ritual celebration. I realised that my refusal had been rude. Time is not as important as acknowledging and respecting others. I was then shown around the classrooms with their concrete floors and rows of desks.

As I moved into my dance space I found that far more students wanted to participate than we had the room for. I was asked to select the students I wanted to work with. I divided the students into two groups. We were hoping that we would have time to conduct two sessions, but it wasn't to be. The first group of students engaged with passion, boys and girls worked together, they laughed, they played, and they worked creatively to problem solve. I followed a similar format to the other workshops I'd conducted and made the focus the "Spider Dance". This was a great success with the primary students, just as it had been with tertiary students. One of the teachers loved the fact that the students were learning about spiders and said that it was a topic she had taught her students. At the time, I was fairly focused on the fact that I was teaching ternary form in dance and the spiders were a vehicle

Picture 11.1 Students engaging in dance during the workshop, Pic. Barbara Snook personal collection.

for creativity. I have since worked intensively with arts integration and have found that indeed, the Spider Dance is an excellent way of teaching about spiders. As the students develop the need for a greater level of development and understanding of spiders, the dance activity can be adapted to suit. It all seemed to be over very quickly, we were having so much fun, and I reluctantly left to be driven back to my accommodation.

Case Study Five

This school was a private boarding school in Balipara, Tezpur, that accepts students from the age of ten years. I couldn't help but be impressed by the imposing buildings and grounds as I was driven into the complex. According to their website, this school is ranked as the fourth best co-educational residential school in India. There appeared to be a huge focus on extracurricular activities, such as arts, equestrian events, and sports.

I was taken to the visual art studio where there were two teachers, six students, and large tables filling the space. The teachers didn't seem particularly interested in what I was there to do, quite a different response to what I was used to when visiting other Indian schools. They asked if I could come back tomorrow instead, but as we couldn't, it was decided to go ahead. It was apparent that the desks would pose a problem, but there were only six students after all, so we could work around the tables. I felt a little more nervous than usual as I felt that there might be some judgement coming from the teachers. I fell back on the activities that I knew worked well and we launched into the "Spider Dance". The senior students who had been influenced by their teachers started slowly, but as they warmed to the activity, they began to enjoy themselves and have fun. The desks didn't pose too much of a problem and in the end, they showed their completed dances to the others in the room. By this stage, the teachers were quite enthusiastic and asked if we could come back tomorrow and teach another class. It wasn't possible unfortunately, but they gave me a tour around the campus, and I was quite amazed by the standard of the student's art works.

Conclusion

The main finding to emerge from the five different case studies was the fact that students adjusted well to a new teaching pedagogy that involved dance, and even in one small workshop, there was evidence that students were thinking both critically and creatively. The students worked eagerly to engage with each task with which they were presented. They enjoyed learning through the creative pedagogy of dance and were proud to show their work when completed. There did not appear to be any moments that were "lost in translation". The difficult moments were with the teachers. Educational change is difficult (O'Neill, 2000) and where change is imposed upon teachers without due consultation and involvement, the change may result in being unsustainable (Buck & Snook, 2020). Change involving the development of critical and creative thinkers in Indian classrooms seems an almost insurmountable problem following years of instructional and rote teaching and learning. When teachers feel insecure in their teaching, they tend to revert to the way that they themselves were taught, so change can be a long time coming. As stated earlier, the size and scale when implementing change is difficult to overcome within an Indian context. It was possible to see that in Case Study Five, students had advantages over the students in other schools. Arts were encouraged and students were working at a sophisticated level from my observations, but this would not apply to most schools in India.

While dance may not be the only way to teach or encourage creative and critical thinking, it is certainly an excellent way in which to engage kinaesthetic learning. Associate Professor Rajshree Vaishnav's (2013) study revealed that,

> Kinesthetic learning style was found to be more prevalent than visual and auditory learning styles among secondary school students. There exists a positive high correlation between kinesthetic learning style and academic achievement.
>
> (p. 1)

While there has been a continuous flurry of interest since Howard Gardner (1983) proposed that students learn through seven different intelligences, it seems that the bodily-kinaesthetic intelligence is least understood by educators. Ren (2013) examined several different studies on the dominant learning styles of students where kinaesthetic learning generally scored highly. Ren (2013) cites Karp (2003) who found that 45% of pilots were kinaesthetic learners. While my research here is broad due to the constraints of this chapter, there are many students who are either kinaesthetic or multi-sensory learners. At this point in time, educational establishments continue to focus on "a tradition of schooling that places a premium on the uniform attainment of prescribed goals as an ideal" (Eisner, 2004, p.35).

The students involved in the documented case studies enjoyed their learning. According to Lumby (2010) "Children learn better when they are excited and engaged" (p.3). Over many years, in both western and eastern contexts, learning was considered something very serious that required silence and concentration. There are times when this might be appropriate, but in general if students are enjoying themselves, they are more likely to retain what they have learned.

Another aspect of learning creatively through the arts is the amount of group work that students engage in. Students learn from others as they engage in group problem solving, finding new ways to process information. The group members realise that they will not be able to succeed on their own, that they need a consensus to be reached, and so they engage in a process to reach that consensus. In doing so they not only come to understand the value of others' creative processes, but they learn a great deal about themselves and others, assisting in the development of the whole person.

Although the five case studies reflect one-off individual events, it was clear that everyone involved engaged in critical and creative thinking. Students (and teachers) worked together well in groups to problem solve and achieve an "end result". Most importantly, everyone enjoyed themselves, and I suspect that if I asked them now "What did you learn in that dance workshop you did four years ago?" they would be able to tell me.

References

Amans, D., (2017) *An Introduction to Community Dance Practice*, McMillan Education, Palgrave, London.
Appel, M., (2006) Arts integration across the curriculum. *Leadership*, 36(2), 14–17.
Boden, M., (1998) What is creativity? In Mithen, S. (Ed.), *Creativity in Human Evolution and Prehistory*, Routledge, London.
Bruner, J., Goodnow, J., Austin, G., (1956) *A Study of Thinking*, Wiley, New York.
Buck, R., Snook, B., (2020a) How might creative learning through dance support resilience? *Journal of Human Behavior in the Social Environment*, 30(3), 289–305.
Buck, R., Snook, B., (2020b) Reality bites: Implementing arts integration. *Research in Dance Education*, 21(1), 98–115.
Buck, R., Snook, B., (2016) Teaching the arts across the curriculum: Meanings policy and practice. *International Journal of Education and the Arts*, 17, 29. Retrieved from http://www.ijea.org/v17n29/.
Buck, R., Snook, B., Martin, B., (2020) Arts integration in Northland, New Zealand: A case of socially empowered learning. *Journal of Artistic and Creative Education*, Melbourne.5–11.
Burnaford, G., Aprill, A., Weiss, C., (2013) *Renaissance in the Classroom: Arts Integration and Meaningful Learning*, Chicago Arts Partnerships in Education (Cape), Lawrence Erlbaum Associates Inc., Mahwah, NJ.
Darling-Hammond, L., (1999) *Professional Development for Teachers: Setting the Stage for Learning from Teaching*, The Centre for the Future of Teaching and Learning, Santa Cruz, CA.
Dello-Iacovo, B., (2009) Curriculum reform and 'quality education' in China: An overview. *International Journal of Educational Development*, 29(3), 241–249.
Denzin, N., Lincoln, Y. (Eds), (2008) *The Landscape of Qualitative Research*, Sage Publications Inc., Thousand Oaks, CA.
Eisner, E., (2004) Multiple intelligences: Its tensions and possibilities. *Teachers College Record*, 106(1), 31–39.
Fasko, D., (2001) Education and creativity. *Creativity Research Journal*, 13(3/4), 317–327.
Fisher, R., (2004) *Unlocking Creativity: Teaching across the Curriculum* (Fisher, R., Williams, M., eds.), David Fulton Publishers, London.
Fosnot, C., (2005) *Constructivism: Theory, Perspectives, and Practice*, Teachers College Press, New York.

Gardner, H., (1983) *Frames of Mind: The Theory of Multiple Intelligences*, Basic Books, New York.

Gullatt, D., (2008) Enhancing student learning through arts integration: Implications for the profession. *The High School Journal*, 91(4), 12–25.

Karp, R., (2003) *Maximizing Learning and Knowledge Transfer*, Author, Tempe, AZ.

Keun, L., Hunt, P., (2006) Creative dance: Singapore children's creative thinking and problem-solving responses. *Research in Dance Education*, 7(1), 35–65.

Klein, E., Riordan, M., (2009) Putting professional development into practice: A framework for how teachers in expeditionary learning schools implement professional development. *Seeking New Visions and Possibilities*, 36(4), 61–80.

Loughran, J., (2002) Effective reflective practice: In search of meaning in learning about teaching. *Journal of Teacher Education*, 53(1), 33–43.

Lumby, J., (2010) Enjoyment and learning: Policy and secondary school learners' experience in England. *British Educational Research Journal*, 37(2), 247–264.

McKeown, D., Brindle, M., Harris, K., Sandmel, K., Steinbrecher, T. D., Graham, S., Lane, K. L., Oakes, W. P., (2019) Teachers' voices: Perceptions of effective professional development and class-wide implementation of self-regulated strategy development in writing. *American Educational Research Journal*, 56(3), 753–791.

Martin, B. H, Snook, B., Buck, R., (2018) Creating the dance and dancing creatively: Exploring the liminal space of choreography for emergence. *Journal of the Canadian Association for Curriculum Studies*, 16(1), 162–174.

NEP, (2020) Policy document released by Government of India. Retrieved fromhttps://www.education.gov.in/sites/upload_files/mhrd/files/NEP_Final_English.pdf.

O'Neill, J., (2000) Fads and fireflies: The difficulties of sustaining change. *Educational Leadership*, 57(7), 6–9, Retrieved November 16, 2020, from https://learntechlib.org/p/90602/.

Rambo, C., Ellis, C., (2020) *Autoethnography*, Wiley Online Library, Accessed https://doi.org/10.1002/9781405165518.wbeosa082.pub2.

Ren, G., (2013) Which learning style is most effective in learning Chinese as a second language. *Journal of International Education Research*, 9(1), 21–32.

Richards, R., (2007) Everyday creativity and the arts. *World Futures*, 63(7), 500–525.

Silverstein, L., Layne, S., (2010) Defining arts integration, the John F. Kennedy centre for the performing arts, U.S Department of Education and the Dana Foundation. Washington. U.S.

Rinne, L., Gregory, E., Yarmolinskaya, J., (2011) Why arts integration improves long-term retention. *Mind, Brain, and Education*, 5(2), 89–96.

Snook, B., (2012) Someone like us: Meanings and contexts informing the delivery of dance in New Zealand primary classrooms, Unpublished PhD thesis, University of Auckland.

Snook, B., (2021) *Using the Arts across the Curriculum: Arts Integration Lesson Plans*, NZCER Press. Wellington.

Sriprakash, A., (2006) *Pedagogies for Development: The Politics and Practice of Child-Centred Education in India*, Springer, Dordrecht Heidelberg, London.

Sternberg, R., (2001) What is the common thread of creativity? It's dialectic relation to intelligence and wisdom. *American Psychologist*, 56(4), 360–362.

Tuhiwai Smith, L., (2012) *Decolonising Methodologies: Research and Indigenous Peoples*, 2nd edition, Zed Books Ltd., London. ISBN 978 1 8481 3950 3, 256 pp

Vaishnav, R., (2013) Learning style and academic achievement of secondary school students. *Voice of Research*, 1(4), 1–4.

Whitworth, B., Chiu, J., (2015) Professional development and teacher change: The missing leadership link. *Journal of Science Teacher Education*, 26(2), 121–137.

12 Echoing the rhythm
Voices of school dance teachers

Juri Gogoi Konwar

Introduction

Dance is not a compulsory subject in the school curriculum of Assam, and hence, there are few dance teachers in government schools. Any subject teacher with a basic knowledge of dance may end up teaching dance in school. In certain cases, the school authorities arrange for dance teachers as per their requirement on a contractual basis, but in some private schools, dance is taught from primary school up to the high school by a designated dance teacher. Generally however, there is little or no dance in schools, therefore most dance in the Brahmaputra Valley is offered by teachers who have their own dance schools where interested students can take private lessons. The Indian government's New Education Policy 2020 aims to foster languages, arts, and culture in the school curriculum. Students will be supported in choosing a balance between different courses for themselves so as to develop their own creative, artistic, cultural, and academic paths. The hiring of leading local artists as master instructors in various subjects has been recommended by the 2020 policy so that there is an accurate inclusion of traditional knowledge systems including tribal and other local knowledge throughout the school curriculum. The following voices provide an insight into dance in Assamese schools.

Sri Khagen Kalita

Sri Khagen Kalita is a Sattriya nritya (dance) teacher in Assam Jatiya Vidyalaya, Noonmati, Guwahati, Assam. He is a recipient of the prestigious Senior Fellowship from the Ministry of Culture, Government of India. He runs the Lohor Dance Academy, a private dance school for Sattriya nritya.

I was born in the Bamokhata Sattra, in Pathshala within the Barpeta district of Assam, and so I was exposed to the *Sattra* at a very early age. When I was studying in class 6 (ten years of age), my Guru Sangeet Natak Akademi Awardee Ramakrishna Talukdar created a learning atmosphere for teaching us music and *Sattriya nritya* (dance). Every year, we went to Guwahati to take part in the *bhaona* (theatre festival of plays) such as "Rama Vijay", and "Rukmini Haran". We would only return after taking part in several events.

After I passed higher secondary school, I was admitted into the Rudra Barua Music College in Guwahati and graduated with a Bachelor of Music degree.

In 2003, there was an advertisement for a *Sattriya nritya* teacher in Assam's Jatiya Vidyalaya, Noonmati (a private sector school). I applied for that job and was selected even though there were many talented candidates for the post. I took the job and started my journey as a dance teacher. I have been working as a *Sattriya nritya* teacher there for the past 18 years. I only teach *Sattriya nritya* but I am trained in Kathak as well.

In 2020, the State Government of Assam introduced dance as an elective subject in matriculation for school students studying in classes 9 and 10 (aged 14–15). Every year my students passed their exams with the highest marks in the subject across the region and within the state. I believe the reason for this outstanding success is the curriculum of Assam's Jatiya Vidyalaya School which includes *Sattriya nritya* as an elective subject from class 2 (aged 6). It is compulsory to pass the school exams in dance at every year level just like any other regular subject. Currently, there are 180 students from class 2 to 10 pursuing the *Sattriya nritya* elective in the school. We have two *Sattriya nritya* teachers in the school and we have classes every Saturday, so we have divided the classes between us.

We have ensured that the basic syllabus of *Sattriya nritya* is delivered in a gradual manner from class 2 to 10. The students are taught *Sattriya nritya* as a practical subject till class 5 but a theory paper is also included in the syllabus from class 6 onwards. We cover the *gayan* (musician), *bayan* (drummer), *taal-maan* (rhythmic note), *haj-par* (costume), *baidyo-jontro* (musical instrument), *aa-alonkar* (jewellery), and Srimanta Sankaradeva's life history in the theory paper. We have designed the school syllabus in such a way that we can cover the basics even though we have only one class per week.

It gives me immense pleasure to see that my students are learning with utmost dedication. They are so involved in the process, and they often ask me, "Sir, why did you choose dance?" I believe that these questions come from their understanding of the traditional societal norms where people choose medicine or engineering as career options and not something like dance; it is even more unlikely for a man to choose something as unconventional as dance. I always tell them that training to be a doctor, engineer, or something else is rewarding if you learn with full discipline and concentration. It doesn't matter what kind of work you are doing if you love your work and keep pursuing it seriously. I have been following this mantra throughout my life.

Students often keep up with their dance even after finishing school. Some of my students have gone on to do the *gunin* (seven years diploma in *Sattriya*) under Sangeet Sattra in Guwahati. However, most of my students follow their own career paths by taking admission in the prestigious Cotton College for their higher education. They have the choice of seeking admission under Cotton College's music quota policy (which includes dance) and in doing so students benefit from their prolific background in *Sattriya*. This is a major advantage in having *Sattriya* in the school curriculum.

As a *Sattriya nritya* teacher, I have observed physical exercise in the form of *mati-akhora*. *Mati-akhoras* are ground exercises and are considered the basic grammatical forms of *Sattriya* dance. They not only help students to remain healthy but they also increase their concentration power. *Mati-akhoras* are the foundations to set up healthy learners; physically, mentally, and spiritually. Some of these *mati-akhoras* are similar to some yoga steps which are used to help the students maintain physical and mental discipline. In my experience, most of the students who learn *Sattriya nritya* have managed to achieve extremely good academic results. My belief is that dance improves their back posture which helps increase their concentration while ridding themselves of laziness, thereby enhancing their productivity. In fact, last year the Ministry of Cultural Affairs gave me a Senior Fellowship for two years to study *mati-akhora*. The objective of my study is to research how *mati-akhora* is being used to benefit students in *Sattriya nritya* and to find new ways to improve *mati-akhora*.

Apart from teaching this classical dance form, I teach semi-classical dance that includes *mati-akhora*, that is accompanied by the *baidyo-jontra* (musical instrument) and *khol* (a percussion instrument traditionally made of clay). I dance, play the *khol*, and even sing the *borgeet*. The *borgeets* are Vaishnava devotional songs which were composed by Srimanta Sankaradeva and Sri Madhavadeva in the 15th to 16th centuries and they are required for *Sattriya nritya* as delivered to my students.

I also take private classes in five different dance schools during the weekends. Two of these private schools belong to someone else and three are my own. One of my schools, the Lohor Academy, is run in my home premises. This school is completely mine, and currently there are around 35 students. I have been running the Lohor Academy for more than 18 years now. Most of my students are young Assamese girls, but students of different faiths and tribes are also showing an interest in learning *Sattriya*, and although I teach a few boys, they are generally not showing an inclination towards *Sattriya* dance.

Mainly, I am a *Sattriya* teacher, but I cater to the needs of my students who might have approached me with a request to choreograph a dance to music. I oblige their request by choreographing a dance using *mati-akhora* as the base. I make certain that the students keep in mind the dress code for *Sattriya nritya*. The dress code needs to be respected as the entire dance form is run on the principles of *bhakti bhabona* (devotion). The *bhaakti bhabona* runs on *guru–shishya parampara*, a tradition of spiritual relationship and mentoring where teachings are transmitted from a *guru* (teacher) to a *shishya* (disciple), wherein the disciples touch the feet of their guru before they begin their practice to pay their respects. Such principles teach discipline and focus to the students from a very young age.

Recently, many schools in Assam have appointed dance teachers who specialise in *Sattriya nritya* but these teachers do not enjoy the freedom of teaching *Sattriya* solely. These teachers are bound to fulfil the needs of the school programmes and forgo the formal curriculum of *Sattriya nritya*. This kind of curriculum diversity makes it difficult to emulate the *Sattriya nritya* curriculum in the schools.

Sri Binay Bora

Sri Binay Bora is an eminent Bihu dance teacher and dhol exponent. He is an active member of the Bihu Sangrakshan Samiti, Assam, a committee that works towards the preservation of the authenticity of Bihu.

I hail from Da Parbatia, a quaint little village 1.5 km west of Tezpur town in the Sonitpur district, Assam. From the young age of eight years, I was attracted towards the cultural environment in my native village where young boys and girls regularly practised and participated in various dance and music programmes including the *Bihu* dance and *Bihu* songs. Gradually, I started learning *Bihu* from them.

In due course of time, I started teaching *Bihu* myself and organised my own *Bihu dol* (*Bihu* troupe) with my students. I received my formal training as a *ghai bihua* (master *Bihu* dancer) from the *Bihu* Sangrakshan Samiti, Assam, and after being recognised as a *ghai bihua* I started working towards teaching the *Bihu nach* (*Bihu* dance), *naam* (bihu song), *bhangima* (body gesture), *dhulor sapor* (drum beats) to my students. This is how I started the journey of my life.

I began my training by learning how to play the *dhol* from one of my neighbours who happened to be a *dhulia* (a drummer) who used to perform in the marriage ceremonies held in our village. I was enchanted by the mesmerising drum beats and the *Bihu* performances of my elder brothers and sisters who were part of the *Bihu dol*. Mostly, I learnt the *Bihu* songs and dance at home from my grandparents. For me, *Bihu* has always been in our blood, it is as old as the River Brahmaputra.

I also teach *Sattriya* dance. I picked up this dance as my village followed a *Sattriya Samaj* (society with *Vaishnavite* faith) back in those days. For over a hundred years, the Sankaradeva's Rukmini Haran *bhaona* performance has been organised annually in our village on the eve of the *Kaati* month (15 October to 15 November). This is an age-old tradition in the village and there is a strong belief that if this ritual is not performed on the exact date, it will bring great devastation to the people of the village. In this *bhaona*, I first learned to play the *khol* followed by the *geet*, *maat*, and *bol* (codified beats and rhythms) of the instrument from the elderly *bayans* (drummers). I took formal training of *Sattriya* dance from different *sattra* institutions in Lakhimpur, Majuli, and Barpeta. Apart from this, I have trained in *sutradhari nach* (narrator's dance) and *dashabatar nritya* (a dance that depicts ten incarnations of Lord Vishnu). I try to teach whatever I have learned to my students, who are the upcoming generations of our society. I teach all of the musical instruments associated with *Bihu* like drum (*dhol*), horn pipes (*pepa*), jew's harp (*gogona*), flute (*banhi*), cymbal (*taal*), bamboo slapstick (*toka*), and a crescent-shaped small indigenous instrument made of clay (*xutuli*).

As an artist, I have had the experience of accompanying renowned music maestro Dr. Bhupen Hazarika. In the year 1976, I played the *dhol* on the stage of Nehru Maidan in Tezpur. I was part of the chorus for revered artists Ajit Sinha, Rubi Sinha, and Dr. Bhupen Hazarika. When Atal Bihari Bajpai became the Prime Minister of India and visited Assam for the first time, it was my *Bihu* troupe, "Bishnu Jyoti *Bihuwa Dol*", that was entrusted with the responsibility of receiving him at the airport. I have also performed *Bihu* at the Rashtrapati Bhawan (the Indian President's House) when Shankar Dayal Sharma was the President of India.

Every year I am invited to conduct various *Bihu akhora* (*Bihu* dance workshops) just ahead of the Rangali *Bihu*. Due to extreme modernisation, we seem to have lost our traditional *Bihu* art form, but I am trying to revive the forgotten beats of *dhol*, through dance steps, hand movements, body language, and gestures as much as possible. I am trying my level best to transfer my knowledge of this folk dance tradition to my students, the future of our society. I am faced with the challenge of translating the theoretical aspects of *Bihu* to the English language as most of my students are English medium educated, and because of this they have a poor grasp of their mother tongue, Assamese. This causes multiple problems with the main essence of the art form. Therefore, it is my earnest request to all the students and their parents to educate themselves in their mother tongue so that they can learn *Bihu* in its authentic form.

The Coronavirus pandemic situation has put a halt to most of our efforts. But despite the lockdown, maintaining all Covid-19 protocol, along with my wife, I have trained several enthusiastic boys and girls from our village in *Bihu* dance, playing *dhol*, *pepa*, and *gogona* with the motto of propagating the traditional moral values among the children of the new generation.

Priyanka Kalita

Priyanka Kalita completed her post-graduate education in Cultural Studies at Tezpur University, Assam (India). She has participated in several dance programmes organised by the Government of India through the NEZCC (North-East Zonal Cultural Centre). She has travelled to almost all the states of India and abroad representing Assam.

I grew up in my maternal grandmother's home. There was a lady in the immediate neighbourhood who used to teach *diha naam*. *Diha naam* is a type of congregational prayer derived from Vaishnava religious scriptures. She also taught *dashabatar nritya*, a dance that depicts the ten incarnations of Lord Krishna. When I was very young, the lady approached my parents to ask if she could train me. There have been absolutely no dancers in our entire family, so naturally, my parents had never even thought about letting me take dance classes. In fact, they had never felt that I had any inclination towards becoming a dancer, as I had never displayed any interest in dancing. But because of that lady, I was allowed to dance and to learn the *dashabatar nritya*.

The good lady had actually approached my parents to train me for the *dashabatar nritya* for a dance competition which was organised by the *Dikhoupuriya samaj* (a cultural body) during the *Bihu* festival. Therefore, with my mother's permission, I entered the competition and even managed to get the third prize. At that time, I was only five years old. I was in kindergarten and had not even started going to school. Bagging a prize at such a young age made my parents very happy and they decided to allow me to take up formal dance classes.

When I started primary school, my mother saw a banner which read "Learn Bharatnatyam on Sundays". My mother discussed this with my father, and they decided that these dance classes would be very convenient. That is how I started taking formal dance classes in my school. I used to go to school for studying from Monday to Saturday and then again on Sunday for my dance classes. Since all the classes were taking place in my school, I used to think that the dance classes were also part of my school curriculum. I was unaware of the fact that these classes were not a part of the regular school curriculum and were only conducted within the school premises as it was large enough for dance classes. As a result of this, I took my dance very seriously, focusing on the dance classes as much as I did on the Maths and Science classes taught in school.

When I reached my 5th standard, my dance teacher started teaching *Sattriya nritya* and I enrolled in these classes. By then, I had also started learning *Bihu* dance during the month of *Bohag* (spring). Every Sunday, my schedule became such that I used to learn Bharatanatyam from 9.00 am to 12.00 pm and then *Sattriya nritya* from 12.00 pm to 2.00 pm. This is how dance became an integral part of my life. Eventually, I completed my training in Bharatnatyam to the 9th standard and practised *Sattriya nritya* until the 12th standard.

Dance is one of my greatest strengths. When my father passed away after my high school examinations my family was suddenly under extreme financial stress. I was offered several jobs as a Bharatanatyam teacher as I already had a *visharad* (Bachelor's degree) in Bharatanatyam. My family was completely dependent on the income from my Bharatanatyam classes which was around INR6000–6500 per month. I started giving private dance lessons by going to my pupils' homes every day after school hours while running multiple dance classes in private dance schools on Sundays.

Dance has been an important asset in my life. After high school, I sought admission to a good higher secondary school, but my high school results were not very good. I couldn't fulfil the minimum eligibility requirements for admission to that school. Fortunately, when I approached the school authorities and showed them all the medals and certificates that I had won while participating in various dance competitions, I was finally admitted into that school as I was a *visharad* in Bharatanatyam and a practicing *Sattriya* dancer. In my higher secondary examination, I managed to get only 75% which was again not enough to pursue a major in Economics from the prestigious Cotton College in Guwahati, Assam. By then however, I had come to know about the ECA (Extra-Curricular Activity) quota at Cotton College and so I applied for my admission through this quota. I was selected as the best dancer from the 60 students shortlisted for auditions from a pool of about 600 applications under this quota. Therefore, I was given the opportunity to pursue my undergraduate studies in the Department of Economics, Cotton College, under the ECA quota.

When I moved to Guwahati to pursue my higher education, my mother was struggling to make ends meet. She could only afford to send my hostel fees from what she earned. I started teaching dance in different dance schools across the city after my college classes were finished. As a student under the ECA quota, I was given the opportunity to dance in various cultural events in both corporate and government functions, for which I was also paid a decent remuneration. I also represented Assam in various regional, state, and national level dance programmes organised by the Government of India through the NEZCC (North East Zonal Cultural Centre). Basically, it was dance which made it possible for me to sustain my family as well as my studies.

After my graduation, I was admitted to Tezpur University for Post-Graduate study in the Department of Cultural Studies. During this time, I was associated with the Dance Club called Nrityangan where I was a dance instructor. I also continued taking private dance classes at the university campus so that I had a regular income to sustain my expenses till I completed my post-graduate degree.

Currently, I am working as a school teacher. In the selection schema for this job, there was a bonus criterion for national or international representation. When I applied for this job, I got an additional ten marks due to my participation in the national as well as international dance events. Dance has even helped me to gain employment. I joined the school as an Assistant Teacher. Assistant teachers are not given any specific subjects to teach but have to work according to the requirement of the subject teachers. Since the principal of the school knows about my dance background, he has asked me to teach dance as many students of the school are very interested in learning dance but have been unable to find appropriate guidance. Occasionally, he also asks me to prepare some dance performances by students for different cultural events and farewell ceremonies held in the school.

Prior to this, I was working in a Kendriya Vidyalaya – I in Solmara, Tezpur, where I gathered ample experience in teaching dance to young children. I noted that some students are hyperactive in class whereas some have typically slow physical movements. When all the children are taught dance together, it brings them to the same energy levels despite their inherent differences and helps them understand the importance of learning step by step.

In my experience, dance helps the students in improving their flexibility while allowing good physical and mental development. I believe that dance can do wonders for young children. Dance connects the mind, the heart, and the soul thereby enabling the dancer to feel good.

I would like to mention that I mostly teach folk dances of Assam to younger students. Through dance, these children are introduced to different lyrics, rhythms, and the unique attires worn by different tribes, each having their own distinct textile designs or motifs. Each tribe has different folk instruments that are used while performing a particular dance form. In a multicultural classroom, I have observed that students are very enthusiastic about learning information about new cultures, and seem open to adopting different dance steps and music. It seems as though these children have learned so many new things through dance, that may not be obvious to some adults.

I also worked in Kendriya Vidyalaya – II School in Goroimari, Tezpur, for about three months. Although I didn't get much time to develop relationships with the students while I was working in that school, there was a cultural week called "Ek Bharat Shresth Bharat". For a week, the school organised various events based on the culture of an Indian state other than their home state. Our school was assigned the state of Haryana. During that week, the school organised dance, drama, singing, and literary events all of which were related to the state of Haryana. I was asked to prepare the dance event, but I had no clue about Haryanvi dance. Luckily, the students as well as the teachers of the school come from various parts of India and there was one teacher who hailed from the state of Haryana. He helped me in teaching the Haryana dance forms to the students. So even though we were in Assam, we successfully choreographed a Haryanvi dance performance that was performed by approximately 150 students. I think such events help the students in understanding other Indian states through dance forms, clothing, and music.

Personally, I am very much interested in doing research in the field of dance studies. But right now, my family needs me. At the moment, I am working in the capacity of a teacher, but I aspire to do a Ph.D in dance studies. I think dance is a very broad field and it includes many different things that are still unexplored. I want to give back to dance what it has given me at every crucial juncture of my life.

Mitali Borthakur

Mitali Borthakur is a well-known dance teacher. She has her own dance schools in Tezpur and Nagaon. She has worked in Kendriya Vidyalaya I and II in Tezpur on a contractual basis. While representing the school, her students have been able to win laurels in various dance competitions.

I was inclined towards dance from a very young age. In simple words, I loved to dance, so, I joined the Kalaguru Sangeet Vidyalaya (dance school) in Tezpur and started my formal training. My Guru, Sri Tileswar Tamuly, was the first person to teach me the basics of *Sattriya nritya*. I persevered throughout my training and went on to receive my Bachelor of Music degree in *Sattriyanritya* from Kalaguru Sangeet Vidyalaya and my Bachelor of Music degree in Kathak under the guidance of Sri Shanti Charan Dasgupta who was a renowned Kathak dancer from Tezpur.

Even after completing my formal training, I took further training in Kathak from Ms. Moloya Nidhi, an eminent dancer from Guwahati, and *Sattriya nritya* from Padmashree Bayanacharya Ghanakanta Bora Borbayan. My parents were always very keen on my learning dance, and that is why they left no stone unturned to help me reach my goals. I have been very fortunate to have been born in a family who have relentlessly supported my dance.

I started teaching dance way back in 1999 from a small place in Nagaon, Assam. Today, I run a dance school named Shreejani Nritya Mahavidyalaya which has several centres in different parts of Assam. More than 300 students learn different dance forms in our school and go on to obtain their B. Music degrees. As a formal learning centre, we are affiliated to Assam Sattra Mahasabha for *Sattriya nritya* and Lucknow Bhatkhande Sangeet Vidyapith for Kathak. Therefore, we have theory classes alongside practical dance lessons as these are necessary for a student to obtain a conventional B. Music degree. We ensure that the prescribed syllabus and books suggested by the respective systemic organisations are religiously followed. Typically, a student has to study dance for about six years to obtain a formal degree in dance.

In my schools, we follow the correct dance curriculum for systematic learning. Apart from this, I encourage my students to try creative dance and supplement it with new *Sattriya* choreography using the music of revered artists such as Rupkonwar Jyoti Prasad Agarwala, Kalaguru Bishnu Prasad Rava, and Sudhakantha Bhupen Hazarika. I do this so that my students can understand the various *rasas* where the dancer can evoke different emotions through aesthetic dance movements emoted through the eyes, facial gestures, and body movements. As an institution, we have the good fortune of training students from different parts of India who aspire to learn dance from our dance schools but it is particularly overwhelming to see students from different states like who want to learn the *Sattriya* dance form of Assam.

As a teacher, I have always tried to motivate the students who are weak in learning dance. Many times, I have seen that there are some students who are irregular in their dance classes as they feel that they are not good enough to learn dance. So, I particularly try to encourage such students and give them more attention in class. I often praise them even for the minimal progress that they manage to achieve so as to boost their morale. In my experience, this method of motivating students works wonders and these students become much more regular and enthusiastic in the subsequent dance classes.

Our school organises several dance competitions within the school to encourage our students to perform their own dance movements, as it helps us to keep a check on the progress of all the students. Teaching the same dance moves day in and day out makes the class monotonous and stagnant, therefore I also conduct one-day acting classes when teaching the *rasas* which are important in any classical dance form. This allows some fun with physical activity to keep up the spirit of the class. In this way the students also improve their ability to work in a group.

In all these years, the students who have come to learn dance from me have always been very enthusiastic about dance. They take dance as seriously as their studies in any other school subject. I have witnessed that most of my students get good grades in school and have never complained that their grades in school have slipped due to learning dance. In fact, I have had many students who have gone on to become successful professionals in their respective fields of work.

For a short period of time, I worked as a dance teacher in Kendriya Vidyalaya – I (Solmara, Tezpur) and Kendriya Vidyalaya – II (Goroimari, Tezpur), respectively. It was a contractual job of about four to five months where I was entrusted with the responsibility of preparing their students for various dance competitions in the regional cluster, as well as for national competitions as per the theme for that year. Generally, the theme for such competitions is folk dance of any state apart from their home state. This is done with the intention of generating awareness about the different cultures of India and to promote the feeling of "Unity in Diversity". It has been observed that dance is a unique medium to spread this message because it directly impacts the psyche of a general audience. In my time at these schools, I had the experience of accompanying my students to regional and national competitions held in Kolkata and Jaipur. This allowed me to learn more about the importance of multiculturalism.

Due to the ongoing pandemic situation, it has become very difficult to conduct dance classes for my students. Since dance is very different from other school subjects, it is very complicated to conduct the online live classes. Several other factors like poor internet connectivity and lack of access to proper infrastructure make it onerous to have a class at a constant pace through the digital medium. It is required for the students to learn each and every movement made by the teachers but these challenges multiply our problems making it difficult to reach our students. We often have to keep repeating what we are trying to teach the students. Therefore, instead of having live classes, our teachers are trying to record videos and send them to the students. The students then respond by sending back their video recording of practice sessions so that we can ascertain their progress.

Dr Madhurima Goswami

Dr Madhurima Goswami is a classical dancer who is known for her proficiency in Odissi. She is a faculty member in the Department of Cultural Studies, Tezpur University, Assam. She has been practising Odissi for the past 35 years. She received her formal dance training from Odissi Gurus who were the direct bearers of the Odissi tradition. She has been an honorary member of the Advisory Committee, Sangeet Natak Akademi, New Delhi, and a recipient of the national scholarship of dance from the Government of India. She runs a dance school called Kashianth Krishnapriya Institute of Odissi dance. Presently she is working on a production, Doudini, as a protagonist, based on the folk culture of the Bodos, an ethnic group of Assam.

When I was in school, my parents took me to the Sri Jagannath temple in the Haus Khas village, New Delhi, to start my Odissi dance classes. At that time, I was not interested in dance and liked to read books or write poems instead. I had no passion for dance. Guruji Mayadhar Raut understood this. He saw a petite little girl who he believed lacked the charisma to become a dancer. One day, during the Jagannath festival, I was sitting silently in the temple and happened to experience some higher power. I was in a *chowk* position (*chowk* is a basic Odissi stance where the weight of the body is distributed equally on both the sides) when renowned dance exponent Padmashree Ranjana Gahar *didi* (sister) saw me and said something to Guruji, "*uska aankh dekhiye, aankh ka chamak dekhiye, lagta hain sakshat Jagannath ka ashirbaad hain*" (Look at her eyes, they are so bright as if she has been blessed by Lord Jagannath himself). Guruji told Gahar *didi* that even though I had the body of a dancer, I had no interest in dance. That day, Gahar *didi* empowered me with the belief that I had all the qualities of a dancer within myself.

I started taking dance very seriously and learned whatever Guruji dictated to his disciples. I vividly remember that Guruji often made us take a Jagannath *shthiti* (position) and then leave to go to the nearby market to do his shopping. We would wait in that stance for hours together and thus undergo his traditional teaching/learning process. At that time Gurus were considered as the repositories of artistic temperament and knowledge and we would religiously do as we were told. Today, I know that this initial training formed the fundamental steps for gaining power, agility, patience, and balance.

As time passed, I started feeling as though I was about to do something big, but I lacked a sense of beauty. There was a sense of great power which came from within. I would often feel a certain energy inside me when I placed my feet on the dance floor with vigour. Observing my increasing dedication towards dance, my father took me to Odisha where the Odissi dance originated and has premier institutions dedicated to the propagation of traditional art forms in music and dance. He brought me all the volumes of Natyasashtra which is a detailed treatise and handbook on dramatic art in Sanskrit. I was so engrossed in the process that I went through all these books word by word.

As I continued my dance classes, I received the National Scholarship for dance from the Government of India. Renowned actor Zohra Segal's daughter Padmashree Kiran Segal and Padmashree Madhabi Mudgal were my seniors in dance school, and there is no doubt that this school was the best learning platform for any aspiring dancer. At a certain point in time I had to leave New Delhi, so my Guruji gave me permission to train students so as to raise awareness and promote the age-old dance legacy of our revered Gurus.

After coming back to Assam, a group of students came to me and said that Odissi dance exponent Guru Kelucharan Mahapatra had suggested that they take dance classes from me. At that time, I had recently got married and joined Tezpur University as a faculty member, so I did not oblige.

In 1996, the North-East India Vice Chancellors' Meet was hosted by Tezpur University and I was requested by the Vice Chancellor to perform *Sattriya nritya* in the cultural programme; so I performed a *Sattriya* dance in that event. After my performance, the people of Tezpur came to know about me and started requesting that I start a dance school. It was then that I decided to start my own dance school and named it Kashianth Krishnapriya Institute of Odissi dance.

My teaching pedagogy is mainly based on the *guru–shishya parampara* (a tradition of spiritual relationship and mentoring where teachings are transmitted from a guru (teacher) to a *shishya* (disciple). When I start my dance class I say, "*Natyarambhe*! Now we are going to start dance. Calm down, be attentive, seek divine blessings, you are going to a different world now. When you are dancing you are not you, you transform into Radha or Krishna". Odissi is deeply spiritualistic in nature, it is through this dance form that a relationship between God and his adherents is established or performed.

As a dance teacher, I often organise Odissi dance recitals with my students. One of the senior teachers at my institute also takes *Sattriya* dance classes. She was trained under Bayan Acharya Ghanakanta Bora Borbayan and Padmashree Jatin Goswami. I am also trying to teach the various folk dances of the indigenous tribes in Assam such as the *bordoi sikla* dance, *deodhani* dance of the Bodo community, and the *tauling porota* of the Tiwa community in order to help my students understand the differences and plurality of the Assamese culture. One cannot learn *Sattriya* in isolation, as it is a mixture of various folk dances of Assam. This inclusion of musicality variety has assisted *Sattriya* with its rich tradition.

I would like to mention that CBSE (Central Board of Secondary Education, Government of India) has introduced Visual Art, Yoga, and Music as regular subjects in their recommended school curriculum and now it has included Dance as well. But why is it that Assam has always overlooked this particular area? If dance is introduced in the school curriculum from 4 to 12 years of age, the children of our state will be physically fit, dynamic, and expressive and way better in their communication skills. We hope that schools in Assam will follow the lead of other Indian states.

In the formative years, everyone wants the overall development of a child's personality. We are starting to realise however, that 2–4% of young students suffer from dyslexia. These children are slow learners and cannot cope with the average pace of their fellow students. If they are taught through movement, they are more likely to be able to learn and achieve the desired results.

In my opinion, dance is a therapy which connects the mind, the body, and the soul. Now the question is whether the people of Assam will understand the social importance of dance in the society and raise their voice for having dance as a subject in the mandatory school curriculum.

13 Dancers' voices

Gaurav Rajkhowa

Madhurima Choudhury

Madhurima Choudhury is a dancer and a leading Assamese film and television actress. She lives in Guwahati, Assam.

I grew up in an environment permeated by traditional music and dance. Belonging to a *sattra*, my father began teaching me *sattriya* dance when I was just three years old. By the time I was five, I was undergoing formal training in *borgeet* and *sattriya* dance under Prabhat Sarma and Rasheswar Saikia Barbayan, whom I consider to be my gurus. In fact, I was among the second batch of students to pass out of Rasheswar Saikia Barbayan's prestigious Sangeet Sattra music and dance school. My interest in *Bihu* was something I cultivated on my own. I would go to my father's home in Jorhat, or my mother's in Gohpur for the *Bihu* holidays every year. *Bihu* was not performed within the *sattra*, but I would be fascinated by the *sattra bhakats* performing the *husori* dance. I would often slip away to the nearby villages to watch boys and girls performing *Bihu* dances and enjoying themselves. Later, I was fortunate enough to learn the *Bihu* dance from the eminent *dhuliya* (drummer), the late Nilakantha Dutta.

I began performing *Bihu* on the stage when I was a little girl in Panbazar Girls School in Guwahati. My father was not particularly pleased about me devoting a lot of time to Bihu, to the detriment of my *sattriya* dance practice. However, people were very appreciative of my performances. One thing led to another, and when I was in secondary school, I began participating in *Bihu* dance competitions held at various venues across Guwahati. I swept the competition circuit in 1978 and 1979, winning the "Bihu Konwari" title at the prestigious Latasil Bihu stage in 1978, followed by the "Bihu Sundari" title at Bharalumukh and "Bihuwoti" at Chandmari. My crowning accomplishment was winning the "Bihu Rani" title in 1979, which had been instituted that year as the most prestigious *Bihu* dance competition in Assam. That day, up on the stage, it felt like I could not put a foot wrong. It felt like I was in some sort of trance where I did not need to make any conscious effort – every movement flowed so naturally and gracefully. My success in the "Bihu Rani" competition made me an instant celebrity of sorts and the accolades came pouring in from all directions. This also marked my last appearance in Bihu competitions – hereafter I would be invited to these as a judge rather than contestant.

It was around this time that I also fell in love when I met my future husband! Fed on a steady diet of Hindi films and romantic literature, it was a heady time for me, and soon after completing my matriculation, we got married. For the next few years, I chose to focus on my family life and public performance took a backseat. My son was born a year after our marriage, followed by my daughter.

Following a long sabbatical, I once again began accepting invitations to perform *Bihu* in the 1990s. No longer tied to the demands of the competition circuit, I spent a lot of time travelling the length and breadth of Assam, meeting folk dancers and learning about the many subtleties of the dance form. It was around this time that I put together my own *Bihu* dance troupe, Ragini, and also began helping out my father in the *sattriya* dance school that he operated out of our home. Our troupe has been fortunate enough to be invited to perform before audiences across India and the world. I was felicitated as a *Bihu* Guru in 2008 by the Government of India, and Ragini was recognised as an empanelled troupe by the Indian Council for Cultural Relations (ICCR). I also took up a few offers to act in films and appeared in a number of successful releases, including *Hiya Diya Niya* (2000), *Kanyadan* (2002), and *Bidhata* (2003).

Bihu competitions these days are dime a dozen and everyone dances *Bihu*. And yet, nowadays even a prestigious competition will have, say, 15 participants. When I became the *Bihu* Rani in 1979, there were 75 competitors, and the selection process went on for three days! The main reason for the decline in both the quality and number of competitors is that the format has changed quite a bit. In most *Bihu* dance competitions, the performers are also required to sing as they dance. The song is merely meant to be an accompaniment. In the last few years, I have noticed a strange trend, that even in a dance competition, the judges place great emphasis on the contestant's singing ability. But there are many girls even in my own troupe who are excellent dancers, but not very good singers. This places them at a disadvantage when they are being judged alongside another who might sing very well but is not a great dancer.

Another thing that often discourages girls from participating in the competitions is the trend of judges asking the contestants questions, as in a beauty pageant. While it would seem justified to ask the contestant about the particular item she has presented on stage, many judges these days like to put the performer in a spot by asking them something really obscure, which an amateur performer can hardly be expected to know. This turns the dance competition into a scholastic affair, and the focus shifts from being able to dance, to knowing about dance. And finally, many judges are biased towards contestants who are conventionally "good looking", much to the detriment of the others.

Together, these factors have created a situation where mediocre dancers come to be recognised as the new standard of performance, and in time they will be passing on their misconceptions to youngsters who look up to them as experts. What had been a problem restricted to the *Bihu* stage has now snowballed into a generalised cultural decline. I feel the only way to intervene in this is to conduct more and more workshops where young dancers can be taught the proper technique, but also encouraged to inculcate a more nuanced approach to interpreting Bihu dance. Since my return to public life, I have dedicated much time and effort to conducting such workshops. Every year I come in touch with about 3,000–4,000 children and I take this aspect of my work very seriously. Our troupe also conducts workshops outside Assam, and has been invited to Delhi, London, and Birmingham.

In our performance repertoire, Ragini has sought to strike a balance between tradition and innovation. One of our most experimental efforts was to perform *Rama Vijaya*, a traditional bhaona dance-drama with an all-women cast. We also sought to introduce some innovations like double stages and ramps, and made extensive use of lighting, colour, and sound effects.

Dr Prasanna Gogoi

A veterinarian by profession, Dr. Prasanna Gogoi is an accomplished Bihu artiste and ethnomusicologist. He lives in Guwahati, Assam.

My father is from Konwargaon, North Lakhimpur, and my mother is from Dhakuakhana, but I was born and brought up in Ziro in Arunachal Pradesh, where my father was posted as a government employee. I have really fond memories of our time in Ziro. Located near the main bus stand, our house was always alive with visiting guests and cultural gatherings of song, dance, and poetry. Both my parents were active in local cultural activities and always encouraged me to explore my musical talents. During the *Bihu* holidays we would return to our parents' homes and I would spend my days with the local youths, performing *Bihu* from house to house.

I joined the College of Veterinary Sciences, Guwahati, in 1991 and immediately took to the local cultural scene. I avidly participated in college competitions, playing the pepa (a wind instrument made from buffalo horn) as part of a *Bihu* folk dance group. Before long the judges began to take notice, as my style and repertoire were quite different from the usual fare presented by most Guwahati-based pepa players. In 1993, I was invited to join the Rangpuria Silpi Samaj Bihu Dal by two giants of the *Bihu* scene in Guwahati – Dilip Phukan and Mukut Bora. That year, I was judged as the best pepa player in a number of *Bihu* competitions across Guwahati, including the prestigious *Latasil Bihu* competition. It is a bittersweet feeling that for the next 12–13 years, I did not get to go home for the *Bihu* festivities, instead performing at and judging various *Bihu* events in Guwahati. From

1995 onwards, I also began to travel abroad with the Rangpuria Silpi Samaj Bihu Dal. To date, I have performed in 27 countries around the world. In 2003, the Government of India recognised me as a *Bihu* Guru – at the time the youngest person to have been thus honoured. I am also a member of the Sangeet Natak Akademi's advisory board for North-East India.

Each community's dances represent an aspect of their unique culture – be it in their attire, jewellery, or rhythmic patterns. Many tribal communities across North-East India have been able to preserve their authentic folk dance forms. But I cannot say the same for Assam. I feel that commercial pressures here have forced performers to introduce too many contemporary elements in the folk forms. For instance, one would invariably come across folk dance performances that use recorded music tracks rather than musicians playing live. In such situations, it is convenient to lay the blame squarely on the performers. But the fact remains that they are often forced to make such compromises on account of event organisers. The current trend of inviting a folk group for a "cultural evening" on the side-line of some conference, trade expo, or sports event has meant that organisers see them merely as "fillers", and feel no responsibility towards the dance form itself. With most of them unwilling to bear the extra cost of musicians to accompany the dance troupe, it is ultimately the performer who must accommodate their performance to the available budget.

No doubt, much of the spontaneity and beauty of folk dance forms is lost when they are adapted to the confines of the proscenium stage. Not only must the basic rhythms and movement patterns be modified, the dances also need to be squeezed into whatever time is allotted to the performance. Moreover, when a dance is a part of a more elaborate choreographed performance – where it is preceded and followed by other items – the entry and exit for each segment must also be tailored to maintain the overall flow of the programme.

At the same time, folk dancers are not entirely without blame. In an effort to stand out in the sea of *Bihu* performers, they are not averse to include all sorts of bizarre acrobatics and sensation in their performances. Worse, there seems today a complete disregard for the traditional conventions of dressing and attire. It is no longer a surprise to see a dancer performing Bihu wearing a *Bodo aronai* or *dokhona* – anything goes, as long as it all evokes "ethnic culture" in some vague way, with utter disregard for the cultural meanings associated with these elements of folk culture. Audiences also seem to enjoy this, all in the name of novelty and experimentation. I must confront these dilemmas every time I choreograph a folk dance programme. For instance, in 2019, I was the choreographer and music director of the Rashtriya Sanskriti Mahotsav, where I had to bring together folk dances from 22 states across India.

One of the major obstacles to further development of folk music instruments in *Bihu* has been the lack of standardisation – in terms of instrument design, construction, size, and materials. As early as 1993, I was constructing and tuning my own pepas. As I began to record in studios, I explored the possibility of developing notation for various folk instruments so that they may be suitably harmonised in a studio as well as live performance environment. Out of my experiences in recording folk instruments in the studio, I also began to study the effects of humidity and weather conditions upon the acoustic properties of instruments. This is something that I had first encountered when we tried to use the bamboo "gogona" (jaw harp) in a studio setting. The change in humidity levels would often shift the pitch, which caused serious difficulties when it was paired with other instruments like the *banhi* (flute) or *dhol* (drum).

I had tried to get around the problem by designing a steel gogona – an experiment that, I am proud to say, met with great success. My interest in folk music instruments eventually led to a junior research fellowship from the Ministry of Culture in 2005, as I sought to explore the possibilities of improving the acoustics of the "been", a traditional bow-and-string instrument. This fellowship allowed me the opportunity to develop a new 25-stringed instrument, the "hansa been".

In 2014, I received a senior research fellowship from the Ministry of Culture to work on the semantics and semiotics of *Bihu* dance. My research looked at the *bhangima* – or, vocabulary of gestures – in *Bihu* dance. I sought to systematise all the traditional steps of the dance into a system of eight major *bhangima* and eight minor *bhangima*. One of the motivations behind this research was to make an intervention in the pedagogy of *Bihu* dance. I developed this system for new learners to help them learn the *Bihu* dance vocabulary in simple steps, and in a systematic way that is easy to remember and pass on to others. This is all the more important today when so many children are learning through dance schools and workshops, and are often imparted incomplete or incorrect knowledge by uninformed instructors. I am hopeful that this approach will help young students truly appreciate the beauty of the dance form, and will perhaps help them to resist the temptation to arbitrarily introduce contemporary elements in *Bihu*, all in the name of innovation and experimentation.

Irean Rozamliani

Irean Rozamliani is a 40-year-old high school teacher at St. Lawrence School, Ramthar. She is from the Mizo community and lives in Tlangnuam, Aizawl, in Mizoram, India.

It's very important to me that folk dance is always a collective experience, and every dance performance – big or small – is an occasion to renew the sense of community. In fact, through dance, I have found many friends. My earliest memories of dance are of learning the steps with other children from my locality for performances in the *Chapchar Kut* festival. It was in these informal "workshops" that I learned and came to love the traditional *Cheraw* dance. The most popular and oft-performed dance among the Mizos, it features a group of men sitting on the ground facing each other as they tap long bamboo staves open and shut in rhythmic beats while the female dancers step in the spaces between them. This dance is performed in almost all festive occasions. Traditionally, gongs and drums are used as accompaniments, though some also use modern instruments nowadays.

Over the years, I have worked with a number of cultural troupes, living, travelling, and performing together, and making friends along the way. It was actually my elder sister who really inspired me to take up dancing. She was a dancer herself and along with her friends, would often travel to different parts of India to participate in folk dance festivals. Like her, I too wanted to see the world and travel to different places. And I loved dancing. These two things seemed to come together perfectly, and I decided to undergo formal training in folk dance at the Institute of Music and Fine Arts (IMFA), run by the Department of Art and Culture, Government of Mizoram.

I am also a member of the Mizoram Cultural Artiste Association (MCAA). This group undertakes many activities like participating in festivals, making documentary films on Mizo folk dance culture, fundraising for social causes, and so on. As members, we often travel to different places for performances. I have also been involved in teaching schoolchildren different folk dances. However, as a school teacher, there are limitations on how much time I can devote to these activities.

My most memorable experience as a folk dancer was on a visit to Siauliai, Lithuania, in 2017. Our troupe was representing India in the Flower of the Sun International Folk Contest Festival. Performing the *Cheraw* dance before hundreds of people and competing against dancers from so many countries filled me with pride, but also made me nervous. Our performance was a grand success and the IMFA Performing Troupe won the bronze medal in the folk dance category. We returned home to a grand reception, as we were the first troupe from Mizoram to have won a medal in a competition abroad.

The pressures of modern life have placed folk culture in a strange predicament. Youngsters today love to watch movies, play online games, and spend much of their time on social media. Many of them are not really interested in learning folk dance. Of course, some enthusiastic individuals have tried to popularise our folk dances by uploading videos on YouTube and other social platforms. They are doing their bit to preserve our traditions, and many people watch these videos too. But keeping a tradition alive is not quite so simple. First of all, enjoying a video of a dance is not quite the same thing as being interested in learning the dance. I love to watch football but that does not make me play football and undergo the intense training which is required to become a serious player. Likewise, all Mizos are not interested in learning folk dance even though they enjoy watching it. The second problem is how our dances are being represented in these videos. Quite often, the steps and movements are done incorrectly. To make the situation worse, many youngsters are not open to criticism and advice – they try to justify their incorrect form by saying that they are performing a "modern" version of the traditional steps. While one is not against modern interpretations of traditional dances, it is dishonest to pass them off as authentic.

These challenges, I feel, cannot be confronted on an individual level. It might be more appropriate for the Department of Art and Culture to take steps to disseminate authentic knowledge, especially when school and college troupes are practising for competitions and festivals. But, despite all the difficulties, one must be optimistic. It is heartening to know that there are still many youngsters who are interested in folk dance and are willing to learn. Their enthusiasm gives me hope that as long as there are Mizos in this world, there will be Mizo folk dance.

J. Lalsangzuala

> *J. Lalsangzuala works as a lecturer for the District Institute of Education and Training (DIET) and currently lives in Chaltlang, Mizoram, India. He is 40 years of age and belongs to the Mizo community.*

I have always enjoyed dancing and first began to participate in folk dance performances when I was in school. We would perform in special events such as our school's Annual Day or in opening ceremonies for sports events. In the beginning, it was simply about doing something enjoyable and fun with my friends, who would also participate in the performances. But by the time I entered college, I was entering folk dance competitions and was taking things more seriously. Upon graduating from college, I went for a three-month course in Mizo folk dance under the Department of Art and Culture, Government of Mizoram. This turned out to be a wonderful learning experience, as I got to know a lot about the wealth of folk dance cultures in Mizoram. Through instruction and dedicated practice, I became intimately familiar with the nuances of dances such as *Chailam*, *Sarlamkai*, *Cheraw*, and *Khuallam*.

Of these, I am most attracted to the *Sarlamkai* dance. *Sarlamkai* is a martial dance originating from the Pawi and Mara communities. In bygone times, it was a dance to commemorate victory in war. The dance is part of an elaborate five-day ceremony to ensure that the souls of the vanquished remain as slaves to the victor even after death. Accompanied by gongs and drums and dressed in colourful attire, men and women stand alternately and move in circles. For me, the most enjoyable aspect of the *Sarlamkai* dance is that men and women participate with equal enthusiasm and energy.

As a member of various cultural troupes under the Department of Art and Culture, I participate regularly in the annual *Chapchar Kut* festival. I have also had the good fortune of travelling to various parts of India as well as abroad. I was a member of the Institute of Music and Fine Arts (IMFA) cultural troupe that won the bronze medal at the Flower of the Sun International Folk Contest Festival, held in Siauliai, Lithuania, in 2017.

I also conduct training and workshops in schools and localities across Mizoram. In my interactions with the young people who attend these workshops, I have noticed that their ideas about folk dance are quite different from those of the older generation. Most notably, they are very comfortable with new technology. Many people are making videos on folk dance these days, which are shared through social media. In fact, YouTube, Facebook, Instagram, and WhatsApp are playing an important role in disseminating information and popularising Mizo folk dance – they are sources of entertainment as well as knowledge. Online presence has also helped in gaining recognition and admiration for Mizo folk culture in the rest of India and abroad.

Mui Yamak

Mui Yamak is a 40-year-old farmer and folk dance practitioner. A member of the Nyishi community, she lives in Raga village, Kamle district, Arunachal Pradesh.

I have been a dancer for about 25 years now. For me, dance has always been associated with an idea of tradition and a sense of community. Our folk dances have been passed down the generations, and performing them brings people closer together. I began when I was about 15 years old, learning by watching my parents and grandparents dancing during festivals. I remember practising the steps in our yard with my grandmother and how meticulously she would examine my attire before I headed out to join the rest of the village in performing the songs and dances that accompanied the ceremonies during the *Boori-boot Yullo* festival. Alongside the dancing I also learned to sing *Nyishi* folk songs. Despite having no formal training, I have been invited to sing and dance on radio and television programmes by All India Radio and Doordarshan. Other times, I go to perform wedding songs if someone invites me from one of the nearby villages.

One of the most important annual festivals for the *Nyishis* of Kamle district is *Boori-boot Yullo*. The five-day festival is celebrated in the first week of February, or Rajo Pol – the first month of the *Nyishi* calendar. Song and dance are an important part of the ceremonies as we follow the *Nyib* (priest) in praying for the well-being of the community in the year ahead. Alongside the sacrificial rituals, the festival is an occasion for all of us to get together and perform traditional dances such as the Jhulum-Pongnam and Jajin. While Jajin is performed only by young girls, men and women of all ages can participate in Jhulum-Pongnam. Other dances, such as Nitin and Punu are usually performed by the older married women of the community. I particularly enjoy the festival as it really draws enthusiastic participation from the younger people. Especially in the weeks before the festival, I devote time teaching the dance to young boys and girls. Many youngsters from the neighbouring villages also come to learn. I try to pay attention to all aspects of the dances – from the rhythms and movements, to their attire and headgear. I have noticed that while most of them have a broad idea about these things, they are not quite aware of the finer details. For instance, the dress and ornaments of different Nyishi clans vary slightly, and one must pay attention to these nuances.

I feel a great sense of responsibility when I teach young children. Our folk dances are part of our tradition that was passed down to me by my parents. They, in turn, learned it from my grandparents. In this way, knowledge about our dances and traditions has been passed down through the generations. It is my duty to pass on the same to the younger generation. I think this has become all the more important today, with so many young people having to travel outside in search of work. It makes me sad that many people today no longer speak our language and are unfamiliar with our culture. It is my hope that through our songs and dances, we can keep some part of our tradition alive.

Amarsing Bey

> *Amarsing Bey is a 42-year-old farmer and folk dancer. A member of the Karbi community, he lives in Dhentaghat, Karbi Anglong, Assam, India.*

All communities are culturally unique, and one cannot maintain their distinct identity without keeping alive their distinctive culture. Folk dance, music, food, and attire are thus part of our cultural identity for the world. Over the course of almost three decades as a cultural performer and activist, this has been a guiding principle of sorts for me. As a young teenager, this first took shape in the form of a cultural troupe I formed along with some of my friends. In 1993, some of us young people in the village formed the Nirdan Cultural Troupe. We wanted to do something to practise and preserve our folk cultural practices within our own community, but also to showcase our distinctive culture to those outside the community. We would perform at festivals and folk dance competitions across Assam. In 1997, our troupe was also invited to Delhi to perform at an event hosted by Assam Association and the Ministry of Tourism, Government of India. A highlight of our visit was a performance at the Doordarshan television station.

While the troupe has continued to perform, these days I am more involved in conducting folk dance workshops. Conducted with the aim of teaching folk dance to Karbi youth, these workshops vary in duration from one to three weeks. Organisations such as the Karbi Cultural Society have been very supportive in this regard, inviting me for workshops held in Karbi Anglong and Sonitpur districts in Assam. In fact, I have been closely associated with the Karbi Cultural Society since 1993, and have been involved in their efforts to strengthen Karbi culture and identity. I was also the cultural secretary of the Tekelanjung area committee in 1996. I am also sometimes called upon to judge folk dance competitions during the Karbi Youth Festival.

One of the biggest challenges today is to keep alive our folk culture in the age of the internet and digital media. On the one hand, television and the internet have exposed today's youth to a wide range of cultural influences, not all of which are positive. At the same time, platforms such as YouTube and Facebook also help in making the youth familiar with Karbi folk dance. Beyond the question of whether a medium – say, television or the internet – is good or bad, I think we should instead focus on helping the youth understand that while their cultural tastes may change with the prevailing trends, Karbi folk dance and music signify a deep aspect of our distinct social identity. Having met so many young people through workshops and our cultural troupe, I have found them to respond to this idea in two ways. While there are some who find our folk practices to be "backward" and are embarrassed by them, there are also others who take great pride in their cultural heritage.

That being said, one must be realistic in understanding the place folk music and dance hold in the hearts and minds of the youth. No doubt, they are exposed to a wide range of cultural influences today. Consequently, it is all the more important to think of how folk culture must respond to the pressures of modernity. The annual Karbi Youth Festival, for instance, tries to strike a balance by having separate slots for folk and modern dance and music. I feel that people sometimes get too hung up on maintaining the "authenticity" of folk culture by insulating it from modern influence. Culture must always have an aspect of continuity but also change. In a certain sense, this is what gives a culture its vitality, its life.

For me, this is not simply a matter of principles and ideas – it is something we deal with within our troupe all the time. Karbi folk dances fall in two broad categories. First, we have the dances that are part of our death ceremonies. These include *Nimso Kerung*, which is performed together by men and women; and *Banjar Kekan* and *Chong Kedam*, which are performed only by men. Then we also have a number of dances that are connected with our traditional practice of *jhum* (shifting) cultivation. For instance, *Rit Nong Chingdi* is performed at the time of sowing the *jhum* fields, in April–May, while *Hacha Kekan* is a style for song and dance accompanying festivities after the harvest, in January.

When performing these, say, in a folk dance competition, of course the dance itself is being taken out of its original context. Moreover, it is factors such as the size of the stage that will determine how we move, where the singer stands, and so on. In spite of this, we do everything we can to keep intact the essence of the dances, even as we try to make them more aesthetically pleasing and suited for the proscenium stage.

Debashish Reang

Debashish Reang is a 40-year-old social worker and the Founder of the Gachirampara Hojagiri Cultural Troupe. A member of the Reang community, he lives in Gachirampara, North Tripura District, Tripura, India.

I learned dance and music from our elders in the village and have not had any professional training. A major influence on my journey as a performer has been the Gachirampara Cultural Society (GCS). Set up in 1980, it functions as a local youth club as well as cultural society. It was here that I met a lot of other artists and had an opportunity to learn about Reang folk music and dance. It was around this time that I first began to play cymbals (*sota*) and drums (*kham*), which have since become my area of expertise. I have been involved in public performances since 2007, when I joined the GCS.

In 2015 I formed the Gachirampara Hojagiri Cultural Troupe and have been working with them ever since. I am also the Secretary of the troupe, and am involved in all of the day-to-day aspects, from organising rehearsals to managing invitations and competition entries to managing the finances of the group. Our troupe presently has 22 members, including 16 dancers and 6 musicians. Most of the members are young college and senior school students. We are an active group and even when we aren't preparing for a show or competition, we meet twice a week to practise and discuss contemporary cultural issues. Our troupe specialises in three dance forms – namely, Hojagiri, Dailo, and Goroiya. Of these, Hojagiri is the most popular and a recognisable Reang folk dance. Performed widely towards the end of October, the Hojagiri dance is part of a number of ceremonies to propitiate Mailuma, the goddess of the paddy fields and seek her blessings for bountiful crops and the well-being of the community. The dance features women performing acrobatic feats, such as balancing plates and lit lamps in their hands and on their head as they stand on an earthen pitcher while moving to the rhythm of drums, cymbals, and the flute. Men participate in the dance by providing musical accompaniment. There are other dances such as the Dailo and Goroiya that are performed only by men. While the Dailo dance is associated with harvests, gaiety, and merrymaking, the Goroiya dance is part of festivities on the first day of the Reang calendar (mid-April) to seek the blessings of Goroiya, the god of prosperity.

In the last four or five years, we have performed at a number of events across India, sponsored by the National School of Drama, Sangeet Natak Akademi, and the Ministry of Tourism, Government of India. Of these, my most memorable experience was at the Rashtriya Sanskriti Mahotsav, held in New Delhi in 2016, where I had a wonderful opportunity to learn about the many folk cultures from across India, and interact with musicians and dancers from so many different regions and communities.

Despite working full-time with the group, I feel that we have not been able to fulfil our potential as folk artists. The members of our troupe are very dedicated, but the most serious difficulty is in the financial side of things. The costumes and musical instruments are very expensive these days. The costumes have to be made to order and require high maintenance. The instruments we use are made by traditional techniques. These are not readily available in the market, primarily because the process is expensive and time-consuming, and secondly, many traditional craftsmen are abandoning their expertise as it is not enough to make ends meet. Most of the members of our troupe are from modest backgrounds, mainly attached to farming. A lot of them are also students. To financially support the group, we have to take every opportunity that comes our way, be it an invitation from the Tourism Department, or a competition with prize money, or performing for tourists.

The financial difficulties aside, another problem is the availability of dancers and musicians. The older artists are now retired and also getting on in age. The youngsters, however, are not very interested in taking up folk dance seriously as it does not offer great career prospects. For instance, in our own troupe, most of the members will continue performing while they are in school and college. Thereafter, they will either have to go out of the state for higher education or in search of work. Some of them will get married and will not be able to commit as much time to the group. In fact, before the coronavirus lockdown, our troupe had 12 excellent dancers who could be called upon to perform at any time, anywhere. But during the lockdown itself, four of them have married and are no longer members of the troupe.

That being said, I am still optimistic about our troupe's prospects. Our performances always meet with much praise and appreciation, and we receive a lot of support and encouragement from many people, young and old. Despite all the new cultural influences that society is exposed to these days, people are still receptive to folk dance and music.

Babita Reang

Babita Reang is 23 years of age and is pursuing her Master's degree in History at Tripura University. She is a member of the Reang community in the Ambasa, Dhalai District, Tripura, India.

The Hojagiri dance literally runs like blood in my veins. My father, Chulaihum Reang, is a dance teacher and he has been a major source of inspiration and support. He began teaching me the Hojagiri dance from a very young age. One of my fondest memories associated with Hojagiri goes back to when I was about 10 or 11 years old. My father had already been teaching me for a few years, and at his urging, I took part in a public performance in our hometown of Ambasa. Young as I was, I thought of it all as just another occasion to do the dance. But people really enjoyed the performance and I was suddenly a minor celebrity in the locality. It was around this time that my father started a cultural troupe, and I joined it as a dancer. Our dance team is called the Baba Longtharai Cultural Troupe and was formed in 2008. We have 15 members at present, including 8 dancers and 6 musicians.

We started off performing at various competitions and government-sponsored events across Tripura, but from 2012 onwards we began touring and performing outside the state as well. In the last few years, we have performed in 22 states across the country. One of the most important events is the two-day annual Hojagiri festival organised by the Government of Tripura, which draws cultural troupes from across Tripura in various competition categories. The event also sees participation from cultural troupes from Bru (Reang) and villages in neighbouring Mizoram as well. Traditionally, the Hojagiri dance is performed in the month of October, but nowadays we receive invitations around the year to perform at various government-sponsored events, trade, and tourism exhibitions, and sports events.

Since 2018 when I completed my undergraduate studies, I have performed in music videos. I have appeared in 14 modern as well as folk dance videos. Music videos on television channels and on the internet, I feel, have played a significant role in bringing the Hojagiri dance, and Reang culture in general, to viewers across India. Having performed on stage for so many years, I now want to set up a dance and music school after I complete my postgraduate education. I will have been able to put together some savings from my performance earnings, which will be sufficient to get things off the ground. Of course, this cannot be an individual effort, and I will be depending on my father and the members of our troupe and community for support.

The surging popularity of Hojagiri over the last few years has encouraged many people to learn the dance. With my experience, I feel I can help young girls who are interested in learning this unique dance form. Beautiful as the dance looks, it takes years of practice to become a proficient Hojagiri dancer. I feel it is best if girls start training early, when they are between eight and ten years old. Admittedly, some of the movements might look quite dangerous to a lay person, for instance, balancing a bottle or a burning lamp on one's head while standing on an earthen pitcher, but proper instruction at this early age can really help them develop good technique and the requisite skills, and with about two years' practice they can become proficient performers.

Special thanks to Kamsing Kro, Lincoln Reang, Rotom Yater, and Joseph Zoliana for their help in conducting these interviews.

14 Dance through the performers' lens

Mandakini Baruah

Padma Shree Nrityacharya Jatin Goswami

Picture 14.1 Jatin Goswami.

DOI: 10.4324/9781003398776-15

Padma Shree Nrityacharya Jatin Goswami is a renowned Sattriya artist of Assam. He was born on the 2nd of August 1933 at Aadhar Sattra, Dergaon, Assam, India, into a family Sattra which was established by their priest Jadumani. He started his formal education studying at Dadhara LP School in Dergaon and then matriculated from Dergaon High School. He was awarded the prestigious Padma Shree in 2008. He also received a Sangeet Natak Akademi award and Sangeet Natak Akademi Ratna (Fellow) in 2004 and 2019, respectively. Padma has received many other awards.

I was born into and brought up in a Sattra environment and so was automatically attached to Sattriya dance and culture from my early childhood. I met Kalaguru Bishnu Prasad Rav in November 1954, and received dance training from him. With his inspiration I formed the cultural foundation, named Pragati Kala Parishad, the headquarter of which was in Tinsukia. On the advice of Bishnu Rava, I invited Raseswar Borbayan of the Sri Sri Kamalabari Satra to organise an *Ankiya Naat Bhaona* named *Rukmini Horon* in 1962. The main objective of arranging this Bhaona was to popularise and uplift *Ankiya Bhaona*. I, along with a few other performers, planned to stage it in various places throughout Assam, but we could not make it happen due to the Chinese aggression in 1962. In 1966, I was employed in the cultural section of the Department of Public Relations. For me, it was a bitter experience, and after working for three years, I left the job. I then formed the *Bhaskar Theatre,* a small theatre group. It was running nicely but in 1990 I had to shut down the theatre group, as military rule was imposed in the state of Assam to fight insurgency. After that I started the Ranganath Kalakshetra in Sivasagar and the Sattriya Academy in Guwahati and have been busy with these two organisations to date.

As I have already mentioned, a Sattriya environment was familiar to me from the day I was born, so it has always been normal to hear the sounds and tunes of *Khol*, a one act play, *Taal*, percussion instruments, *Borgeet*, songs *Naam Prasang*, devotional prayers, and other religious and Sattriya cultural activities. I used to participate in almost every event. In fact, in some events, my participation was mandatory. I received my first dance training from my father, the late Dharanidhar Goswami, and then I received training in dance and music, (playing *Khol*) from two Bayans of our Sattra, the late Gopiram Bayan and the late Babula Bayan. After meeting Bishnu Rava, I took his advice to train in dance and music under the late Rasheswar Saikia Borbayan of the Sri Sri Kamalabari Satra. He introduced me to the rich storehouse of Sattriya culture.

The ambit of the Sattriya culture is huge. I worked only in the segments of dance and Bhaona. Sattriya dance received national recognition in 2000. Dr. Maheswar Neog and many others had been trying to have Sattriya dance recognised as a major dance form since 1958. In 1999, Dr. Bhupen Hazarika, a cultural hero of Assam, was appointed as the president of the Sangeet Natak Akademi and I was selected as one of the members of that body. Dr. Hazarika formed a sub-committee to scale the standard of Sattriya dance. I was the only person who was directly associated with Sattriya dance on that committee. Finally, on the 15th of November 2000, with the consent of this committee, the general body of Sahitya Akademi declared Sattriya dance as one of the major dance forms of India. Thus, I have been engaged in the process of expanding Sattriya culture.

The Sattras were originally influenced by Bengali culture where the Dhura Bhaona, Faujia Bhaona, Gaanar Bhaona, and Juri Bhaona were played. Bengali culture had a strong impact on dress, and Assamese music. Some foresighted Assamese people made priceless efforts to keep these traditional assets alive, and for this we feel really proud. If we try to mix another culture with our traditional songs, dances, or music then we would be laughed at. The Sattriya dance would lose its individuality, and if that happened, we would not have anything to feel proud of.

Sattriya culture will retain its existence as long as the Sattras exist. In present times it is becoming tough to retain Sattra culture due to the unavailability of young boys to be appointed as *Bhakats*. These days it is very common to have only one or two males in most of the families, so it is difficult for the families to send a son to a Sattra.

In earlier days, the *Adhikaras* (senior or elderly *Bhakats*) were looked after and hospitality was provided by the young *Bhakats* or the disciples. It is gradually becoming difficult in the present changing society, because many people are afraid of the insecurities that may present in old age. The Sattras must be well organised and provide security. The *Bhakats* must also receive economic security; otherwise the Sattras will cease to exist. Both government and the public must take the responsibility to save the Sattras of Assam.

Dance is a good physical exercise. An education in Sattriya dance has two parts – the first is the dance, and the second is the physical exercise. The physical exercise has a relationship with the mind so the mental as well as the physical growth are very much associated with the process. Dance impacts on both mental and physical health. If people are physically and mentally healthy then their society will more likely be healthy. It is an art form which requires a complete physical involvement. One cannot achieve success in dance without physical effort. There is no other way but to engage in hard work to achieve success. I believe that with regular dance practice people will remain physically healthy and mentally determined.

Ghanakanta Bora Bor Bayan

Picture 14.2 Ghanakanta Bor Bayan.

Ghanakanta Bora Bor Bayan is one of the most eminent exponents and gurus of the Sattriya dance of Assam. He is also a renowned instrumentalist, choreographer, and author. He won the prestigious Sangeet Natak Akademi Award in 2001 and has also achieved the most coveted Padma Shree for his dedication towards Sattriya art and culture.

I was born in a village called Kalitagaon near the Dakhinpaat Sattra in Majuli, Assam. After my father's death when I was just an infant, my mother took me and my sister to her brother's residence at Bamungaon in Kamalabari, Majuli. One day two *Bhakats* saw me playing outside my maternal uncle's house and took me with them to the Sattra where I received a ritualistic bath and was dressed in new clothes. The *Burha Bhakat* (older monk) made me take a bath again and told me to bow in the *Kirtan Ghar where the monks go for prayers*. Later he took me to the Satradhikar's abode to pay my respects to him. I met a few other boys of my age in the *Boha*. Though I was away from my home, I was not that sad because of the love and affection bestowed on me by Maniram Dutta Muktiyar (the eldest monk of our *Boha*) and Bhugiram Hazarika, and a few others. I was about four years old during that time. Every evening I was directed to sing Gunamala-Bhatima along with a few of my fellow students in the *Kirtan Ghar*. This was how I entered into the Sattriya life and culture. After a few days the *Burha Bhakat* of our

Boha took me to a *Deka Bhakat* (younger monk) from another *Boha* to teach me how to play the *Khol*. First however I had to offer betel leaf and areca nut along with *Xarai* as a mark of respect. My first Guru, Rasheswar Saikia Bor Bayan, taught me how to play the *Khol* and also the basics of dance. Even though he was strict, he was also caring and fond of me, and I learned my lessons well and quickly. He took me to the late Bapuram Borbayan to learn the art of singing. We addressed our teachers as *Adhyapak*. After learning the basics of playing *Khol* and singing, the *Burha Bhakat* taught me advanced lessons on the same topics. We started participating in various festivals of the Sattra from time to time, and were able to display our skills and what we had learned in the arts on such occasions. All of us needed to participate in the special *Kirtan* during the month of *Bhaada* and our skilful performances on such occasions led to greater participation and responsibilities in the works of the Sattra. During a difficult time, I had to take charge of the *Barbayan* at the young age of 15–16 and had to teach singing *Borgeets* and *Nam prasanga*, playing the *Khol*, and dancing to younger students residing in the Sattra. Our *Burha Bhakat* could no longer perform his duty because of his age. In the meantime, we had to shift our Sattra from its original abode to a different place due to erosion of the Brahmaputra river. Because of this situation, I decided to marry and become a householder. After coming to Guwahati with the help and encouragement of the late Rudra Baruah I joined the Government Music College as a teacher of Sattriya arts. Before that, I had started an institution called Sattriya Kalakendra to teach Sattriya art and culture and impart my knowledge to younger generations. I am still doing the same even now. Many of my students have established themselves in their respective fields of Sattriya art and culture after the completion of their courses.

In a Sattra, the inmates are formally taught dance and music and they are innately connected with the lifestyle of a Sattra. In today's modern environment, this art is taught formally. Students join such a course just like any other course in an educational institute. Sattriya art and learning in such situations cannot be said to be a part and parcel of daily life. Even amid such a situation, few students do make Sattriya art and culture as part of their life as it requires hard labour and perseverance.

Music and dance have always been innately connected. Indian people recognise the oneness of mind and body found through practice of both. The teaching and practice of Sattriya art has a resemblance to the art of yoga. As the artists excel in their arts, the unification of mind and body required to develop excellence helps them gain mental and physical growth. *Mati-Akhora*, exercises done on the ground, are how the Sattriya learning starts, and is nothing but a physical workout. We can improve the exercises of the *Mati-Akhora* with the help of modern science and help attract a younger generation towards it. This *Mati-Akhora* has immense potential to help children and adolescents in their mental and physical development.

Padma Shree Indira P.P. Bora

Picture 14.3 Indira P.P. Bora.

Padma Shree Indira P.P. Bora is an acclaimed Sattriya dancer from Assam who contributed in establishing Sattriya dance as a Classical dance form of India. She is also known for her performances in Bharatanatyam and Kuchipudi. She was awarded the Sangeet Natak Akademi in 1996 and has been awarded many other awards since this time. She promoted Indian Classical dance as "World Dance" at the Edinburgh Festival Fringe in 2011 at the National Centre for Dance in Edinburgh, Scotland. She also promoted Indian Classical Sattriya dance as a principal choreographer and dancer in the critically acclaimed Sattriya Dance Series: UK 2007. She is an empanelled Sattriya dance artist of ICCR, 1992. She received the Guru Gopinath Natya Puraskaram awarded by the Department of Cultural Affairs, Government of Kerala, India, on 22 February 2021 for her lifelong dedication for the recognition and patronage of Sattriya as a Classical dance form of India.

It was more than seventy years back when I was a child. I belong to a very cultural family. Dance runs through my veins. During those days, there was no dance in the real sense. There was dance, but it was mainly popular dance. There was a belief that "ideal" Indian girls did not dance. Most of the dancers were males in those days. My Gurus were Rukmini Devi Arundale for Bharatanatyam and Dr. Pradip Chaliha, Ghankanta Bora Bor Bayan and Rasheswar Saikia Bor Bayan, pioneers in the Sattriya tradition of Assam. I do not know when I started loving this art form, but it was when I was a very young girl that I started learning Sattriya dance. There were dance competitions held in 1957, 1958, and 1959 and over these three years I travelled to Jorhat, Nagaon, and the Dibrugarh districts of Assam. Radha Govinda

Baruah was the main person in the organisation of the whole Sattriya programme. There were happy moments for me then as I got first prize in all the Sattriya competitions for three consecutive years. During that time, great dancers and musicians from all over India, such as Santa Prasad and Roshan Kumari were very happy to see different forms of dance. This was memorable for me and it was this programme that inspired me to dance. The great dancers performed different dances which started in the evening at 6.00 o' clock that lasted till the morning. Being a child, I learnt that if you want to learn, you must learn whole-heartedly. Probably I danced from my heart from then onwards.

If anyone wants to learn Sattriya properly they must go to the Sattras. That was how my journey started. After that I spent 13–14 years in Chennai continuously learning Bharatanatyam. I was a direct disciple of Rukmini Devi Arundale at Kalakshetra in Chennai and was the first Assamese girl who was awarded a Post-Graduation Diploma with Distinction in Bharatanatyam.

I was also attracted towards the Kuchipudi dance form, one of the most prominent dance forms of India. I learnt Kuchipudi for another five years from the late Guru Vempatti Chinna Satyam at the Kuchipudi Art Academy in Chennai. After completing these years, I came back to my homeland, Assam. After having developed a great deal of experience in Classical dance, I wanted to take up Sattriya dance more seriously. I married Prafulla Prasad Bora who was a chief engineer and director of an oil company. We loved each other and he always encouraged me to carry on with Sattriya dance along with Bharatanatyam and Kuchipudi. With the help of the late Dr. Maheswar Neog, Ghanakanta Bor Bayan, and Raseswar Saikia Bor Bayan, I started learning Sattriya once again from a new perspective. *Abhinaya* is a very important component of Sattriya dance which was earlier absent in this art form. I introduced *Abhinaya* as a solo Sattriya dance form. We also took the initiative to bring *Borgeet* into the Sattriya dance form. During the 1990s, we gave Sattriya dance major national exposure across metropolitan cities of India where there was a mingling of *Borgeet* (Vaishnava devotional songs) with the Sattriya dance form. Texts such as *Stri Hastamuktavali* have had a great influence in articulating *Abhinaya* in Sattriya dance. One has to understand the meanings of the lyrics which are used for the performance of Sattriya dance, e.g. *Kanaira kamala mukha* (lotus-like face of Lord Krishna). When I came back to Assam, I applied the thoughts of the Margi technique into Sattriya dance and people started liking it more. I also danced Bharatanatyam and Sattriya using the lyrics and music of Jyotisangeet, Rava Sangeet, and Bhupendra Sangeet. I am still performing this in a Classical way using *Abhinaya, Hastamuktavali* or *Abhinaya Darpan*, an ancient book. People were thrilled by the addition of such new components that I had added into Sattriya dance.

Along with my Gurus, I pioneered making Sattriya dance a solo performance rather than a group dance. For instance, *Nadu Bhangi*, and *Krishna Bhangi* are different categories that we perform as a solo dance form. I then travelled to different places outside of India and performed Sattriya. In 1985, I was the first woman from Assam to fully record a Sattriya dance on the BBC. People were eager to know about Sattriya dress, music, and instruments, along with the dance.

Dance unites everyone; it creates universal emotions and dance requires dedication. Dance to me is a natural extension of who I am as a person in life. To become a great dancer, one needs to maintain a strict training discipline and regular maintenance of the body through healthy food habits and body conditioning. One must deliberately instil a sense of deep understanding of how dance inspires people of different generations, nations, and cultures as it is a fundamental embodiment of infinite well-being and joyful existence. I do exercise in the morning and always enjoy nature. I love nature. We can learn a lot from nature. I always take simple food. I can walk very fast and still walk 10,000 steps every day. My strength in my mind comes from my life of dance.

Ramkrishna Talukdar

Picture 14.4 Ramkrishna Talukdar.

Ramkrishna Talukdar was born and raised amongst the Bhakats at Bamakhata Sattra, in the district of Barpeta, Assam, in the year 1963 to the late Gajendra Nath Talukdar and Dhaneswari Talukdar. His father was a senior artist of that locality on Lokogeet (folk songs) and Borgeet (Vaishnava devotional songs). He is a third-generation artist in his family. His many achievements in the field of Sattriya dance include becoming an "A" grade artist from Prasar Bharati Doordarshan, Delhi, and an ICCR empanelled artist of Sattriya dance. He has received the Sangeet Natak Akademi Award in Sattriya dance for the year 2017 from the Ministry of Culture, Government of India, for his lifetime achievement towards the field of Sattriya culture. He has been felicitated and honoured with various titles in different sociocultural organisations such as Axom Gaurav, Nritya Ratna, Kala Gaurav, and NE TV People's Choice Award. International Students from Belarus, France, Japan, U.S.A., and Kazakhstan have received training under his guidance. He has produced and directed more than 12 dance dramas (the latest being the Mahatmar Drishtit Axom where he played the role of Mahatma Gandhi).

I was fortunate enough to grow up in a family who provided a good cultural environment for my childhood. I used to listen to the sounds of *Borgeet Daba*, a traditional drum, *a Sankh*, conch, and cymbals coming from the *Naamghar* (prayer house for congregational worship) that was located in front of my house. The Assamese community is associated with the Ekasarana sect of Hinduism that is native to Assam. These factors contributed to my interest in learning about Sattriya dance and culture at a very young age. I have worked for the propagation of this dance form my entire life and am still doing so. For the young generation to take an interest in this Classical dance form, I have invented new methods of teaching in my institution. Nartan Kala Niketan in Guwahati is designed in such a way that the students who receive their education from me will have opportunities to establish themselves as future dance artists. I have devised various choreographies and compositions, productions, workshops, seminars, and lecture demonstrations for the development of Sattriya dance.

I have to acknowledge many Gurus who have inspired me to learn this dance form since childhood. I received my first lesson of Sattriya from Sonamal Das in the Bamakhata Sattra and later from Gurus Gobinda Saikia, Ananda Mohan Bhagawati, Raseswar Saikia Borbayan, Jatin Goswami, and Ghanakanta Bora in Guwahati. Dharanidhar Bayan and Basanta Talukdar helped pave the way to my learning Sattriya dance under the guidance of these renowned gurus. In those days there were no opportunities to learn Sattriya dance in the Bamakhata Satra which led me to join the Assam State College of Music as a student in 1982. I took Sattriya Nritya as my major and completed a five-year Bachelor of Music degree from Guwahati University (1982–1987). Apart from studying Sattriya dance I also pursued a four-year Nritya Visharad from B.S.V Lucknow, a two-year Master of Music, a Nrityalankar diploma course from A.B.G.M.V Mandal, Mumbai, in 1992 and then a two-year M.A. degree from I.K.S. University, Madhya Pradesh, in Kathak in 1997.

The *Mati Akhora* (basic exercises of Sattriya dance) is divided into eight parts; *Ora, Sota, Jolok, Sitika, Pak, Jaap, Lon,* and *Khor*. The *Lons* are yoga-like exercises such as *Dhanurasana* and *Padmasana*, that are good for promoting immunity and overall health if practised every day. These exercises were created by Mahapurush Srimanta Sankaradeva many decades ago, before the advent of yoga. It is believed that the *Lons* have immense health benefits if performed on a regular basis.

If we included Sattriya at the school level rather than only at the college level, then I believe that more students would take an interest and study it as a major subject in their later years. The educational institutions of Assam could reform their syllabi and include Sattriya as a subject in their Fine Arts departments so that interested students could take up Sattriya as one of their subjects. Perhaps the Sattriya dance institutions could spread to other parts of the country to teach students throughout India.

Fusion in Sattriya dance is a common concept nowadays. It happens not only in Sattriya dance but also in the other Classical dances of India. I am not against the idea of this fusion because it helps to attract a large variety of audiences. Care is needed to ensure that the traditional culture and roots of Sattriya dance are not affected. Change is inevitable and change is necessary to move forward in a new era.

Subhalakshmi Khan

Picture 14.5 Shubhalakshmi Khan.

Subhalakshmi Khan is an accomplished artiste who has learnt Bharatanatyam under the direct tutelage of Rukmini Devi Arundale of Kalakshetra. She is the wife of India's legendary Sarod Maestro Ustad Amjad Ali Khan. She has been a presenter/organiser of Classical music concerts and festivals all over India since 1985. She has presented concerts under the banner of SLK Promotions, the Sarod Ghar-Museum of Musical Heritage (the only private museum that houses musical instruments of the great music legends and is a 300-year-old haweli of her husband's ancestors). She is the managing trustee of the Haafiz Ali Khan Memorial Trust, named after her father-in-law, Ustad Haafiz Ali Khan Saheb.

I was born in Sivasagar in the well-known Borooah family. My father, Shri Parashuram Borooah also known as Phunu Barooah, played the role of Gadapani in the first Assamese film Joymoti (1935). This was one of the first six talkies of Indian cinema. My uncle (my father's elder brother) Shri P.C. Borooah, a former Member of Parliament, was the first Assamese gramophone artist of great repute and was also associated with that film. My father and Jyotiprasad Agarwala were very close friends and were involved in making that film together. I can remember from my very childhood that there was a musical environment in our family. My grandfather Sangeetacharya Lakhiram Barooah was a pioneering figure in the history of Assamese Classical music. They created an orchestra for the first time in the Ban Theatre, in Tezpur, Assam. My grandfather was the only person who knew the English notation at that time. He could also play instruments like the Cello, which was not at all common during that time. He also played the Violin, Sitar, and other Indian instruments. From my childhood I was inspired by the artistic activities in the family. Our home was a hub for political, cultural, and business people. Dignitaries from all walks of life visited our home. I had the great opportunity to meet world-famous personalities like Pt. Nehru, Vinoba Bhave, Acharya Kripalani, Dr. Sarvepalli Radhakrishnan, Humayun Kabir, Gopala Reddy and many more who visited our home or the town. Later in my life I also had the privilege of meeting Indira Gandhi, Rajiv Gandhi, Atal Bihari Vajpayee, Narendra Modi, and all the Presidents and Vice Presidents just to name a few. I also met many Ustads and Pandits of the musical field. We had a habit of creating a musical atmosphere amongst our family members every evening till dinner time. Guru Rash Bihari Sharma, our Manipuri Guruji stayed at our home for six months to teach me and my elder sister Bijaylakshmi Barooah the Manipuri style of dance. In this context, I would like to state that my name was originally Rajyalakshmi but when I was a child, my parents saw the movie called "Meera" and were totally inspired by the Meera Bhajans sung by none other than Smt. M.S. Subbulakshmi (the great singer from south India) and then they changed my name to Subhalakshmi. I participated in the "All Assam dance competitions" organised by the All Assam Music Conference and I was awarded 1st prize for a few consecutive years. They were indeed inspirational moments for me.

It was with good foresight that my parents encouraged me to travel to places outside Assam for study. They argued that I would not only broaden my views towards life, but I would also have an opportunity to meet people from different parts of India. I was, therefore, sent to Kolkata for studies along with my elder sister. All my siblings were sent outside Assam for higher studies and God has been so kind that wherever we have gone, we have made an impression. I came to Kolkata to study when I was ten to eleven years old. I visited Jaipur and Lucknow to participate in different dance competitions, accompanied by my sister and my father. Once in 1955 when I was in Kolkata, I had the opportunity to witness a live dance performance which was held in the famous cinema hall called the New Empire. I was ten years old at that time. I was extremely delighted to watch that dance ballet and later I got to know that that was called "Bharatanatyam" (one of the six Indian Classical forms of dance), and that it was performed by students from the famous Rukmini Devi Arundale's school, who later on became my Guru. The dance had a great impact on me. When I returned home, I told my parents that I will learn that dance form only, come what may. During childhood, I had little interest in my studies. My uncle took me to Kalakshetra in Chennai to learn Bharatanatyam. It was like an Ashram or Gurukul. It was a totally different world for me. We had to get up at 4.45 a.m. and go for a bath, go to the prayer hall, work on serving duty, clean our rooms, attend classes, practise, wash clothes, and more. They would decide after one year whether or not we could continue. We had been learning only the basics of Bharatanatyam that year. Rukmini Devi Arundale whom we respectfully and affectionately called *Athai* (Aunty or *pehideu* in Assamese), came to examine our dance steps at the end of that year and selected me as her disciple.

It was a happy moment for me when I received a first-class award in a five-year diploma course in Dance in the year 1967. I just wanted to continue and so I undertook a Postgraduate degree in Dance Studies in 1969, and again got a distinction. I made Kolkata my base and started my solo performance career. My first foreign tour with Kalakshetra was in 1970 when we went to Hungary, Czechoslovakia, Romania, West Germany, England, France, Belgium, and Holland. Following that, in 1971, I was selected in a group of nine girls and three boys to go to Montreal, Canada, for "Man and His World Exhibition". We were both hosts and artists in that exhibition. We had to perform three shows every day. That was a very great experience. I was very enthusiastic and inquisitive. From then on there was no looking back in terms of dance performances all over the world.

I met Khan Sahab (Ustad Amjad Ali Khan) in 1974 and in 1975 he came to Kolkata and watched my stage performance. By the grace of God, I have been very lucky, not to receive a single review anywhere in the world that was negative. I went to Cairo, Abu Dhabi, Dubai, and the Scandinavian countries. I went to London with my husband Amjad Ali Khan Saheb to perform and we held joint concerts of my dance alongside his recital in the late 1970s. I had my older son Amaan in 1977 and Ayaan in 1979. It was after Ayaan's birth that I began performing for charity causes in a few cities. In 1985, eight years into my marriage, I performed for an event organised for an Eye

Hospital, sharing the stage with my husband. My final dance performance on stage was when my Guru, Rukmini Devi Arundale, asked me to perform a solo dance on the occasion of the Golden Jubilee of the Kalakshetra. My Guru blessed me immensely after that concert.

Dance is a visual form of art, and for me an artist does not present that artistry only on the stage. We can contribute to art in our own ways, which can be through anything we do in our life, whether it is housekeeping, cooking, climbing a tree, dressing, looking after somebody, everything is a part of art. We can feel a holistic pleasure, a calm feeling through a Classical performance that can also be felt when engaging wholeheartedly in other activities.

People's lives are like diamonds. We become better and better if we polish ourselves. While I no longer perform, it does not mean that I have given up. An artist is always an artist no matter what he/she does. If somebody is taking any performance seriously, this is to be applauded. Keeping the tradition intact and moving with time is very important. It is our duty to make Classical dance and music interesting for the next generation by presenting the art form in the most interesting manner we can so that the next generation can understand the value of our traditional wealth. Learning a Classical art form is a slow process. It requires lots of patience. It is our culture and heritage.

Dr. Lima Das

Picture 14.6 Dr. Lima Das.

Dr. Lima Das is a dentist by profession. She is a renowned Sattriya dancer who won accolades at the India International Dance Festival (IIDF) in Bhubaneswar. She has also played the role of the female protagonist in a recently released Assamese film Aamis directed by Bhaskar Hazarika.

Ours was a family where art and science co-existed because my father was a doctor and my mother worked as a Professor at Cotton College, Guwahati, Assam, in the Department of Chemistry. My mother was also a singer and an artist on All India Radio. I saw her juggling life between her two different worlds, the artistic and the scientific. She would attend her classes at Cotton College, and on her way home she would record a song at All India Radio. That convinced all of us that we do not have to compromise one for another if we want to follow our passion. My mother, being a singer, wanted me to pursue music. I had a very strong inclination towards dance, and because of this my mother enrolled me in a programme to study a Classical dance curriculum so that I could explore the world of dance. There was a new institution that I was enrolled in at the age of eight. It was the Odissi Institution established by my Guru, Sangeeta Hazarika, where I was trained in Odissi under her. As she was a disciple of Guru Gangadhar Pradhan, she would have Guruji come over to take workshops with us. This was back in the early 1990s. At a very early age, we got a glimpse of what Classical dance was all about; we saw the dedication of the gurus towards this art form. I think that really influenced us as children, even though we did not realise it at the time. We were fascinated by the amount of hard work and precision they put into teaching and development of the art form. That is how I got drawn towards that art form. Odissi and Odisha were so much a part of my growing up. What is good about that is that the same kind of discipline is used in the Sattriya dance that I am now pursuing. The similarities and differences of ideologies of both the dance forms are relatable. One art form can draw inspiration from the other and so the Odissi dance form has helped me today to think about how to develop Sattriya dance and to work towards the promotion of this dance form.

After completing my class 12, I enrolled myself in the BDS curriculum at the Regional Dental College and completed my MDS from there. I was married in 2004 and we had a son. After he was born I began a second innings in the world of dance, taking it more seriously. Initially when I was studying, it was more like a hobby but once I had my son and started working as a lecturer at the Regional Dental College itself, I realised that I also needed to do something else, and that it would be Sattriya dance. So that is how my second innings started and my Guru, Padma Shree Nrityacharya Jatin Goswami, has mentored me well. He is like a guiding light. I began taking dance very seriously from 2012 and started performing in various parts of the country. Now it has become an integral part of my day and my life. It's a passion that I hold dearly in my heart.

I once danced a fusion of Bharatanatyam, Odissi, and Kathak when learning Odissi as a young person, but personally, I am a worshipper of Classical dance. There are certain aspects of the modern stage that attract particular audiences. The quality of the fusion is important because when a western dance is fused with an India dance, both dances have a uniqueness which must be maintained and resonate with the audience. I feel however, that Indian Classical dance has a spiritual aspect, and it seems wrong to take that away by fusing it with another genre. Classical dance provides immense peace and happiness, and from my point of view, this dance should be learnt and preserved as Classical dance. Sattriya dance has a strong history, with 600 years as a living tradition. This dance form is still performed today in the Sattras as a form of worship. There are certain changes when it is brought to the stage. For instance, when a *Jhumura* or *Sali Nritya* is performed in the Sattra, it is repeated three times. When it is brought to the stage, it cannot be repeated because of the audience's expectation, and because of the time that is given for a particular performance. Sattriya dance was recognised as a Classical dance form in 2000, however when we are performing it now, in 2020, without bringing anything new to the table, it can become monotonous. People want something new from the dance form, and from the performer. We must remember all these aspects. Therefore, we should know the history and philosophy of the dance form while incorporating something new to the dance form.

Dance for me has become an inseparable part of my life. I draw solace and peace of mind from dancing. Any art helps us to go through life in a better way. In some ways it makes us better people. Initially, it started as a hobby and passion, but now it has become more than a passion. It is a passion which I cannot do without because it gives me immense pleasure, happiness, and peace of mind. Dance is like a sea and anyone who dives into the depths of the sea of this beautiful art, will be nourished and will find a greater meaning in life.

Dance has a positive impact on the human psyche. When we dance, immediately afterwards, we feel so good, so liberated. If we want to explain it more scientifically, endorphins are released from the body when we exercise, uplifting our mood. That physical aspect is always there, and the humane or spiritual aspect cannot be denied. It helps us to uplift ourselves spiritually and helps us to develop a more positive outlook which is very important in today's time where life is so stressful. Dance can be liberating from all the pains and sorrows of day-to-day life.

Dance like any other art forms has no boundaries of gender, religion, and race. It helps us to build a more inclusive society because the goals are common. When we dance and work towards developing a dance form, our vision is for peace and prosperity. Dancing together helps us to forget our differences. Art can help us to create inclusive societies.

When I was very young, maybe at the age of eight or nine, there were two dancers who had come from Oddissa, to perform *Dashavatara*. The kind of symmetry and synchronisation that I watched was something I had never seen before. It was unique, amazing, and absolutely out of this world. That performance strongly influenced me. I had also watched Guru Gangadhar Pradhan's choreography of Abhimanyu with all male dancers. It was a beautiful piece. Each of these experiences contributed towards me as a dancer. I can gain inspiration from everyone who does good work; even if it is from a little child who has dedication towards her/his performance.

Dr. Menaka P.P. Bora

Picture 14.7 Dr. Meneka Bora.

Dr. Menaka P.P. Bora is a multi-award winning Indian Classical dance soloist (Sattriya and Bharatanatyam), contemporary choreographer, actor, ethnomusicologist, and broadcaster. Educated at London and Oxford University, Menaka became the first Affiliated Artiste at the Bodleian Libraries, University of Oxford, soon after completing her Ph.D and post-doctoral research fellowships as a Wingate Scholar in Ethnomusicology at St. John's & Faculty of Music, University of Oxford. She became an elected Fellow of the Board of the highly prestigious Royal Asiatic Society in London. After winning India's most prestigious national award for young artists in Classical Sattriya dance, Sangeet Natak Akademi Yuva Puraskar, she won Britain's highly coveted Leverhulme Early Career Fellowship (2016–2019). Menaka combines the best of the Eastern and Western intellectual and artistic traditions. She was a Finalist in the BBC Radio 4's Journey of a Lifetime Award for radio broadcasting featuring music and monks of Assam and appeared as a Guest Speaker on BBC Radio's "World music" programmes. She has also appeared on Radio New Zealand and SBS National Radio in Australia. Her performances as a dance soloist have seen her in prestigious festivals and venues across the world. Menaka participated in the Inaugural ceremony of the Auckland Festival where her performance was appreciated by the then Prime Minister of New Zealand, John Key.

I was born into a world of dance from a very early age. My mother, Guru, Smt. Padma Shree Indira P.P. Bora was a pioneer in the field of Sattriya dance and introduced Bharatanatyam and Kuchipudi dance in the North-East of India. As her daughter, born into a dance world, I was automatically drawn into Classical dance, folk dance, music, and literature. My training began at a very young age. In fact, I started performing when I was two years old. I was performing *Borgeet*, Krishna roles, and plays.

I was literally very excited to be on the stage long before I started my Classical training. Dance, for me, was a dream and a very organic way of expressing myself as a young child. I also observed my mother, my Guru, and her students performing when she was teaching at her institution, Kalabhumi, which is a 38-year-old pioneering dance institution in North-East India. I was very young when I started to observe dance and learned many methods through observation of body language. I initially trained in Sattriya and Bharatanatyam and completed my first graduation ceremony *Arangetram* at the age of nine years in Chennai. Like my mother, I was also trained with some of the top gurus of the Kalakshetra School of Bharatanatyam. For 13 years I was a disciple of Rukmini Devi Arundale. I had a good understanding of the South Indian Classical dance style along with the family language of dance where we had to learn everything including the Carnatic system of music.

Dance education was not just about moving one's limbs, dancing and singing in a particular way, but it was about learning the culture and the language, learning Tamil, learning Sanskrit, learning Carnatic music and learning the history of the Dravidian culture. It was very important for us to get that exposure. Gradually, as my mother began to work on Sattriya, there was a revival, and it became more popular, finally being recognised as a Classical dance in 2000. The developmental work began in the 1990s onwards through various scholars and gurus from the monasteries of Assam and Indian artists. My mother, along with other gurus, started touring some of the major cities of India, introducing Sattriya for the first time to mainstream audiences. Until then Sattriya was very much confined within the monasteries and very few dancers had been seen outside of a monastery. This was the first time that such a series of concerts had been organised. Documentation and conferences on these very important performances were arranged. The following scholars were all involved in the 1990s systematically giving major exposure to Sattriya as a solo art form; Dr. Kapila Vatsayan, Dr. Sunil Kothari, Rasheswar Saikia Bor Bayan, Ghanakanta Bora Bor Bayan, Dr. Maheswar Neog, and Dr. Pradeep Chaliha. I was a child during that time, performing Sattriya and having many experiences as I learned this dance form. Of course, I also had a parallel training in Bharatanatyam. I eventually went to Chennai for my schooling because that was where the centre for Bharatanatyam was. I studied there for three years for a direct degree under Guru Padma Bhushan

Dhananjayans. For me, it was very important because being an artist of Assamese origin I needed to learn something that was not our own. It was a big challenge for me. I was very fortunate that after my *Arangetram* at the age of nine, I was asked to perform. That gave me the confidence to take up dance very seriously and that is when my parents started thinking that I should be trained more seriously. Of course, coming back to Assam, I started training in Sattriya and continued to learn the Classical dance form, with my mother as one of my main gurus. I also kept up with my academic study and I went to London University. I did my M.A. in Transnational Communication because I wanted to show dance as a form of communication. I was very keen that dance was not only confined to a set group of dance-loving audiences. I was also interested in dance as a structured form of communication as I wanted to present an ancient art form from India to a national and global audience. It was a turning point in my life. I literally absorbed everything; whether it was ballet, contemporary dance, or western classical art, it was a huge experience for me. I think that diverse dance forms have much to offer society. I took up a Ph.D in Ethnomusicology, studying Indian music. Eventually I did my Post-Doctoral study at Oxford University in Sattriya dance. For the first time I was studying ethnomusical research. I worked with some of the monks and musicians back in Assam and prepared tracks as a musicologist. I used traditional music and we played it on BBC Radio.

Dance has certainly had an impact on the human psyche because it is primarily a way of life and everyone performs in their own way. Essentially, we are all human beings, and we know that dance is a symbol of being alive at its highest form. When we are happy, we move our arms, we jump, we dance, we energise. I think there cannot be any other form of art which symbolises the highest form of being alive. It is a universal experience. Dance is an art form that brings immense joy. A good dance can be transformational. For example, a very good ballet dance performed in a village in Africa or in India, can bring immense joy. Similarly, when we bring Sattriya to a western audience, people understand the essence of it if we are very good at presenting its authenticity.

Dance, for me, is another form of meditation. When I perform, I perform from a different mental geography. My geography is in my mind. I always leave scope for improvisation within the technique and so I am literally in a state of meditation. It takes me away from physical spaces. These days, a lot of studies on dance are about the therapeutic value of dance. There is a subject called Dance Science which is prevalent in London University which comes together with physiotherapy to understand human anatomy from the perspective of dance.

I try to see western classical ballet. I think it is unbelievably beautiful and it made me change the way that I looked at dance when I first saw it. Dances can transform themselves into completely different worlds. I do watch Indian Classical dance and contemporary dance, and observe the way artists have transformed me into a moment of joy.

I always try to connect with nature. Learning dance and appreciating dance have very close relationships and to do that one needs to appreciate nature. Whether it is observing the plants or the weather or animals or even a butterfly in a small pot of flowers, I think nature enriches an artist's work. Nature always inspires me to be creative. It is important to be conscious about our body posture in our everyday life. We can change our lives through body conditioning, yoga, exercises, and dance.

Dr. Jashodhara Bora

Picture 14.8 Dr. Jashodhara Bora.

Dr. Jashodhara Bora is a Bharatanatyam performer, teacher, choreographer, and director. She was awarded the Sangeet Ratna from Rabindra Bharati University. She, along with her younger sister Kalashree Upasana Bora, received the title, "The Assam Sisters" from Guru Dr. Saroja Vaidyanathan in the year 2010. In 2014, she started a Bharatanatyam Dance School at Nagaon, Assam, named Saroja Natyalaya. She was the Founder President of the Nrityangan Dance Club (the Official Dance Club of Tezpur University) which was established in 2015. She was honoured with the National Nritya Shiromani Award in 2016 and a Nritya Kanaka Jyoti Samman in 2018 for her contribution to the promotion, preservation, and popularisation of Indian Classical dance – Bharatanatyam. She completed her graduation and postgraduation in Hindi from the Lady Shri Ram College, New Delhi, and worked as an Assistant Professor at Handique Girls' College, Guwahati, Assam, in 2013. She received her Ph.D degree from Tezpur University and is presently working as a Guest Lecturer at Guwahati University.

I started learning dance at the age of six and completed my *arangetram* (graduation) when I was 19 years old in 2005. My mother, the late Rina Saikia Bora introduced me to dance and has been an inspiration throughout my life. Smt. Mandira Bhattacharjee was my first Guru in this field. Then I moved to Delhi for further studies and started my training under Guru Padma Bhushan Dr. Saroja Vaidyanathan at Ganesa Natyalaya, New Delhi. After completing my Masters, I started teaching dance at Guruji's institute till 2013. Later I came back to Assam and founded *Saroja Natyalaya*, a Bharatanatyam Dance Institute in Nagaon, Assam.

As I dance I am enlightened with so many things, such as historical facts or mythological facts or social awareness. Dance leads me to a positive life of happiness, professional independence, and it makes me a better person.

I perform the oldest style of Bharatanatyam known as Tanjore. Definitely the mathematics of the movements remain the same, but we can add to the dance's beauty through our own imagination and choreography. With time, our art also needs some changes but without disturbing the originality of the form. I hope the New Education Policy, 2020, of the Indian government plays a significant role in the promotion of dance in academic fields so that the students have a wide choice of dance to study.

For me, the major aspect of dance is as a discipline, and by discipline I mean both mental and physical discipline. To have a disciplined body, you need to have a disciplined mind. You need to eat healthy food, workout, have healthy thoughts, and sleep well. Dance is not limited by gender, age, caste, or status. Dance is practised by both Hindu and Muslim. We do not have any age limits nor gender preferences. The themes we use in our performances could be from any mythological story and speak to many social causes.

Presently I have no late-night activity, I like to wake up early so that I can read something, for at least for two hours. I prepare a bath of lukewarm water and turmeric. After bathing I do *Pranayam*, *Yoga*, and some stretching exercises which keep my muscles strong and flexible for dance. After warming up, I eat breakfast where curd is mandatory and then I go for my regular dance practice for three to four hours as we do not have regular university classes now because of the pandemic. When I say "dance practice", it does not mean only physical movements. It may include theoretical and research work, watching dance videos, composing music and *jati*, and writing scripts or drafts. After having lunch, I take a rest for one to two hours depending on my workload. In the evening I conduct dance classes (now online). If I have time after class, I go for a walk. I try to eat dinner early so that by 9:00 pm I am in bed. This is my usual schedule unless I have a programme or event.

Nganbi Chanu Leima

Picture 14.9 Nganbi Chanu Leima.

Nganbi Chanu Leima was born in 1982 as the third daughter of Kamal Toijamba and Y. Thabatombi Devi in Churachandpur in the district of Manipur. Dancing has been her hobby since childhood. After matriculation, she studied in Imphal, the capital of Manipur and completed her Master's degree and Ph.D from Manipur University in 2014. She married the renowned Manipur singer, Konthoujam Bobin Singh and has two daughters. Along with her husband, she founded an Institution called ATINGA – An institute of Performing Arts & Cultural Identity. She served as a government primary teacher from 2011 to 2017. Since that time she has been working as an Assistant Professor at the Manipur University of Culture in the Department of Umang Lai Haraoba. Nganbi has received numerous awards from organisations throughout India.

Being brought up in Manipur, where festivals are dominated by dance, music, and rituals, I am inclined towards Manipuri dance. Most of the Manipuri youths including me, were easily drawn towards the various Performing Arts of the State, be it Lai Haraoba, Thang-ta, Ras Leela, Sankirtana, Khubak-esei, folk songs, dances, or Sumang Leela. I chose Lai Haraoba as a dance to concentrate on. It is an indigenous ritualistic dance performed at festivals to please gods and goddesses. Since Manipur is known to be the land of gods and goddesses, the festival is held in most state localities once in a year, running for several days. Dances are performed as a means of religious offerings and not as mere entertainment. When I was young, I simply loved dancing but as I grew up, I gradually started realising that every dance step performed by the *Amaibis* (Priestesses), one of the main functionaries of the festival, held meaning about our history, identity, and culture.

Guru Ngathem Ranjit Singh (Senior Guru, Ras Department, JNMDA [Jawaharlal Nehru Manipuri Dance Academy], Imphal) was my first Guru who introduced me to Manipuri Dance in JNMDA. My other gurus are Guru P. Dhanajit Singh (State Kala Awardee), M. Kaminikumar Singh (SNA Awardee), E. Indira Devi (Padma Shree Awardee), Ph. Iboton (SNA Awardee), Th. Chourajit (State Kala Awardee), Th. Bimola, G. Raseshori (State Kala Akademi). I started dancing from a young age without training, however when I met my Guru, N. Ranjit, I started undergoing proper training in dance. He encouraged me to learn dance under different gurus in JNMDA after my school studies and Post-Diploma courses. Further, I pursued my MA in Manipuri Dance from Manipur University and completed a Ph.D as well. When I was young, I simply danced as an additional activity. However, with my coming of age, dance became my way of life, my heart, and soul.

I have performed fusion dance. However, in regards to the maintenance of authenticity, I believe it depends upon the dancer who composes the dance. If the fusion is done for the purpose of reviving the old and indigenous elements in innovative ways, it will definitely lead to a positive impact. Everything in this world is subject to change, so Manipuri dance will change too. It is really challenging in our current time of innovation to balance the new while retaining authenticity. For me, I will always try to maintain the essence of Manipuri.

Educational institutions do have significant roles in promoting dance in academia. I would proudly say that we are an example of those who are working in colleges and universities. Many regard dance as some kind of extracurricular activity. However, with the inclusion of dance as a subject within educational institutions, people gradually realise that dance is also an important subject worthy of study.

I recently joined an interesting online workshop on Art Therapy which also includes Creative/Dance Movement Therapy. From the workshop, I learned a lot regarding the therapeutic value of dance. It really has an impact on the human psyche by exploring different layers of psycho-motor skills through different body movements. Movement is the medium of therapy.

I would say that dance can help in building a more inclusive society. Moreover, the physical and mental states of dance practitioners are improved by participating in dance. Dance has helped young people build their character and personality while also developing artistic skills and 21st century competencies.

I faced challenges in the field of dance as a woman. I was married in 2010 and because of an infertility problem and the need to undergo treatment for five years, I did not perform any dance during that time. Following many hormonal injections, I gained a lot of weight. However, with the grace of

God I finally had two little daughters who are five and three years old at present. I was working as a primary school teacher during that time and also doing my research. During those eight years, I gave only two performances. However, with the help of my husband along with my Guru's support, I have now resumed my profession through a dancing career.

I used to watch dance performances mainly held in JNMDA (Jawaharlal Nehru Manipuri Dance Academy) as I was there for quite some time. To be frank, I would say that whenever famous non-Manipuri dancers like Guru Devjani Chalia, Guru Darshana Javeri, and Didi Preeti Patel, performed, I enjoyed them, while at the same time I felt ashamed for not adequately being a quality Manipuri dancer. I was thinking of their zeal to support our dance forms and I wasn't doing that, but I found my courage from them, and I am now working to uplift the status of Manipuri dance. They really had an impact upon my dance journey.

Sinam Basu Singh

Picture 14.10 Sinam Basu Singh.

Sinam Basu Singh hails from the state of Manipur, Imphal, India. He is the second son of the late Sinam Nimai Singh and Sinam Anandini Devi and also the grandson of Maestro Meitei Pung *(Manipuri Classical drum player and Guru of the late Shri Sinam Bokul Singh)*. He completed a diploma from the Jawaharlal Nehru Manipur Dance Academy, Imphal, in 2003 and also completed a Master's degree in Manipuri dance from the Visva-Bharati University with first class honours in 2011. At present he is pursuing a Ph.D in dance from the same university. Besides dance, he has learned various aspects of art such as Thang-Ta *(Martial Art of Manipur)*, Pung Cholom, Kartal Cholom, Pena, Mime, Natasankritan, and folk songs.

He has received many accolades from art connoisseurs and scholars for the grace, beauty, lyricism, and power of his vibrant dances and choreographic techniques. He has received many awards and has been privileged to perform across the length and breadth of India and abroad in Bangladesh, Malaysia, Australia, Russia, Thailand, Vietnam, Japan, and America. He has given more than 300 lecture/demonstrations and workshops at various institutions in India and abroad. At present he is working as a choreographer for the production unit *"Progressive Artiste Laboratory"* (PAL) an organisation of dance and music.

I was brought up in an environment where dance and music was a part of the life of Manipuri people. There are two traditions of Manipuri dance: a pre-Vaishnava dance form, namely Lai-Haraoba and a post-Vaishnava dance form connected to the Ras Lila tradition of Hindu philosophy. Both these dance forms are still alive in the temples and are observed in an annual festival at particular times, respectively. Manipuri people practise dance and music as a medium of worship in both pre-Vaishnava and post-Vaishnava situations. Since my childhood, I witnessed the traditional festivals and also took part regularly, like all Manipuris. My grandfather the late Sinam Bokul Singh was a great Guru of *Meitei Pung* (Manipuri drum). It might be the reason why I was inspired by dance and related art forms.

My first Guru was Haorongbam Rabikanta Meitei, who is not a traditional dance Guru but teaches a popular dance form. When I started formal training in Manipuri dance I practised under Guru Kh. Ibomcha, Guru N. Tiken Singh, Guru W. Lokendrajit Singh, Guru Y. Hemantakumar Singh, and Vidushi N. Amusana Devi. In the very beginning I was involved in the training as Guru Sishya Parampara.

I perform fusion dance sometimes as it gives artists an opportunity to understand other traditional dance forms. Fusion dance has become very popular in India. The government and private institutions strongly encourage fusion works. Sometimes I get an invitation to perform a fusion dance. I feel however that we lose the opportunity or the platforms of our own art forms if we only do fusion dance. There is no articulation of philosophy, aesthetics, political meaning, or authenticity in fusion dances. We have to take care not to compromise our traditional art forms. We cannot establish a scholarly institution based on fusion dance because there is no academic input of integrity in this art form. Here I would like to mention that fusion works often lead to commercialisation of our traditions to create popular art. If we continue this practice more and more, I am sure that there will be a negative impact on the integrity of many authentic dance forms.

However, art forms cannot be stagnant and therefore we should keep our eyes open to contemporary trends and societal changes. It is obvious that any art form changes with time. We are always facing challenges with this process of change because we have to keep the traditional values and the authenticity of our art form. On the other hand, we should also keep our focus on history, philosophy, and the literature of our art form so that we can preserve traditional art forms. Conservation of all traditional arts practice is important in India as is the recognition of an evolving social context.

As a professional dancer, I have tried my level best to uplift the most devotional dance form of India in international arenas by performing and giving lecture/demonstrations. As a dancer and choreographer, I composed a number of solo dances and choreographed a number of dance ballets. Recently in 2018 and 2019 the Government of Manipur appointed me as a choreographer and I choreographed consecutively two closing ceremonies and choreographic works for the International Sangai Festival namely "*Laigi Machasing*" (Children of Gods and Goddesses) and "Manipur", (The Jewel of India), respectively.

Dance is a part of life and it supports a peaceful and happy life. It has a pivotal impact on the human psyche irrespective of one's age. In my view, dance includes mental and physical exercise, and as such recommend dance as a good therapeutic practice.

As a professional dancer, I have witnessed a number of memorable dance performances performed by various gurus in various dance forms and I was truly inspired by their performances. I was particularly inspired by the Odissi dance form in my creative faculty of dance, particularly when performed by Guru Kelucharan Mohapatra.

As a Manipuri, I belong to a family where there is no question of privacy. Therefore, if I want to practise, I have to go to my Guru's house. After I joined the Progressive Artiste Laboratory, founded by Late Thiyam Tarunkumar, I found an area to practise my dancing. Sometimes I experiment with my expertise when teaching the junior dancers of this institution. Every day I practise for four hours and then after the practice, as a hobby, I spend two to three hours in the kitchen garden of this institution.

I would like to acknowledge Indrashis Baruah, Bijit Borthakur, and Jashodhara Bora for assisting me during the process of preparing this chapter.

15 Studio dance teachers' journeys

Mayuri Bordoloi

Bhabananda Barbayan

Inducted into the revered Uttar Kamalabari Sattra at the age of three and half years, Bhabananda Barbayan learned the nuances of Sattriya culture under the guidance of many gurus. Today, he is an exponent himself, imparting lessons, as well as conducting workshops. He holds lecture demonstrations on Sattriya, travelling far and wide. At the age of 16 years, he became the youngest Barbayan, a master of Sattriya dance and music of the Sattra. The Sattra authority conferred the Adhyapak title on him in 1997. He is the first person who has taken the dance form beyond Sattra boundaries in India and abroad. He has taught, demonstrated, and performed regularly in France, England, United State of America, Hong Kong, Switzerland, Germany, Italy, Portugal, Mexico, Columbia, Brazil, Russia, Denmark, Norway, Belgium, Belarus, Chile, China, and Bangladesh. Bhabananda introduced Sattriya dance into the curriculum of different overseas universities and has also been a regular visiting scholar. He has been associated with Paris-VIII University, King's College, University of London, Brown University & Drexel University, USA, Jawaharlal Nehru University, the National School of Drama, and Dibrugarh University. He has established three Sattriya training institutions in Sattraranga, a foundation for cultural relation in Majuli, Assam, in 2000; Rongayan, an academy of Sattriya dance theatre and music in Guwahati, Assam, in 2003; and the Sattriya Akademy in New Delhi in 2008.

I was fortunate to be born and raised on a unique river island of natural beauty, a place surrounded by the Sattras. Following the family tradition where one child is offered to the Sattra, I was "given" to the Uttar Kamalabari Sattra at the tender age of four. Since then, I have learned all activities of the Sattra, very much in a very practical way, not only to maintain the ritual but also to sustain livelihood as a *bhakat* (devotee) in the Sattra.

Although I received training in different disciplines in Sattriya arts and music from the renowned *Adhyapaks* of the Sattra, my passion is chiefly devoted to the dance, drama, and *khol* playing. I received an opportunity to explore my artistic self when I was at 16 years of age, being placed in charge and becoming an *Adhyapak* (teacher) of the Sattra immediately after being conferred with the Barbayan. I still continue my artistic activities as a practitioner, teacher, composer, and choreographer. I moved from this Sattra to grow the Sattriya culture, and I established a training institute in Delhi in 2008. This was the first time that Sattriya training had been facilitated outside of Assam.

In the same year, I led my group to Europe for a one-month performance and teaching tour. Gradually my work expanded to different parts of the globe, not only for performance and workshops but also academic research. Since then, I have maintained teaching for three distinct platforms: Sattra rituals; stage performances within India; and, performances overseas. As I am committed to teach in Delhi as well as abroad, it is not possible for me to maintain the daily rituals of the Sattra. Despite this, I manage to teach the special training courses for occasional ceremonial occasions and stage performances.

Of course my mind is sculpted with so many beautiful memories of teaching experiences in the Sattra, where I imparted physical training (*Mati-akhora*) and dance to the children of the Sattra in the very early morning. At noon there were *khol* lessons for adults and in the afternoon dance lessons for advanced students. The evening was the main learning period for all disciplines of Sattriya art and music where I supervised dance, *khol*, and drama (*Ankiya Bhaona*) sessions. As I mentioned earlier, the training procedure of the Sattra has been sustained through oral tradition along with day-to-day activities that are completely unwritten, yet still exist under a systematic somatic curriculum.

Each curriculum area in the Sattra was supervised by a principal *Adhyapak*. In the case of dance and drama, there were some assistant *Adhyapaks* who assisted the principal *Adhyapak* during the teaching and performance sessions. It is compulsory for each and every member of the Sattra to enrol in dance from their first entry to the Sattra at a very tender age. Thereafter, they can choose the subjects that they like to pursue. It is usual that they learn some knowledge from each subject so that they can enhance their interest and decide what they enjoy the most. That's why most of the Sattra people are accomplished in different disciplines.

There are some differences in the teaching methodology between Sattra and non-Sattra students. A strong teaching methodology cannot be imposed on non-Sattra students who consider the art as a profession, and they have to complete the course in a specific period of time.

I would like to say it's our duty to propagate the philosophy of Srimanta Sankaradeva on the devotional deeds of Krishnaism. This ethos is very beneficial, not only for the Assamese community, but for others: it is a universal asset. Through theatre and dance we can distribute this beautiful notion of life.

Dr. Anjana Moyee Saikia

Dr. Anjana Moyee Saikia was initially trained in Odissi under the tutelage of Garima Hazarika, a Sangeet Natak Akademi Awardee at Guwahati. She has performed extensively in many festivals within the country and abroad and won accolades for her performances. She is an empanelled Odissi soloist of the ICCR (Indian Council of Cultural Relations), Ministry of External Affairs, Government of India, New Delhi, and an "A" grade artiste in both Odissi and Sattriya dance from Doordarshan. Dr. Anjana is noted for her fluidity in dance and her choreographic technique. Her works are staged at major dance festivals throughout India.

Anjana has been a leading name in the media over the years for her unique productions and performances on stage. She was invited to grace the occasion of the Indian Independence Day Celebration at the residence of the President of India in 2019. She was also invited to perform Indian classical dances at the 40th Assam Convention at Vancouver, Canada, under the aegis of the ICCR, Ministry of External Affairs, Government of India. Besides dance, theatre has also been a passion for Dr. Anjana Moyee Saikia. She has acted in leading roles for some renowned drama productions, namely *Chitralekha, Purush, Jerengar Sati, Nisanga Nayak, Mouse Trap, Chitrangada,* and *Shyama.*

I am excited by dance. Anything related to dance, theatre, or poetry is very close to me. My mind is automatically settled, when I hear different beats of music or I perform dance movements. I find rays of happiness through dance. Students come to me with great hopes and dreams to be a part of this dance world, and my satisfaction comes from looking at their little feet and their smiling faces. Introducing someone new to this beautiful dance world is my happiness and I consider myself their mentor. It is my responsibility to shape them into dancers. I take care of them. I do this, not for any monetary profit, but to bring about change in society through creating beautiful work.

Besides my passion in dance, I am engaged in an academic job, teaching students from the medical profession. The subject is related to statistics, and within science I deal with counts and measures and interpret research studies that have to be perfectly presented. After hours of long duties at college when I come back to the world of dance, I get a very different flavour, but with the same sense of perfect counts, through the beats and again with a need for precise presentation. For me, both statistics (close to mathematics) and dance go well together. I face the same challenges while doing difficult movements in dance as I do when working on different puzzles and statistical modelling.

While teaching dance for the students, I do concentrate on their maximum physical and mental capabilities. I never ponder upon the particular duration of a class. It depends on their natural urge or concentration while practising the lessons. Conducting classes for them is my great pleasure and satisfaction. If any of them shine, my soul smiles with love and respect. Moreover, most of my students are from middle-class families and few are able to afford the expenditure related to stage performance. Keeping this in mind, the fee structure of my dance institute is very nominal. Students from a poor economic background avail classes free of charge. My motto is to learn to dance without the pressure of competition. I try to develop the learners' inner knowledge, their senses, their confidence, and personality. I try to teach them the meaning of life and social responsibilities through dance.

I feel that dance teaches many things in life besides its pure *Bhangimas* (gestures), techniques, and history. It makes us disciplined, it brings an awareness of responsibility, and improves concentration and memory. I would say, teaching dance also gives me the same qualities. But, nothing arrives perfectly, and we must apply dedication and love for the medium that we choose, be it music, dance, theatre, or visual art. Therefore, my responsibility or duty as a mentor to the aspirant plays a vital role. I have set up an institution, "Darpan Dance Akademi" at Guwahati, where I offer training in the Classical dance form, Odissi, along with experimental dance forms. Besides training, I also work on ideas for choreographic creations with special emphasis on developing innovative work. Apart from my own institution, I am associated with several other institutions and organisations as a dance guru.

As an academic and a dance teacher, I enjoy the company of students. My role in society is to bring happiness, peace, and harmony. If I am able to contribute, that is my great satisfaction and I try my level best to bring a change in the society. I believe that a new generation will shine in the near future with more innovative and creative work keeping our educational foundations strong. Our society will be enriched by good human beings with beautiful minds and pure hearts.

Dreamly Gogoi

Born and brought up in Guwahati, Dreamly Gogoi completed her Visharad (vocals) from the Public Guwahati Music School in 1998. She received training in Sattriya Nritya from Sri Gobinda Saikia. In 2002, she received the state's highest title in Bihu "Bihu Samragyee". She was conferred with a Bharat Kala Ratna Award in 2015 and has received many awards since. She acquired a scholarship in "Folk" from the Ministry of Cultural Affairs during 2002–2004 to promote the folk art of Assam. Dreamly was recognised as a graded artist in Sattriya dance (solo) from Prasar Bharati Doordarshan Kendra in the year 2005. In 2007 she was empanelled as a Sattriya artist under the ICCR, Government of India. During the pandemic in 2020, online short-term workshops were conducted where she delivered lectures on the topic "Introducing Cultural Inputs in Curriculum Teaching".

My penchant for art and culture can be attributed to my belonging to a place that is known for its rich and vibrant culture. Assam, my home state, is the meeting ground of different ethnic groups and diverse cultures. My interest in the arts was fuelled by my mother, Shishir Gogoi, a prominent drama artist, and my father, a cultural enthusiast and retired district judge from Assam's Dhemaji. Hence, my eternal tryst with art and culture began at the age of six when I started learning Hindustani Classical Music under the guidance of Vivekananda Sarma. Later, I realised that I was more interested in dance, and at that juncture, I was introduced to Sri Gobinda Saikia Sir where I received training in Sattriya Nritya, a 15th–16th century classical art form of Assam. Sattriya Nritya was composed by a great Vaishnavite Saint, Mahapurush Srimanta Sankaradeva to spread Vaishnavism, also known as Ek Saran Hari Naam Dharma (Believing in One God, i.e. Vishnu or Lord Krishna). According to the Hindu Vaishnava Cult, Lord Krishna is the ultimate role model and the sole medium from whom salvation is sought. I was charmed by the images and idols of Krishna, the descriptive elaboration through the borgeet and Prasanga style of Naam Kirtan and the prayers. I enjoyed the entire Krishna style presentation (costume/sharya) with its yellow glazing beauty, the peacock feathers and the flute in his hands. I always insisted my Guru allow me to dance as Krishna and my first opportunity was provided to me by my mentor on the occasion of Janmashtami at the ISKCON temple located at Guwahati. Since then there has been no looking back. I carried on with my Sattriya performances travelling around the state with my Guruji's group from the year 1987. In 1997, I was sponsored by the Cultural Ministry and the Cultural Zonal Centres of India to perform for a month with my Guruji in Andaman and the Nicobar Islands. Along with Sattriya, I simultaneously had the opportunity to perform Bihu, as my parents had formed a group called the "Rongpuria Bihu Husori Band". At the time, when I was pursuing both art forms, Sattriya was not recognised as a classical art form. In 2000, Sattriya was awarded the status of a classical dance form. The early part of my dance journey rendered a different perspective of looking into life. It taught me to be independent and confident and enhanced my capacity to tackle obstacles and challenges on my own.

I take pride in the fact that whatever I have been able to achieve to date is entirely through my own hard work and dedication. There have been many challenges on both personal and professional fronts, but by handling them as I did, I have become a stronger person. I am indebted to my Gurus for their invaluable support and encouragement in pursuing my dreams. It's under the tutelage of my revered Gurus that I have learned the advanced performing art form, including "Abhinaya", which prepared me to participate in various classical festivals across the country and to gradually establish myself as a professional Sattriya dance artist. I feel blessed for the opportunities to participate in the group and solo categories at the Sattriya Nritya Parva festival, the prestigious event organised by Sangeet Natak Akademi, New Delhi, in collaboration with Sattriya Kendra, Guwahati, under the guidance of my Gurus.

Since 2010, I have been regularly invited to judge television shows run by local media channels. I have participated in many talk shows concerning women's empowerment, commercialisation of Bihu, and modernisation of the classical dance form Sattriya. In 2003, I started Gandharva Kala Kendra, a government-registered and Sangit Sattra-registered institute which imparts training in both Sattriya classical art as well as Bihu folk art. Courses on classical *borgeet*, *dhol badan*, and other popular ethnic art forms are provided in the institute. I believe that my classical dance training has assisted me when it comes to the use of *taal* and *maan* (rhythm and music). I became familiar with notations while learning Sattriya, which helped me in understanding the rhythmic beats of the *dhol* (drum) in Bihu. The students who learn Bihu do not understand the notations involved in its performance, and it was through my own study and analysis that I connected the classical form to folk form and taught the students rhythmic systems through notation. Thus, I used the classical patterns in folk to understand the rhythmic beatings on the *dhol* and specifically taught the notations. Young artists in the contemporary dance scene are familiar with these patterns, but I am proud of the fact that at the time I began imparting training, there was no such institute. I was the pioneer in rendering formal institutionalised training in Bihu. Earlier, Bihu would only be practised prior to a performance, but I introduced the concept that training in Bihu can be conducted throughout the year. Due to my training in vocals, I could train the students to understand the sense of controlling the breath and the use of the throat. Under my banner, an active group of 32 artists perform all throughout India on invitation. We showcase classical as well as Bihu and other folk art forms of Assam through our performances.

When I judge a performance, I basically focus on the technical aspects such as, how the entire stage is used in a proscenium performance, the position of the microphone, lights, entry, exit, ability to constantly grip the audience's attention, together with keeping true to the ethnicity of Bihu. Moreover, either in group, duet, or solo, being in sync with the music is essential. My classical training background helped me in this regard. It's worth mentioning that Sattriya art is all about devotion, while folk art is associated with fertility, love, and expression of various emotions, even costume modifications can be made to some extent. It is, therefore, imperative to control the variety of moods in folk dance, which is different from devotional art. Folk dance has the scope to be re-created, using a colloquial language form. In the classical art form there is a grammar, a particular limitation, and we cannot go beyond it or remake it. Sankardev culminated all the tribal cultures of Assam to compose a classical art form. In terms of the costume too, Sattriya has its rigid set of rules.

It's been a blessing for me that I could make my passion my profession. The entire journey has been very enriching so far. Till now, 47 of my students have graduated (*gunin*) in Sattriya dance and 9 students managed to achieve a Central CCRT (Centre for Cultural Resources and Training) scholarship both in the fields of Sattriya Nritya and Bihu under my training and guidance. It is my hope that my students carry on with their endeavours towards the development of the art forms and that they excel in their life. This would be the ultimate reward.

Anita Sharma

Anita Sharma is a leading Sattriya exponent. She is considered one of India's most experienced and compelling dancers. She has devoted herself to learning Sattriya dance under Padmashree Nrityacharya Jatin Goswami. Born into a distinguished family with a rich cultural heritage, Anita was initiated into the field of Sattriya when she was barely seven years old. She had her early training under the late Guru Rasheswar Saikia Borbayan. Anita was trained in the art of Odissi by Guru Garima Hazarika and the late Guru Pad mabibhusan Kelucharan Mahapatra of Bhubaneswar. She is the founder and director of her own institution, "Abhinaya Dance Academy" at Guwahati where she imparts training in Sattriya dance to young aspirants. On behalf of the Abhinaya Dance Academy she annually organises "Parampara", a national dance and music festival. Anita has completed extensive research related to the Sattriya. She has researched "Ojapali", a rich cultural tradition of Assam. She is an "A" grade artist of Doordarshan Kendra, New Delhi. She is an empanelled solo artist of the ICCR and an active artist of Spic Macay. A widely travelled danseuse, she has presented her art in the United Kingdom, Sweden, the United States, Turkmenistan, Kazakhstan, Kyrgyzstan, Russia, Bangladesh, and Australia. Anita was conferred with the prestigious Sangeet Natak Akademy Award in 2014 by the Government of India.

I don't remember the exact date but I remember that it was a rainy monsoon evening when my mother took me to a renowned Guru, the late Raseswar Saikia Borbayan of the traditional Sattriya dance of Assam, to learn Sattriya dance. My parents felt that exposing me to the traditional classical art form at an early age would help me stay connected to my heritage and culture. I am from an eminent cultural family of Assam, my father was a historian, the late Benudhar Sarmah. As a result, I started going to dance classes when I was only nine years old. I trained in the style of Sattriya, starting from *Mati-akhora* (basic exercises of Sattriya) which originated from the monks of Assam more than 500 years ago. Since then, I've spent countless hours, days, and years learning not only the physical movements that define this style of dance, but also the meaning behind the movements and the age-old traditional Bargeet songs and other compositions that Sattriya dancers have been performing for generations.

I do not believe that I ever thought of becoming a professional dancer. I was doing my regular classes at "Sangeet Sattra" when I received an offer to act in a dance drama, "Panchatantra", directed by renowned choreographer and dance Guru, Garima Hazarika. I performed in the roles of "butterfly" and "rabbit" and that was the turning point of my career in dance. In 1982, I joined Mitali Kala Kendra, of Guru Garima Hazarika and started learning Odissi. Originally, Odissi was performed by temple dancers known as Maharis. They are unmarried and dedicated their lives to dancing for the Gods. They performed at night under candlelight and sometimes their bodies were clad only in ornaments. Guru Garima Hazarika was an amazing dancer of both Odissi and Sattriya. I was closely associated with her between 1982 and 1991 and performed with her extensively within the state and throughout India. During this period, I kept learning the techniques and styles of Odissi and Sattriya, and also learned different choreographic presentation styles as I assisted my Guru in many successful productions. In 1991, I performed my auspicious Mancha Prabeshin Odissi dance at Rabindra Bhawan, Guwahati.

I was very fortunate to have been trained in Odissi under a great maestro of this art form. It was in 1993 that I had the opportunity to meet Padma Vibhushan Guru Kelucharan Mohapatra and started learning advanced techniques of Odissi. During this period, I was introduced to a different world of dance. I learned about the soulfulness of Indian Classical dance and connected myself to the world of devotional dance. I have learned that Classical dance is about dedication, patience, commitment, devotion, and giving time to body conditioning in order to achieve the stamina needed to perform. At Guruji's academy, I learned the mantra that to be a successful, professional dancer, one must seek perfection through rigorous practice, and as we all know, that requires both time and commitment.

I must say that although I began my dance journey because of my parents' dream, I've continued pursuing my passion because of the great impact it has had on my life. To me soulful, traditional, Sattriya dance not only gives me a strong connection to my heritage and culture, but also often provides me with a space to let go of my worries and step into a poignant and creative part of my life. I love the deep-seated, devotional Vaishnava narrative texts, music, and every aspect of Sattriya tradition. When I perform either on stage or in my own space, I immerse myself into the characters of the stories in such a way that I find a different world.

I started my dance academy "*Abhinaya*" in 1995 with the blessings and able guidance of Guru Kelucharan Mohapatra, who himself along with eminent dance Guru, Ratikant Mahapatra and Sujata Mahapatra inaugurated the academy. Thus, the journey of being a guru of dance began. I performed and taught Odissi until 1999, but one day when I was coming down from the stage after my performance, the late Dr. Keshabananda Deva Goswami, a renowned Sattriya scholar came to me and asked me to study and work on traditional Sattriya dance in order to reach the masses. He said that there are many dancers that promote Odissi, but Sattriya needs proper attention as the living tradition of Assam. With his encouragement and as a good dancer, I felt some responsibility and started my journey as a Sattriya dancer.

I started fine tuning my Sattriya dance technique under the guidance of Nrityacharya Padmashree Jatin Goswami in 1999. I have found my Guru to be very contemporary in his mindset as he always allows and encourages me to work with new thinking, creativity, and transformation while keeping the traditional values and style of the dance form. With his blessings from the year 2000, I have pursued my dream to work as a solo Sattriya dance artist and to encourage young dancers to pursue their dreams, as well as uphold the tradition of Sattriya dance. I have created my own repertoire group of *Abhinaya* and we have travelled extensively in India and abroad namely, United Kingdom, Sweden, United States, Turkmenistan, Kazakhstan, Russia, Australia, and Bangladesh.

Apart from dancing, choreography is also my passion. I have transitioned from simply learning and performing to also choreographing, and have choreographed the religious Vaishnava texts, scriptures, and mythology using music and other traditional expressional works to praise the deities. I have also created the famous dance dramas of Rabindranath Tagore such as *Ritu Ranga* and *Chandalika* and choreographed to a famous Assamese ballad, *Sonit Konwari* by Jyotiprasad Agarwala. Dance is poetry in motion, something that is very elegant and beautiful to observe and that was the first time I had choreographed to a dance ballad. I went on to choreograph Sattriya movement with poetry, *Kobitar Chandot Nrityarata Godhuli* (dancing evening in the rhythm of poetry).

A change has been observed in the Indian Classical dance forms, including Sattriya. Changes and transformation of traditional art forms through new approaches or experiments in choreography are setting new benchmarks in performance styles. We, as senior Sattriya performers, have to think of new ways to contribute to the making of new works. Rather than relying on traditional conservative choreographic concepts and simply reproducing old works and movement we must work creatively. I believe that dancers no longer have to work in isolation the way that previous generations might have, or to be under pressure to perform in a conservative presentation manner. Undoubtedly, we are world class with new creative thoughts and ideas and we can hold our own on the world stage. Whether you're just starting or you've been dancing for years, never underestimate the power of trying something new. This may mean learning a new move, experimenting with a completely different style, or choreographing a piece on your own.

Now, let me also share something about my experience and observation as an Indian classical dance Guru. Apart from a professional dancer, I have spent around two decades as a dance educator. I feel that being a teacher in a school or a master in spirituality, one has a great responsibility to help their disciples progress and to build a strong guru–shishya (student–teacher) relationship. A true disciple's duty is to grasp all that the guru has to teach them with the utmost sincerity. In changing times, the guru–shishya traditional practice of the teaching–learning process of an art form is facing new challenges. I feel that guru–shishya parampara (traditional system of education in India) has a great role to play in the case of Indian classical dance, therefore, I make sure that whatever knowledge I have, is correctly passed to the shishya (my students) through a spiritual, intellectual, and emotional bond. At the same time, the relationship requires the student to be obedient and devoted to their gurus. Teachers and students should connect with each other with devotion and dedication during teaching–learning sessions. I always give instances of my soulful attachment with my gurus following every teaching session.

It is easy to be a dance teacher by opening a school and educating students with weekend classes, but to be a true *Guru* is a difficult job. Dance teachers are available, but there are not many *Gurus*. Gurus are actually complete artistes who have mastered an art form. Dance gurus, apart from mastering dance techniques and movements, must use correct dance grammar and become knowledgeable regarding the *sahitya* (literature), *sangeet* (music), and *shastras* (scriptures) associated with the dance.

As an educator, I have observed that there is only so much that is possible to teach student groups in a dance school through weekend classes. Every student's experience, imagination, and capacity is different and this can be best enhanced by one-to-one lessons through the guru–shishya relationship. For this reason, only around 5% of weekend students go on to become successful performers or dancers from the large group. Certain aspects of teaching are beyond the scope of learning in a school group.

School is important, but later the *guru–shishya* bonding plays a pivotal and important role in shaping a bright, soulful, true dancer who may carry forward the legacy. In other words, a true young dancer or artist is not born overnight, but as a result of immersive training over a prolonged length of time. This is very serious and involves more than weekly technical class sessions. A contemporary version of the *guru–shishya* relationship bears some resemblance to its precursor, where some element of "shadowing" one's teacher over a prolonged period assists the dancer's growth. The art form is imbibed through observation, discussion, devotion, and interpersonal contact. It is very important for an inspirational teacher to be up to date in imaginative thinking, dance techniques, choreography, and other related elements of the dance form.

However, what I dislike most is the fast-moving attitude of most of the parents and students of the current generation. They do not choose to invest much time or effort, and everything needs to be fast in respect to learning, performing on a stage, and the accomplishment of fame and awards. As an educator of classical dance my sincere endeavour is to teach the moral values of life, to teach how to work in a team, and to be a responsible person. Besides making students understand the theoretical aspects of classical dance through practical learning, I want them to comprehend the traditional grammar of dance and music, the *Natysastra*.

The transformations in dance pedagogy and the teacher–disciple connect in recent times is undoubtedly complex and fascinating. The revered teacher–student bond is not a generation gap, it is a generation's desire to reshape the hierarchy and rewrite the rules. As a teacher and educator my goal lies in transforming the student into a good human being. As a guiding force, I try to understand the need to connect and evolve with the students. The students' patience and perseverance will go a long way in conserving the tradition of learning. As Albert Einstein quoted, "It is the supreme art of the teacher to awaken joy in creative expression and knowledge".

Whatever the reason, my message to future dancers remains, you must develop fierce dedication to your art form with genuine interest, and to give your best in every day of performance and practice. I know it is not easy "but when the going gets tough the tough get going". I am proud to be a Sattriya dancer from the land of blue hills and the red river.

Dr. Mallika Kandali

Dr. Mallika Kandali was amongst the first female doctoral researchers in dance giving her a rare blend as an excellent performer and distinguished scholar of Sattriya dance. She obtained her Ph.D degree in 2005 from the Gauhati University on "The Sattriya and the Odissi Dances: A Comparative Study". Currently, Dr. Kandali is an Associate Professor at the R.G. Baruah College, Guwahati, and the founder director of "Parampara Pravah", an institution of Sattriya dance. Dr. Kandali is also a visiting professor in the Performing Arts Department at the Dibrugarh University and at the Srimanta Sankaradeva University, Assam. She is an empanelled artist of the ICCR, Festival of India, and graded artist of Doordarshan. Of significance is Dr. Kandali's imaginative choreography based on traditional and contemporary issues. She prepared the nomenclature of many foot positions and Sattryia hand gestures. She added eight new gestures for each of the nayikas *(heroines) in the* Ashta-nayikas *(performing arts). She has also written scripts and verses in* Brajawali *for dance compositions. Dr. Kandali has performed in various Indian locations as well as abroad. She is equally hailed for her lecture-demonstrations, as her workshops and other academic activities for the promotion and expansion of Sattriya culture in its broad context. She was awarded state and national level awards for her contribution to Sattriya dance, both in the practical and theoretical aspects. Dr Kandali is the author of three books, two in Assamese and one in English:* Nrityakala prasanga aru Sattriya Nritya *(Sattriya Dance in Context of the Art of Dance, 2007);* Sattriya Sanskritir Surabhi *(Glimpses of Sattriya Culture, 2008); and Sattriya: The Living Dance Tradition of Assam (2014).*

My childhood was colourful and vibrant. In our extended family, all the members were busy with their cultural activities. When I was seven years old, my father took me to Bardowa, a place where Srimanta Sankaradeva, the architect of Sattriya dance, was born. My father described the bhakti saint, his versatile life, and the huge contribution he had made to Assamese society. That day, although I was just a little girl, I decided with firm determination that I would be a Sattriya dancer.

My uncle was my first *Adhyapak* or teacher. I saw my uncle the late Dimbeswar Kandali visiting many nearby villages, to teach people Ankiya nat, the Vaishnava theatre introduced by the great bhakti saint Srimanta Sankaradeva. My uncle gave me my first lesson in life when discussing the basic definition of dance and the aesthetic beauty of art. One day he asked me, "Can you earn your bread through dance?" I answered, "I don't know, but whatever, I just want to dance, dance is in my soul". He seemed immensely happy as if he had been waiting for such a reply, but perhaps he also wanted to give me a warning that life would not be easy as a dancer. He was right. It was difficult as I grew up to take up dance as a profession. Things are now changing. The present generation can take dance as a profession and earn an income, which is indeed a very welcome development. However, everything hasn't changed, and there are many more hurdles to overcome, both economically and socially.

My father once told me, "Remember dance is a meditation, and a strong instrument for physical well-being. Through dance, you can change society". My father worked at Diphu, a small hilly town in the Karbi Anglong district of Assam that had immense scenic beauty and multicultural diversity. During my childhood, I experienced the vibrant environment at Diphu. Sattriya culture and a colourful "tribal" culture was sown into my childhood. Dance taught me to love nature and human beings, to live life with positivity, thereby creating potent energy for a joyful life. Gradually, I too realised what my father had once told me, that dance is a meditation and physical exercise and a powerful medium of intervention in society. Through this medium, I can raise my voice and protest against societal issues of concern.

Sattriya dance is a living dance tradition. This dance form has thrived and been nurtured through the Sattra institution (Vaishnava monastery of Assam) for almost six hundred years. For the last 25 years of my life I have been visiting the Sattras and especially those in the famous island of Majuli on the River Brahmaputra, learning not only the dance form and the associated cultural tradition, but also the overall life style and philosophy of the bhakti tradition and the Sattra institution. Sri Sri Uttar Kamalabari Sattra has become my abode in my cultural and spiritual journey. I have had countless visits and stayed in the Bohas (the residential dwelling where the *bhakats* or the monks live), and have explored a beautiful and layered life narrative; a narrative of art and philosophical engagement.

For the last two decades, I have been engaged in this wonderful artistic journey as a dancer and have been performing traditional repertoire. However, besides the traditional dances I have composed some dance compositions that address contemporary issues which I think, were essential in order to intervene as an artist in society. Yes, I support my father's view and position, that dance is a strong medium to create awareness amongst people. I have created compositions about environmental issues, ecological crisis, gender and women's issues, the horrendous evil of child trafficking, alongside traditional and mythological themes and subject matter. When the students come to learn Sattriya dance in my institution Parampara Pravah, I teach them on the very first day that dance is not simply a performing art, it is a way of life with a deeper philosophy than a mere means of entertainment and fun.

I believe that to carry forward a dance tradition to a wider arena we must have theoretical knowledge alongside the practical knowledge. There are certain sections of society who consider dance as a mere form of entertainment and amusement and show a certain kind of prejudice toward dancers. When a dancer is equipped with both dancing skill and an in-depth knowledge about the dance's origin, philosophy, and the cultural context, they may gain the prestige and dignity they deserve. Theory gives an analytical power, providing an orientation toward research, providing dancers with the required knowledge, and capacity to better articulate the root of the dance. For this reason, I decided to do my doctoral research on Sattriya dance. To sum up, dance provides a great path for mental, physical, and spiritual upliftment while also being a joyous means for artistic attainment in life.

Dr. Pratibha Sharma

Dr. Pratibha Sharma, a dedicated artist of the Sattriya dance form was born in Tezpur, considered the cultural capital of Assam. She started her formal lessons in Sattriya as a young child under the guidance of Guru Tileshwar Tamuli in 1982. Besides Sattriya, Pratibha was trained in Kathak dance. She has performed innumerable Kathak dances with Guru Bipul Das in his choreographic works. She is also trained in Deodhani dance under Sri Gunakar Dev Goswami. Pratibha is an empanelled artist of ICCR (Indian Council of Cultural Relations) and is also an empanelled artist for the "Festival of India Abroad". Pratibha is a "B" graded artist of Guwahati Doordarshan. She received the award of Junior Fellowship from the Ministry of Culture for Sattriya dance in 2009 and has received numerous other awards.

Pratibha has contributed to society through the "Nrityakalpa" National Dance Festival, a festival of young Classical dancers in Tezpur, which allow the young exponents to speak and share their thoughts and ideas through dance, and communicate to the youth in a contemporary world.

I never thought that I would be a dancer, but I have had an interest in dance since my childhood. When I was young, I had a fever almost every week and was in poor health. My physician advised my parents to encourage me to do some regular exercise. My parents noticed my interest in dance and decided to enrol me in dance. At that time, they were not aware of any Classical dance forms and did not know what form would be the best. I was admitted into the Kalaguru Sangeet Mahavidyalaya of Tezpur, Assam, which was very near to my house. The late Punyabarata Dev Goswami, Principal of Kalaguru Sangeet Mahavidyalaya, who was also the Sattradhikar of the Sri Sri Nikamul Sattra, advised my parents to allow me to be trained in Sattriya. My journey of learning Sattriya dance started at age five under the guidance of Sri Tileswar Tamuli Borbayan. At that time, he was a young monk from the Kamalabari Sattra, Majuli. I was his first student. He was and is a very dedicated and hardworking teacher. He has such an incredible knowledge and amazing experience and due to his guidance, I was able to receive first position in the "All Assam Classical Dance Competition" organised by the Department of Culture. I continued learning under him until the age of 15. During this period, I was given many opportunities to perform in different parts of Assam and in other states.

When I was a fourth standard student (nine years old) I was given an opportunity to perform at Seppa, Arunachal Pradesh. At that time, the late Punyabrata Deva Goswami, Sattradhikar of the Nikamul Sattra, had established a very good relationship with the local tribes of Arunachal Pradesh and he was trying to spread the neo-Vashinavism culture amongst them. Holding his father's (the late Gahan Chandra Goswami) legacy, he initiated an integration and cultural exchange programme and sent my Guru, Sri Tileswar Tamuli Barbayan, and myself to Arunachal Pradesh to teach Sattriya dance and Borgeet to the local people.

After my class 10 board exam, I learned another Indian classical dance form, Kathak, under Sri Santi Shankar Das Gupta and completed Visharad in Kathak at Jyotikala Sangeet Mahavidyalaya in Tezpur. The Jyotikala Sangeet Mahavidyalaya is the first music school of Assam and was established by Rupkonwar Jyoti Prasad Agarwala, the cultural icon of Assam. Later, I worked there as a teacher.

I completed my Master's in Botany and also completed my Doctoral study at Gauhati University. Along with my study, I continued with my passion for dance. I worked with my Guru, Sri Bipul Das for Kathak, and Nritycharyya Jatin Goswami in Sattriya dance, and learned to see the world of dance in a broader context. I was fortunate enough to meet Kathak Maestro Pandit Birju Maharaj at that time. He taught me a sense of simplicity and subtleness of life, which I feel is essential to be a true artist. I am always mesmerised by his performances, knowledge on the subject, and his innovative compositions. It fuelled my obsession to dance.

All Classical dance forms of India have some basic exercises that are related to yoga and well-being. I experienced the strength of dance during the period of my Doctoral study. When I felt low or stressed, I always visited my Guru's place and spent a few hours practising dance. Dance acts like medicine and relieves my overwrought mind.

Dancing before an audience is the most challenging task for a dancer. An audience is seeking entertainment and a dancer should meet that end no matter what the personal situation a dancer may be facing offstage. I can still remember one incident when I was only nine years old. I had to portray the role of Krishna in an *Ankiya Naat*, "*Kalia Daman*". During the day's rehearsal, I cut my foot on broken glass. It was painful, but still I had to perform in the evening with a smiling face as I was the main character of that dance drama.

In my Kathak dance performances, I mostly present Pandit Birju Maharajji's compositions as taught by my Guruji. My Sattriya Guru, Nrityacharyya Jatin Goswami is well known for his choreographic works. He composed and choreographed some special compositions for me such as *Sitar Patal Prabesh*, *Pancha Kanya*, and *Prakiti Vandan*. The core of *Sattriya Nritya* is usually mythological stories. This is an artistic way of presenting mythological teachings to the people in an accessible, immediate, and enjoyable manner. *Sitar Patal Prabesh* focuses on how women were tortured by describing the agony and sorrows of Sita. At the end of the item, there is a message that in present times, the act of Ram against Sita is like violence against women. Another research-based composition is *Prakriti Vandan* that is based on environmental issues. Further to contemporary issues, I often blended traditional stories with new choreography. *Panchakanya* is a group of five iconic Hindu heroines, extolled in a hymn and whose names are believed to dispel sin when recited. They are, *Ahalya*, *Tara*, and *Mandodari* from Ramayana and Draupadi and Kunti from Mahabharata. I enacted the role of five characters in five different *taal* (rhythms) in the *Sattriya* idiom. Such productions were unique experimental works within the *Sattriya* style.

One of my own choreographed productions is *Sonit Kuwari*, a dance drama in the *Sattriya* style. It was a very successful production which earned great appreciation and encouragement. Another experimental and memorable production was *Chitrangada* based on the dance drama of Kaviguru Rabindra Nath Tagore's *Chitrangada*. The composition was based on both the *Sattriya* and Kathakali dance forms.

In my experience as a teacher, I have seen that most guardians fail to guide the interests of their children in a serious way. I feel that parents mostly yearn for glamour, awards, and prizes. They appear to search for an easier and faster method for their children to reach their destination. They expect a fixed time of learning and a technical duration and do not understand that there is no end to any learning, and it cannot be completed throughout a lifetime. Classical dance/music is like an ocean and therefore, I suggest that everyone should concentrate on learning their subject with a long-term vision. Nowadays, there are many scholarships and fellowship schemes from the government and other agencies that may support students. When I received a junior research fellowship for *Sattriya* dance from the Ministry of Culture (now CCRT) during 2009, I was given an opportunity to study deeply in this field. Now, I find the meaning of life in engaging myself in performing and teaching dance.

I think we have responsibilities as dancers to be innovative and to do something for society. I established a sociocultural organisation named *Saptaswa* "the rays of performing art" to provide a clear vision for Indian Classical dance and also to share knowledge about the folk dances of Assam. For the past nine years I have organised "Nrityakalpa" a national/international Classical dance festival that receives funding to pay local and professional dancers to perform. Other artists work collaboratively. It is the first Classical dance festival organised in Tezpur by a private organisation. We regularly organise seminars and workshops, which help students and other people to extend their knowledge by learning from great gurus. Even very recently (2020), our organisation successfully ran an awareness programme on COVID-19 where approximately 35 artists from different fields expressed the need of awareness through their own art form.

Experiences nourish us. When I started the festival and invited people to watch, they asked me whether it was a kind of competition or a programme where their children could perform. People seem to have little idea about the objective of a festival, seminar, or workshop. I have noticed that most of the people take interest in "functions" (as they are generally called in India) only when their child performs. They do not feel it necessary to see others' performances. Parents should encourage their child to observe and learn from others.

At present, I feel that people now value our festival, not only in Assam but all over India. Artists apply to perform in our festival from different parts of India. We have received coverage in national/international media and journals. Nationally recognised critics have come to witness our festival. This gives me immense satisfaction, because at the same time they also come to know about my small town, our culture, and our heritage. I feel rewarded and recognised after receiving empanelment in ICCR (Indian Council of Cultural Relations, Government of India) along with my group of students.

Marami Medhi

Marami Medhi is an internationally acclaimed Kathak exponent from Assam. She received her initial training under the late Guru Charan Bordoloi and later became a disciple of renowned Kathak maestro, the late Surendra Saikia ji of Kathak Kendra. She is the founder of "Sur Sangam", an institute of kathak dance and music. She is presently working as a lecturer at the LKRB State College of Music, Guwahati. An empanelled artist of ICCR, Marami is also considered an A grade artist by Doordarshan Kendra, New Delhi. She was awarded a two-year fellowship in the year 2000–2001 from the Ministry of Human Resource Development. She has performed in more than 30 reputed national dance and music festivals throughout India. Marami has represented India in festivals through tours to London, Egypt, Israel, Palestine, U.A.E, Bangladesh, and New Zealand. Marami has received numerous awards for her dancing and has also worked successfully in the field of choreography. Apart from being a Kathak dancer, she is also an actor in the Assamese film industry and has acted in more than 15 films including feature films, television films, and serials.

My dance journey started when I was two and half years old. My mother told me how excited and interested I was about dance from my very early years. My parents were interested in art and culture: my mother used to sing and my father was a theatre artist. They guided and encouraged me to follow my interest in dance.

In our early days we only had access to radio as a means to listen to music and very few people had access to tape recorders. My mom recalls that I used to dance to one of my favourite radio programmes every day for an hour whenever it was broadcast. At times my mom used to sing for me and I used to choreograph with her help and dance to her tunes.

I received many opportunities to perform on stage because of my father, as he was very active in sociocultural activities. I mostly danced to Dr. Bhupen Hazarika's compositions. And so, my dance journey started.

It was around the 1970s when I was about five years old when my father was transferred to the beautiful town of Tezpur in Assam. Our entire family moved in with him. This town gave me a lot more exposure to the world of art, music, and dance. I received many opportunities from my school and even my teachers encouraged me to work on different forms of art that interested me apart from dance, like painting, singing, and recitation. I also received an opportunity to learn *Sattriya* dance and creative dance at Tezpur. The cultural environment in Tezpur influenced me a great deal.

After five years my father was transferred again and we moved to a small town called Nalbari in Assam. Here I learned painting from Guru Aidya Sharma. He guided and motivated me a lot in my life, not only in painting but also in drama, dance, and many other aspects of the arts and cultural world. Guru Aidya Sharma gave me opportunities to perform not only in Assam but also in many national-level programmes around the country. In our art school in Nalbari I learned various folk dances of Assam and received some preliminary knowledge of Kathak and Sattriya dance. This was a very important phase of my life and was the beginning of my future career in dance.

In 1981, I passed my tenth standard at school and moved to Guwahati, and admitted myself to Cotton College. I was enrolled in Kathak dance classes under Guru, the late Charu Bordoloi who was the founder and principal of the State College of Music, Assam. This was my first formal training in Kathak dance and the beginning of my journey. I boarded in the college's girls' hostel and our hostel supervisor Mrs. Aparna Bezbarua was kind enough to allow me to use the hostel common room as my dance practice hall. She always supported me, and also excused me if I was ever late to the hostel from any dance-related work.

After learning Kathak for three years under the late Charu Bordoloi, I had to stop my training because of his health issues and his advanced age. After a few months, I continued my learning in Kathak under another legendary Guru, the late Surendra Saikia. He was the Guru of Lucknow Kathak Kendra. Although Guru Surendra Saikia was originally from Assam he then settled in Lucknow, therefore I only got the opportunity to meet and learn from him once or twice a year. He would either travel to Guwahati or I would go to Lucknow. He made me explore the Lucknow Gharana of Kathak dance and I learned the dance form intensely.

During this phase of my life, I decided to get married to Mr. Joy Prakash Medhi who is a Hindustani vocalist and the man who supports, loves, and cares for me. This was a turning point in my life. He was a great influence on my musical journey. He encouraged and helped me a lot in my field of work. From performing live and accompanying my dance with his Hindustani vocals to creating music tracks for my performances, he took care of everything. In the beginning of my married life, along with Kathak dance I also started formal training in *Sattriya*, the Classical dance form of Assam under the guidance of Guru Padmashri Sri Ghantakanta Bora.

In 1989, I joined the State College of Music, Guwahati, Assam, as a teacher of Kathak dance. Thus, my passion became my profession. I rehearsed and prepared myself for my performances as well as teaching my students. Teaching the dance form really helped me gain more knowledge about it. I found that learning and teaching is a give and take process where one continually gives and gains knowledge.

Initially when I was learning Kathak dance, I noted that few people in my region were interested in classical forms of dance. However, as time passed, I noticed that gradually different classical dance forms were becoming popular amongst people and more and more people started taking interest and learning various Indian classical dances in Assam. Many dance festivals emerged throughout the entire country. I did not have an opportunity to perform in the beginning, and was unhappy with my own performances as there were not many platforms for me to develop my dance form. During this period of struggle, I planned to begin a Kathak dance Institute in Assam.

This was the beginning of *Sur Sangam*, an institute of classical dance that I established in the year 1990 with the motive to spread this form of Classical dance in my region and to popularise Indian Classical dance and music. Initially, I started the classes at my home but when students started increasing more and more each day, I decided to move the institute into a proper studio space. The growing interest motivated me to work more in this field and carry forward the knowledge I had gathered from my Gurus. I tried to modify and beautify the dance in my own way, keeping the traditional grammar of the dance form. At *Sur Sangam* we organise a festival every year to give a platform to young upcoming talents to showcase their artistic skills. We also invite various nationally and internationally acclaimed artists to perform at our show and try to give the audience of this region a taste of fine Indian Classical dance and music.

I have always tried to give my best teaching to my students in order to help them develop into good dancers. I feel satisfied and proud when the students from *Sur Sangam* become successful dancers, teachers, choreographers, or social activists.

My husband and I have always loved to create new compositions and choreographies and we have made numerous compositions together to date. As a resident and a native of Assam, I also have a duty towards *Sattriya* dance and hence, I am working in the field of *Sattriya* to popularise the form outside Assam. We have made various compositions blending *Sattriya* and Kathak dance that have gained many laurels from audiences in India and abroad.

I am a mother of two children, one son, Surya Prakash Medhi and a daughter Meghranjani Medhi. Both are working in the field of music and the arts. My daughter Meghranjani is a Kathak dancer and an actor, and my son Surya enjoys western singing. Apart from music, he is currently doing his training to become a pilot.

During my journey, the cooperation of my children was always with me. Specifically, my daughter, Meghranjani has helped me in my choreographies and teaching. My son also helps me in various aspects of my dance career, and takes care of all the technical needs and feeds me with the updated information of today's digital world. I am always grateful to my entire family including my parents for their support in pursuing my dream.

Meghranjani Medhi

Meghranjani is a young and acclaimed artist of Kathak dance. She is the daughter of Marami Medhi a renowned Kathak exponent and Joy Prakash Medhi a renowned vocalist, composer, and music director of Assam. Born on 15th November 1989, in Nalbari, Assam, Meghranjani started learning Kathak at the very tender age of three years under the guidance of her mother. She has also further undergone training under the great legend, Kathak Maestro Padmavibhushan Pt. Birju Maharaj. Currently she is training under a Jaipur legend, Gharana Guru Pt. Rajendra Gangani. Meghranjani is also a renowned actor in the Assamese Film Industry.

In 2009, she was awarded a senior scholarship from the Ministry of Culture, Government of India. Meghranjani has completed her Master's in Kathak dance under Indira Kala Sangeet Vishwavidyalaya at the Khairagarh University. She has also undergone training in Sattriya dance and completed her Nritya Gunin from Sangeet Sattra Pariksha Parishad, Assam, in the year 2017. Meghranjani is an A grade artist of Doordarshan Kendra in the field of Kathak dance. She has many national and international performances to her credit.

Meghranjani performed as Mumtaz in a dance theatre production entitled TAJ and was well received by the audience. She has acted with renowned Bollywood stars such as Kabir Bedi and Canadian actress Lisa Ray.

I am a very blessed child to be born to a cultured family where my mother, Guru Marami Medhi, is a Kathak exponent herself and my father a renowned vocalist, Guru Joyprakash Medhi. I did not choose dance as my life but dance chose me and became my life. As a child, I was brought up in a very beautiful environment which was full of positivity, independence, open discussion, and sensitivity. I became attracted to dance and music from the age of two. I cannot recall my memories very clearly, but my mom says that I gave my first performance at the age of three in Rabindra Bhawan, Guwahati. I was very active as a child, taking part in all of the cultural and academic activities in school. My first schooling started at home, as I received my mother as my dance Guru and my father as my music Guru. Gradually I started to dance every day and it became a scheduled part of my life. My parents had established an institution named *Sur Sangam* the year I was born. Now, the institution has completed 30 years. My informal training started with the students in the institution. My mother also gave me some private lessons. At that time, I never took Kathak dance seriously, I just took it as a fun hobby because I loved the dance form and I loved to see my mother dancing so gracefully with her jewellery, beautiful costumes, and make-up. I also enjoyed the dance form in Hindi movies. I was called the "dancing queen" in school as I usually took part in every cultural activity and won laurels from my teachers. I took dance as my elective subject in my 10th Year board exams and secured the state's highest grade that year in 2006. I also received the Junior Scholarship in the year 2004 from the "Center for Cultural Resource and Training" in the field of Kathak dance. I completed my Visharad in the field of Kathak from Bhatkhande Sangeet Vidyapith in the year 2004, and that year was a turning point in my life when the legendary exponent of Kathak Padmabivushan Pandit Birju Maharaj came to Guwahati to conduct a workshop. My mother took me along with a few other students from our institution to take part in the workshop and earn blessings from Panditji. I was a very shy girl and stood in the third line of the class with around 40–50 dancers. He was teaching us a *bol* and immediately when we were asked to dance the same movements he taught us, he noticed me and asked me to join the first line in the centre. He told me that I danced well and from that day during the entire workshop, I should stand in the first line. I was extremely happy and blessed. The next year he invited me to Delhi to perform a solo for 45 minutes in one of his festivals at Triveni Auditorium. From that point, I really became serious with my dance, and dance forever became my passion. My mother prepared me for three months with vigorous rehearsals for my first solo performance and it was a huge success. I started to fall in love with Kathak and Kathak dance became my life.

I was admitted to Cotton College, Guwahati, which is one of the best colleges in Assam. I graduated from Cotton College and at that time, I was the best dancer for five consecutive years, earning gold medals for the college in youth festivals. In the meantime, I also completed my Master of Music in Kathak from Bhatkhande Sangeet Vidyapith, Lucknow. I also received the senior scholarship for two years from the Human Resource of Cultural Development. I started to earn in my professional career as a dancer from the year 2008 when I also recorded a video CD of a few of my dances. I used my small earnings at that time to fund the KD production while also applying for empanelment in ICCR. I was lucky to be selected as an empanelled artist to represent the country abroad. With the blessings of my Guru, parents, and my hard work I was offered one opportunity after another and every opportunity was a turning point of my life. I travelled with my mother to perform abroad to Egypt, Israel, Palestine, U.A.E, and London. My first tour as a solo performer was in the year 2016 to New Zealand.

Abhinaya (acting) plays a vital role in dance and I was always attracted to the *abhinaya* aspect of performance and explored it in some depth. I was offered many opportunities to act in many movies, music videos, and advertisements. My parents always encouraged me in my interests, and always inspired me to follow my heart; I had had a dream to become an actor someday. I first started my acting career at the age of 18 and worked in numerous films, music videos, advertisements, and short serials. My first video film "Lakhimi" was widely appreciated and was a super hit. After that, people all over Assam came to know me as an actor. I had previously been known as a Kathak dancer but now people know me as an actor.

Later, I thought that I should use my name and fame in a way to popularise Kathak dance in all parts of Assam so, I started another journey by sharing the beauty of the dance. Every year my parents organised annual programmes in the institute, apart from the showcases for student performances. During the last five years, on completion of 25 years of the institution, we have started to organise festivals and invite different legendary artists of different dance forms to perform, especially for the students. I have also been teaching in the institute for the last seven years and I feel my teaching has improved me as a performer. I have also started choreographing, as well as assisting my mother with many dance ballets. I also conduct workshops nationally and internationally. I completed my Master's in Kathak from Khairagargh University. I received an opportunity to choreograph with the great legend, Guru Kumudini Lakhiaji in Canada in the year 2010 for a Dance Ballet "TAJ".

Now my aim is to carry forward the legacy of my parents and become a role model for the next generation. The question asked by many is, "can dance be a career?" Yes, it can. Beyond being a career, dance provides physical and mental development, helping me to become stronger. To be successful what is required is a passion, dedication, and hard work and a thirst for the craft. Young dancers need to also remember that gurus and teachers are always there to help, motivate, inspire, and guide their growth and journey.

Seetarani Hazarika

Seetarani Hazarika is a well-known Sattriya exponent, actor, and Bihu dance artist. She has given many Sattriya Nritya lecture demonstrations and was associated with Spicmacay. She has received a number of invitations from various government and non-government associations to perform Bihu and Sattriya nationally and internationally. Of particular note are performances of Bihu and Sattriya Nritya in the London Nehru Centre and the House of Lords, South Hall in 2011. She also performed at the London Olympics when India campaigned for the Olympics. She has received a number of scholarships and fellowships and was awarded the Tanmay Bordoloi Memorial Award in the field of Bihu. She has also received blessings and praise from many people. She received the titles of Mou Kuwori, Bihu Kuwori, Bor Bihuwoti, Bihu Rani, and Bihu Samragi in Latasil (the utmost honour of Bihu). Besides Bihu and Sattriya, Seetarani has also performed various regional dance forms of Assam such as, Bodo, Jhumoor, Tiwa, Hazong, Gowalporia, Karbi, Deuri, and Mishing. She is recorded as an A-grade artist nationally in Doordarshan Prachar Bharti. She has also been engaged as an actor in innumerable series on private channels. Amongst the tele films she performed in, Dr. Bhabendra Nath Saikia's "Srinkhal" was a milestone in her career. She is a "B-high" grade artist in AIR (All in Radio) and is happy to be a part of this industry.

My deep passion and involvement in dance began in childhood. As I grew, I started expressing my feelings through dance and music. Random expressions and movements turned into dance forms and from the age of six I began my formal dance training alongside my other studies.

My mother, Srimati Amal Prava Hazakira and my father the late Jagannath Hazarika recognised my interest in dance and allowed me to start my institutional learning in the field of the Sattriya dance in Sangit Kanan, Panbazar, under the blessings of my Guru, Padmashree Bayanacharya Ghanakanta Bora Borbayan. Gradually, I became increasingly involved in Sattriya dance. After learning the first lessons of Sattriya Nritya namely *Mati-akhora*, I went to Madras (Chennai) to perform *Mati-akhora* along with my guru Ghanakanta Bora Borbayon Dev and with the cultural executor of the Assam Government at that time, the late Anand Mohan Bhagawati. *Mati-akhora* builds the body up for dancing. It simultaneously develops our bodies to grow physically, mentally, and spiritually.

Gradually, I started receiving invitations for the performance of Sattriya Nritya from all over Assam, and other states of India. Along with the completion of my studies and subsequent graduation, I also completed my institutional learning of Sattriya Nritya and I became a *Gunin* of dance.

Besides performing, I have been working as a teacher in the field of Sattriya Nritya. To be an efficient teacher, I never stop learning. I participate in lecture demonstrations, discussion cycles, and workshops. I interact with eminent and experienced persons in the field, so that I can provide accurate and systematic knowledge to my students. I also feel that to be a good teacher in the field of dance, perfection as a performer is inevitable.

Following my achievements, and with others' blessings I started an institution for Sattriya and Bihu in Rupnagar, Guwahati. At present, I am training approximately four hundred students. The name of my institution and centre for Sattriya Nritya and Bihu is "Jagannath Hazarika Sanskritik Kendra".

I hope that our next generation will respect and have the desire to learn our culture and traditions correctly and wholeheartedly and spread its importance both nationally and globally.

In the process of training my students, I am aware of keeping the authenticity of the dance form, particularly when a student is learning more than one form of dance. One dance may become influenced by the other.

Nowadays, Sattriya Nritya is not only attached to the Sattras, but it is spread all over the globe with its webs extended everywhere. Therefore, it is important to keep intact the original identity of the dance form. In recent times, some artists and students, without an awareness of the basic knowledge of the dance or without proper training, reworked some of the movements to gain more popularity in front of an audience. This can ruin the identity of a dance. Being a teacher, I always try to adhere to the proper style of dance and not to damage or ruin the originality and purity of the art form.

In earlier days, Sattriya Nritya lessons were given only in Sattras, but nowadays lessons are also taught outside the Sattras following a particular formula or protocol. I aim to maintain such protocols. Firstly, I begin by teaching my students about the *Matras, Taalas,* and *Layas*. I am careful to speak the *bols* (beat) in a particular speed and rhythm. I let students use their hands and legs to keep the *talas* and rhythm perfect at a particular speed. That means, by uttering numerically, 1, 2, 3 or so on, they learn the timing for the different postures. I also instruct the students to utter the *bols* themselves. It is important to have a perfect understanding of the *geet, taalas, layas* to learn the dance form.

The primary dance lessons, *Mati-akhora* are practised daily to make the body capable of dancing. Many dancers can face the problem of a slipped disc, therefore, before starting my dance lessons I instruct my students to practise warm up drill for at least ten minutes every day so that they do not face any severe problems during performances.

In Sattriya dance, before starting the daily lessons it is a culture or tradition to take the blessings of the Guru or the teacher. It is believed that we should start our lessons by showing respect and devotion towards the Guru. Moreover, we should also show respect and devotion by taking blessings and pray to the area where we perform and also to the instruments that are played during the entire performance. These things should be given importance by the students.

In recent years, our society is becoming crowded with various disorderly and unwanted situations. In such circumstances, I feel dance has a great role to play. Dance can communicate required messages to society. It can also develop the mental and physical health which is very necessary to survive in this chaotic world.

Dipjyoti Dipankar: (Dipjyota Das and Dipankar Arandhura)

"JibonSindhuBohuBindure Hoi Jodi Kormere Hoi BinduPurno"
Dr. Bhupen Hazarika

Dipjyoti Das and Dipankar Arandhara are popularly known as, **Dipjyoti-Dipankar,** *the duet exponents of Sattriya and modern dances of Assam. The duo completed their Master's in performing Arts (Sattriya) at Dibrugarh University in the year 2016 and completed a "Gunin" (Diploma) of Sattriya dance at the Sangeet Sattra Pariksha Parishad. They were selected as empanelled Artistes of the ICCR duet category in the year 2017 and are declared as A Graded Artists from Doordarshan, Guwahati. The duo were trained under Ramkrishna Talukdar, Boby Rani Talukdar, and Dolly Rani Talukdar. In 2010, they won the 1st Prize in the "National Level Classical Dance Competition" in the duet category organised by Doordarshan Kendra, Guwahati. They have received numerous awards since then and have received blessings from Padmabibhusan Dr. Sonal Mansingh. Dipjyoti–Dipankar were the first duo to perform Sattriya dance on a national television reality show (Bharat kiShan Rum Jhum) and the duo have performed throughout India.*

The sweet scent of mud from the paddy fields during the rainy season has never left me. My journey in dance started with a decision to seek admission to the State Music College in Guwahati. My father always knew and understood my love for the art of dance. A new chapter of my life unfolded with the step towards Guwahati.

During my college days, the bright young boy sitting next to me in all of my classes turned out to be the best dancing partner of my entire life. He was Dipjyoti Das. Apart from Sattriya, both of us (Dipjyoti and I) opted to learn a secondary subject, Kathak Nritya, under the guidance of Guru Marami Medhi. We also had the opportunity to receive the guidance of Gurus Smt. Bobby Rani Talukdar and Smt. Dolly Rani Talukdar on the subject of Sattriya. The idea of the duo Dipjyoti–Dipankar was initially proposed by Guru Ramkrishna Talukdar during the time when the Sattriya Kendra of the Sangeet Natak Academy was established in Guwahati. The first events organised by Sattriya Kendra were held in places like Goa, Aurangabad, Pune, and Mumbai where both of us had the pleasure to dance as a part of Guru Ramkrishna Talukdar's troupe. These few performances marked the beginning of our duo – Dipjyoti–Dipankar.

The year 2013 was very memorable for the both of us as we had the opportunity to showcase Sattriya Nritya on a national platform through various reality shows. In one of those reality shows we were indeed blessed and honoured to have Padma Visbhushan Dr. Sonal Man Singh as one of our mentors. One of the most memorable moments of our dance career would be the time when we had the privilege to perform in front of Pandit Birju Maharajji on the occasion of his birthday. We performed a Sattriya-Kathak jugalbandi as a part of Marami Medhi's troupe. At the end of the performance, we received a standing ovation from Panditji and he also urged us to wear the Muga turban which we wore during our performance. He highly praised our Sattriya dance and claimed that our performance of Sattriya had overshadowed the Kathak Nritya. This praise has had a lasting impact on us.

Sometimes people ask us why we choose to dance. We actually breathe dance. Dance is the freedom of movement in the chaos of life. When we dance we feel secure under the shade of Krishna and the presence of the Supreme is experienced everywhere around us. We are Sattriya practitioners, still striving to reach an ultimate goal and propagate the teachings of the great Vaishnavite saints, Srimanta Sankaradeva and Sri Sri Madhavadeva. Dance made us recognise ourselves. Dance gave purpose to our lives. Dance gives us energy, happiness, satisfaction, and spirituality.

Being a Classical dancer is not a one-day job. It takes years and years to grasp the spiritual essence of the dance forms. To become a Classical dancer, one should have sheer dedication, concentration, devotion, practice, confidence, and faith towards the dance and the Almighty. Apart from this, the dancer should be able to sacrifice themselves completely at the feet of their Guru. These are the significant characteristics that help in the shaping of a good dancer.

No story of a dancer is devoid of hurdles put forth by the society. We have faced many queries such as "Why do we dance?" "How will we earn a living?" "Do boys even dance?" We never pay much heed to such questions and comments and instead focus on the path on which Krishna chose to lead us. We always believed that with supreme dedication we could achieve anything. We also feel proud for being the agents of propagation of such a great art form. We feel that what little we have been doing can be compared with the spiritual attainment of a monk. Dance is our humble service at the feet of the Almighty.

During the very short span of 20 years of our dancing life we have successfully performed in many revered festivals across the nation. Among these, the Khajuraaho Dance Festival (2014), Kalaghoda Art Festival (2015), Raindrops Festival (2017) which are some of the most prestigious as well as cherished dance festivals for us. In this way, through our performances, we have tried our best to spread the sweet nectar of the divine creations of Srimanta Sankaradeva and Sri Sri Madhavadeva. We have been conferred upon with accolades such as "Yuva Kala Ratna" from the Andhra Pradesh Kuchpudi Art Academy (2015), "AtulyaNrityaPratibhaSammaan" from the Pratibha Nritya Mandir, Nagpur (2019). Apart from receiving the graded title from Doordarshan Kendra, Guwahati, we have also been the first duet dancers to be selected as empanelled artists by the Indian Council for Cultural Relations (ICCR) in the category of Sattriya dance.

We consider the establishment of our dance academy in 2008 – Manikanchan Kala Manjari – as a milestone in our career. Currently, we render our humble services to almost 200 students from places including Canada, England, Chile, Abu Dhabi, and Dubai. With an attachment to our institution, we feel that our students are like flowers. They bloom at different times with different qualities and talents and we therefore, try to guide our students in a way that they are comfortable. We try to understand them, know them in every way so that they won't face any difficulties while learning. The happiness which we receive in teaching them can't be compared to any other thing in this world. The relationship that we share with our students seems to us as precious as the relationship of a mother and her child. We think that both students and teachers should be in a relationship where there is respect, devotion, and love so that they both can support each other. Most of our students of the young generation are learning Sattriya Nritya with great enthusiasm and devotion. They enjoy learning this dance form. We also try to guide them in a creative way to draw their focused attention towards this art form.

For the past three years we have organised an annual dance festival, Manikanchan Nritya Mahotsav, offering a platform to showcase new and evolving classical dances of India.

We have created successful dance projects based on Sattriya Nritya. These include: *Narasimha* – the half man half lion incarnation, *Moksha*, *Govinda Govardhana Dhari*, and *Shakuntala*. Our dream project, *Shakuntala* – the

Love Saga, which was based on Kalidasa's *Abhijyana Shakuntalam*, was staged on the 16th of February 2020. To our surprise, the show witnessed one of the biggest audiences of all time. Irrespective of the chilly winter and the scarcity of seats, the people's response was overwhelming. We were encouraged and felt there was a positive future for the Sattriya culture. Today, almost every other house in Assam has at least one Sattriya dancer. We feel very grateful to be agents of this great art form. We promise to uphold the spiritual as well as cultural ideals of our revered saints and walk into the path that has been guided by them through music and dance traditions.

16 The performers of folk dances

Mandakini Baruah

Dharmeswar Nath Oja

Dharmeswar Nath Oja is a renowned performer of Ojapali art from the Satghariya village of the Sipajhar area of the Darang district of Assam, India. He was honoured with a One-Time financial award of Rs. 10,000 and also received a Silpi Pension from the Assam government in 2014.

I was born into a very poor family. With very little formal education I have involved myself in the art of Ojapali as I have had a deep interest in it since my childhood. My father was a poor farmer and we did not have any land. We had cows and buffaloes and when I brought them to the paddy field, I used to sing the tunes of Ojapali and I just felt happy. Later I came to know that Ojapali is a very beautiful and precious part of Assamese culture. I used to enjoy Ojapali when it was sung by others, and then I believed that this would be the perfect cultural activity for me and nothing could be better. Thus, I established myself in that field and simultaneously tried to carry it forward into society. The late Santiram Nath, who was a prominent Oja, was my Guru for Ojapali.

Concentration is the key to success. Keeping this in mind I proceeded towards my goal, even as I faced various conflicts in my life, but I was determined to recognise myself as an Oja of Byas Sangeet. Culture is the backbone of a religion or community. Culture will expand forever, but we are responsible for keeping it alive. With this mindset, I have been trying to teach Ojapali to the young people in our community so that it will continue to be spread amongst new generations. Life is more than eating and sleeping, it consists of other important factors such as a responsibility towards society, a development of one's own culture, and the creation of an awareness of that culture amongst others. Ojapali is a type of fine art which is performed in a group. It has four different characteristics: song, dance, expression (mudra), and dialogue. In a formal performance Ojapali can be categorised as acting to some extent, but it cannot be described completely as acting since there is no individual character development. It is noted that no specific religious idealism is expressed through Ojapali. Even though it is similar to other arts, I feel it cannot be combined with them to make a fusion, as I believe the integrity of Ojapali would be lost.

DOI: 10.4324/9781003398776-17

A culture or an art form should not be constrained to a certain locality for the sake of the existence of a religion. A rich culture like Ojapali has infinite importance in carrying out various messages concerning social reform. Ojapali singing can be an effective medium for showcasing various positive and negative aspects of society. I believe that we have to bring Ojapali to an international platform.

Within Assam, educational institutions play significant roles in shaping one's personality and in school, all students study together without any discrimination. Music, games, and sports are important components of education, therefore I feel that Ojapali can also play an important role in the context of education. It is necessary that subjects like Ojapali are included in the syllabus as Ojapali serves multiple roles beyond art and culture. Presently Ojapali has helped to develop an awareness amongst people regarding various diseases such as Aids and Ebola. Awareness campaigns to fight against the on-going worldwide pandemic of the CoronaVirus (COVID-19) is also being carried out through the performance of Ojapali.

Guru Shree Rajendra Nath Oja

Guru Shree Rajendra Nath Oja was born in 1952, and is a renowned Oja of the Suknani Ojapali who belongs to the Sipajhar area of the Darang district of Assam. His late father was Seniram Nath and his mother was Baneswari Nath. He twice won first place in a competition on Suknani Ojapali organised by Darangi Kala Krishti Unnayan Sangha, and was the first recipient of the Narayan Sarma Shield. He was recognised as a regular artist in the All India Radio in 2007 and also participated in the Assam State Aids Control Society 5-day workshop held in New Delhi in 2011. In 2012, he delivered a One-Month Training Course on Xuknani Sangeet to a team of 27 boys and girls in Rashtriya Natya Vidyalaya, supported by the Government of India, after which time he was designated with the title of Guru. In the years 2016–17 an organisation from the North Eastern region known as Jon Sangskritik Kendra, awarded him the title of Guru by involving him in the tradition of Guru and Sishya.

I was born into a poor landless farmer's family in a village called Nayakpara under Sipajhar in the Darang district of Assam. We had nothing in the way of land and property. In spite of the hard efforts of my parents, I was unable to succeed in the 10th class examination, and at that point in time I concluded my studies forever. From my childhood I have had a deep interest in folk songs, acting (in Assamese Bhaonas), games, and sports. I used to be a regular narrator of *Nagara Naam* from the 8th standard (13 years of age). After I dropped out of school, I married Smt. Dharmeswari Nath from our village in 1971 for the sake of looking after my parents. During that year I started practising *Suknani Sangeet* which was one of my favourite performing art forms. Soon after, my father left us and I had to work to gain a daily wage and look after my family. I worked during the day and practised Ojapali at night. We did not always have food to eat but I often practised Ojapali for the entire night. It would be a long chapter if I started telling my whole life story here. Presently I am 69 years old. For the past 50 years I have been striving to carry forward our culture despite facing many tough and unhappy moments.

I can remember when I was in the 6th standard (11 years of age) when some students of class seven performed *Suknani Sangeet* in the Annual Function of our school. The Oja elder was well dressed with a silk kurta, chador, and dhoti with a beautiful white turban on his head. He was narrating the Ojapali so well that I was just looking at him, and thought that I would like to become an Oja of his level in the future. In 1972, when I was imagining myself as an Oja, a group of elderly people of our village were planning to construct a team of *Suknani Oja*. The group was led by the famous Oja of that time, the late Chandra Kanta Nath Oja, who was a stout and handsome person respected by all, and a Godfather to me. The entire process was on the verge of finalisation but the question was, "who will be the Oja?" Eight or nine Palis were confirmed. The Palis accompany the Oja by performances of a continuous rhythm played on folk instruments. After a long discussion, a person near our house was selected for the role of Oja. The Guru and other villagers went to meet and talk to the parents to gain their permission. The parents did not allow their son to be the Oja. I was accompanying the group of people that day. Suddenly, pointing towards me, the Guru said, "I will give him *Puthi* (training) and he can be the Oja of the group". It was an honour for me, thus with the blessings of my Guru and with no stone left unturned I dedicated myself to the practice of being an Oja. I was very fond of Ojapali after seeing the performances of the famous Ojas such as the late Lalit Chandra Nath, the late Deben Bora, and Muktaram Baruah.

My first Guru was the late Chandra Kanta Das Oja who was a Silpi Pension holder under the Government of Assam. I was then associated with Suknani Sahityacharjya and the late Lalit Chandra Nath Oja who was a winner of the Sangeet Natak Academy Thakur Award and also a Silpi Pension holder under the Government of Assam. With my limited knowledge and experience, I have been whole-heartedly performing Ojapali for the last 50 years for various occasions like Pujas, government programmes and private programmes to carry forward this folk culture.

I believe that this art form has had a great impact on creating people's worldview. A community cannot live without a proper language and culture. It helps people to live. Exercise, meditation, good thoughts, happiness, and a smile, assist people in leading healthy lives. A cultured person can be a human being with qualities like intelligence, intellectuality, soberness, and politeness. One can hold an exceptional position in society when engaged with such qualities.

A tradition should stay true to its origins and does not need any kind of fusion or mixing. If any kind of fusion is introduced into a tradition, it will be tough for the new generation to understand and accept the origins and it may be confusing for them. They may end up being less interested in acquiring cultural knowledge and may ignore their own culture. I believe that the Ojapali as an art form has not been changed to date and I believe that Ojapali experts would not allow the art form to be changed.

To bring Ojapali into an international platform we have to be socially conscious and alert. Instead of going forward as before, in supporting the traditional Ojapali, we need to gain the interest of the next generation and try to involve them in the process of learning the Ojapali art form. This will assist in creating more interest and bringing Ojipali to an international platform. Schools and other educational institutions can definitely play an important part in this. I strongly believe that if educational institutions, social organisations, or the intellectuals of our society take the initiative to encourage new generations in learning Ojapali, then it will not be a very big deal to take this culture to the international level.

Ojapali, as an art form, can help people in supporting their mental growth, as this cultural art form is related to religious and auspicious occasions. There are two types of Ojapalis – Byas Ojapali and Suknani Ojapali. These forms are closely related to Vaishnavism and Shaktism, respectively, and therefore, they include many religious rituals. By way of example, after taking a bath in the morning, a person completes their religious rituals, such as worshipping God, and narrating Puthis (holy books). These rituals help to make a person become calm, polite, cultured, honest, sober, and also mentally strong and pure. Ojapali rituals have arguably helped our communities in dealing with social issues. Normally an Ojapali team consists of a minimum of six members who are honoured by people of their society. These six leaders can play a major and important role in supporting people as they cope with social concerns. The leadership role of Ojapali cannot be underestimated in contemporary Assamese society, as they are highly respected by members of their society.

Ranjit Gogoi

Ranjit Gogoi is a renowned Bihu performer and esteemed player of the Dhol and Pepa from the Charaideo area of the Sivasagar district of Assam. He is the author of a book, titled "Bihu Sanskritir Itibritta" (2017) and is currently writing about the current situation of Bihu, and hopes to have it ready by the end of 2021. He runs an organisation named Aviskar in Guwahati, where he teaches the younger generation folk performances and folk instruments. He was the choreographer of different national and international events such as the South-East Asian Games, National Games, 2007. He was the segment Director in the BRIC (Brazil, Russia, India, and China) Festival of Goa. He was involved with SPICMACAY (The Society for the Promotion of Indian Classical Music and Culture Amongst Youth) and CCRT (Centre for Cultural Resources and Training).

I always want to experience life and develop myself through the ideology of art and culture. I have had a deep interest in Bihu music from my childhood and learned to play *Dhol*, *Pepa*, *Gagana*, and *Sutuli*, and sang Bihu songs to make myself mentally happy. I was instinctively wrapped by the thread of Bihu.

Originally Bihu was an ancient folk dance born from an agricultural context. Normally the term Guru is not prominent in folk dance because the creators are anonymous. Even so, the history must be acknowledged, where each generation has handed down the Bihu tradition to the next. I learned Bihu music through this process from the seniors of our village and that is why they can be known as my first Gurus, and my village as my first informal platform. I learned the art of playing *Dhol* (being the Oja) under the supervision of Sjt. Tulashi Oja who himself was a disciple of the Great Moghai Oja.

In my view Bihu can be a medium of economic support for livelihood. It not only contains physical, mental, spiritual, and entertainment elements, but also can be the source of the living process. Many Bihu artists are receiving opportunities to study in good institutions, and are also getting jobs and pensions from the government. Many more are running their own dance schools to make themselves financially stable, and are helping others to support families.

Music is a traditional vehicle through which people can develop their intellectual capacity. Music is the soul of our traditions. Music can refresh a tired person or it can boost them when they want to be refreshed. Music is also a therapy that heals and inspires people's mental state. In simple words, music benefits everyone. Even though music does not directly address social disorders, it can make indirect changes. We cannot ignore the importance and contribution of music in making social change, developing brotherhood, and fostering friendly relationships.

Jina Rajkumari

Jina Rajkumari is a prominent figure in the context of Bihu performance. She completed her Higher Secondary education at Barooah College, Guwahati, and then completed her Bachelor's degree at the Gorgaon College, Sibsagar. After that she studied a Diploma course in Civil Engineering (in Draftsmanship) at the Girls' Polytechnic in Guwahati. She completed her Post-Graduation in Classical Music at the Chandigarh University. She has been honoured with the title of "Guru" of folk dance by the Eastern Zonal Cultural Centre, Kolkata, under the Government of India. She also received a Junior Fellowship for "A comparative Study on Bihu and Tribal Folk Dances" from the Ministry of Culture, Government of India. She is an approved artist of the Indian Council for Cultural Relation under the Department of External Affair, Government of India and also a "B-High" grade artist of All India Radio and Doordarshan, Guwahati. She is an approved radio artist of Borgeet, Kamrupiya Lokogeet, Goalporiya Lokogeet, and Bihu. The Tai Ahom Development Council, Government of Assam has honoured her with an award of excellence, the "Bishesh Parodorshi Award". She also received the "*Anil Sarkar Smarak Lokosilpi Award*" in Cumilla, Bangladesh, from the Pratidin Times.

I was born and brought up in Lakowa, in the historical place of Sivasagar, Assam. Since my birth place is the hub of petrochemicals, I grew up with the smell of oil and gas along with the aroma of beautiful nature. My mother worked for the Oil and Natural Gas Corporation, so we lived in the official quarters, but I did not miss any opportunities to visit my father's village, Ujoni Kunwor Gaon, which was also near our quarters. I really enjoyed the rural atmosphere and environment and felt happy to work with my hands in rice cultivation and in many other rural activities.

The Bihu dance is an appeal to nature. It has an internal power of attraction which attracts people towards it. In our village and at my home, everyone was very fond of Bihu. My father was a very popular Bihu artist, my brother plays *Dhol* and *Pepa* and my sisters were also good at Bihu dance. I was attached to Bihu from my early childhood. In other words, I can say that Bihu is in my blood. Each and every tribe in Assam has a Bihu that is similar to that of other tribes. The ways of celebration may differ but the central motifs are similar.

Bihu is not taught or learnt as a course or study. It is a spontaneous outcome of internal happiness. Just as the tree leaves are shaken naturally by wind, the happy feelings of people's minds are expressed automatically in the form of Bihu. For the Assamese there is no need to go to any dance school to learn how to dance, sing, or enjoy Bihu, it is an instinctive process. Four decades ago there were no workshops or any kind of training on Bihu, we simply learned it by watching the performances of our seniors. Bihu has gained popularity in recent times and schools have been set up to teach this traditional art form.

I am running a school teaching Folk Dance titled *Borluit Kala Kristi Vikash Kendra* in Bamunimaidam, Guwahati. We have 100 students from the financially weaker section of the city where I, along with a few other experienced facilitators, have been providing training in Bihu and other folk dance forms. Every year we arrange workshops on Bihu dance under the banner of my school. I always love to teach Bihu dance when I participate in cultural exchange programmes abroad. I have taught Bihu dance to many of the students in Tripura, Thailand, and China.

Bihu is an expression of nature that cannot be limited to a few phrases. The cultural and economic, or in a nutshell, the entire rural life of Assam is related to and connected with Bihu. In a real sense it is the showcase of the typical, simple, and easy-going mentality of Assamese people. It speaks to the hospitality and the sociocultural system of the people of Assam.

Index

Note: Page locators in italics refer to pictures.

Aap ke aa jane se (song) 128
A. Appadurai 130
Abhijyana Shakuntalam 245
Abhinaya 140, 201, 224, 239
Abhinaya Dance Academy 226, 227
Abhinaya Darpana 3, 27
Abhinaya Darpana lasya 16
Adhikaras 197
Adhyapak 199, 220, 221, 230
Adi Yogi 42
agrarian communities 80, 88
aharya 37, 38
Ahom Bihu team 109
Ahom Kings 140; *see also* Rudra Singha (King)
Aidya Sharma 236
Aji Lhamu 10
Aji Lhamu pantomime 15
Ajit Sinha 173
Ali-ai-Ligang 11, 99
Ali East 160
"All Assam dance competitions" 205
Amal Prava Hazakira 241
Amarsing Bey 190–191
Amjad Ali Khan Saheb 206
Ananya Chatterjea 3
ancient martial art, Thang-Ta 12
Anita Sharma 225–229
Anjana Moyee Saikia 221–223
Ankiya Bhaona 25, 27, 196
Ankiya Naat Bhaona 196
Ann Daly 149
Anwesa Mahanta 45–47, 160, 162
Aoleang Lokpu 14
Aparna Bezbarua 236
Arangetram 211, 212
Arshiya Sethi 40, 41
arts integration 156–158

Arunachal Pradesh 10, 15, 232, 233
Arup Senapati 127
A. Seier 126, 127, 133
A. Sriprakash 159
Assam 2, 6, 17, 19, 51, 170, 190, 236; "All Assam dance competitions" 205, 232; Bhakti Movement 24, 25; Bihu *see* Bihu; Bodo community 136; culture and heritage 29–32; dance education workshops 154–166; indigenous tribes, folk dances 180; Mishing community 11; nationalist litterateurs 18; Sattriya *see* Sattriya; TikTok celebrities 129; Tiwa community 11, 95; traditional cultures 11; tribal folk dance *see* folk dance amongst tribal, Assam; western Assam, dance forms 11
Assamese Film Industry 143, 235, 238
Assamese television 123
Atal Bihari Bajpai 173
"AtulyaNrityaPratibhaSammaan" 244
authenticity 133, 191, 216, 241
auto-ethnographic approach 155
Avirupanurupini 147
Ayoti (young women singers) 100

Baba Longtharai Cultural Troupe 193
Babita Reang 193–194
Babula Bayan 196
Bachan Rabha 40
Bagarumba 11, 74
Baik (words) 109
Baikhu/Baikho festival 99
Bamakhata Satra 203
bamboo dance 13, 14, 132
Banjar Kekan 97, 191
Bapuram Borbayan 199

Index

Baran dance 84
Barbara Snook 45, 102
Bari Dhoka 87
Bari Ghura 87
Barman, P. 5, 91
Barua, Birinchi Kumar 108
Baruah, Radha Govinda 143
Basanta Talukdar 203
Bashani 82
Bas-puja 11
Bathou, structure 69–72; *Arkhala janai* 70; *Bathou gidingnai* 69; *Bathou kharnai mosanai* 69; *Dahal thungri sibnai mosanai* 70; *Daukhe longnai* 70; *Gandula bonnai mosanai* 70; *Gorai dabrai nai* 70; *Govo khungriao gana mosanai* 70; *Jaraphagala dia* 71; *Khamao barkhona mosanai* 71; *Kherai golao* 69; *Kherai gusungnai* 70; *Khezoma phonai* 70; *Nao bonai* 71; *Paizam banai mosanai* 69; *Raigung sibnai* 71; *Ranchandri mosanai* 71; *Xat hengra sifai na* 71
Bathou gidingnai 67, 69
Bathou kharnai mosanai 69
Bayanacharya Ghanakanta Bora Borbayan 177, 241
B. Bagdikian 131
B.C. Allen 29
Behdienkhlam 13
Bengali culture 197
Benudhar Sarmah 226
Bhabananda Barbayan 220–221
Bhabendra Nath Saikia 240
Bhagavata 42
Bhagavata Purana 25, 28, 36
Bhakats 147, 197, 198
bhakti 25–28, 141, 146
bhakti bhabona 171
Bhakti Movement 24, 25, 27, 141
bhangima (body gesture) 172, 186, 223
bhaona 169, 172
Bharata Muni 147
Bharatanatyam 174, 175, 201, 206, 211, 214
Bhaskar Theatre 196
Bhuban Chandra Ray 86
Bhugiram Hazarika 198
Bhupen Hazarika 173, 197, 235
Bibar Bathou 144
Bihu 10, 100, 136, 137, 139–140, 142, 182, 251; celebration 12; committees 143; folk music instruments 185; holidays 182, 184; music 249, 250; performance *see* Bihu performance, morans of Assam; posture 57; video compact disk 144, 145
Bihu akhora 173
Bihu-Geet 115
Bihughar 112, 114, 115
Bihu Husori 112
Bihu Konwar 145
"Bihu Konwari" title 182
Bihu Kuwori 145
Bihu nach (*Bihu* dance) 172
Bihu performance, morans of Assam: Bihu among morans 109–112; Bihu Husori 112; Dhormo Husori 112; Log Bihu 112; methodology 107; Raati Bihu 112, *112*, 114–115; songs, Morans 115–119
Bihu Rani (Bihu Queen) 143, 145
"Bihu Rani" (title) 182, 183
Bihu Sanskritir Itibritta (2017) 249
"Bihu Sundari" title 182
Bihu Uruwa 110, 111, 118
Bihuwoti 136, 143, 145, 146, 150, 151, 182
Bijaylakshmi Barooah 205
Bijhu 14
Bilambita Laya 88
Binu Goswami 141
Biodiversity Park 102
Bipul Das 232, 233
Birendranath Datta 84
Birju Maharaj 233, 238, 239, 243
"Bishnu Jyoti *Bihuwa Dol*" 173
Bishnu Prasad Rava 196
Bisu see Bihu
Bobby Rani Talukdar 242, 243
Bodo community 49, 50, *50*, 57, 61–63, 73, 136, 180
Bodo music 73–75
Bodo Sahitya Sabha 101
Boha 198, 199
Bohag Bihu 108–111, 116, 119; Bihu Husori 112; Dhormo Husori 112; Log Bihu 112; Raati Bihu 112, *112*, 114–115; *see also* Bihu performance, morans of Assam
Bohagi Utsavs 144
Bollywood 128; dance films 123; dancing stars 121; Govinda (actor) 128
Boori-boot Yullo festival 189
Borbil region 75

borgeet 171, 182, 196, 201, 211
Borgeet Daba 203
Borluit Kala Kristi Vikash Kendra 251
Bor Namati 112
Borot dance 101
Borot festival 100, 102
Bowari (film 1982) 127
Brahmaputra valley 139, 145, 169
Brajabuli 38
Buiya 10
Buka nac (Mud Dance) 100
*Buranji*s 16, 140
Burha Bhakat 198, 199
Bushu 12
Byas Ojapali 249

C. Abidin 128
Central Board of Secondary Education, Government of India (CBSE) 180
C. Geertz 77
Chailam 13
Chak Chani *113*, 114
Chalo 10
Cham 14
Chanalaw bana 67
Chandalika 228
Chandra Kanta Das Oja 248
Chandubi festival 102
Changsang 14
Chapchar Kut festival 186, 188
Charan Bordoloi 235
Charu Bordoloi 236
Chathar dance 11, 98, 101, 102
Chatka 88
Chat-mari 110, 111
Cheraw dance 13, 186–187
Cheru 14
Chheihlam 13
Chihnayatra 25, 26
China 159
Chi Rimu 14
Chitrangada 234
Chomangkan 12, 97
Chong Kedam 191
C. Horrocks 1
Chotrali 67
chowk position 179
Chu Faat 14
Chulaihum Reang 193
Chyabrung 15
classical dance 79, 207–209, 223, 227, 229, 233
C. Moser 126

Cotton College 170, 175, 208, 236, 239
creative thinking 155–156, 159
creativity 123, 126, 155–156, 164
Criminal Act 2013 Offence 354C 146
cultural exchange 48–49
cultural heritage 18, 103
Cultural Museum 48
cymbals (jotha) 12, 54, 73, 192

Dailo 192
Daimary, I. 138, 144, 146
Dalimi Boro 64
D. Amans 156
dance 4, 77, 90, 93, 125; allow artistic freedom 5; as auto-mediated practice 133; categorisation, Kherai 75–76; "impurity" 3; performance, virtual sphere 124–126; political economy in social media 130–131; in political purpose 6; practice 214; reality television programmes 122; as restored behaviour 75; scholarship 4; *see also individual entries*
dance act 125
Dance Ballet "TAJ" 240
dance education workshops, Assam: case studies 159–166; creative thinking 155–156; dance/arts integration 156–158; methodology 154–155; new Indian curriculum 158–159
Dance Ethnography: International Field Trip 45
dancers' voices: Babita Reang 193–194; Bey, Amarsing 190–191; Debashish Reang 191–193; Irean Rozamliani 186–188; J. Lalsangzuala 188–189; Madhurima Choudhury 182–184; Mui Yamak 189–190; Prasanna Gogoi 184–186
dance school teachers: Madhurima Goswami 178–181; Mitali Borthakur 176–178; Priyanka Kalita 173–176; Sri Binay Bora 172–173; Sri Khagen Kalita 169–172
dance through performers: Ghanakanta Bora Bor Bayan *198*, 198–199; Indira P.P. Bora *200*, 200–202; Jashodhara Bora *213*, 213–214; Jatin Goswami *195*, 196–197; Lima Das *207*, 208–210; Menaka P.P. Bora *210*, 210–213; Nganbi Chanu Leima *215*, 215–217; Ramkrishna Talukdar *202*,

203–204; Sinam Basu Singh *217*, 217–219; Subhalakshmi Khan *204*, 205–207
Dao thoi longnai 67
Darpan Dance Akademi 223
dashabatar nritya 172–174
Dashavatara 209
Daukhe longnai 70
D. Best 5
D. Das 82
Debashish Reang 191–193
Deborah Hay 148
Deepali Das 142
Dehing Patkai festival 102
Deka Bhakat 199
Dekachang 95
Deodhani 11, 51, 99–100
Deodhani Nritya 88, 99–100
Deoghar Parva 87
Deori community 50, 103
Deori tribes 94, 104
desi (regional) 2, 28
Dhamail 14
Dharanidhar Bayan 203
Dharanidhar Goswami 196
dharma kamarthamokshadam 22
Dharmeswar Nath Oja 246–247
dhol (drum) 172, 173, 225, 250
Dhormo Husori 112
dhulia 172
dhulor sapor (drum beats) 172
Dhultang 100
Dhyana Padam 41
Dibrugarh University 55
digital networks 126, 128
diha naam 173
Dinesh Pawar (TikTok celebrity) 128
Dipak Kumar Roy 85
Dipali Goswami 141
Dipankar Arandhura 242–245
Dipjyoti Das 242–245
Dipjyoti–Dipankar 242–245
District Gazetteers of Assam, Sibsagar 29
diya 41
D.I.Y. video 128
Dolly Patowari 142
Dolly Rani Talukdar 242, 243
Dombaley 81
Doordarshan 40, 104, 122, 190
Doordarshan Kendra 235, 238, 242, 244
Doudini 4, *63*, 72, 76, 136, 138–139, 143, 144; choreography 68; costume 64–65; gait (chali) 64; hand gesture 65; initiation ritual 65–68; mediator between community and God 63–64, 146; priestess dance 71
Dreamly Gogoi 223–225
"drop in the bucket" 159
drums (kham) 73, 192
Druta Laya 88
D. Straub 133
dugdugi 114
Duncan, Isadora 152
Dunner 126
DY365 123
DY Bihurani 123

ECA *see* Extra-Curricular Activity quota
educational change 164
Edward Gait 108
E. Hanley 80
E. Indira Devi 216
Einstein, Albert 229
"Ek Bharat Shresth Bharat" 176
Ekkushiya 80–85, 87, 89
E. Klein 159
Ek Saran Hari Naam Dharma 224
ethnic identity, tribes 96
ethnographic reconnaissance 160
Extra-Curricular Activity (ECA) quota 175

Facebook 126, 131, 189
fandom 129
Farkanti 98
field trip 45
flute (siphung) 73
folk art 89, 225
folk dance 2, 79, 123, 186, 225; category 11; Chailam 13; Dhan Nach 15; Faat 14; Karbi 191; Kherai 62; Lepcha 14; Mizo folk dance 188, 189; Thabal-chongba 13
folk dance amongst tribal, Assam 93; dance forms 97–100; ethnic identity of tribes 96; ethnographic profile 94; identity revivalism 100–104; Karbis 96; methodology 94; Mishing 96; Rabha 95; Tiwa 94–95
folk dance performers: Dharmeswar Nath Oja 246–247; Guru Shree Rajendra Nath Oja 247–249; Jina Rajkumari 250–251; Ranjit Gogoi 249–250
forbidden behaviour 87
fusion dance 122, 216, 218

Gachirampara Cultural Society (GCS) 192
Gachirampara Hojagiri Cultural Troupe 192
gait (chali) 65
Gajan 14
Ganakkuchi 147
Gandharva Kala Kendra 224
Gandiya, J. 138
Gandoula bonnai 67
Gangnam style 124
Garia 14
gender and dance: Bihu 139–140; Doudini 138–139; gender dimension 140–149; Kherai 139–140; methodology 136–137; Sattriya 139–140
George, E. 43
George Haokip 132
G. Gobo 1
ghaat 84
ghai bihua 172
Ghankanta Bora *198*, 198–199, 200, 201, 211, 236, 241
gharanas 122
Ghile Kighile harvest-dance 14
Ghunghroos 41
Gidali 82, 84, 87, 89
Gitthanee 87
Gnungnala Gnunghey 14
gogona (jaw harp) 186
The Golden Bough 81
Gopiram Bayan 196
Gorai dabrai nai 70
Goroiya 192
Goru Bihu 110, 111, 115
Goshani 100
Government of Assam's Ministry of Cultural Affairs 102
Government of India's Ministry of Cultural Affairs 103
Government of Manipur 219
Gramsci, A. 125
G. Raseshori 216
Greater Karbi Tribe 104
G. Ren 165
Grushka, K. 56
"Guerrilla Girls" 150
Gumrag 99, 101
Gumrag Mishing Bihu 102
gunin 170, 241, 242
Guru Darshana Jhaveri 217
Guru Devjani Chalia 217
Guru Gangadhar Pradhan 208, 210

Guru Garima Hazarika 142, 226
Guru Kelucharan Mohapatra 227
Guru Ngathem Ranjit Singh 216
Guru N. Tiken Singh 218
Guru P. Dhanajit Singh 216
Guru Rash Bihari Sharma 205
guru–shishya parampara 180, 228
guru–shishya relationship 229
Guru Shree Rajendra Nath Oja 247–249
Guru Vempatti Chinna Satyam 201
Guru W. Lokendrajit Singh 218
Guru Y. Hemantakumar Singh 218

Hacha Kekan 98, 102, 191
Hahn 159
Hamjhar/Girkay 98
hansa been (instrument) 186
Haorongbam Rabikanta Meitei 218
Hari Prasad Saikia Barbayan 36
Hen up ahi kekan 98, 102
Hill Tiwas 95
Hindi cinema *see* Bollywood
Hojagiri dance 192–194
home dance 129
Howard Gardner 165
Hozagiri 14
H. Schiller 124
H. Simon 133
Huchori 140, 142
Hudum 81, 82, 84–86, 90, 91
Hudum and *Hudumi* 81
Hudum Deo 5, 79, 80, 89; dance performance 81–82; structure and songs 82–89
Hudum Khuti 80–83, 85, 89, 90
Hudum Puja 11, 79–81, 84–86, 88–90
Husori Bihu 100
Husori song 117
Hwrw Khañw 10

ICCR *see* Indian Council of Cultural Relations
Igu 10
IMFA *see* Institute of Music and Fine Arts
Indian cinema 121, 122
Indian Council of Cultural Relations (ICCR) 183, 222, 230, 232
Indian government's New Education Policy 2020 169
Indian satellite television channels 123
Indira P.P. Bora 142, *200*, 200–202, 211
Indra 83, 84
"Influencers" 128

Instagram 127, 189
Institute of Music and Fine Arts (IMFA) 187, 188
Irean Rozamliani 186–188

Jagan 80, 82, 86
Jagani 82, 83
Jagannath festival 179
Jagannath Hazakira 241
Jagannath Hazarika Sanskritik Kendra 241
Jaintias 13
Jajin 189
Janmashtami 224
Jaraphagala dia 71
Jashodhara Bora *213*, 213–214
Jatin Goswami 141, 142, *195*, 196–197, 208, 226, 227, 233
Jatiya Vidyalaya School 170
Jawaharlal Nehru Manipuri Dance Academy (JNMDA) 216, 217
J. Baudrillard 133
J. Brooks 1
J. Descutner 90
Jean-Baptist Chevalier 17
Jeng 140
J. Frazer 80, 81
J. Ganguly 97
jhamtas 89
Jhijhian dance 84
Jhulum-Pongnam 189
jhum (shifting) 191
Jibeshwar Goswami 141
Jina Rajkumari 250–251
J. Kandali 140, 141
J. Konwar 138, 139, 145
J. Lalsangzuala 188–189
J. Lumby 165
Joan Frosch 58
John F. Kennedy Centre 157
Joymoti (film) 205
Joy Prakash Medhi 236, 238
JÜmÜ Nyichi 14
junga 95
J. Wasko 130, 131
Jyotikala Sangeet Mahavidyalaya 233
Jyoti Prasad Agarwala 177, 205, 228, 233

Kalaghoda Art Festival 244
Kalaguru Sangeet Mahavidyalaya 232
Kalakshetra School 206, 211
"*Kalia Daman*" 233
Kali-chandi 11
Kalika Purana 16
Kaliya-Riha 114
Kamala Goswami 141
Kamarupa 16
Kameshwar Brahma 75
Kapila Vatsayan 211
Karbi Cultural Society 103, 190
Karbi folk dance 191
Karbis 96, 98
Karbi Youth Festival 191
Karp, R. 165
Kashianth Krishnapriya Institute of Odissi dance 179, 180
Kathak 233, 236–238, 240
Kathak Nritya 243
Kati-puja 11
Katyayani Brata 81
Kaziranga National Orchid 102
Keith, A. 23
Kendriya Vidyalaya–I 175, 176, 178
Kendriya Vidyalaya–II 176, 178
Keshabananda Deva Goswami 227
Khajuraaho Dance Festival 244
kham (Bodo traditional drum) 74
Khamao barkhonai 67
Khamao barkhona mosanai 71
kham beats 74
Khan Sahab 206
Khapri chipnai 67
Khasis 13
Kherai: Bathou see Bathou, structure; Bodo community 61–63; Bodo music 73–75; dance as restored behaviour 74–75; dance categorisation 75–76; dance performers 72–732; Doudini see Doudini; festival 4, 61–62, 139–140; music types 73–74; performance 76; ritual space 71, 72; space for performance 62
Khermuthi 111
Kh. Ibomcha 218
Khoijama phonai 67
khol 171, 172, 196, 199, 221
Khuallam 13
Khubakesei 13
Khubak-ishei 13
Khuksi 99
khuti 84, 85
kinesthetic learning style 165
Kirtanaghosa 36
K. Landing 152
K. Medhi 35

Index

Kobitar Chandot Nrityarata Godhuli 228
Koch Rajbangshis 79, 80, 82, 84, 88; dance 89; fertility ritual, women 91; society 90; women 90
Koloh loi 66
Koni-Jujj 111
kontha 114
kotwal 147
Krishna Bhangi 201
Kuchipudi dance 201
Kulu-tsen head-hunting dance 14
kumbha 41
Kushan-gan 11
Kuwari (young girls) 100
K. Vatsyayan 79, 81, 90

Labdinga dance 65, 72
Labdinga music 74
"*Laigi Machasing*" (Children of Gods and Goddesses) 219
Lai haraoba 12, 13, 15, 215, 218
Lakhiaji, Kumudini 240
"Lakhimi" (video film) 239
Lakhiram Barooah 205
Lalit Chandra Nath Oja 248
Lasya 86–88
Latasil Bihu competition 184
Lavanya Bhakat 81
Lebang Boomani 14
Leisha Lokpu 14
Lepcha 14
Lima Das 207, 208–210
Lincoln, Y. 154
Linda Tuhiwai Smith 154
Llonen, Maarit 57
Log Bihu 112, 140
Lohor Academy 171
Lons 204
Lora (male) 139
Lora Bihu 145
Lora-Huchori 145
Lord Krishna 12, 24, 224
Lord Vishnu 11, 146

Maanen, John Van 58
Madhaba (Madhabadeva) 115
Madhurima Choudhury 182–184
Madhurima Goswami 178–181
Madhya 88
Madhya Laya 88
Madison, S. 56, 57
maduli 114

Mahabharata 16, 234
Mahapurushia Vaishnavism religion 108
Maibas 12
Maibis 12
Mainland India 8
Majuli festival 102
Majuli Island 46, 52–53, 54
MAK *see* Mising Agom Kebang
Makhoni Goswami 141
malita 15
Mallika Kandali 150, *151*, 230–232
"Man and His World Exhibition" 206
Mandira Bhattacharjee 214
"Mandodari pusoyo Ravanak" 150
M. Andrejevic 130, 131
Manikanchan Kala Manjari 244
Manikanchan Nritya Mahotsav 244
Manipur 12–13, 15, 215
"Manipur" (The Jewel of India) 219
Manipuri dance 2, 12, 18, 216–218
Maniram Dutta Muktiyar 198
Mansingh, Sonal 242
mantra 83, 170, 227
Manuh Bihu 110, 111, 115
Maoji mambrand galena 67
Marami Medhi 235–238, 243
Marciniak, L. 1
margi 2, 4, 28, 204
Martin, Brittany Harker 157
Maruni 15
Mashakhaori moshanai 67
mati akhara 27, 171, 199, 204, 226, 241, 242
M. Bhattacharya 84
meaning-making process 133
Meera (film) 205
Meghalaya 13
Meghrani Brata 81
Meghranjani Medhi 237–240
Meitei Pung (Manipuri drum) 218
Mekhela pindha 66
Melo Phita 14
Menaka P.P. Bora *210*, 210–213
M. Erickson 130, 131
merrymaking 87
Methoni 114
M. Ghosh 23
M. Goswami 138, 144, 146
microcelebrity 128
Mileswar Patar 101
mime farming 88
mimetic dances 76
Ministry of Culture in 2005 186

Mishing Bihu 99
Mishing community 11, 46, 52, 53, 99, 102
Mising Agom Kebang (MAK) 102
Mitali Borthakur 176–178
Mitali Kala Kendra 226
Mizo folk dance 187–189
Mizoram 13, 187, 188
Mizoram Cultural Artiste Association (MCAA) 187
M. Kaminikumar Singh 216
M. Kandali 138, 142, 150
Moamoria rebellion 110
Moghai Oja 250
Mon-Dryak-Lok dance 14
Mon Hira Doi (song) 127
Moran *see* Bihu performance, morans of Assam
Moran Bihu 114
Mota-Bihu 145
moving objects 33–34; body existence 36–40; dance narrativisation 41–43; object spatialisation 41–43; space and extended body 40–41; spatial frame and visualisation 34–36
M. Reilley 35
M. Soha 124, 130–131
M.S. Subbulakshmi 205
mudra 84, 86
Muhudi 100
Mui Yamak 189–190
Mukha nritya (Mask dance) 100
Mukhopadhyay, Durga Das 89
Mun Hait Lok dance 14
M. Woodhouse 133

naam (bihu song) 172
Naamghar 203
Naam Kirtan 224
Naam Prasang 196
Nadu Bhangi 201
Naga groups 14
Nagaland 14
Nagara Naam 247
Naharkhura Saikia 110
Naidu, Y. 122
Nalbari 236
Namani 82
Namghar 25, 27, 30, 34, 36, 42, 53, 62, 65, 111
Nancy, J. 43
Nao bonai 71
Narasimha 244

Nara-singa Bihu 99
Nartan Kala Niketan 203
Narzary, Bhaben 75
Nasoni (dancer) 63, 139, 146
Nataraja idol 41, 42
National Education Policy 159
Natyasastra 3, 16, 22, 23, 27, 28, 147, 229
N. Denzin 154
Neog, M. 17
Neog, Maheswar 141, 196, 201, 211
Neogi, P. 85
networks 125
New Education Policy 2020 214
new Indian curriculum 158–159
New Zealand curriculum 156
Nganbi Chanu Leima 215, 215–217
Nikamul Sattra 232
Nimso Kerung 97, 101, 191
N. King 1
North-East India 6, 132, 185; archaeological specimens, dance reference 16; Arunachal Pradesh 10; Assam 10–12; heritage commodification and dance 17–20; indigenous communities 4; Manipur 12–13; Meghalaya 13; Mizoram 13; Nagaland 14; oral traditional resources, dance reference 15; region and people 8–9; Sikkim 14–15; trajectories, dance traditions development 2–3; Tripura 14; Vice Chancellors' Meet 180; written resources, dance reference 16
nritya and *natya* (dance and drama) 23
Nrityakalpa 232, 234
Nrityangan 175
N. Sharma 88
Nyib (priest) 189
Nyishi folk song 189

Odisha 179, 208
Odissi dance 178–180, 208, 219, 223, 226, 227
Odra-Magadhi 16
Ojapali 11, 51, 57, 226, 246–249
Ojapali singing 247
"The old couple and the jackals" 15
"Outward Bound" 159

Pad (beginning song) 115–116
Padam Nyani 10
Paizam banai mosanai 69

Pakeha 154
Palis 248
Pallud, J. 133
Pam Burnard 55
Panchakanya 234
Panchatantra 226
Papu and Puja (TikTok celebrity) 129
Papu MDR (YouTube channel) 129
Para Berani 87, 89
Parampara 226
Parampara Pravah 231
Parampara Pravah institution 231
Pârlam 13
Paro uruwa 66
Pasi Kongki 10
Patra Mudra 86
Paul, P. 90
P.C. Borooah 205
P. Chakravorty 122, 123
pepa 114, 184, 249, 251
Pessar, P. 138
Peters, K. 126, 127, 133
Pharkanti 11
Ph. Iboton 216
Phidimba 12
photography 132
phul-tulasi 84
Phunu Barooah 205
Pisu 12, 100
Plain Tiwas 95, 100
political identity 6
Ponty, Merleau 36
Ponung 10
Popir 10
Porag 11, 99
post-Vaishnava dance 218
Pouliot, V. 94
Prabhat Sarma 182
Pradeep Chaliha 200, 211
Pradip Mahanta 46, 48
Prafulla Prasad Bora 201
Pragati Kala Parishad 196
Pragjyotishpura 16
Prajnananda, S. 22, 23
Prakriti (female/feminine) 147
Prakriti Vandan 233
prasad 88
Prasanna Gogoi 46, 184–186
Pratap Chandra Choudhury 17
Pratibha Sharma 232–235
Preeti Patel 217
pre-Hindu ritualistic dance 12
pre-Vaishnava dance 218

primary dance 76, 242
privatisation 124
Priyanka Kalita 173–176
Progressive Artiste Laboratory 218, 219
Promila Ray 82, 84
Psy 124
Punyabrata Dev Goswami 232
Purnima Goswami 141
Purusha (male/masculine) 147
Pushpa Bhuyan 142
Puthi (training) 248
Putuli Hazarika 141

qualitative research 137, 154, 155
Queen's University Belfast 38

Raati Bihu 112, *113*, 114–115
Rabha 95, 98, 103, 104
Rabha community 11, 40, 99, 102, 103
Rabindranath Tagore 228, 234
Rabindra Nritya 14
Radha Govinda Baruah 200–201
Raghab Moran 110
Raghudeva (King, Koch) 147
Raigung sibnai 71
Raindrops Festival 244
Rajaghariya Cali Nac 27
Rajbangshi Nareer Hudum Puja 81
Rajendra Gangani 238
Rajini gerba 12
Rallulam 13
Ralph Buck 102
Ramakanta, A.D. 110
Rama Vijaya 35, 184
Ramkrishna Talukdar 169, *202*, 203–204, 242, 243
Ranchandri mosanai 71
Ranganath Kalakshetra 196
Rangpuria Silpi Samaj Bihu Dal 184, 185
Ranjit, N. 216
Ranjit Gogoi 249–250
rasas 177, 178
Rasheswar Saikia Barbayan 141, 182, 196, 199–201, 203, 211, 226
Rashtriya Sanskriti Mahotsav 185, 192
Rasleela 12
Ras Lila tradition 218
Rati Bihu 140, 142
Ratikant Mahapatra 227
Ray, D. 88, 89
R. Chawla 84
R. Dev 90

reality dance shows 123
reality television 122
Reang folk dance 192
"reflective community of practice" 55
restored behaviour 75
Rig Veda 23
Rina Saikia Bora 214
Riordan, M. 159
Rit Nong Chingdi 191
Ritu Ranga 228
R.M. Emerson 56
Rongali Bihu *see* Bohag Bihu
Rongker 96
Rongpuria Bihu Husori Band 224
Roppi 10
R. Schechner 75, 87
R. Sternberg 155
Rubi Sinha 173
Rudra Singha (King) 142
Rukhyo-sharu war-dance 14
Rukmini Devi Arundale 200, 201, 206, 207
Rukmini Horon 196
Ryle, G. 69

Sagol Pheikhai 14
Sagra Misawa 11, 100
Sahitya Akademi 197
Sahitya Sabha 101
Sali Nritya 209
Salita khowa 65
Sangeeta Hazarika 208
Sangeet Natak Akademi 31, 103, 197, 224, 243
Sangeet Sattra 226
Sangita Ratnakara 22
Sanjay Srivastava 128
Sanjeev Shrivastava 128
Sankh 203
Sannidhi/a confluence: concept 46–47; cultural exchange 48–49; dancing with village communities 49–52; embodied participation 57–58; field trip 45–46; learning 47–48; Majuli Island 52–53; Sattra communities 53–55; shared interest communities 55–56; somatic sensibility 57–58; testing 55; trans-locational teaching 47–48
Saptaswa 234
Saradi Saikia 142
sarailau instrument 100

Sarathi Ray 89
Sarlamkai 13, 188
Saroja Natyalaya 214
Satradhikar Gosain 109
Sattra 10, 24–31, 58, 139–141, 169, 182, 197, 199, 220, 221, 241; *see also* Namghar
sattra bhakats 182
Sattra communities 53–55
Sattradhikar 141
Sattra institution 32, 140, 172, 231
Sattriya 2, 4, 10, 11, 18, 19, 22–24, 136–142, 151, 171, 182, 196, 197, 201, 209, 220, 224, 226, 236, 237; art 199, 220, 225; Assam's culture and heritage 29–32; culture 197, 199, 231; dancer 33, 42; female dancer costume 37, 39; fusion in 204; inspirational expression 27–28; male dancer costume 37, 39; music 31, 140, 221; performance 41, 42; place of dance 25–27; Sattra throughout history 28–29; telecast 40; tradition 24–25, 37, 147
Sattriya Kalakendra 199
Sattriya Kendra 243
Sattriya Nritya 169–172, 174, 177, 180, 203, 224, 240, 241, 244; *see also* Sattriya
Sattriya Nritya Parva festival 224
Sattriya Samaj 172
Scheduled Tribes 94
secondary dance 76
Seetarani Hazarika 240–242
Serene calm music 74
serja (Bodo traditional violin) 73
Seroso 97
Shakuntala 244
S. Hall 133
short videos, applications 127–130
Shreejani Nritya Mahavidyalaya 177
Shri Astabhuja Dev Tithi 111
Shringara 146
Shringar Rasa 88
Shri Shri Astabhuja Dev 110
Shri Shri Chaturbhuja Dev 108, 110
shthiti position 179
Sidney Endle 107
Sikkim 8, 14–15
simhasana 42
simulacra 133
Sinam Basu Singh 217, 217–219

Sinam Bokul Singh 218
Singapore's Ministry of Education's Thinking Skills, Learning Nation 158
Sitar Patal Prabesh 233
Skovira, R. 133
S. Mahler 138
Smit 13
social media, dance: authentic in representative reality 133; dance performance, virtual sphere 124–126; dance performer 126–127; political economy 130–131; short video applications 127–130; staged television performances 121–124; staging local at global festivals 132
Sodou Rabha Kristi Sanmilan 103
Solakia 13
somatic sensibility 57–58
Sonal Man Singh 243
songs, Morans: of love and attachment 115–119; Pad (beginning song) 115–116; prayer and supplication 115
Sonit Konwari 228
Sonit Kuwari 234
Sonowal Kacharis 11
spatial frame 34–36
Spider Dance 162–164
splashing sound 87
Sri Aniruddha Deva 108
Sri Binay Bora 172–173
Sri Gobinda Saikia Sir 224
Sri Gunakar Dev Goswami 232
Srihastamuktavali 16
Sri Khagen Kalita 169–172
Srimadbhagavata Purana 36
Srimanta Sankaradeva 11, 18, 24–26, 28, 29, 34, 35, 115, 139, 142, 150, 171, 204, 221, 224, 230, 243
Srimanta Sankaradeva Kalakshetra 101, 102
Srimanta Sankaradeva Temple 48
Sri Santi Shankar Das Gupta 233
Sri Sri Kamalabari Satra 196
Sri Sri Madhavadeva 26, 33, 37, 139, 147, 150, 171, 243
Sri Sri Nikamul Sattra 232
Sri Sri Sankaradeva 108
Sri Sri Uttar Kamalabari Sattra, Majuli 231, 232
Sri Tajuram Narzary 61
Sri Tileswar Tamuli Borbayan 232, 233
S. Springgay 37

Stage Bihu 143
staged television performances 121–124
State Government of Assam 170
studio dance teachers: Anita Sharma 225–229; Anjana Moyee Saikia 221–223; Bhabananda Barbayan 220–221; Dipankar Arandhura 242–245; Dipjyota Das 242–245; Dreamly Gogoi 223–225; Mallika Kandali 230–232; Marami Medhi 235–238; Meghranjani Medhi 238–240; Pratibha Sharma 232–235; Seetarani Hazarika 240–242
Sualkuchi Weavers' village 48
Subhalakshmi Khan *204*, 205–207
subject–object body 36–40
Suhtah Lam 14
Sujata Mahapatra 227
Suknani Oja 248
Suknani Ojapali 247, 249
Suknani Sahityacharjya 248
Suknani Sangeet 247, 248
Suli ghurua 66
Sunil Kothari 211
Surendra Saikia 235, 236
Suren Goswami 142
Sur Sangam 235, 237, 238
Surya Prakash Medhi 237
Suwali (female) 139

Taal 196
taal and *maan* (rhythm and music) 225
taka/gagana 115
Takam Mising Mime Kebang (TMMK) 102
Takam Mising Porin Kebang (TMPK) 102
Tanjore 214
Tanjua Devi 142
Taruwal ghurua 66
Tashi Zaldha 15
Tea community 49, 50, *50*
Tel bati 66
Tendong Lho Rum Faat dance 14
Terank 98
Tezpur University 104, 173, 175, 178, 180
Thabal-chongba 13
thans 95
Th. Bimola 216
Th. Chourajit 216
Theresa Buckland 57

Therk 88
Therka dance 90
Thiyam Tarunkumar 219
Thomas Metcalf 132
Thungri nac 66
TikTok: ban in India 129; stars/celebrities 128, 129
Tileshwar Tamuli 232
Tiwa 11, 94–95, 100
Tiwa Tauling dance 104
Tiwa Tribe Official 104
TMMK *see* Takam Mising Mime Kebang
TMPK *see* Takam Mising Porin Kebang
Toby Miller 131
trance music 74
trans-locational teaching 47–48
Transylvania 80
Traube, S. 43
Tripura 14
T. Spry 56
Tuan, Y. 34
Tulashi Oja 250
Twitter 126

Uddam 88
"Unity in Diversity" 178

Uruka 110, 115
Uttar Kamalabari Sattra 53, 54, 220

Vaidyanathan, Rama 41
Vaidyanathan, Saroja 214
Vaishnav, Rajshree 165
Vaishnavite Bhakti movement 142
Vedic hymnology 22
Vidushi N. Amusana Devi 218
Virginia Woolf 34
visharad 174, 175, 239; *see also* Bharatanatyam

Wangala festival 13, 88
Wan sawa 12
W. Gamson 124, 125, 133
WhatsApp 126, 189
W. Wang 133

Xat hengra sifai na 71
Xutuli 115

Yoginitantra 16
YouTube 124, 128–131, 189
"Yuva Kala Ratna" 244

Z. McDowell 124, 130–131